Resources, Governance and Civil Conflict

Civil war is the greatest contemporary threat to peace. Well over 90 per cent of all armed conflicts are civil conflicts, and the human suffering they generate is staggering. If we are to understand civil conflict adequately, it is particularly important to grasp two sets of conditions that may critically affect its incidence and resolution. One is resources, including both the distribution of material resources in society and its dependence on natural resource endowments. The other is domestic and international governance structures. This book explores this interplay between governance structures and resources in the onset and termination of civil conflict.

This book includes a series of novel contributions to the study of three different aspects of civil conflict, including case studies on India, Sudan, Costa Rica and the Basque Country. The first part of the book contains an introduction to the subject and a broad overview of civil conflicts worldwide since 1945. Chapters in the second part analyse the onset and dynamics of civil conflict. They examine the effects of democratization and constitutional engineering, how the process of resource extraction can contribute to civil conflict, how changes in agricultural practices affect the pattern of civil conflict and how inequalities and ineffective governance structures can combine to create a market for insurgency. The second part of the book includes original contributions on the external dynamics that civil conflicts generate, including third-party interventions and their impact on regime stability. The third and final part is devoted to conflict termination and the stability of peace agreements. The chapters here analyse how dependence on natural resource rents affects the possibility of settling civil conflicts through competitive elections, and how the inclusiveness of peace agreements affect their stability.

Resources, Governance and Civil Conflict will be of particular interest to students and scholars of Politics, International Relations and Conflict Studies.

Magnus Öberg is Director of Studies at the Department of Peace and Conflict Research, Uppsala University, Sweden and Research Associate at the Centre for the Study of Civil War, International Peace Research Institute, Oslo (PRIO), Norway.
Kaare Strøm is Professor of Political Science at the University of California, San Diego, USA and Research Professor, Centre for the Study of Civil War, International Peace Research Institute, Oslo (PRIO), Norway.

Routledge/ECPR studies in European political science
Edited by Thomas Poguntke
Ruhr University Bochum, Germany on behalf of the European Consortium for Political Research

The Routledge/ECPR studies in European political science series is published in association with the European Consortium for Political Research – the leading organization concerned with the growth and development of political science in Europe. The series presents high-quality edited volumes on topics at the leading edge of current interest in political science and related fields, with contributions from European scholars and others who have presented work at ECPR workshops or research groups.

1 **Regionalist Parties in Western Europe**
   Edited by Lieven de Winter and Huri Türsan

2 **Comparing Party System Change**
   Edited by Jan-Erik Lane and Paul Pennings

3 **Political Theory and European Union**
   Edited by Albert Weale and Michael Nentwich

4 **Politics of Sexuality**
   Edited by Terrell Carver and Véronique Mottier

5 **Autonomous Policy Making by International Organizations**
   Edited by Bob Reinalda and Bertjan Verbeek

6 **Social Capital and European Democracy**
   Edited by Jan van Deth, Marco Maraffi, Ken Newton and Paul Whiteley

7 **Party Elites in Divided Societies**
   Edited by Kurt Richard Luther and Kris Deschouwer

8 **Citizenship and Welfare State Reform in Europe**
   Edited by Jet Bussemaker

9 **Democratic Governance and New Technology**
   Technologically mediated innovations in political practice in western Europe
   Edited by Ivan Horrocks, Jens Hoff and Pieter Tops

10 **Democracy Without Borders**
   Transnationalisation and
   conditionality in new democracies
   Edited by Jean Grugel

11 **Cultural Theory as Political Science**
   *Edited by Michael Thompson,
   Gunnar Grendstad and Per Selle*

12 **The Transformation of Governance in the European Union**
   Edited by Beate Kohler-Koch and Rainer Eising

13 **Parliamentary Party Groups in European Democracies**
   Political parties behind closed doors
   Edited by Knut Heidar and Ruud Koole

14 **Survival of the European Welfare State**
   Edited by Stein Kuhnle

15 **Private Organisations in Global Politics**
   Edited by Karsten Ronit and Volker Schneider

16 **Federalism and Political Performance**
   Edited by Ute Wachendorfer-Schmidt

17 **Democratic Innovation**
   Deliberation, representation and association
   Edited by Michael Saward

18 **Public Opinion and the International Use of Force**
   Edited by Philip Everts and Pierangelo Isernia

19 **Religion and Mass Electoral Behaviour in Europe**
   Edited by David Broughton and Hans-Martien ten Napel

20 **Estimating the Policy Position of Political Actors**
   Edited by Michael Laver

21 **Democracy and Political Change in the 'Third World'**
   Edited by Jeff Haynes

22 **Politicians, Bureaucrats and Administrative Reform**
   Edited by B. Guy Peters and Jon Pierre

23 **Social Capital and Participation in Everyday Life**
   Edited by Paul Dekker and Eric M. Uslaner

24 **Development and Democracy**
   What have we learned and how?
   Edited by Ole Elgström and Goran Hyden

25 **Do Political Campaigns Matter?**
   Campaign effects in elections and referendums
   Edited by David M. Farrell and Rüdiger Schmitt-Beck

26 **Political Journalism**
   New challenges, new practices
   Edited by Raymond Kuhn and Erik Neveu

27 **Economic Voting**
   Edited by Han Dorussen and Michaell Taylor

28 Organized Crime and the Challenge to Democracy
Edited by Felia Allum and Renate Siebert

29 Understanding the European Union's External Relations
Edited by Michèle Knodt and Sebastiaan Princen

30 Social Democratic Party Policies in Contemporary Europe
Edited by Giuliano Bonoli and Martin Powell

31 Decision Making Within International Organisations
Edited by Bob Reinalda and Bertjan Verbeek

32 Comparative Biomedical Policy
Governing assisted reproductive technologies
Edited by Ivar Bleiklie, Malcolm L. Goggin and Christine Rothmayr

33 Electronic Democracy
Mobilisation, organisation and participation via new ICTs
Edited by Rachel K. Gibson, Andrea Römmele and Stephen J. Ward

34 Liberal Democracy and Environmentalism
The end of environmentalism?
Edited by Marcel Wissenburg and Yoram Levy

35 Political Theory and the European Constitution
Edited by Lynn Dobson and Andreas Follesdal

36 Politics and the European Commission
Actors, interdependence, legitimacy
Edited by Andy Smith

37 Metropolitan Governance in the 21st Century
Capacity, democracy and the dynamics of place
Edited by Hubert Heinelt and Daniel Kübler

38 Democracy and the Role of Associations
Political, organizational and social contexts
Edited by Sigrid Roßteutscher

39 The Territorial Politics of Welfare
Edited by Nicola McEwen and Luis Moreno

40 Health Governance in Europe
Issues, challenges and theories
Edited by Monika Steffen

41 Republicanism in Theory and Practice
Edited by Iseult Honohan and Jeremy Jennings

42 Mass Media and Political Communication in New Democracies
Edited by Katrin Voltmer

43 Delegation in Contemporary Democracies
Edited by Dietmar Braun and Fabrizio Gilardi

44 Governance and Democracy
Comparing national, European and international experiences
Edited by Yannis Papadopoulos and Arthur Benz

45 **The European Union's Roles in International Politics**
Concepts and analysis
Edited by Ole Elgström and Michael Smith

46 **Policy-making Processes and the European Constitution**
A comparative study of member states and accession countries
Edited by Thomas König and Simon Hug

47 **Democratic Politics and Party Competition**
Edited by Judith Bara and Albert Weale

48 **Participatory Democracy and Political Participation**
Can participatory engineering bring citizens back in?
Edited by Thomas Zittel and Dieter Fuchs

49 **Civil Societies and Social Movements**
Potentials and problems
Edited by Derrick Purdue

50 **Resources, Governance and Civil Conflict**
Edited by Magnus Öberg and Kaare Strøm

Also available from Routledge in association with the ECPR:

Sex Equality Policy in Western Europe, *Edited by Frances Gardiner*; **Democracy and Green Political Thought**, *Edited by Brian Doherty and Marius de Geus*; **The New Politics of Unemployment**, *Edited by Hugh Compston*; **Citizenship, Democracy and Justice in the New Europe**, *Edited by Percy B. Lehning and Albert Weale*; **Private Groups and Public Life**, *Edited by Jan W van Deth*; **The Political Context of Collective Action**, *Edited by Ricca Edmondson*; **Theories of Secession**, *Edited by Percy Lehning*; **Regionalism Across the North/South Divide**, *Edited by Jean Grugel and Wil Hout*

Resources, Governance and Civil Conflict

Edited by
Magnus Öberg and Kaare Strøm

LONDON AND NEW YORK

First published 2008
by Routledge
2 Park Square, Milton Park, Abingdon, Oxon OX14 4RN

Simultaneously published in the USA and Canada
by Routledge
711 Third Avenue, New York, NY 10017

Routledge is an imprint of the Taylor & Francis Group, an informa business

First issued in paperback 2012

© 2008 Selection and editorial matter, Magnus Öberg and Kaare Strøm; individual chapters, the contributors

Typeset in Garamond by Wearset Ltd, Boldon, Tyne and Wear

All rights reserved. No part of this book may be reprinted or reproduced or utilized in any form or by any electronic, mechanical, or other means, now known or hereafter invented, including photocopying and recording, or in any information storage or retrieval system, without permission in writing from the publishers.

British Library Cataloguing in Publication Data
A catalogue record for this book is available from the British Library

Library of Congress Cataloging in Publication Data
A catalog record for this book has been requested

ISBN13: 978-0-415-51263-3 (pbk)
ISBN13: 978-0-415-41671-9 (hbk)
ISBN13: 978-0-203-94071-6 (ebk)

Contents

List of illustrations xii
List of contributors xiv
Series editor's preface xvi
Acknowledgements xviii

PART I
Introducing civil conflict 1

1 **Introduction** 3
  MAGNUS ÖBERG AND KAARE STRØM

2 **Civil conflict in the contemporary world** 23
  KRISTINE ECK, BETHANY LACINA, AND
  MAGNUS ÖBERG

PART II
Causes and dynamics 43

3 **Insights from macro studies of the risk of civil war** 45
  BETHANY LACINA

4 **Civil wars and interstate disputes** 58
  KRISTIAN SKREDE GLEDITSCH AND
  IDEAN SALEHYAN

5 **Robin Hood or Al Capone? Natural resources and conflict in India's Naxalite insurgency** 77
  WILLIAM NOËL IVEY

6 Government restructuring and reallocation of resources in the face of ethno-nationalist insurgency in the Basque Country (1979–2005)   101
ENRIC MARTÍNEZ-HERRERA

7 Political marginalization and economic exclusion in the making of insurgencies in Sudan   125
ALEKSI YLÖNEN

8 Military intervention, democratization, and post-conflict political stability   147
SCOTT GATES AND HÅVARD STRAND

PART III
Termination and post-conflict stability   163

9 Enforcing alone: collective action in ethnic conflicts settlement   165
THEODORA-ISMENE GIZELIS

10 From bullets to ballots: using the people as arbitrators to settle civil wars   178
MARGARETA SOLLENBERG

11 Democracy after war: causes and consequences of the 1948 Civil War in Costa Rica   205
FERNANDO F. SÁNCHEZ

12 Democracies, disengagement, and deals: exploring the effect of different types of mediators in civil conflict   227
ISAK SVENSSON

13 Rebels on the outside: signatories signaling commitment to durable peace   247
DESIRÉE NILSSON

**PART IV
Conclusions**   267

14 Conclusions   269
MAGNUS ÖBERG AND KAARE STRØM

Index   283

Illustrations

Figures

2.1	Number of civil conflicts by type, 1946–2003	24
2.2	Global trends in number of civil conflicts, average conflict age, and number of new conflicts, 1946–2003	25
2.3	Number of countries in civil conflict by region, 1946–2003	26
2.4	Percentage of all states affected by civil conflict	27
2.5	Battle deaths worldwide, 1946–2002	29
2.6	Peace keeping operations in civil conflict, 1946–2003	35
6.1	Murders of ETA, 1968–2005	108
6.2	Rate of regional public spending out of the total public spending corresponding to the Basque Country, 1981–2002	109
8.1	Hazard function of the log-logistic regression	151
8.2	Hazard function of the log-logistic regression, comparing the duration of democratized polities to all other polities	158
8.3	Hazard function of the log-logistic regression, comparing the duration of polities experiencing loss of war in an intervention to all other polities	158
11.1	Voter participation in Costa Rican elections, 1897–2002	215

Tables

2.1	Democracy and civil conflict	32
2.2	Conflict termination by type of incompatibility, 1946–1999	38
4.1	Interstate conflict (MID) and civil conflict	63
4.2	Logit of likelihood of MID, monadic data	64
4.3	Replication of Oneal and Russett (2001), including civil conflict	65
5.1	The number of Naxalite incidents and deaths, 2000–2004	87
6.1	Variables utilised in the modelling of the number of murders	111

6.2	Negative binomial event count regression of ETA murders	116
6.A-1	Negative binomial event count regression of ETA murders with a forecasting approach	120
8.1	Descriptive statistics	154
8.2	Comparing median duration of regimes across conflict experience	154
8.3	Comparing median regime duration across types of political change	155
8.4	Log-logistic estimates of polity survival time ratios, 1945–1996	156
10.1	Logit regression results	191
10.2	Cross-tabulation of negotiations secondary party and competitive elections	193
10.1A	List of all war endings 1989–2000	197–8
10.2A	Summary statistics	198–9
11.1	Costa Rican election results, 1953–2002	222–3
12.1	Distribution of conflict with one or several rebel groups	232
12.2	Where do mediators mediate?	236
12.3	Measuring the effect of mediation	238
13.1	Exclusion of rebel groups and the hazard of peace failing	257

Contributors

Kristine Eck. PhD candidate, Department of Peace and Conflict Research, Uppsala University.

Scott Gates. Professor, Department of Sociology and Political Science, Norwegian University of Technology (NTNU) and Director of the Centre for the Study of Civil War, International Peace Research Institute, Oslo.

William Noël Ivey. PhD candidate, Department of Government and Politics, University of Maryland at College Park.

Theodora-Ismene Gizelis. Lecturer, Department of Politics and International Relations, Rutherford College, University of Kent.

Kristian S. Gleditsch. Reader, Department of Government, University of Essex.

Enric Martínez-Herrera. M. García-Pelayo Fellow, Centro de Estudios Políticos y Constitucionales (CEPC), Madrid.

Bethany Lacina. PhD candidate, Department of Political Science, Stanford University.

Desirée Nilsson. Assistant Professor, Department of Peace and Conflict Research, Uppsala University.

Magnus Öberg. Senior Lecturer and Director of Studies, Department of Peace and Conflict Research, Uppsala University.

Idean Salehyan. Assistant Professor, Department of Political Science, University of North Texas.

Fernando F. Sánchez. Postdoctoral Research Associate, Latin American Centre, University of Oxford.

Margareta Sollenberg. PhD candidate, Department of Peace and Conflict Research, Uppsala University.

Kaare Strøm. Professor, Department of Political Science, University of California San Diego and Senior Research Fellow, Centre for the Study of Civil War, International Peace Research Institute.

Håvard Strand. PhD candidate, Department of Political Science, Oslo University, and Researcher at the Centre for the Study of Civil War, International Peace Research Institute.

Isak Svensson. Assistant Professor, Department of Peace and Conflict Research, Uppsala.

Aleksi Ylönen. PhD candidate, Department of Political Science and International Relations, Universidad Autónoma de Madrid.

Series editor's preface

While we all know by now that the 'peace dividends' that were so widely expected after the end of the Cold War were as elusive as the profits generated during the 'dot.com bubble' (at least for many!) another form of conflict is still present. The editors of this volume draw our attention to the depressing fact that civil conflicts have accounted for more than '90 per cent of all armed conflicts' since that time. Despite the enormous human suffering they often bring about, and their devastating effects on the development of the countries involved, many of these conflicts largely escape the world's attention. This is predominantly due to their low level and the fact that they generate few external consequences that would compel the global public to take notice. As long as civil conflicts do not produce a large number of refugees seeking shelter in other countries, as long as they do not endanger the flow of goods and resources crucial to the performance of the world economy, and as long as they do not threaten to generate terrorist attacks outside the conflict-ridden state – to name but a few of such external consequences – the world is likely to turn a blind eye to those who keep the fighting going.

The sheer frequency of civil conflict, which is documented in Chapter 2, underlines the editors' statement that it is one of the most important objects of political analysis. The range of theoretical and empirical questions is enormous and while the editors and their contributors address many they do not claim to cover all of them as this would certainly be beyond the scope of a single edited volume. Essentially, these questions centre around causes of civil conflict and strategies to terminate it and ensure a lasting peace thereafter.

While we may think of some of the causes as being almost self-evident, empirical evidence is less clear-cut. There is a considerable debate about the role of poverty and inequality as causes of civil conflict. Similarly, large natural resources certainly play a role in explaining the duration of civil conflict, but their role as a cause is still an open question. The short-hand for this debate is 'greed versus grievance' and it is also related to different paradigms in social sciences. As the editors write in their introduction, 'if rebels are in the business of rectifying collective grievances, they are providing a collective good' and hence they are likely to 'face serious collective action problems'. In contrast, challenging the state order in pursuit of private gain is easier to explain from this perspective.

Another set of explanations for the emergence of civil conflict relates to governance structures and this book also focuses on this often underestimated perspective. It is not entirely surprising that established and strong democracies are not alone in guaranteeing domestic tranquillity. Arguably, strong autocracies are also effective in ensuring domestic peace. Clearly while established, strong democracies can rely on responsiveness and participation, autocracies use repression. When it comes to domestic peace, they can be quite effective while the 'in-between category' of non-established democracies with ineffective governance structures seem to be particularly conflict-prone.

In a globalizing world, governance no longer exclusively refers to domestic governance structures but necessarily includes transnational governance structures like, for example, the UN, the OSCE or NGOs. Here, much attention is on the termination of conflict and it is far from evident that even the most well-meaning military intervention is helpful in successfully settling a conflict. Post-conflict intervention, on the other hand, may be a very different matter.

While the editors point to a considerable number of questions where more research is still needed, the book shows that politics matters. In other words, designing political structures which provide for effectiveness, efficiency, responsiveness, fairness and competitiveness goes a considerable way in ensuring domestic peace. Yet, the history of Europe tells us how difficult it is to bring this about – and to maintain it.

Thomas Poguntke, Series Editor
Bochum

Acknowledgements

Civil conflict is one of the most important issues in world politics today. It is not (yet) among the phenomena that political scientists best understand. These were the most important realizations that led us to the collaborative project that this book represents. To be precise, this book is the fruit of a workshop that was held at the Joint Sessions of Workshops of the European Consortium for Political Research (ECPR) at Uppsala University in April 2004, under our direction. This was a workshop that brought together students of conflict and students of institutions, students of what is traditionally known as international relations and students of what has come to be known as comparative politics. It was a type of partnership that was new to both of us, but in which we both believe.

We thank all of those who made this partnership and this book possible. First among them must be the European Consortium for Political Research, who allowed us their venue for the workshop. No less deserving of our thanks is the Centre for the Study of Civil War (CSCW) at the International Peace Research Institute in Oslo (PRIO), where one of us (Strøm) is a senior research fellow. The CSCW has supported us both generously. Moreover, it was at a CSCW meeting that the idea of this collaboration was born. At the CSCW we are especially grateful to its director, Scott Gates, its chief administrator Marsha Snodgrass, its 2004 acting director, Nils Petter Gleditsch, and to PRIO's director, Stein Tønnessen. Uppsala University has our sincere gratitude for the excellent way that our workshop and the larger conference was organized and run. The University's Department of Peace and Conflict Research has continued to support our research in various ways after the workshop, and we are again most grateful for this continued commitment to our cause. Finally, it is the home institution of one of us (Öberg) and has earned our thanks for all the large and little ways in which it has facilitated our work. The same thanks go to the University of California, San Diego (UCSD), Strøm's home institution.

We thank a number of our colleagues and the contributors to this book for all the different ways in which they have helped develop the ideas that are expressed here. Special thanks are also due to those workshop participants whose work is not represented here. We nevertheless learned much from their contributions to the workshop. For assistance in preparing the typescript, we are indebted to Johan Brosché.

Thomas Poguntke has our thanks for the cheerful and efficient way in which he has guided our book to publication in the ECPR Routledge book series. We thank our editor and the production staff at Routledge for the excellent way in which they have shepherded the book to publication.

Finally, we thank our families and friends for whatever sacrifices this project has meant for them. We hope that they will find the end product worthwhile.

Magnus Öberg
Kaare Strøm
La Jolla and Uppsala

Part I

Introducing civil conflict

1 Introduction

Magnus Öberg and Kaare Strøm

The meaning and importance of civil conflict

Human societies have always known group violence, and the contemporary world continues to be a violent place. Ruth Sivard (1996) estimates that between 1900 and 1995, armed conflict caused over 40 million deaths in three countries alone: Russia/the USSR, China, and Germany. Almost half of these victims were civilians. World Wars I and II were indeed cataclysmic events, which caused suffering on an unprecedented scale. And even after the conclusion of World War II, the number of armed conflicts tended, until 1992, to increase, rather than decrease, over time (Harbom and Wallensteen, 2005).

Violent conflict comes in many different forms. Some such events take the form of communal violence, that is, organized violence between non-state actors. Others may be massacres or genocide in which a government or ruling group inflicts deadly violence on individuals that may not be armed, organized, or capable of resistance. Yet, the most important and costly forms of conflict in the contemporary world are civil conflicts. A civil conflict is commonly understood as organized armed violence for political purposes between the government of a state and some organized opposition group. Sometimes, one or both of these parties are aided by outside parties such as the governments of other states or transnational armed groups.

Civil (or intrastate) conflict has been the predominant form of war at least since the end of World War II. After the end of the Cold War well over 90 percent of all armed conflicts have been civil conflicts (Harbom and Wallensteen, 2005). These sobering statistics make it a pressing need for scholars and political leaders alike to understand why civil conflicts occur and how they can be resolved or prevented. Yet, in comparison to interstate conflict, there has been little systematic research on civil conflict, and we do not well understand its causes and dynamics. This is now beginning to change and the present volume is one example of the increasing scholarly interest in the problems of civil conflict.

Although for a long time overshadowed by the issues raised by the Cold War, civil conflict has been a problem of great importance long before it came to the fore in the mass media and the scholarly community in the early 1990s. In the post-World War II era civil conflicts have been much more frequent than international conflicts, and they have typically been of much longer duration. Many civil conflicts last for a decade or more. Some that started in the first couple of decades after World War II are still ongoing today (e.g. the Karen insurgency in Myanmar and the civil conflict in Colombia). At any given time since World War II, an average of 14 percent of all countries has been affected by civil conflict. By comparison, only 1–2 percent of all countries are typically affected by international conflict. Although the number of civil conflicts has declined since its peak in 1992, there were 30 conflicts still active in 2004 (Harbom and Wallensteen, 2005).

The human suffering generated by civil conflicts is staggering. We do not have accurate estimates of total casualties generated by civil conflicts since 1945, but they clearly number many millions. At the beginning of 2005 there were approximately 19.2 million displaced people in the world, of which 2.2 million were uprooted in 2004 alone.[1] The vast majority of forced migrants were fleeing countries in civil conflict. The economic costs of civil conflicts are also tremendous. Civil conflict destroys physical infrastructure as well as social infrastructure, and it drives off labor, especially skilled workers (Melander and Öberg, 2006). Civil conflicts have been and continue to be a major obstacle to economic development in several regions of the world (Collier et al., 2003). Moreover, civil conflicts hamper economic growth and development not only in the war-torn country but also in neighboring countries and the surrounding region (Murdoch and Sandler, 2002).

Most civil conflicts are minor armed confrontations generating more than 25 but fewer than 1000 battle-related deaths per year. This fact tells us something about the magnitude of fighting, but this measure is in itself not always a good indicator of the amount of suffering associated with the conflict. The casualties of civil conflict include not only those who die and their immediate families, but also all those who get seriously abused, deprived of their possessions, or driven out of their jobs, neighbourhoods, and homelands. In terms of geographical displacement, civil conflicts generating more than 1000 battle-related deaths do not on average generate a significantly larger number of forced migrants than minor armed conflicts (Melander and Öberg, 2004). In the most extreme case of the post World War II period – the genocide in Rwanda – fewer than 1000 people died in battles. Yet an estimated 500,0000–800,000 people were slaughtered and 2.7 million were displaced (Wallensteen and Sollenberg, 1995).

The prevalence of civil conflict, and its staggering human and material costs, pose two pressing questions for the student of international peace: What the causes of civil conflict might be? and How this kind of conflict might be contained, or better resolved or even prevented? Since antiquity at least, scholars have pondered such questions, and through the evolution of modern social science at least some shared and commonly accepted lessons have been learned. In this volume, we examine the contributions of contemporary scholarship. Our purpose is to shed light on civil conflict in present-day societies, so that we can better understand its causes, termination, and prevention. And if we are to understand civil conflict more adequately, two causal factors seem to us particularly critical. One is the contribution of resources, and particularly natural resources, to the outbreak and sustenance of conflict. The second cause of civil conflict that strikes us as especially important and worthy of our attention lies in governance structures, within and between existing states. While such political institutions can help contain or resolve group conflict, they can also fuel or exacerbate such conflagrations. Furthermore, while resources and governance structures may separately and independently greatly affect the likelihood of civil conflict, their interplay may be especially interesting and important. Could it be, for example, that the impact of natural resource endowments on civil conflict is contingent on the institutional environment? These are the kinds of questions that have motivated the editors and contributors represented in this volume. Thus, in this book we especially explore the role and interplay of governance and resources in the onset, dynamics, and termination of civil conflict.

Resources

Ever since Thucydides (Thucydides, 1954), students of conflict have known that resources matter to the incidence and resolution of disputes, including civil conflict. Disputes over the control over resources, or the distribution of resources, are potential reasons for civil conflict. In this context, the absolute level of resources in a given country has a strong effect on the likelihood of civil conflict. A great number of studies have found that conflict is related to poverty and lack of economic development (Collier and Hoeffler, 1998, 2001; Fearon and Laitin, 1999, 2003; Gurr and Moore, 1997; Hegre et al., 2001). There are several reasons why countries plagued by poverty and lack of economic development may end up in civil conflict. Poverty and underdevelopment imply a lack of economic opportunities which means that in these circumstances the opportunity costs of joining a rebellion are low (Collier, 2000; Gates, 2002). Low economic development also suggests weak state capacity, and hence greater opportunities for rebellion and insurgency (Fearon and Laitin, 2003).

These findings also suggest that a society's distribution of material resources may be closely related to its risk of conflict, since there is a close relationship between income or wealth inequality and the extent of poverty. Countries that are poor also tend to have very uneven distributions of whatever resources they possess. Such inequalities give rise to various grievances upon which rebel groups can mobilize. Yet, the empirical findings on the consequences of inequalities are mixed. Recent studies suggest that inequality between groups may matter more than individual inequalities for civil conflict (Regan and Norton, 2005; Østby, 2005).

Thus, two aspects of material resource endowments are particularly important to the risk of civil conflict: the overall prosperity of the state and inequality in the distribution of material resources. As we have noted, prosperity generally lowers the risk of civil conflict. Yet, more resources are not always better. This is because resources, and particularly lootable natural ones, provide tempting targets for greedy potential rebels. Besides, armed conflict in itself requires resources, so that the presence of such resources can enable potential belligerents to mobilize and act. Whether derived from looting, taxation, or foreign patronage, material resources are a principal means used to contest political authority in violent ways.

This book sheds new light on these complex relationships. Chapter 2 surveys the existing data on civil conflict in the contemporary world. As Kristine Eck, Bethany Lacina, and Magnus Öberg show, the incidence of civil conflict has varied in interesting and important ways over time. In fact, not only has the incidence of civil conflict gone down in the Post-Cold War period, but civil conflict has also become less intense and less atrocious (Lacina, 2006; Melander et al., 2006). Eck, Lacina, and Öberg raise the question whether these trends are coincidental, or whether the fact that the end of Cold War superpower rivalry resulted in decreasing funding for states and rebel movements alike may in part account for the decline in civil conflict. The decline – in many cases the end – of superpower funding has shifted focus to alternative ways of sustaining civil conflict in general, and rebel movements in particular.

The resource perspective calls our attention to the micro-foundations of civil conflict, to the question of how rebel groups are organized, financed, and sustained. In this context, it is important to keep in mind the depressing fact that sometimes what prevents overt conflict is nothing nobler than the costs of organizing and fighting a rebellion. Armed conflict is a very costly endeavor even for its perpetrators. Clothing, feeding, training, and arming a rebel movement is expensive. Organizing and sustaining a rebellion also involves serious collective action problems, and an 'entrepreneur' who wishes to overcome these problems needs to have sufficient resources to create selective incentives (Collier, 2000; Gates, 2002; Lichbach, 1994, 1995). Moreover, being a rebel is a dangerous proposition, and mobilization is often competitive – the government may also offer selective incentives to buy off potential rebels or recruit them into the government army. In their contributions to this volume, William Noël Ivey (Chapter 5), Enric Martínez-Herrera (Chapter 6), and Aleksi Ylönen (Chapter 7) help shed light on such micro-foundations of civil conflict.

Onset and dynamics of civil conflict

Resources may affect civil conflict at different stages and in different ways. One of the most obvious effects they might have is the onset of overt conflict in the first place. In recent years, scholarship on civil conflict has been greatly invigorated by several innovative and important studies focusing on exactly these problems. The debate began with a series of studies by Paul Collier and Anke Hoeffler, who juxtapose and critically examine two competing assumptions about the motivations of rebels in civil conflict: greed versus grievance. There is a long-standing literature on civil conflict which emphasizes the importance of political and economic grievances, inequalities, and deprivation as the driving force behind rebellions (Davis, 1962; Gurr, 1970; Midlarsky, 1988; Muller and Seligson, 1987; Russett, 1964).[2] Collier and Hoeffler, however, argue that for two reasons rebels are more often driven by greed than by grievance (Collier and Hoeffler, 1998, 2002, 2004).[3] First, if rebels are in the business of rectifying collective grievances, they are providing a public good. This implies that potential rebels face serious collective action problems and that it would be difficult to recruit and sustain a rebel army. In contrast, rebels engaged in predation will produce private gain and be much less troubled by collective action problems.

Second, Collier and Hoeffler found that civil conflict is more likely to occur where there is more opportunities for armed predation, e.g. in the form of lootable natural resources.[4] Thus, with respect to the potential for civil conflict, resources are not all alike. For potential rebels, it is the rents and the lootability or obstructability of the relevant resources that matter most (Ross, 2004b). In particular, conflict may be exacerbated by the existence of easily accessible natural resources with a relatively high value to weight ratio, such as diamonds, oil, precious timber, or illicit drugs. Furthermore, the precise location of minerals and other valuable goods may generate fierce conflicts between areas blessed (or cursed) with such resources and those without them. Such regional conflicts over resources have, for example, contributed to the civil conflicts in Congo and Nigeria in the 1960s. Thus, Ross (2004a, 2004b) argues that in more general terms resource-rich peripheral regions generate separatist incentives.

Collier and Hoeffler's argument and findings sparked a fierce debate, and subsequent studies have not found the same strong relationship between primary commodities and conflict onset (de Soysa, 2002; Fearon, 2005; Fearon and Laitin, 2003). A possible explanation, as Ola Olson and Heather Condon Fors argue, is that appropriable resources also render the government better equipped to deter and suppress rebellions (Olsson and Fors, 2004).

In sum, research to date suggests that natural resource wealth is important in explaining the incidence and duration of civil conflicts, while the role of natural resources in the onset of conflict is still an open question. There is also some disagreement as to why natural resources may be important. A few recent studies suggest that natural resources are related to conflict not because they provide rebel financing, but because government extraction of such resources often generate local grievances (Swanson, 2002; Switzer, 2001).

This volume provides further evidence of such ramifications of resource endowments. In Chapter 7 Aleksi Ylönen examines the civil conflict in Sudan and the role of natural resources, especially oil. Ylönen suggests that the oil in Sudan may indeed be related to rebel motivations and the civil conflict, but not through greed in the way suggested by Collier and Hoeffler. His argument is that natural resource endowments may in themselves give rise to grievances, which in turn may fuel rebellion.

Similarly, in Chapter 5 William Noël Ivey reconsiders Collier and Hoeffler's argument about grievance and rebellion in light of another case of civil conflict. Ivey examines the linkages between the distribution of resources, the availability of lootable resources (in this case precious timber) and the incidence and duration of civil conflict in the Naxalite insurgencies in India. Evidence from the Naxalite cases suggests that in societies in which the majority of the population directly depends upon natural resources for their subsistence civil conflicts will tend to be localized and of short duration. Only when and where some form of redistribution of natural resources creates opportunities for insurgents to sustain an insurgency and reduce the power of the resource controllers should we expect to see sustained insurgencies. Thus, the distribution of wealth and resources seems to matter, albeit not exactly in the way suggested by previous grievance arguments. The role of predation and the availability of lootable resources in the form of precious timber, on the other hand, seems to play only a marginal role in the Naxalite insurgency, and it cannot account for the variations in activity within the Naxalite case.

Termination and post-conflict stability

Resource availability may also have implications for conflict resolution and post-conflict stability. Previous research implies that conflicts with resource abundance are harder to terminate (Collier *et al.*, 2004; Fearon, 2004). Where lootable resources are easily accessible, rebels will be better able to sustain their activities and more tempted to revert to them after a potential ceasefire. Such resources create opportunities for political rents: gains or spoils created through political (or armed) intervention. Rents in turn attract rent seekers, individuals or groups that prefer to prosper through political means rather than through the economic marketplace.

Yet, the problem of rent-seeking and lootable resources has not yet had a big impact on the conflict resolution literature proper – although there are a few exceptions. Michael Doyle and Nicolas Sambanis find that resource abundance has a negative effect on peace-building efforts and thus on post-conflict stability (Doyle and Sambanis, 2003). Leonard Wantchekon argues that dependence on rents from natural resources makes warring parties in inconclusive conflicts less likely to agree on putting their conflict to the people for arbitration, whereas dependence on the citizens' productive investments make them more likely to do so (Wantchekon, 2004). Margareta Sollenberg's study in Chapter 10 is in part an empirical test of this proposition.

Governance structures

Governance structures are the established means of resolving conflicts of interest and coordination problems within or between societies. Politics involves resolving differences and incompatibilities, and the differences that are most difficult to resolve often have to do with the allocation of important values. These are often the most serious governance challenges that political communities face. Even under everyday circumstances, governance is a critical task. In communities where people interact repeatedly, significantly, and with peaceful intentions, they need some minimum of governance mechanisms, and they need these structures to meet certain minimal criteria.

Governance and governance structures are at the heart of civil conflict. To rebel is to rise up (in arms) against, reject, or challenge government authority. Civil conflict follows when the government attempts to forcefully reassert its authority (Öberg, 2002: 18). Thus, whatever the concrete demands made by the rebels, a civil conflict is a violent contest over political authority, over the right and means to make authoritative resolutions to conflicts of interest. The rebels are either questioning an authoritative resolution to a conflict of interests, or they want an authoritative resolution to a conflict of interest; or more commonly they wish to obtain for themselves, or deprive the government of, the competence to make authoritative decisions on some issue or issues, or for all issues concerning some people or geographical area (Öberg, 2002: 87–88). The termination of civil conflict then, involves the re-establishment of functioning governance structures.

When governance structures work, they allow groups or individuals to reach agreements and resolve their differences. Governance structures that are perceived to be fair and effective tend to diminish the risk of conflict. All else equal, the more responsive and effective the governance structures, the lower the likelihood that conflict will break out. And the more positive governance expectations the parties to any conflict have, the more easily any existing conflict can be resolved. While these are clearly not the only conditions that affect the onset, incidence, duration, and resolution of civil conflict, we believe that governance structures are critical parameters in this picture, and that their importance has too often been overlooked.

But what exactly are governance structures, and which are the ones that matter? In the traditional study of international relations, this question has tended to be addressed in overly simplistic ways because of the assumption of a Westphalian world, that is to say, a world in which the only actors that matter are a set of sovereign and equal states. This is indeed the normative principles by which Europe was organized following the 1648 Treaty of Westphalia. This treaty established the principle of sovereign equality, which implies that states are not subject to any higher authority within their respective jurisdictions, that all states are legally equal (so that no state has any formal authority over any other), and that all states have a right to political self-determination and the concomitant obligation to respect the right to self-determination of other states (the principle of non-intervention).

In a purely Westphalian world, it is easy, at least in principle, to identify the critical governance structures. In domestic politics, they are simply the formal and informal political institutions of the relevant states. For a well-contained purely intrastate conflict then, the relevant governance structures would all be comprised by the national government. Outside the various states, the governance structures would be thin, consisting only of the treaties, conventions, and supranational institutions that the relevant states had approved and with which they could be expected to comply.

In the contemporary world, which has moved at least some distance away from the theoretical simplicities of the Westphalian peace, it is less simple to identify the relevant governance structures. Clearly, domestic political institutions, such as legal orders, power-sharing arrangements, and federalism, still matter a great deal, especially in situations of purely intrastate contestation. But there is also a growing set of governance structures that are not contained by national borders. The United Nations and its various agencies, especially its peacekeeping operations, is just one example of an effort to project transnational governance even in places where national institutions break down or provide perverse or unacceptable environments for peace. Other international agreements and orders provide additional, though perhaps less enforceable, means of governance. Examples would be the Organization for Security and Cooperation in Europe, the various international war crime tribunals, international economic embargo arrangements that have been established (such as the food-for-oil program for the previous Iraqi regime), and other agreements containing enforceable sanctions of some significance.

For practical purposes, governance structures also include formal or informal alliances of states willing and able to intervene in conflict situations, such as NATO and later the EU in Kosovo and the US- and British-led alliances that intervened in the Gulf War of 1991 and that led the invasions to topple the Taliban regime in Afghanistan in 2001 and Saddam Hussein's regime in Iraq in 2003. Governance structures may also be imposed by great powers acting unilaterally, such as the United States in parts of Latin America or France in some of its former colonies.

Finally, international governance structures include a vast and growing number of non-governmental organizations, from Amnesty International to Al-Qaeda, to the extent that these are able to impose their terms, resources, and conditions on potential participants in any domestic or interstate conflict. The exact array of governance structures in any given conflict will of course depend on time, place, participants, and the stakes involved. But there is no reason to doubt that this whole array of structures, involving national governments and great powers, non-governmental and international organizations, and all the rest, matters to those who are engaged in civil conflict or who are considering that option.

Governance structures may be stable or unstable, simple or complex, coherent or incoherent. They are most likely to be successful if they can gain the consent of all or most significant parties to any potential conflict. We can think of significant groups as all those groups capable of making serious and credible threats to challenge government authority in case their demands or expectations are not met. In order to win popular approval, governance structures have to provide some expectations to all significant groups that at least some minimal expectations will be met.

What properties will make governance structures more or less acceptable to the populations they serve? One criterion is clearly *effectiveness*. Whatever other virtues it might have, a political system that is not able to guarantee its citizens a reasonable measure of personal safety, or a rudimentary protection of their property, is not likely to be valued very highly. Many states have found supranational governance structures such as the League of Nations and at times the United Nations wanting on such grounds. A second demand is *efficiency*. Political governance structures have to 'deliver the bacon' at a price that most citizens are willing to pay. They cannot make unreasonable demands on time or human resources or disproportionate encroachments on the freedoms of those they are designed to serve. Third, political governance structures have to be *responsive* to their citizens, or more broadly to all those groups and individuals that are affected by them and have the power to reject them. Finally, political structures have to be reasonably *fair* and unbiased in their conferral of costs and benefits.

The last of these concerns, fairness or the absence of bias, is especially important in situations in which much is at stake for some or all groups. In such situations especially, governance structures have to secure the consent of actual or potential losers in the political game (Anderson *et al.*, 2005). If losers turn to violence or other 'outside options', then civil peace may break down. Politics involves many contestations or decisions that might produce losers. Elections are the emblematic of such mechanism in democracies. While elections and the uncertainty they represent are hallmark virtues of democracy (Przeworski, 1991), their implications can be deeply disturbing to those that do not prevail, and their consequences can therefore often be destabilizing. Parliamentary, administrative, and judicial decisions can have similar properties: they produce winners and losers and, for better or worse, their decisions often contain elements of uncertainty and surprise.

Many such decisions and contests will inherently generate losers *ex post*, because they are competitive and because efficient solutions often require that some players get advantages at the expense of others. But they can vary dramatically in the extent to which the losses that arise *ex post* are predictable *ex ante*. The *competitiveness* of a political governance structure, for example, an election, is a reflection of the extent to which losses are predictable *ex ante*. The more competitive the election, the more uncertain it is who the winners and losers will be. The same reasoning can be applied to other institutions, such as courts or arbitration agencies. The more uncertain the outcome is *ex ante*, the more competitive the institution.

We can think of fairness in similar terms. The more the outcome depends on the performance of the group rather than its identity, the fairer the institution. The fairness and competitiveness of governance structures are critical to their acceptability. The more political processes seem open, fair, and competitive, the more they will be trusted by all players, and the less likely the *ex post* losers will be to complain about their fate, or worse, to withdraw from the game and resort to force.

Particular kinds of states may run into particular governance problems. Problems of effectiveness and efficiency may be felt most acutely in weak or failed states, where essential public goods are most likely not to be delivered. Responsiveness may perhaps be a particular concern in autocratic or especially corrupt societies, where rulers do not even try to accommodate the desires of their citizens or subjects, until perhaps these subjects' lots get so miserable that they are likely to rebel. But fairness and openness are a somewhat more complicated matter. On the one hand, it is probably important for civil peace that no significant group is permitted to fare too badly, regardless of its performance. On the other hand, there probably needs to be some positive probability of not only avoiding a seriously bad outcome, but also of achieving truly attractive and desired results. Thus, some credible expectation of 'winning', of achieving the results that one greatly desires, is likely to be of great importance in sustaining support for a particular governance regime (see Anderson *et al.*, 2005).

Onset and dynamics of civil conflict

Different political regimes are likely to score differently on the dimensions of governance discussed above: effectiveness, efficiency, responsiveness, fairness, and competitiveness. For example, the domestic political institutions in a democracy are likely to be more responsive, fair, and competitive than in a typical autocracy. Yet, in some circumstances at least, autocracy may be more effective and efficient. Hence, states with different governance structures are likely to have different incentive and opportunity structures for rebellion as well as for repression, and hence be differentially susceptible to civil conflict.

Most research relating governance structures to the onset and dynamics of civil conflict has focused on the forms and degree of democracy. While there does not seem to be a straightforward linear relationship between the level of democracy and civil conflict, recent research has revealed some interesting patterns. Several studies find a parabolic relationship between regime type and civil conflict such that strong democracies and strong autocracies are less susceptible to civil conflict than other types of regimes (Benson and Kugler, 1998; Elbadawi and Sambanis, 2002; Ellingsen and Gleditsch, 1997; Hegre *et al.*, 2001; Muller and Weede, 1990). The argument is that in strong autocracies, the government has the capacity to prevent effective mobilization and suppress would-be rebellions. Strong democracies, on the other hand, are more responsive to grievances and allow for political participation and influence, thereby making rebellion a much less attractive option. The problem in the inbetween group is that they are neither as responsive and open as democracies, nor as effective in preventing or suppressing would-be rebellions as autocracies are. In short, in democracies there are fewer incentives to rebel, and in autocracies there is less opportunity, while in anocracies (the inbetween category) there may be both strong incentives to rebel and the opportunity to act on them. The development over time in the Basque conflict illustrates this pattern. In Chapter 6, Enric Martínez-Herrera analyzes how the Spanish transition to democracy, together with counter-insurgency activities and international cooperation, has affected the level of violence in the Basque conflict since 1975. He examines the effects of a range of counter-insurgency strategies, such as constitutional engineering, policing efforts, and international cooperation, upon the levels of violence.

The problem can also be framed in terms of the consistency and stability of institutional arrangements. Democracies with consistent political institutions have well-developed mechanisms for executive recruitment and tend to be stable. Autocracies with consistent political institutions and well-developed mechanisms for executive selection are also relatively stable. Regimes with inconsistent political institutions (mixtures of democratic and autocratic institutions) tend to be less stable and more prone to civil conflict (Gates *et al.*, 2001; Przeworski *et al.*, 2000). Moreover, institutional instability is in itself associated with a heightened risk of civil conflict (Hegre *et al.*, 2001), and there is good reason to believe that the relationship between institutional inconsistency, instability, and civil conflict is endogenous (Gates *et al.*, 2001). In other words, conflict tends to breed institutional instability, and institutional instability breeds conflict.

While we know relatively little about how different types of autocratic systems of governance might affect the likelihood and dynamics of civil conflict, recent studies have shown that some types of democratic systems reduce the likelihood of civil conflict more than others. Marta Reynal-Querol finds that among parliamentary democracies, more inclusive forms of governance arrangements, such as proportional systems, are less prone to civil conflict than less inclusive arrangements, such as majoritarian ones (Reynal-Querol, 2002). Similarly, supporters of consociational democracy have argued that such structures provides better guarantees for minority groups than do more majoritarian systems, and hence better prospects for civil peace in divided societies (Lijphart, 1977, 1999). Proportional and consociational democracies tend to impose fewer clear-cut losses on any significant group and may therefore be perceived as fairer. On the other hand, majoritarian systems may be more open and competitive and provide better long-run incentives for politicians to build more inclusive constituencies (Roeder, 2005; Strøm et al., 2003).

How well a nominally democratic system works in practice may also affect the likelihood of it being rejected in a rebellion. Repeated electoral fraud may make elections predictable and undermine losers' consent. As Fernando Sánchez shows in Chapter 11, repeated electoral fraud in Costa Rica in the 1940s was an important catalyst in bringing about the civil conflict in 1948. In some societies electoral outcomes may be similarly predictable due to ethnic or religious composition.

Multiethnic societies do not seem to be inherently more prone to civil conflict. In fact, most studies find that if the level of ethnic and religious fragmentation is related to civil conflict at all – if anything, ethnic fragmentation seems to reduce the risk of conflict (Collier and Hoeffler, 2004; Sambanis, 2001). However, when ethnicity and religion become politicized, this may affect how governance structures fare in terms of competitiveness. Strong mobilization along ethnic or religious lines may make electoral outcomes determinate if there is a dominant group, thus undermining losers' consent. This might at least partly explain why recent studies of the onset of civil conflict have generally found that countries with ethnic dominance also have a higher propensity for civil conflict (Collier and Hoeffler, 2004; Elbadawi and Sambanis, 2002; Ellingsen, 2000; Hegre et al., 2001; Reynal-Querol, 2002).

State formation is a conflictual process in and of itself, and newly formed institutions tend to be less stable than well established ones. Several studies have found that the time since independence is associated with the likelihood of civil conflict (Fearon and Laitin, 2003; Hegre et al., 2001). Governance structures in many former colonies suffer from a lack of effectiveness, efficiency, and responsiveness. Departing colonial powers often leave behind social and political structures associated with colonial rule and exploitation, and they also often continue to intervene in the internal affairs of their erstwhile possessions.

Termination and post-conflict stability

The high cost of civil war means that most parties are keen to find ways to resolve the conflict short of fighting it out to the bitter end. Moreover, most civil conflicts are inconclusive, and do not end in clear victories and defeats. In inconclusive conflicts the parties may find it difficult to settle even as their expectations about the final outcome of continued fighting converge, because revealing to your opponent that you have had enough may influence his expectations such that the bargaining range moves further from your ideal point. To avoid this problem, assistance from third parties may be helpful. It has been suggested that measures that invoke supplementary penalties and rewards linked to the negotiation process can help overcome informational impediments (Wilson, 1995) and that third parties may manipulate the costs of continued fighting so as to shorten the conflict (Licklider, 1995). Thus, in finding a settlement and establishing a new, or re-establishing an old, governance structure, outside intervention may be helpful.

Yet, not all types of intervention are likely to be helpful. Recent research on third party intervention suggests civil conflicts with international intervention generally tend to be longer than conflicts without such intervention, but that intervention on the side of the government may shorten the conflict (Regan, 1996, 2000, 2002). Patrick Regan also finds that opposing interventions on both sides in a civil conflict tends to prolong the conflict, which may explain why we see a peak in conflict terminations at the end of the Cold War. Furthermore, biased intervention tends to shorten the conflict, while neutral intervention does not. Finally, the timing of the intervention does not seem to affect the likelihood of termination in the next period (Regan, 2002). Thus, the available evidence suggests that economic and military interventions have generally not been very helpful in terminating civil conflict or promoting post-conflict stability, but again the evidence is mixed. In Chapter 8, Scott Gates and Håvard Strand examine the ways in which military interventions affect regime stability and democratization. Gates and Strand also look at the democratization effects of interventions, examining whether countries that after an intervention shift from autocracy or semi-democracy to democracy are more stable than regimes that do not experience such political reform.

While recent research suggests that in terminating conflict and establishing viable post-conflict governance structures, military and economic interventions may be more problematic than helpful, political, and diplomatic mediation, and post-conflict interventions may be a different matter. In Chapter 12 Isak Svensson asks whether mediation by different types of mediators increases or decreases the likelihood of a settlement.

Conflict parties may also attempt to settle the conflict with little or no outside intervention. As Fernando Sánchez shows in Chapter 11, holding free and fair elections is one way to produce a settlement to the contested issues in a civil conflict. The opportunity to do so, however, may be contingent on some uncertainty as to the outcome of potential elections. As Leonard Wantchekon has argued: in inconclusive armed conflicts warring parties are more likely to settle their conflict through competitive elections if the outcomes of such elections are not foreseeable (Wantchekon, 2004; Wantchekon and Neeman, 2002). Thus, if the electoral outcome is predictable, this may be a barrier to this mechanism of conflict resolution. In other words, competitiveness matters in a positive way. Given the propensity to vote along ethnic lines, especially in conflict-ridden societies, ethnic dominance would make the outcome predictable, while ethnic heterogeneity or homogeneity would make outcomes less predictable. In Chapter 10 Margareta Sollenberg tests this proposition empirically.

Maintaining a stable peace once a settlement is at hand is particularly complicated in civil conflicts, since it typically implies that one side will have to give up its outside option, its ability to resort to force. Hence, a credible peace agreement requires confidence among the conflict parties that the party that retains its coercive means (usually the government) does not exploit the disarmed side at some later time. It is difficult to create conditions that allows the government credibly to commit not to renege on the agreement once the opposition has been disarmed. Barbara Walter has therefore argued that outside interventions that provide security guarantees in the post-conflict period are necessary to create stable peace agreements (Walter, 1999, 2002). In contrast to military and economic interventions in ongoing conflicts, interventions to provide security guarantees in the post-conflict period seem to promote peace (Walter, 2002). The question is who can or should intervene and produce guarantees to sustain a peace agreement? In Chapter 9, Theodora-Ismene Gizelis argues that interventions to provide such guarantees is a public good and that settlement therefore requires a privileged actor or group of actors willing to bear the costs of enforcing it.

Peace agreements establish new, or re-establish old, social and political orders, and it is often argued that for a peace agreement to be stable, all or almost all of the major warring parties have to be included (Darby and Mac Ginty, 2000; Hampson, 1996; Zahar, 2003, 2006). The idea is that any excluded groups will either continue fighting or try to destabilize the agreement. Evidence that inclusive agreements make for more stable settlements is sketchy, but a number of studies point to rebel groups standing on the outside as potential threats to the stability of agreements (Kydd and Walter, 2002; Newman and Richmond, 2006; Stedman, 1997; Zahar, 2003, 2006). In her contribution to this volume, Desirée Nilsson asks whether these propositions conform with the experiences in recent peace agreements. Looking at all peace agreements between 1989 and 2004, Nilsson examines whether the exclusion of rebel groups in peace agreements affects the signatories' commitment to peace.

Contributions in this volume

This volume raises several important issues in the study of civil conflict. Our particular aim is to focus on the role of resources and governance structures in the onset, incidence, and duration of civil conflict, as well as in its termination and in outside interventions. Among the questions we raise are the following:

- How are natural resources linked to civil conflict? How do such resources affect the onset, incidence, and duration of civil conflict? What role do natural resources play in the termination of civil conflicts? In different ways, the contributions of Ivey, Ylönen, Gleditsch and Salehyan, and Sollenberg all address these questions.

- How do changing governance structures, such as domestic political institutions, international peace-keeping efforts, or armed interventions by other states or coalitions of states, affect civil conflict? The chapters by Sanchez, Martinez-Herrera, and Gates and Strand all address questions of this nature.
- What is the role of governance factors in ending civil conflict? On this point, we are aided by the contributions of Svensson, Nilsson, and Sollenberg.

The first part of this book introduces the problem of civil conflict and the topics covered in the remainder of the book. In addition to the present chapter, Part I contains a chapter by Kristine Eck, Bethany Lacina and Magnus Öberg which gives a global overview of the scope and magnitude of the problem of civil conflict since 1946. Part II deals with issues of onset, incidence, and duration of civil conflict. In Chapter 3 Bethany Lacina details what we know about the causes of civil conflict based on large-n studies, while also providing an assessment of some of the strengths and weaknesses of this approach. In Chapter 4, Kristian S. Gleditsch and Idean Salehyan analyze some of the international dynamics that civil conflicts may generate. They ask whether civil conflict increases the risk of international disputes and describe a number of mechanisms through which civil conflict may give rise to international disputes. In Chapter 5 William Noël Ivey examines the linkages between natural resources and the incidence and duration of civil conflict in India's Naxalite insurgency. In Chapter 6, Enric Martínez-Herrera analyzes the influence of the transition to democracy and changing governance structures, together with counter-insurgency activities and international cooperation that has affected the level of violence in the Basque conflict since 1975. Martínez-Herrera examines the effects on conflict of a combination of counter-insurgency strategies, such as constitutional engineering, policing efforts, and international cooperation. In Chapter 7 Aleksi Ylönen examines the role of oil in the conflicts in the Sudan. He contrasts the explanation that insurgencies in the Sudan have been driven by responses to the national government's repressive policies related to oil extraction and exploration with a focus on rebel opportunities generated by the presence of oil in contested areas. In Chapter 8, Scott Gates and Håvard Strand study how military interventions affect regime stability and democratization. They find that interventions per se do not affect regime stability, but that interventions associated with military defeat and the imposition of a new government lead to greater instability, whether the new regime is democratic or not.

In Part III we shift attention from the causes and processes of civil conflict, toward the termination and resolution of civil conflict. In Chapter 9 Theodoea-Ismene Gizelis analyzes the settlement of ethnic civil conflict as a collective action problem. She argues that due to its adverse regional effects, the settlement of ethnic civil conflict is a public good. Settlement therefore requires a privileged actor of group of actors willing to bear the costs of enforcing a settlement. In Chapter 10 Margareta Sollenberg asks under what circumstances warring elites decide to let the public settle their dispute through competitive elections. In Chapter 11, Fernando F. Sánchez sets out to explain the stability of democracy in Costa Rica since 1948 by examining the breakdown of democracy leading to a civil conflict in 1948 and the major institutional reforms undertaken after the armed conflict. Sánchez examines the effects of corruption, nepotism, progressive land reforms, international support for the opposition, a weak military, a controversial and unstable ruling coalition, and electoral fraud. In Chapter 12, Isak Svensson argues that an important source of mediator influence stems from the potential to withdraw from the process, and that the credibility of the threat to withdraw, and hence leverage of the mediator, depends in large part on whether the mediator is a democratic state, a non-democratic state, or an organization. He finds that in active civil conflicts mediation by non-democratic states are more efficient. In the last study, Chapter 13, Desirée Nilsson examines why and how the stability of peace agreements is affected by the exclusion or inclusion of different rebel groups. Finally, in Part IV, which contains the final chapter of this book, we offer some general conclusions about the role of resources and governance structures in civil conflict.

Notes

1 Numbers from UNHCR: www.unhcr.org/cgi-bin/texis/vtx/basics/opendoc.htm?tbl=BASICS&id=3b028097c
2 There are also a number of studies that in various ways incorporate both grievance and mobilization perspectives (Gurr, 1993, 2000; Regan and Norton, 2005).
3 This debate is reminiscent of the old deprivation (Davis, 1962; Gurr, 1970) versus opportunities (Tarrow, 1994; Tilly, 1978) debate, although there are important differences.
4 The argument made by Collier and Hoeffler is reminiscent of that made by Charles Tilly (1978). Tilly argues that grievances are basically always present, and it is the ability to mobilize that determines the extent overt conflict.

References

Anderson, C., Blais, A., Donovan, T., and Listhaug, O. (2005) *Losers' Consent: Elections and Democratic Legitimacy*. New York: Oxford University Press.
Benson, M. and Kugler, J. (1998) 'Power Parity, Democracy, and the Severity of Internal Violence', *Journal of Conflict Resolution* 42(2): 196–209.
Collier, P. (2000) 'Rebellion as a Quasi Criminal Activity', *Journal of Conflict Resolution* 44(6): 839–853.
Collier, P. and Hoeffler, A. (1998) 'On the Economic Causes of Civil War', *Oxford Economic Papers* 50(4): 567–573.
Collier, P. and Hoeffler, A. (2001) 'Greed and Grievance in Civil War', www.worldbank.org/research/conflict/papers/greedandgrievance.htm.

Collier, P. and Hoeffler, A. (2002) 'On the Incidence of Civil War in Africa', *Journal of Conflict Resolution* 46(1): 13–28.
Collier, P. and Hoeffler, A. (2004) 'Greed and Grievance in Civil War', *Oxford Economic Papers* 56(4): 563–595.
Collier, P., Elliot, L., Hegre, H., Hoeffler, A., Reynal-Querol, M., and Sambanis, N. (2003) *Breaking the Conflict Trap: Civil War and Development Policy.* Washington, DC: The World Bank and Oxford University Press.
Collier, P., Hoeffler, A., and Söderbom, M. (2004) 'On the Duration of Civil War', *Journal of Peace Research* 41(3): 253–273.
Darby, J. and Mac Ginty, R. (2000) *The Management of Peace Processes.* Basingstoke: Macmillan Press Ltd.
Davis, J. (1962) 'Toward a Theory of Revolution', *American Sociological Review* 27(1): 13–28.
de Soysa, I. (2002) 'Paradise Is a Bazaar? Greed, Creed, and Governance in Civil War, 1989–99', *Journal of Peace Research* 39(4): 395–416.
Doyle, M.W. and Sambanis, N. (2003) *Alternative Measures and Estimates of Peace Building Success.* New Haven, CN: Yale University, Department of Political Science.
Elbadawi, I. and Sambanis, N. (2002) 'How Much War Will We See? Estimating the Prevalence of Civil War in 161 Countries, 1960–1999', *Journal of Conflict Resolution* 46(3): 307–334.
Ellingsen, T. (2000) 'Colorful Community or Ethnic Witches' Brew? Multiethnicity and Domestic Conflict During and After the Cold War', *Journal of Conflict Resolution* 44(2): 228–249.
Ellingsen, T. and Gleditsch, N.P. (1997) 'Democracy and Armed Conflict in the Third World', in K. Volden and D. Smith, ed., *Causes of Conflict in Third World Countries.* Oslo: International Peace Research Institute (69–81).
Fearon, J.D. (2004) 'Why Do Some Civil Wars Last So Much Longer Than Others?' *Journal of Peace Research* 41(3): 275–301.
Fearon, J.D. (2005) 'Primary Commodity Exports and Civil War', *Journal of Conflict Resolution* 49(4): 483–507.
Fearon, J.D. and Laitin, D.D. (1999) Weak States, Rough Terrain, and Large-Scale Ethnic Violence Since 1945. Paper presented at the 1999 Annual Meetings of the American Political Science Association, 2–5 September, Atlanta, GA.
Fearon, J.D. and Laitin, D.D. (2003) 'Ethnicity, Insurgency, and Civil War', *American Political Science Review* 97(1): 75–90.
Gates, S. (2002) 'Recruitment and Allegiance – The Microfoundations of Rebellion', *Journal of Conflict Resolution* 46(1): 111–130.
Gates, S., Hegre, H., and Gleditsch, N.P. (2001) 'Democracy and Civil Conflict after the Cold War', in D. Berg-Schlosser and R. Vetik, ed., *Perspectives on Democratic Consolidation in Central and Eastern Europe.* New York: Columbia University Press (185–194).
Gurr, T.R. (1970) *Why Men Rebel.* Princeton, NJ: Princeton University Press.
Gurr, T.R. (1993) 'Why Minorities Rebel: A Global Analysis of Communal Mobilization and Conflict since 1945', *International Political Science Review* 14(2): 161–201.
Gurr, T.R. (2000) *People Versus States: Minorities at Risk in the New Century.* Washington, DC: United States Institute of Peace Press.
Gurr, T.R. and Moore, W.H. (1997) 'Ethnopolitical Rebellion: A Cross-Sectional

Analysis of the 1980s with Risk Assessments for the 1990s', *American Journal of Political Science* 41(4): 1079–1103.

Hampson, F.O. (1996) *Nurturing Peace: Why Peace Settlements Succeed or Fail*. Washington, DC: United States Institute for Peace Press.

Harbom, L. and Wallensteen, P. (2005) 'Armed Conflict and its International Dimensions, 1946–2004', *Journal of Peace Research* 42(5): 623–635.

Hegre, H., Tanja, E., Scott, G., and Gleditsch, N.P. (2001) 'Toward a Democratic Civil Peace? Democracy, Political Change, and Civil War, 1816–1992', *American Political Science Review* 95(1): 33–48.

Kydd, A. and Walter, B.F. (2002) 'Sabotaging the Peace: The Politics of Extremist Violence', *International Organization* 56(2): 263–296.

Lacina, B. (2006) 'Explaining the Severity of Civil Wars', *Journal of Conflict Resolution* 50(2): 276–289.

Lichbach, M.I. (1994). 'Rethinking Rationality and Rebellion – Theories of Collective Action and Problems of Collective Dissent', *Rationality and Society* 6(1): 8–39.

Lichbach, M.I. (1995) *The Rebel's Dilemma*. Ann Arbor, MI: University of Michigan Press.

Licklider, R. (1995). 'The Consequences of Negotiated Settlements in Civil Wars, 1945–1993', *American Political Science Review* 89(3): 681–690.

Lijphart, A. (1977) *Democracy in Plural Societies: A Comparative Exploration*. New Haven, CN: Yale University Press.

Lijphart, A. (1999) *Patterns of Democracy: Government Reforms and Performance in Thirty-Six Countries*. New Haven, CN: Yale University Press.

Melander, E. and Öberg, M. (2004) 'Forced Migration: The Effects of the Magnitude and Scope of Fighting', Uppsala Peace Research Papers No. 8.

Melander, E. and Öberg, M. (2006). 'Time to Go: Duration Dependence in Forced Migration', *International Interactions* 32(2): 129–152.

Melander, E., Öberg, M., and Hall, J. (2006) 'Are "New Wars" More Atrocious?' Paper presented at Jan Tinbergen Peace Science Conference, June 26–28, Tinbergen Institute Amsterdam.

Midlarsky, M.I. (1988) 'Rulers and the Ruled: Patterned Inequality and the Onset of Mass Political Violence', *American Political Science Review* 82(2): 491–509.

Muller, E.N. and Seligson, M.A. (1987) 'Inequality and Insurgency', *American Political Science Review* 81(2): 425–452.

Muller, E.N. and Weede, E. (1990) 'Cross-National Variations in Political Violence: A Rational Action Approach', *Journal of Conflict Resolution* 34: 624–651.

Murdoch, J.C. and Sandler, T. (2002) 'Civil Wars and Economic Growth: A Regional Comparison', *Defence and Peace Economics* 13(6): 451–464.

Newman, E. and Richmond, O. (2006) *Challenges to Peacebuilding: Managing Spoilers During Conflict Resolution*. New York: United Nations University Press.

Öberg, M. (2002) 'The Onset of Ethnic War as a Bargaining Process: Testing a Costly Signaling Model. PhD dissertation, Department of Peace and Conflict Research, Uppsala University, Uppsala.

Olsson, O. and Fors, H.C. (2004) 'Congo: The Prize of Predation', *Journal of Peace Research* 41(3): 321–336.

Østby, G. (2005) 'Horizontal Inequalities and Civil War'. Paper presented at the Annual National Political Science Conference, January 5–7, Hurdalsjoen, Norway.

Przeworski, A. (1991) *Democracy and the Market: Political and Economic Reforms in Eastern Europe and Latin America*. Cambridge: Cambridge University Press.

Przeworski, A., Michael, E.A., Cheibub, J.A., and Limongi, F. (2000) *Democracy and Development: Political Institutions and Well-Being in the World, 1950–1990*. Cambridge: Cambridge University Press.

Regan, P.M. (1996) 'Conditions of Successful Third-Party Intervention in Intrastate Conflicts', *Journal of Conflict Resolution* 42(2): 336–359.

Regan, P.M. (2000) *Civil Wars and Foreign Powers: Outside Intervention in Intrastate Conflict*. First paperback 2002 edn. Ann Arbor, MI: University of Michigan Press.

Regan, P.M. (2002) 'Third Party Intervention and the Duration of Intrastate Conflicts', *Journal of Conflict Resolution* 46(1): 55–73.

Regan, P.M. and Norton, D. (2005) 'Greed, Grievance, and Mobilization in Civil Wars', *Journal of Conflict Resolution* 49(3): 319–336.

Reynal-Querol, M. (2002) 'Ethnicity, Political Systems, and Civil Wars', *Journal of Conflict Resolution* 46(1): 29–54.

Roeder, P. (2005) *Sustainable Peace: Power and Democracy after Civil Wars*. Ithaca, NY: Cornell University Press.

Ross, M.L. (2004a) 'How Does Natural Resource Wealth Influence Civil War? Evidence from 13 Cases', *International Organization* 58: 35–67.

Ross, M.L. (2004b) 'What Do We Know About Natural Resources and Civil War?', *Journal of Peace Research* 41(3): 337–356.

Russett, B. (1964) 'Inequality and Instability: The Relation of Land Tenure to Politics', *World Politics* 16(3): 442–454.

Sambanis, N. (2001) 'Do Ethnic and Nonethnic Civil Wars Have the Same Causes? A Theoretical and Empirical Inquiry', *Journal of Conflict Resolution* 45(3): 259–282.

Sivard, R.L. (1996) 'Wars and War Related Deaths, 1900–1995', *World Military and Social Expenditures 1996*. Washington, DC: World Priorities.

Stedman, S.J. (1997) 'Spoiler Problems in Peace Processes', *International Security* 22(2): 5–53.

Strøm, K., Müller, M., and Bergman, T. eds (2003) *Delegation and Accountability in Parliamentary Democracies*. Oxford: Oxford University Press.

Swanson, P. (2002) 'Fuelling Conflict: The Oil Industry and Armed Conflict: Fafo', Program on International Co-operation and Conflict Resolution.

Switzer, P. (2001) 'Armed Conflict and Natural Resources: The Case of the Minerals Sector', International Institute for Environment and Development.

Tarrow, S. (1994) *Power in Movements: Social Movements, Collective Action, and Politics*. Cambridge: Cambridge University Press.

Thucydides (1954) *History of the Peloponnesian War*. London: Penguin Books.

Tilly, C. (1978) *From Mobilization to Revolution*. New York: McGraw Hill.

Wallensteen, P. and Sollenberg, M. (1995) 'After the Cold War: Emerging Patterns of Armed Conflict 1989–94', *Journal of Peace Research* 32(3): 345–360.

Walter, B.F. (1999) 'Designing Transition from Civil War', in Barbara F. Walter and Jack Snyder, eds, *Civil Wars, Insecurity, and Intervention*. New York: Columbia University Press (38–69).

Walter, B.F. (2002) *Committing to Peace. The Successful Settlement of Civil Wars*. Princeton, NJ: Princeton University Press.

Wantchekon, L. (2004) 'The Paradox of "Warlord" Democracy: A Theoretical Investigation', *American Political Science Review* 98(1): 17–33.

Wantchekon, L. and Neeman, Z. (2002) 'A Theory of Post-Civil War Democratization', *Journal of Theoretical Politics* 14(4): 439–464.

Wilson, R.B. (1995) 'Strategic and Informational Barriers to Negotiation', in K.J. Arrow, R.H. Mnookin, L. Ross, A. Tversky, and R.B. Wilson, eds, *Barriers to Conflict Resolution*. New York: W.W. Norton & Co.

Zahar, M.J. (2003) 'Reframing the Spoiler Debate in Peace Processes', in John Darby and Roger Mac Ginty, eds, *Contemporary Peace Making: Conflict, Violence, and Peace Processes*. Basingstoke: Macmillan Press Ltd.

Zahar, M.J. (2006) 'Political Violence in Peace Processes: Voice, Exit, and Loyalty in the Post-Accord Period', in John Darby, ed., *Violence and Reconstruction*. Notre Dame: Notre Dame University Press.

2 Civil conflict in the contemporary world

Kristine Eck, Bethany Lacina, and Magnus Öberg

Introduction

In this chapter we give a global overview of civil conflicts from 1946 to 2003, detailing trends and patterns in the onset, incidence, duration, and termination of conflicts. We also describe interventions, peacekeeping operations, battle deaths, governance, and resources related to civil conflicts. Interesting in their own right, the patterns and trends we uncover in this chapter also put the subsequent chapters into context.

We base most of our analysis on data from the Uppsala Conflict Data Project (UCDP)/PRIO collections. In this data a civil conflict, or intrastate armed conflict, is defined as 'a contested incompatibility that concerns government or territory or both where the use of armed force between two parties results in at least 25 battle related deaths. Of these two parties, at least one is the government of a state' (Gleditsch *et al.*, 2002: 61–619). In an incompatibility concerning government the issue in dispute is the type of political system, the replacement of the central government, or the change of its composition. In an incompatibility concerning territory the issue at stake is autonomy or secession of some part of the territory of the state.

The structure of the chapter is as follows. First, we look at the magnitude of the problem of civil conflict in a number of different ways, detailing general trends in the incidence, onset, and duration of conflicts, as well as in battle deaths. There has been a post-Cold War decline in the number of ongoing conflicts as well as in the battle mortality associated with those conflicts. We find that rates of conflict onset have not been responsible for this pattern, but rather an increased rate of conflict terminations. Average conflict age climbed throughout the Cold War and dropped in recent years with this increased rate of termination. The average age of ongoing conflicts may be climbing again, however, suggesting that there are currently a small number of highly intractable civil conflicts in the world. Second, we look at various forms of interventions in civil conflicts, ranging from mediation and peacekeeping operations to armed support for one of the parties in the dispute. Peacekeeping by the UN and other international organizations has been increasingly common. However, armed interventions are most commonly undertaken by states that neighbor a conflict or by superpowers. Third, we describe how global patterns in civil conflicts relate to governance and natural resources. Democracy does not seem to relate to lower rates of conflict onset. But, surprisingly, there are more democracies that have remained liberal states throughout the course of an internal conflict than there are cases of a democracy collapsing during civil conflict. Fourth, we detail patterns and trends in conflict termination. There has been a sharp increase in the number of conflicts settled through ceasefire rather than military victory since the end of the Cold War. External interventions also influence settlement types. Finally, we summarize our findings.

The scope of civil conflicts

The incidence of civil conflict (including internationalized civil conflict) shows a distinct pattern in the post-World War II period. In Figure 2.1 we can see that the number of ongoing conflicts increased continually from ten in 1946 to 50 in 1992, after which there was a rather dramatic decline down to 27 in 2003 (the lowest number since 1975). This pattern is very similar to the pattern for all types of armed conflict; other compilations of conflict data have found similar trends (see Gleditsch *et al.*, 2002). This contradicts the commonly held view that civil conflicts have become more common in the post-Cold War era. There was a peak in the number of civil conflicts immediately following the end of the Cold War, but it was followed by the dramatic reversal of the strong increasing trend that had lasted for the entire post-World War II period. The question is: what accounts for these trends?

The long increase in the number of civil conflicts from the end of World War II to the end of the Cold War is not explained by increasing frequency

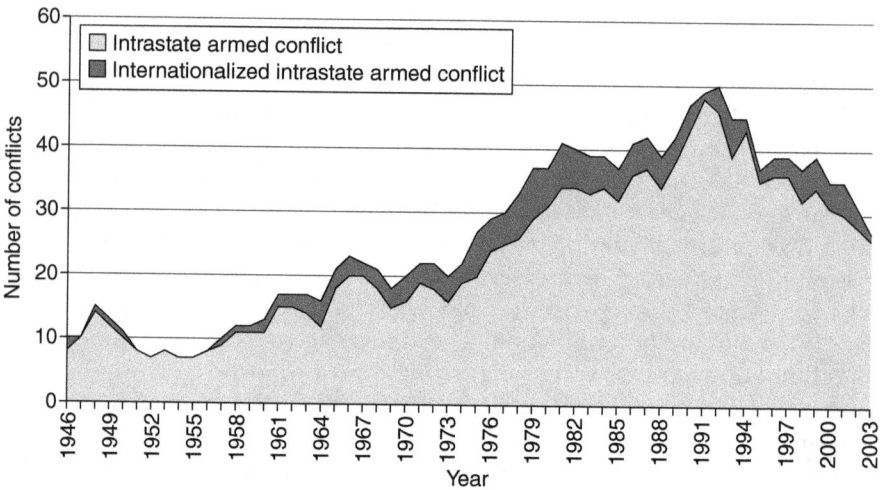

Figure 2.1 Number of civil conflicts by type, 1946–2003.

in conflict outbreaks. The rate of new conflicts does not display any clear trend, although there are peaks associated with decolonization periods in the late 1940s, the 1960s, and the early 1990s. Rather, the primary reason for the long increase is an accumulation of conflicts over time (cf. Fearon and Laitin, 2003). Put differently, the increasing trend is a consequence of the fact that the number of new conflicts every year remained roughly constant while the average age of ongoing conflicts was continually increasing throughout the Cold War period. It should also be noted that the number of states in the system increased throughout the period.

Increasing frequency of conflict termination, as well as a recent decrease in conflict onsets, explains the post-Cold War decline in armed conflict. Figure 2.2 shows some of the patterns underlying the global trends in civil conflicts.

The peak from 1989 to 1992 reflects a peak in the number of new conflicts, associated with the break up of the Soviet Union and Yugoslavia at the end of the Cold War (cf. Figure 2.2). The decline that follows is largely accounted for by a higher rate of conflict termination. The end of the Cold War meant that a number of long-standing conflicts could be ended. The absence of superpower rivalry and an increased interest in conflict management probably also helped shorten the life of the new conflicts following the end of Cold War – most of which were of relatively short duration. By the end of the 1990s most of the conflicts that began in the 1989 to 1992 period and a number of long-standing Cold War conflicts had ended. At the same time, there was a general decline in the number of new conflicts from 1991 to 2003. Taken together, these trends leave us with a lower total number of ongoing conflicts in 2003. However, at the same time, we see an

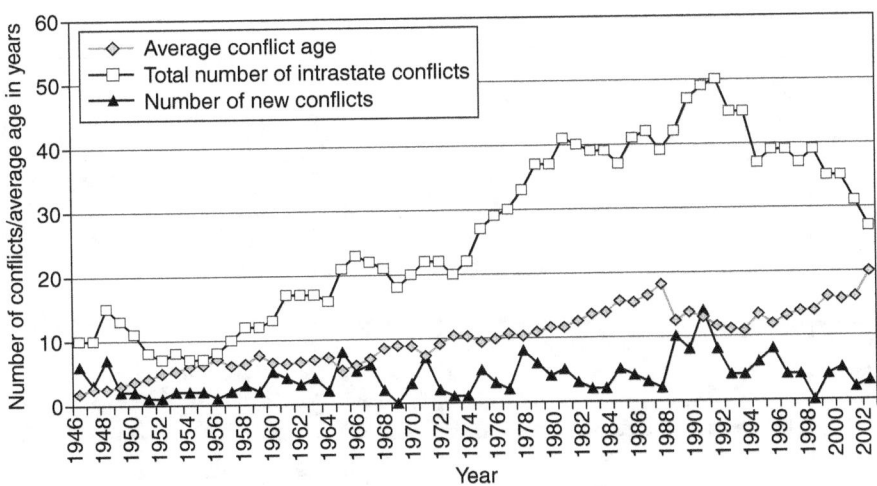

Figure 2.2 Global trends in number of civil conflicts, average conflict age, and number of new conflicts, 1946–2003.

increase in the average conflict age from the mid 1990s to 2003. Thus, at present we seem to be faced with a relatively smaller number of intractable conflicts, some of which have lasted for many decades. On a more speculative note, this might indicate a shift back to the type of cumulative trend we observed during the Cold War. On the other hand, sustaining civil conflicts over long periods of time requires resources. The Cold War superpower rivalry provided some of these resources; such a competitive aid environment is not present at this time, which suggests that we should expect a slower rate of accumulation of conflicts relative to that of the Cold War. However, other sources of funding are still available and recent research suggests that alternative sources of funding, such as the presence of 'lootable' natural resources and illicit drugs, can also increase conflict duration (Ross, 2004a). If we look at some of the oldest ongoing conflicts in 2003 we find three conflicts that are associated with illicit drugs – the Karen insurgency in Burma beginning in 1948, the civil conflict in Colombia beginning in 1965, and the civil conflict in Afghanistan beginning in 1978 – and two conflicts which are not – the Israeli–Palestinian conflict starting in 1965 and the Mindanao rebellion in the Philippines starting in 1970.

Turning to Figure 2.3 we may note that the regional distribution of civil conflicts is uneven. The plight of civil conflict has been felt most in Africa, with 415 country-years of civil conflict since 1946 – the great majority of which occur from the 1960s to 2003. Asia and the Americas have similar numbers of conflict years, 254 and 243 respectively, followed by Europe with 140 conflict years and the Middle East with 114 conflict years.[1]

Figure 2.3 shows the number of countries affected by civil conflict and it displays patterns similar to that observed in Figure 2.1 which displayed the number of conflicts. However, in Figure 2.3, we also see the regional distrib-

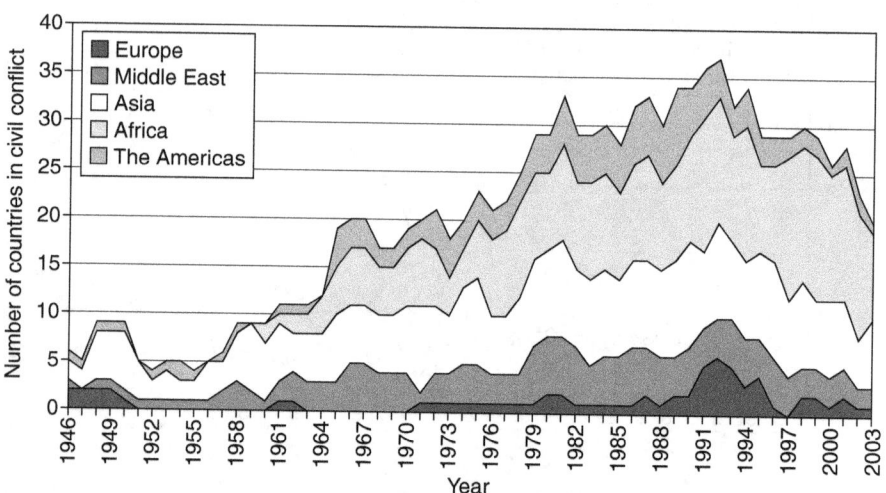

Figure 2.3 Number of countries in civil conflict by region, 1946–2003.

Civil conflict in the contemporary world 27

ution of affected countries. The number of affected countries peaked in 1992 with 37 countries affected, after which there has been a steady decline to a total of 20 countries affected in 2003 — the lowest number of affected countries since 1973. However, while all regions share roughly the same general pattern, there are significant differences in their trajectories. In Africa, fewer countries were affected by conflict prior to 1977 than at any time thereafter. In 1973 only four countries in Africa were affected by civil conflict, in 1992 the figure was up to 13, in 2003 it was down slightly to nine countries. By comparison, in Europe one country was affected in 1973, six in 1992, and only one in 2003. In the Americas four countries were affected in 1973, four in 1992, and one in 2003. In Asia six countries were affected in 1973, ten in 1992, and seven in 2003. In the Middle East three countries were affected in 1973, four in 1992, and two in 2003.

Turning to Figure 2.4 we see that over the 1946 to 2003 period the probability of any given country experiencing one or more civil conflicts increases up until 1992, after which it decreases. In 1992 as many as one country in five (22.5 percent of all countries) were affected by civil conflict, and in 2003 one in seven countries (14.2 percent) were still affected. However, if we disaggregate the numbers we see that the percentage of affected countries is very different in different regions. Europe stands out as the most peaceful region, having a smaller proportion of countries affected than any other region at all times except for a few years in the first half of the 1990s. The highest proportion of affected countries is found in Asia and the Middle East, with an average for the entire period of 25 percent and

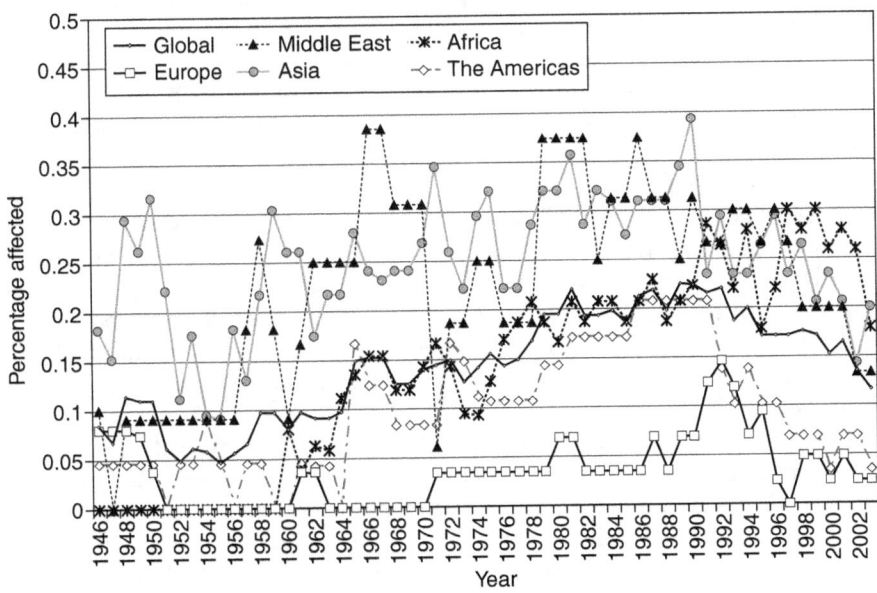

Figure 2.4 Percentage of all states affected by civil conflict.

23 percent, respectively. This can be compared with an average of 3.6 percent for Europe and 9.8 percent for the Americas. However, in both Asia and the Middle East, the proportion of affected countries seems to be falling since the mid-1990s. Africa, which is probably the continent most associated with civil conflict in the public mind, roughly trailed the global average from the 1960s until the early 1990s when the trend in Africa went up for a number of years, while the rest of the world experienced a downturn in conflicts. For the entire period, the average percentage of affected states in Africa was 13.4 percent. In the 1990s, the average for Africa was 25 percent. In 2003 the percentage of all African states affected has dropped quite considerably (to 18 percent) but it is still well above the global average for that year (11.7 percent).

The magnitude of violence in civil conflict

Another plausible measure of the intensity of global violence, rather than the number of ongoing conflicts, is an estimate of how many people are dying in those conflicts. Wars often lead to loss of life not only on the battlefield but through one-sided acts of violence – e.g. criminality, war crimes, genocide – and humanitarian crises leading to excess mortality through starvation and disease. Unfortunately, it is not possible to recover reliable estimates of war deaths across all of these categories for most conflicts over the past half-century. However, data on battle deaths (Lacina and Gleditsch, 2005) are available for the armed conflicts Uppsala/PRIO record from 1946 to 2002. Battle deaths are defined here as deaths, civilian or military, resulting from violence inflicted during contested combat.

Figure 2.5 summarizes the number of battle deaths in state-based armed conflicts from 1946 to 2002 and the number of those deaths in civil conflicts. Total battle mortality during this period is estimated at slightly more than 10 million deaths. Only about 8 percent of these deaths occurred in extrasystemic conflicts, such as colonial conflicts. There were far fewer interstate conflicts than civil conflicts in this period, but interstate conflicts were disproportionately deadly, accounting for about 40 percent of all battle deaths. Since the mid-1970s, however, battle mortality has been increasingly concentrated in civil conflicts and in the post-Cold War period almost exclusively so. In total, about 5.2 million people have died in combat during civil conflict, and far more have died due to starvation and disease caused by these conflicts.

The exceptionally low levels of battle deaths that prevailed in the early 1990s in part relate to the de-escalation of the superpower rivalry and its impact on civil conflict through military aid. Great powers possess the resources and the military technology (such as aerial power and heavy artillery) to inflict large numbers of battle deaths in the wars they start, join, or provide with support. The deadliest combat in the post-World War II period (the Vietnam War, the Korean War, the Chinese Civil War, the

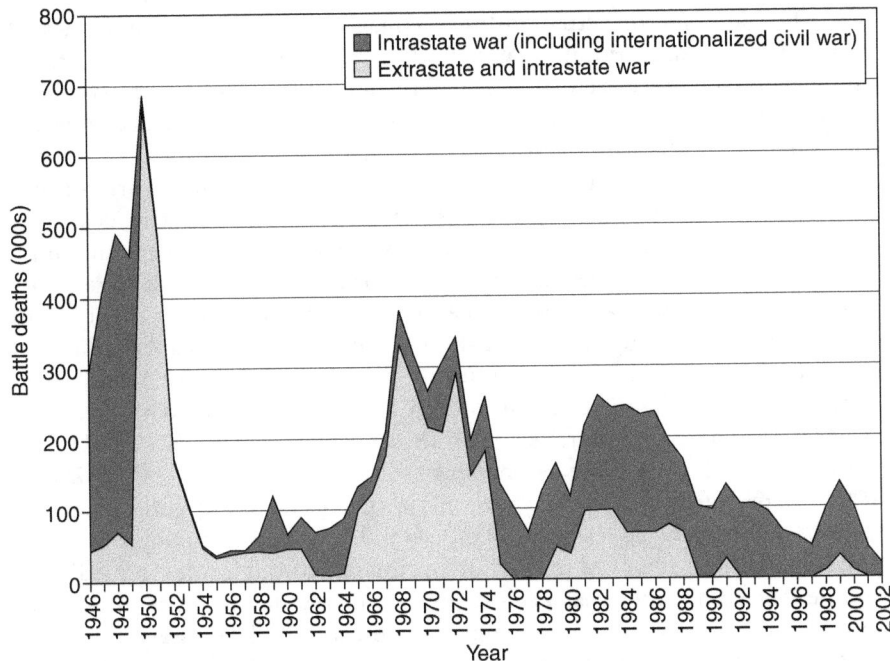

Figure 2.5 Battle deaths worldwide, 1946–2002 (source: Replication data for Lacina and Gleditsch, 2005).

Iran–Iraq War, and the civil conflict and Soviet invasion in Afghanistan) was driven in part by the logic of Cold War politics and the sides were armed by the US and USSR. By contrast, a number of countries emerged from civil conflict as the superpowers ceased fighting in and/or funding these proxy fights (e.g. El Salvador, Nicaragua, Mozambique, Namibia, and Cambodia) and other conflicts continued after superpower interest dried up, but at lower levels, as in Afghanistan through the 1990s or Ethiopia (Lacina *et al.*, 2006; Lacina and Gleditsch, 2005).

This absence of competitive military aid to opposing sides of a civil conflict had an impact on battle mortality by changing the technological profile of warfare. The modal conflict scenario today is a rural insurgency that engages in very low levels of violence, survives primarily by taxing peasants or dealing in contraband, and, though difficult to squelch, has little capacity to expand (Fearon, 2004); examples include conflicts in Burma, northeast India, and Ethiopia. The 1990s also saw several civil conflicts in failed states, where an impoverished society governed by a very weak post-colonial regime descended into warlordism, as in West Africa (Collier *et al.*, 2003; Fearon and Laitin, 2004; Mack, 2005). Both these species of conflicts have been largely neglected by major powers, and the combatants often remain relatively ill-organized and poorly equipped when compared to those who fought in the civil conflicts that turned into proxy wars during the Cold War. The amount of actual military engagement (rather than tactics of insurgency or banditry) in many modern civil conflicts has been quite limited and sporadic, even desultory (Mueller, 2003). Thus these conflicts, though often intractable and devastating, have produced fewer battle deaths than their Cold War counterparts.

On the other hand, although poorly equipped and organized armies may have relatively little capacity to cause large numbers of battle deaths or limited will to engage other combatants, they may still be able to cause high numbers of war-related deaths. In a very poor nation with weak state structures, it may not take very much force to collapse the infrastructure of health and human security and cause a full-blown humanitarian crisis. For example, a small force can cut transportation links vital to food security, as demonstrated by the relatively limited military force required to break the siege of Mogadishu and relieve famine in Somalia in 1992–93 (United Nations, 1996). The most recent spike seen in Figure 2.5, beginning in 1997, is primarily due to the war in the Democratic Republic of Congo (DRC), a conflict has been studied carefully by epidemiologists. Great powers have been involved in the DRC primarily through roles in mediation and peacekeeping; there has been regional military involvement in the conflict but not the dynamics of competitive military aid necessary to sustain battle engagement as many of the groups fighting in the DRC have neither the training nor the equipment to launch cohesive military operations. The result is a distinctive pattern of war-related deaths in that conflict. From 1998 to 2002, the war led to an estimated 145,000 battle deaths (International Institute for Strategic Studies, 2005). The total number of violent deaths, including an upsurge in crime, banditry, and massacre of civilians, is a considerably higher figure of 300,000. The true toll of the war, however, has come through its devastation of the infrastructure of the DRC, much of which was inaccessible to humanitarian aid throughout the war. The result was 2.5 million deaths from all war-related causes, especially disease and depravation (Roberts et al., 2003). These figures imply a battle-to-war-dead ratio of about one to six. Although the major wars of the past fifty years have been associated with larger humanitarian crises in absolute terms, the ratios between the toll of combat and the total toll of the war were quite different. The Korean War, for example, may have resulted in three to four war-related deaths for every combat death.

With a greater percentage of contemporary wars being civil conflicts in poor states, it is likely that the number of global battle deaths has fallen far more precipitously than the count of war-related deaths. Desultory and limited combat combined with extensive predation, anarchy, and humanitarian crisis has been the profile of a number of civil conflicts in very poor countries over the past fifteen years, such as those in Burma, Liberia, Sierra Leone, and Haiti. The Human Security Report (Mack, 2005) estimates that numbers of refugees and displaced persons has climbed dramatically in recent times. The Committee on World Food Security (2005) estimates that civil conflict is now the leading cause of famine.

Governance and civil conflict

Regime type and civil conflict

The type of regime most vulnerable to civil conflict is an anocracy – mixing features of liberal and illiberal government – or an unconsolidated or transitional government (Hegre et al., 2001). Surprisingly, democracy and measures of liberal government do not predict a low risk of civil conflict after controlling for the wealth of a country (Collier et al., 2003; Fearon and Laitin, 2003). Interestingly, there are also several democracies, such as India, Great Britain, and Colombia, which have suffered civil conflict in the post-World War II period without transitioning to autocracy (Table 2.1).[2] Lacina (2006) also estimates that civil conflicts fought in democratic states tend to be less deadly than those fought in autocracies or anocracies.

Surprisingly, few states transform from autocracies to democracies or vice versa during periods of civil conflict. Table 2.1 reveals that shifts in regime type during civil conflict have been relatively rare, with only a small set of countries moving a significant distance toward or away from democracy. The table is based on regime types before and after the war, but not all of these transitions were the direct result of the conflict or the military victory of the opposition. However, regimes may be transformed in part due to the stress of conflict, as in Nigeria during the Biafran civil conflict.

The modal state undergoing civil conflict in the UCDP data was an anocracy and most of these states remained anocratic throughout their years of conflict (47 of 61), although perhaps moving through various regime forms. Most autocracies were also untransformed over the course of conflict. Out of 50 such cases in the data, there were two transitions to democracy in periods of war and three to anocracy. Four democracies collapsed during civil conflict and five were established during war years, although the case of Haiti appears in both these categories.

International intervention in civil conflicts

Intervention by an external party in an ongoing conflict can take many forms. We employ a typology of international intervention based on two dimensions: position and action. Broadly, we distinguish the *position* of the intervening party as being either neutral or biased in regards to the conflict incompatibility. Interventions where the external state seeks to influence the outcome of the conflict in favor of one of the parties are considered to be biased, while interventions where the external state seeks to facilitate an end to fighting or a solution to the incompatibility are considered to be neutral.[3] The other dimension of our typology is based on the *action* of the intervening

Table 2.1 Democracy and civil conflict

State	Years of war	Polity prior to war	Polity after war
Transitions from democracy during civil war			
Bangladesh	1974–1992	8	−7
Haiti	1991	7	−7
Laos	1959–1973	8	−1
Nigeria	1966–1970	7	−7
Transitions to democracy during civil war			
Haiti	1989	−7	7
Macedonia	2001	6	9
Moldova	1992	5	7
Panama	1989	−8	8
Russia	1999–2003	4	7
Democracies in civil war			
Colombia	1965–2003	7	7
Costa Rica	1948	10	10
Gambia	1981	8	7
Greece	1946–1949	8	8
India	1978–2003	8	8
Israel	1949–2003	10	10
Malaysia	1958–1966	10	10
Mali	1994	7	7
Pakistan	1990–1996	8	8
Papua New Guinea	1989–1996	10	10
Spain	1980–1992	9	9
Sri Lanka	1971	8	8
Trinidad and Tobago	1990	9	9
Turkey	1984–2003	7	7
The UK	1971–1998	10	10
Venezuela	1992	9	8

party: namely, if they send troops or not. We believe that this is a salient distinction because by sending troops the external state risks much higher political costs and thus signals its commitment to influencing the conflict.

Biased interventions

Biased interventions are attempts by external parties to influence the outcome of a conflict. It is important to note that biased interventions can support either the government or the opposition group. We distinguish here between two different types of biased interveners: secondary warring parties and secondary supporting parties.

Secondary warring parties are those external states which send their own troops to a conflict in order to actively support one of the primary parties.[4]

The pattern of secondary warring party intervention varied somewhat over the 1946–2003 period.[5] The Cold War period was characterized by a number of superpower interventions (e.g. in Angola, Vietnam, Cambodia, and Central America); with the end of the Cold War, the polarized nature of these interventions disappeared and the remaining superpower (the United States) focused its military interventions instead on the Balkans, Afghanistan, and Iraq.[6] One aspect that has not varied over time, however, is the prevalence of intervention by neighboring states, which has been the dominant type of secondary warring party intervention both during and after the Cold War. The duration of secondary warring party interventions in civil conflicts demonstrates a distinct Cold War demarcation: the length of such interventions during the Cold War was approximately seven years, while after the Cold War this dropped to two years. The obvious critique is that since the post-Cold War period is of shorter duration itself, there has been less time for this type of intervention to occur. Given, however, that there is only one ongoing occurrence of secondary warring party intervention, the average is not likely to rise significantly in the near future.

The timing of secondary warring parties' entrance into conflicts is also worth examining. Looking at all civil conflicts, one finds that of the 36 conflicts which included secondary warring parties, 80 percent of those parties enter within a year of the start of the conflict. Furthermore, over 70 percent of the conflicts where secondary warring parties intervene reach the level of war, raising the question of whether the presence of secondary warring parties leads to an escalation in violence. Without further study, we cannot say whether the presence of a secondary warring party itself leads to an escalation of conflict or if there is a selection effect in which secondary warring parties intervene in those conflicts most likely to escalate to war.

Another type of biased intervention comes from *secondary supporting parties*, which are those actors which give support to a primary conflict party in a way that affects the development of the conflict. The nature of this support can vary: it may be financial, logistical, military assistance short of troop deployments, and so on. Anything relating to normal interaction between states (trade, development aid, etc.) is not considered to be secondary support, even if the consequences of that interaction may be of benefit to the primary party.[7]

Over 70 percent of the civil conflicts between 1989 and 2003 saw some type of secondary support to at least one of the conflict parties. Data from Harbom and Wallensteen (2005) show that while state actors give secondary support to both government and opposition in conflicts, non-state actors support only the opposition side. States contributed some form of secondary support to the government side in 56 out of 79 conflicts, while rebels received support from secondary supporting states in 57 of 79 conflicts.[8] Harbom and Wallensteen note that the majority of the states contributing secondary support – both to governments and opposition groups – were neighbors. Data on non-state actors reveals that there was no instance of a non-state actor supporting a government during the period but that opposition groups received secondary support from non-state actors in 35 conflicts. The majority of this support came from another rebel group, most often from a neighboring country (Harbom and Wallensteen, 2005).

Neutral interventions

Interventions are neutral when they do not seek to influence the outcome of the incompatibility. External states that undertake neutral intervention do so with the aim of facilitating an end to fighting or a negotiated solution to the conflict. We distinguish between two types of neutral interventions here: peacekeeping operations, in which the external state literally interpositions itself between the conflict parties to hinder fighting, and third party intervention, which is a non-military attempt to thwart conflict behavior, usually through mediation and diplomatic intervention.

Peacekeeping is generally a multilateral endeavor, usually undertaken by the UN or other regional actors. There are a few select cases, however, where individual states or groups of states initiate peacekeeping operations. Generally, however, states send peacekeeping troops under the aegis of a regional or international organization. We follow Heldt (2005), who distinguishes between UN and non-UN operations. Heldt's comprehensive study of UN and non-UN peacekeeping operations reveals a number of trends. Between 1948 and 2003, UN and non-UN actors had initiated 40 and 46 intrastate peacekeeping operations respectively. UN and non-UN intrastate peacekeeping operations also have the same average duration in this period (32 mission months). Operational size, however, varied considerably: non-UN operations had on average almost twice as many troops on the ground as UN operations. Troop size has varied considerably over time, with the operation size of both UN and non-UN intrastate operations characterized by peaks and valleys (Figure 2.6). By the end of 2003, there were approximately 60 percent more non-UN peacekeepers than UN peacekeepers on the ground in civil conflicts.[9]

Since the end of the Cold War, there has not only been an increase in the number of peacekeeping operations, but also in the number of countries contributing troops. The type of countries which contribute troops has also changed with an increasing number of developing nations sending troops to UN peacekeeping operations.[10]

Another type of neutral intervention comes through *third parties*, which are actors that are involved in helping the warring parties regulate the incompatibility or the use of violence. These parties act as intermediaries, whether through formal mediation, good offices, or simply by exerting diplomatic pressure.[11] Third party actors are not constrained to being states: a third party may be an individual (for example, Nelson Mandela) or any type of organized entity, such as religious organizations, NGOs, regional or international organizations, and numerous third parties can be actively involved in a conflict at any given time.

Civil conflict in the contemporary world 35

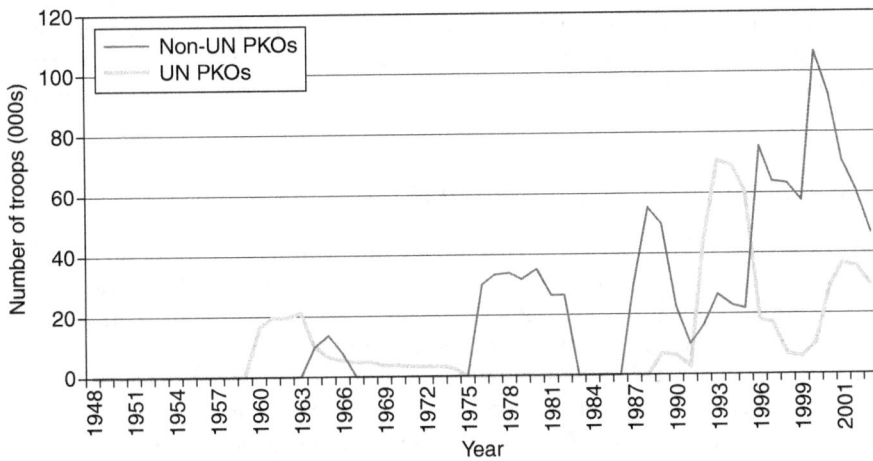

Figure 2.6 Peace keeping operations in civil conflict, 1946–2003.

In the post-Cold War period, nearly two-thirds of all civil conflicts saw some type of third party intervention during the conflict.[12] States were the most active type of third parties, accounting for over 80 percent of third party interventions. Moreover, an average of four states intervened in each of these cases. The nature of this intervention varied, but one distinct attribute is the involvement of regional neighbors: in a vast majority of cases, at least one of the third party states came from the same continent. At the same time, superpower involvement also remained present throughout the period, with the United States as the state most often involved as a third party.

The United States's prevalence as a third party is overshadowed only by the UN, which was the single most active third party: the UN was involved as a third party in almost 30 percent of all conflicts between 1989 and 2003.[13] International and regional organizations acted as third parties in over 40 percent of conflicts. The only other actor with the same global ambitions as the UN was the European Union, which was active in every region except the Americas.[14] Generally, though, the EU has tended to focus on its own neighborhood, with European conflicts as the clear focus for intervention, followed by Africa and the Middle East. Other regional organizations tended to be active exclusively within their regions.

Finally, we also examined UCDP data on other types of interventions, such as by individuals, religious organizations, and local initiatives. The data showed that in over 25 percent of conflicts, third party intervention by some other type of actor than a state or international/regional organization took place. These actors tended in large part to be senior statesmen who were no longer official country representatives; former US President Jimmy Carter and former South African President Nelson Mandela, for example, were commonly cited for their mediation efforts. It must be noted, however, that this category is likely to suffer from coding bias because it probably captures the cases where famous statesmen, like Mandela, intervene but overlooks local initiatives that get little international press. It is therefore entirely possible that this type of intervention is far more common than the numbers here would suggest.

Natural resources and civil conflict

An alternative link between governance and conflict is contained in the literature on rentier states (Collier and Hoeffler, 2002a; de Soysa, 2002; Ross, 2004a, 2004b). Resource dependent regimes, especially petro-states, are thought to be weaker in terms of state capacity than would be indicated by their per capita GDPs. This is because these regimes tend to practice only limited direct taxation of the population and, therefore, provide little in the way of public goods and penetration into the society. Corruption and rent-seeking build up around the state extraction industries, and the government faces little financial pressure for openness or transparency, either domestically or from international donors (Bates and Lien, 1985; Ross, 2001). Thus, these regimes are only thinly present on the ground and may be vulnerable to both peripheral insurgencies and challenges against the center following price shocks in their key industries. The rentier state hypothesis has found the strongest support in the case of states that export large amounts of petroleum products. Fearon and Laitin (2003) find that oil dependence more than doubles the odds of civil conflict onset, while Collier and Hoeffler (2002b) link oil to secessionism. In the UCDP data 23 out of 141 (16 percent) countries that experienced civil conflict drew more than one-third of their export revenue from fuel products at the time when conflict broke out (based on oil dependence data in Fearon and Laitin, 2003); this figure seems notable given that there are only 35 countries that have been this petro-dependent at any time in their history.

There has also been considerable recent attention to the thesis that the export of lootable commodities enables rebellion. Black market goods that are known to have funded rebellion include cocaine and heroin trafficking, timber, gems and lightweight minerals (Berdal and Malone, 2000; Collier, 2000; Grossman, 1999; Keen, 1998). Whether these resources are causal factors in civil conflict is less clear: the data on conflict diamonds are illustrative here. Gilmore *et al.* (2005) report that there are 31 diamond producing countries in the world, 74 percent of which have experienced a civil conflict, as opposed to 43 percent of non-producing countries. However, there is some question as to whether all of these conflicts can reasonably be called diamond related in the sense that one or more warring parties receives a substantial portion of their funding from diamonds. This list of diamond producers that have suffered civil conflict includes a number of cases that are difficult to tie to gem production: China, India, Russia, Thailand, and Venezuela are all examples. Comparing the Gilmore *et al.* list of diamond deposits to the UCDP data reveals that 25 out of 40 countries (63 percent) with known diamond resources have suffered a civil conflict. Although this figure includes some false positives Halvard Buhaug and Päivi Lujala have shown that when controlling for the geographic location of the conflict and the gemstones, a significant association remains (Buhaug and Lujala, 2005).

The termination of civil armed conflicts

How do conflicts usually end? One important aspect for the growing field of conflict resolution is understanding the patterns behind how conflicts actually terminate. Determining when a conflict has ended, however, can be quite problematic. There are a plethora of conceptually problematic situations: a group might be defeated or sign a peace agreement but conflict may continue through the formation of a new group; a ceasefire agreement may be violated after holding for several years; or a lengthy negotiation process may fall apart leading to renewed fighting. We believe a minimum criterion is that the fighting must stop for a substantial amount of time, thus we stipulate that an armed conflict as inactive for five years for it to be coded as a termination; we apply this criterion to UCDP's termination data.[15] This is not to say, however, that even conflicts which have been inactive for five years are solved; many times the conflict issue remains resulting in an unstable situation that risks a return to violence. We have divided conflict terminations into five different categories: victory, peace agreement, ceasefire, low or no activity, and other.[16]

Turning to the data, we see that there is not an even distribution across these categories: victories comprise 50 percent of the terminations, while 28 percent are low or no activity; ceasefires and peace agreements are 7 percent and 11 percent, respectively, while only 4 percent of conflict endings are coded as 'other'. Looking at the development of these different categories over time, there is relatively little change over the decades until after the Cold War, there is a sharp drop in victories reciprocated by an increase in ceasefires. There is another pronounced Cold War distinction: a sharp increase in the average number of terminations per year. During the Cold War, on average, approximately 2.3 conflicts terminated per year; this average shoots up to 6.5 terminations in the post-Cold War period. Since there has been a declining rate in the onset of new conflicts since the early 1990s, the increased rate reflects the termination of numerous Cold War conflicts.

If we distinguish between civil conflicts which see the involvement of secondary warring parties and those that do not, we can observe some intriguing differences. The presence of secondary warring parties appears to be quite important in relation to conflict termination: over 70 percent of civil conflicts which have secondary warring parties end in victory compared to only 47 percent of those that do not. The implication is that the presence of an external warring country can drastically affect the outcome of a conflict by increasing the likelihood of one side winning.

Another relevant factor to consider is the distinction UCDP makes between conflicts over government and conflicts over territory. These two types of incompatibility demonstrate very different patterns of conflict termination (Table 2.2).

Table 2.2 shows that unlike territorial conflicts, conflicts over government end overwhelmingly in victory (67 percent). As a comparison, it is interesting to note that *interstate* conflicts over government only end in victory in 19 percent of the cases. The fact that the vast majority of civil conflicts over government end in victory is perhaps not so surprising since many of them are coups or popular revolutions that are distinguished by quick and overwhelming victories (Fearon, 2004). Moreover, there are factors which may be conducive to prolonging civil conflicts over territory, such as remote location on the periphery of a state, and proximity to porous borders which allow rebels to find sanctuary in neighboring states. Because of the entrenched nature of civil conflicts on the periphery, actors are less likely to be able to establish clear victories and as a result, when these conflicts actually terminate, they do so either through negotiated settlement or little or no activity.

Conclusions

This chapter has reviewed a number of trends in the features of civil conflicts over the past half century. One of the most striking, and positive, patterns described above is the downward shift in number of conflicts after 1992. In 2003 there were 27 active civil conflicts, down from 50 in 1992. Yet, in a longer perspective there is still nearly three times the number of conflicts in 2003 compared to 1946. The number of new conflicts every year does not display any clear trend, although there are peaks in the 1940s, 1960s, and 1990s, coinciding with decolonization processes.

One of the most distinct watersheds in the recent history of internal conflict was the end of the Cold War. In the post-Cold War period conflicts have been of shorter duration and killed fewer people per year than in the previous decades. Many have been rural insurgencies taking advantage of rough terrain and contraband funding rather than extensive military aid. These conflicts have been more likely to see a multilateral or UN neutral

Table 2.2 Conflict termination by type of incompatibility, 1946–1999

	Territory (%)	*Government (%)*
Victory	26	67
Peace agreement	11	11
Ceasefire	17	0
No or low activity	39	20
Other	7	2

intervention force and the frequency of termination in ceasefire rather than military victory has increased. International actors have been quite interested in promoting democracy in post-conflict countries, but it is too early to note the success of most of these efforts. There are also an increasing number of initiatives, such as the Kimberley Process for certifying diamonds, aimed at limiting the use of natural resources to fund civil conflicts.

The essays in this volume take-up and grapple with some of the features of the post-Cold War civil conflicts that have emerged as most salient in the discussion above. Several authors, Gates and Strand, Sollenberg, Gizelis, Svensson, and Nilsson, all address the puzzling question of what explains the diverse ways in which civil conflicts terminate, and, especially, what the role of external players is in generating these outcomes. Sánchez gives a historical perspective on conflict termination, and discusses the successful attempt in Costa Rica to build a post-civil conflict democracy, and Martínez-Herrera also delves into governance during civil conflict. Ivey and Ylönen discuss the nexus between resources and the onset and incidence of civil conflict. This chapter, therefore, serves to set the aggregate context in which their work resides, while the authors provide deeper insight into why the trends we find here have appeared.

Notes

1 Note that the number of countries differs from region to region and it is not constant over time.
2 The criteria for regime type used here is based on the Polity IV (Marshall and Jaggers, 2003) dataset of regime codings. Polity IV gives states an autocracy and a democracy score, which can be summed to compute a regime type on the scale of −10 to 10, with low scores being most autocratic. States were classified according to the their Polity score in the year before and the year after UCDP records fighting. Regime types scored a −7 or less are considered autocracies, scores of 7 or more are classified as democracies, and the remaining regimes are called anocracies.
3 In reality, of course, this distinction can be blurred. Mediating states can have their own agenda or peacekeeping operations can increasingly take sides; what is crucial in our coding is how the external state relates to the actual incompatibility – that is, whether they are trying to support one party's position in the conflict.
4 The secondary warring party must in some way share the incompatibility with the primary party; that is, they enter the conflict in order to support one side's position in the conflict and not for other reasons such as for their own security interests.
5 Analysis here is based on data from UCDP (Uppsala Conflict Data Program, 2005).
6 One might argue, however, that these last two cases demonstrate a new polarization in the world system, between the United States and its allies and those states that have refused to provide military support to oppose the 'war on terrorism'.
7 The data for secondary supporting parties differs from that for secondary warring parties for two primary reasons: first, the temporal domain is more restricted (data on secondary supporting parties is only available for

1989–2003), and second, UCDP allows for a plethora of different actors in this category, rather than restricting the category to states only. As a result, there is a much wider range of forms of external assistance.

8 The section on secondary supporting parties is based in large part on Harbom and Wallensteen (2005). The numbers we present here may differ slightly from their figures because our dataset covers 1989–2003, while Harbom and Wallensteen also include 2004. Moreover, it is worth repeating Harbom and Wallensteen's warning regarding this data: the nature of secondary support is often secretive and the resultant coding problems could lead to undercounting.

9 All data in this paragraph comes from Birger Heldt, who has generously shared his research with us. See Heldt and Wallensteen (2004) for a description of the data through 2000.

10 Data on troop-contributing states is unfortunately not yet available for non-UN operations.

11 The term 'third party' as we use it here differs slightly from the UCDP definition. In the UCDP data both third parties (as described here) and peacekeeping fall under the rubric of 'third parties'. The inclusion of cases does not differ, but we have extracted peacekeeping cases into a separate category, thus employing a narrower concept of third parties.

12 Data is available on third party intervention from 1989–2003.

13 Keep in mind that this number does not include UN peacekeeping operations.

14 A few organizations – such as the Organization of the Islamic Conference – have a global reach but are involved in relatively few conflicts in comparison to the UN and EU.

15 We are indebted to Joakim Kreutz, who is responsible for the UCDP Conflict Termination project, for collecting and sharing his data with us; this section builds in large part on his work.

16 Victory is defined as occurring when one side is either defeated or eliminated, or otherwise succumbs to the power of the other party. Peace agreements and ceasefires both constitute some sort of negotiated settlement, but there is an important distinction between them. While peace agreements are designed to put an end to fighting, they are also meant to settle all or part of the incompatibility or clearly outline a process for doing so. Ceasefires, on the other hand, regulate only the behavior of the warring parties without addressing the incompatibility. Conflicts can also end by simply fizzling out, that is, they cease to be recorded as armed conflict because of little or no fighting. Finally, we have included a category entitled 'other' for those rare cases which do not fit into any of the above categories. Some examples include when a state in conflict ceases to exist, as in the case of conflicts ongoing when the Soviet Union collapsed, or when a conflict changes from being an intrastate conflict to an interstate conflict, as occurred during the Vietnam War.

References

Bates, R.H. and Lien, D.H.D. (1985) 'A Note on Taxation, Development, and Representative Government', *Politics and Society* 14(1): 53–70.

Berdal, M. and Malone, D.M. (eds) (2000) *Greed and Grievance: Economic Agendas in Civil Wars*, London: Lynne Rienner.

Buhaug, H. and Lujala, P. (2005) 'Accounting for Scale: Measuring Geography in Quantitative Studies of Civil War', *Political Geography* 24(4): 399–418.

Collier, P. (2000) 'Rebellion as a Quasi Criminal Activity', *Journal of Conflict Resolution* 44(6): 839–853.

Collier, P. and Hoeffler, A. (2002a) 'The Political Economy of Secession', Washington, DC: World Bank.
Collier, P. and Hoeffler, A. (2002b) 'On the Incidence of Civil War in Africa', *Journal of Conflict Resolution* 46(1): 13–28.
Collier, P., Elliot, L., Hegre, H., Hoeffler, A., Reynal-Querol, M., and Sambanis, N. (2003) *Breaking the Conflict Trap: Civil War and Development Policy*, Washington, DC: The World Bank and Oxford University Press.
Committee on World Food Security (2005) 'Assessment of the World Food Security Situation', in Report from the 31st Session, 23–26 May 2005, Rome: Committee on World Food Security.
de Soysa, I. (2002) 'Paradise Is a Bazaar? Greed, Creed, and Governance in Civil War, 1989–99', *Journal of Peace Research* 39(4): 395–416.
Fearon, J.D. (2004) 'Why Do Some Civil Wars Last So Much Longer Than Others?' *Journal of Peace Research* 41(3): 275–301.
Fearon, J.D. and Laitin, D.D. (2003) 'Ethnicity, Insurgency, and Civil War', *American Political Science Review* 97(1): 75–90.
Fearon, J.D. and Laitin, D.D. (2004) 'Neotrusteeship and the Problem of Weak States', *International Security* 28(4): 5–43.
Gilmore, E., Gleditsch, N.P., Lujala, P., and Rod, J.K. (2005) 'Conflict Diamonds: A New Dataset', *Conflict Management and Peace Science* 22(3): 257–272.
Gleditsch, N.P., Wallensteen, P., Eriksson, M., Sollenberg, M., and Strand, H. (2002) 'Armed Conflict 1946–2001: A New Dataset', *Journal of Peace Research* 39(5): 615–637.
Grossman, H.I. (1999) 'Kleptocracy and Revolutions', *Oxford Economic Papers – New Series* 51(2): 267–283.
Harbom, L. and Wallensteen, P. (2005) 'Armed conflict and its international dimensions, 1946–2004', *Journal of Peace Research* 42(5): 623–635.
Hegre, H., Ellingsen, T., Gates, S., and Gleditsch, N.P. (2001) 'Toward a Democratic Civil Peace? Democracy, Political Change, and Civil War, 1816–1992', *American Political Science Review* 95(1): 33–48.
Heldt, B. (2005) Unpublished dataset on UN and non-UN peacekeeping operations, Stockholm: Folke Bernadotte Academy.
Heldt, B. and Wallensteen, P. (2004) Peacekeeping Operations: Global Patterns of Intervention and Success, 1948–2004, Stockholm: Folke Bernadotte Academy.
International Institute for Strategic Studies (2005) 'Armed Conflict Database', acd.iiss.org/armedconflict/.
Keen, D. (1998) 'Aid and Violence, With Special Reference to Sierra Leone', *Disasters* 22(4): 318–327.
Lacina, B. (2006) 'Explaining the Severity of Civil Wars', *Journal of Conflict Resolution* 50(2): 276–289.
Lacina, B. and Gleditsch, N.P. (2005) 'Monitoring Trends in Global Combat: A New Dataset of Battle Deaths', *European Journal of Population – Revue Europeenne De Demographie* 21(2–3): 145–166.
Lacina, B., Gleditsch, N.P., and Russett, B. (2006) 'The Declining Risk of Death in Battle', *International Studies Quarterly* 50(1).
Mack, A. (2005) *The Human Security report*, Oxford: Oxford University Press.
Marshall, M.G. and Jaggers, K. (2003) 'Polity IV Project. Political Regime Characteristics and Transitions, 1800–2002', College Park, MD: Center for

International Development and Conflict Management, University of Maryland, www.cidcm.umd.edu/inscr/polity/index.htm.

Mueller, J. (2003) 'Policing the Remnants of War', *Journal of Peace Research* 40(5): 507–518.

Roberts, L., Ngoy, P., Mone, C. Lubula, C., Mwezse, L., Zantop, M., and Despines, M. (2003) 'Mortality in the Democratic Republic of Congo: Results form a Nationwide Survey', Kukavu/New York: International Rescue Committee.

Ross, M.L. (2001) 'Does Oil Hinder Democracy', *World Politics* 53(April): 325–361.

Ross, M.L. (2004a) 'How Does Natural Resource Wealth Influence Civil War? Evidence from 13 Cases', *International Organization* 58(1): 35–67.

Ross, M.L. (2004b) 'What Do We Know About Natural Resources and Civil War?' *Journal of Peace Research* 41(3): 337–356.

United Nations (1996) 'The United Nations in Somalia, 1992–1996', New York: United Nations, Department of Public Information.

Uppsala Conflict Data Program (2005) 'Uppsala Conflict Database', Department of Peace and Conflict Research, Uppsala University, www.pcr.uu.se/database.

Part II
Causes and dynamics

3 Insights from macro studies of the risk of civil war

Bethany Lacina[1]

Introduction

The end of the Cold War fundamentally altered the place of civil war in international politics, as well as in political science. In the realms of policy, internal conflict is no longer a proxy in a global struggle for influence between superpowers. In the absence of that dynamic, however, the interests and the normative role of the international community in internal conflict zones is still being debated. Contemporaneously, the 1990s and early 2000s have seen a flurry of media and scholarly interest in civil war. Today it is commonplace to hear that the primary global security threat is not a war between powerful states but zones of internal conflict and contested or absent governance where illegal drugs, human and weapons trafficking, HIV/AIDS, famine, terrorism, and banditry can thrive.

Given the increased policy interest in and growing volume of academic work on civil war, it may be useful to situate the studies in this book within some of the macro-level statistical research on the global incidence of civil conflict. Such models attempt to identify features of civil war that persist across relatively long time periods and/or large geographic areas. This chapter will discuss four sets of variables – economic, political, demographic, and geographic – which have been tested as predictors of civil war onset, noting the major statistical findings and the problems of interpretation some of these findings raise. I will also make suggestions about how new data or micro-level approaches might shed light on the current ambiguities in the statistical literature.

I draw on a variety of well-known, large-n studies of civil conflict, most notably the work of Collier and Hoeffler (Collier *et al.*, 2003, 2004, Collier and Hoeffler, 2001) at the World Bank, the findings of the State Failure Task Force (Esty *et al.*, 1998a, 1998b), and major academic studies by Fearon and Laitin (2003), Hegre *et al.* (2001), and Elbadawi and Sambanis (2002), as well as important investigations of specific risk factors for civil wars. Most of this work concentrates only on the post-World War II period, and the studies use somewhat different definitions of civil war, disagree slightly on the start and end dates of those wars, and investigate various specifications of the dependent variables. The aim of this chapter is not to adjudicate among datasets or statistical methodologies (for a more technical review of this literature see Gates, 2002, Sambanis, 2002, 2004). Instead, I present the work that has been completed thus far, on the assumption that we should have most confidence in findings that persist across a variety of model specifications, and treat variables that have more inconsistent or puzzling results as the areas most in need of future study.

Economic predictors of civil war

Poverty

Perhaps the most persistent regularity in the statistical work on civil war is that various measures of national income or poverty increase the risk of internal conflict. Nations with lower incomes are more prone to civil conflict, as are those with slow economic growth (Collier and Hoeffler, 2001, Elbadawi and Sambanis, 2002, Fearon and Laitin, 2003, Hegre et al., 2001). Conflicts also tend to last longer in poorer countries (Collier et al., 2004, Fearon, 2004). These effects are substantively quite important. Collier et al. find that doubling per capita income approximately halves the risk of civil war onset (2003: 58), and Fearon and Laitin find that, other factors being equal, nations in the bottom tenth percentile of per capita income worldwide have an 18 percent chance of civil war outbreak in a given year compared to 11 percent for a median income country and just 1 percent for a nation in the 90th percentile (2003: 83). The poverty and war correlation is robust whether the independent variable is measured as GDP per capita, energy consumption per capita, or infant mortality rates (Esty et al., 1998a, 1998b).

There are at least two widely-cited explanations of this statistical regularity. Collier and Hoeffler have argued that in poor societies there are low opportunity costs to rebellion. Unemployed young men do not lose much in joining a rebel movement, and may even benefit economically if they gain access to plunder or contraband. Thus, poverty causes civil wars because insurgency is a money-making proposition for poor people. I will return to this theory below, in the discussion of natural resources and conflict. A second explanation for the correlation between poverty and war is that poor societies are governed by weak states that lack the capacity to deliver public goods and enforce security (Fearon and Laitin, 2003). Other interpretations of the poverty and war correlation are also plausible. Wealthy firms and people, for example, are able to move their assets abroad more easily than the poor, and therefore resisting a predatory government by force may be less urgent in a more developed society. Alternately, economic downturns may drive poor people to migrate, possibly causing instability over competing claims for land or overwhelming cities' ability to provide services and employment. Finally, poverty is also a grievance, and rich societies may be less conflict-prone because they have more resources to divide up and can thus pacify groups suffering materially.

One of the drawbacks of this literature to date is that GDP per capita (the most commonly used proxy for theoretical ideas such as low opportunity costs to rebellion or state weakness) is a measure of annual income rather than of specific characteristics of a socio-economic system, such as unemployment, education, gender inequality, limited infrastructure, state corruption, or limited provision of public goods. These characteristics are so closely correlated with each other that many of them can be used to successfully predict civil conflict, provided a sufficiently long time series of data is available. Thus, it is challenging to distinguish among the theories put forward to explain the highly persistent correlation between poverty and internal violence.

Natural resources

The possible linkage between poverty and civil conflict that has been most thoroughly investigated is the thesis that the export of lootable commodities enables rebellion. In the most extreme version of this claim, rebel movements are fundamentally apolitical, motivated by profits from black market goods, such as West African diamonds, Cambodian timber, and Afghan poppies (Berdal and Malone, 2000, Collier, 2000, Grossman, 1999, Keen, 1998). As noted above, one theory tying poverty to civil war is that there are low opportunity costs to rebellion in places where there is little lucrative work – it follows, according to this theory, that the potential to profit from rebellion would make civil war more likely.

On the other hand, a very different set of linkages between resources and conflict emerge in case studies. Examples include high levels of government repression in areas rich in natural resources, economic mismanagement and corruption, and disruption of local communities and economies due to resource extraction (Ross, 2004a). Regimes in countries dependent on the export of primary products may also have little incentive to build the state capacity necessary to collect direct taxes (Bates and Lien, 1985, Ross, 2001) and, as a result, be weak states after the manner suggested by Fearon and Laitin. Thus, resource-financed states might look unusually prone to civil war because they are weaker than would be expected based on their GDP/capita. For example, Fearon and Laitin (2003: 85) find that oil dependence more than doubles the odds of civil war onset, while Collier and Hoeffler (2002) link oil to secessionism.

Collier and Hoeffler (2001) brought the issue of natural resources and civil war into the policy spotlight with findings of a positive, parabolic relationship between primary commodity exports as a fraction of GDP and conflict onset. However, in subsequent work natural resource dependence has not held up as a robust statistical predictor of civil war onset. Collier and Hoeffler's findings have not been replicated in other models (Ross, 2004b) and minor adjustments in Collier and Hoeffler's own data (changing their five year averages to annual figures) overturn their findings (Fearon, 2005). Collier and Hoeffler have also been criticized for their measure of natural resource dependence, commodity exports/GDP, because this actually tabulates more agricultural products than lootable resources. Contraband has been more convincingly tied statistically to increased duration, rather than incidence, of civil wars, implying that these resources can be critical in determining whether a conflict is able to continue, especially as external military aid becomes more scarce following the end of the Cold War (Fearon, 2004, Collier et al., 2004, Regan and Norton, 2005, Regan, 2002). Case-specific research has also made clear that in some cases war can actually become quite lucrative for some elites, creating obstacles to peace negotiations (King, 2001).

Remittances

Perhaps unsurprisingly, conflict is far more likely in nations with recent involvement in a previous civil war (Richardson, 1960). Such a pattern reflects the very real difficulties in resolving the power dilemmas that participants killed to contest in the first place, as well as the fact that a prior conflict is likely to have directly augmented other risk factors for civil war, including political instability and poverty. However, Collier and Hoeffler (2001) have argued that the presence of a large diaspora, which can repatriate funding to ex-combatants, is also part of the reason that civil conflicts often recur. Remittance data are quite scarce, so Collier and Hoeffler measure the number of ex-patriots living in the United States and find a positive relationship to the likelihood of future civil war. These results are quite fragile, however, because Collier and Hoeffler have no way to account for the possibility that people emigrate in anticipation of a civil war, rather than being particularly influential in starting a war once they have left. Nor do Collier and Hoeffler have data on total diaspora size worldwide, but only in the United States. And, unfortunately, there has been almost no further macro-level work on the subject because data are so very poor.

Economic inequality

A final economic finding of note is that cross-country statistical research (Hegre et al., 2003, Collier et al., 2004, Collier and Hoeffler, 2001) has not demonstrated any relationships between measures of income inequality and civil war onset or duration. How economic disparities influence civil conflict remains very much an open question, however, because global inequality data is scarce and very unreliable. Also, the theoretical and case study literature suggests that inequality motivates rebellion only when it takes particular forms, which income inequality data would not necessarily reveal. Stewart (2002) has pointed out that 'horizontal' inequality, or inequality between cultural groups, has not really been captured by most quantitative studies. She argues that wealth differentials are less dangerous than a situation in which economic and political inequalities are reinforced by ascriptive identities. Possibly, rather than measuring income inequality, it is more important to consider political inequality or discrimination; real or perceived bias in social policy; real or perceived changes to economic or demographic relationships caused by differential growth rates; blame attributions; or access to specific resources, such as education or positions in the security service. Statistical studies have found a positive relationship between horizontal inequality and conflict onset (Gurr, 1993) but the measurement difficulties here are even more serious than those with income inequality data.

Economic factors in civil war

In sum, the evidence linking poverty to civil war is overwhelming, but the interpretation of that correlation remains controversial, and many specific linkages that have been tested (natural resource economies, remittances, inequality) have themselves returned inconclusive results. The findings to date should not be dismissed, however. Attention to the poverty and war nexus has already helped to move civil war onto the agenda of economic agencies, such as the World Bank and several of the regional development banks, and underlined the urgent need for development in the global South.

The unclear role of political variables

Revolution and rebellion are political acts. Surprisingly, however, statistical tests of the relationship between political variables and civil violence have yielded neither consistent nor readily interpretable results. Most studies find no relationship between democracy and reduced or increased risk of conflict (Benson and Kugler, 1998, Collier and Hoeffler, 2001, Fearon and Laitin, 2003) or the duration of conflict (Collier *et al.*, 2004, Fearon, 2004). On the other hand, Elbadawi and Sambanis (2002) find that democracy, especially several years of democracy, is negatively associated with the prevalence (onset and duration) of conflict. Lacina (2006) finds that democracies suffer a lower number of battle deaths in their civil wars.

It seems puzzling that it is so difficult to find clear evidence that power-sharing and just government allow for nonviolent resolution of civil disputes. One possible explanation is that civil war and democracy have existed together primarily in relatively poor democracies, for example, the Kurdish rebellion in Turkey during the 1990s or separatist violence in Indonesia. Perhaps the benefits of democracy are enjoyed only above a certain income threshold (Hegre, 2003). Empirically, it is true that there is virtually no incidence of civil war in wealthy, fully consolidated democracies, while even highly consolidated and rich autocracies have been seen to collapse into civil violence (Benson and Kugler, 1998).

More consistent statistical results have been found in investigations of the relationship between regime stability, rather than the nature of regimes, and civil war. A number of studies have found that consolidated democracies and autocracies suffer fewer civil wars than regimes that are classified as not fully of either type (Hegre et al., 2001, Fearon and Laitin, 2003, Ellingsen, 2000, de Soysa, 2002, Reynal-Querol, 2002, Sambanis, 2001). Recent regime instability also increases the probability of civil war (Hegre et al., 2001), as does being a relatively new nation (Fearon and Laitin, 2003).

Yet, it is unclear what the finding that states that are neither autocratic nor democratic are most at risk for civil war really means, because it is difficult to differentiate between nations that truly mix democratic and autocratic features in a single political system (a condition sometimes called 'anocracy') and nations that are simply undergoing the kind of serious instability that is a symptom of conflict. Thus an anocratic governance score may capture the political breakdown that lies behind civil conflict. For example, the widely-used Polity scale (Marshall and Jaggers, 2003) for democracy considers countries more autocratic if they experience violence during elections (Gates et al., 2006). Coups, external war, or governmental upheaval are often reflected in codings for regime instability and regime change. Thus, there is a troubling possibility that the statistical relationships between anocracy and civil war or instability and civil war are tautological.

Also, regime type is very problematic to quantify, especially for these middling cases. In fact, models testing specific institutional characteristics have not always been in line with studies relying on regime scores. Reynal-Querol (2002) has found that the degree of proportionality in government, unlike democracy scores, does predict civil peace. Gandhi and Vreeland (2004) find that the relationship between anocracy and civil war does not hold up when they use a regime type classification that differentiates between autocracies depending on whether they have legislative institutions. These results remind us that common measures for democracy and autocracy, like the Polity Index, are aggregate assessments of a variety of factors, and many features of political systems, such as political rights or minority representation, have not been extensively studied or tested in civil war models.

Current research findings are sufficient, however, to call into question the oft-cited notion that the spread of democratic transitions worldwide since the end of the Cold War is the primary culprit of today's civil violence (Zakaria, 2003). Conflict in 'democratizing' nations may be primarily driven by the fact that the regimes are simply unstable, factional, or have lost the repressive capacities of full autocracies. In fact, some models find that transitions in the direction of autocracy are associated with similar or worse risks of conflict in comparison to transitions to democracy (Esty et al., 1998a, 1998b). And while the number of nations enjoying political openness has generally increased since the end of the Cold War, most conflict monitoring projects have found that rates of civil conflict have fallen since that time (Marshall and Gurr, 2005, Gleditsch et al., 2002). Certainly, the widespread trend toward democratization in the early 1990s has not caused the historically unprecedented pandemic of civil violence that is sometimes portrayed in the media.

The debate over demography

It is a common assumption that ethnic and religious tensions are the driving factors behind many or even most civil wars, especially since the decline of communist movements. However, most macro models find that ethnic and religious diversity do not predict the outbreak or duration of civil conflict (Collier et al., 2004, Collier and Hoeffler, 2001, Fearon and Laitin, 2003, Fearon, 2004, Esty et al., 1998a, 1998b); this is true both for measures of the amount of diversity in a society and for measures of polarization, meaning the division of a society into two large groups. A few studies have found links between cultural heterogeneity and civil conflict onset, but the substantive effect of these variables has not been large (Ellingsen, 2000, Elbadawi and Sambanis, 2002, Hegre et al., 2001). Thus, primordialist explanations for civil war, or claims that ancient cultural hatreds are driving a post-Cold War plague of ethnic wars, are overwhelmingly rejected by quantitative study.

Yet, obviously, ethnicity and religion are central to many civil wars. The risk of such a conflict may not be obvious without a more nuanced account of intra-group relationships than previously tested, as suggested above in the discussion of economic inequality. In the theoretical literature there is increasing agreement that the most dangerous demographic make-up for a nation is polarization, in which the majority (ethnic, lingual, cultural, and/or religious) faces a large minority, especially if economic class lines tend to reinforce rather than crosscut these divisions (Horowitz, 1985, Montalvo and Reynal-Querol, 2005, Reynal-Querol, 2002). Presumably more benign is the situation in which cultural and class divisions do not coincide, so that there are relatively numerous poor and rich members within all cultural groups. This tends to reduce cultural (and class) groups' internal cohesion and should give at least some individuals within each faction a stake in preserving the normal functioning of the economy. The challenge for researchers is to find better ways to describe social composition, and to investigate the possibility that horizontal, or inter-group, inequalities cause civil conflicts.

Country level studies have already made it clear that the role of inter-group disparity in civil war is not simple or even consistent. For example, in Nepal, a civil war began in 1996 after Maoists were barred from contesting elections. This is a society of great horizontal inequality between castes, and these disparities also have ethnic and regional dimensions. Recently, empirical research has demonstrated that regions with higher intensities of violence (a proxy for areas of rebel activity and support) are also those areas that are relatively the poorest and have the highest rates of landlessness (Murshed and Gates, 2003). On the other hand, secessionism has been documented by regions that are disproportionately wealthy relative to the rest of the country and feel they contribute more than they gain from the nation economically (Gourevitch, 1979). Both advantaged and disadvantaged groups may have incentives to engage in conflict, and there is not yet a convincing theoretical account of why it is possible to successfully make such appeals in some societies or at some times and not others.

The role of geography in civil war

To date, the study of geography and civil war has concentrated primarily on natural resource economies, a topic discussed above. However, geography has been tied to opportunities for rebellion and state weakness in other ways as well. Statistics show a correlation between rough terrain, low population density, and conflict onset (Fearon and Laitin, 2003, Collier and Hoeffler, 2001). Fearon and Laitin argue that large tracts of thinly populated land, mountains, swamps, and jungles may make it easier to launch and sustain an insurgency. However, there has not yet been a quantitative study demonstrating that rebellions actually tend to occur in the parts of the country where the rough or sparsely populated terrain is located (for example, by using a GIS matrix instead of national boundaries as units of analysis). Another difficulty for this theory is that Collier, Hoeffler and Söderbom (2004) do not find a relationship between duration of civil war and mountainous or forested terrain, as we would expect if terrain was important as an aid to insurgency.

Neighborhood effects have also been a part of the geographical study of civil war. A state bordering a civil war has an increased risk of internal conflict, as does a state hosting a large refugee population from a neighboring state (Salehyan and Gleditsch, 2006, Esty et al., 1998a, 1998b). Conflicts thus tend to be spatially clustered: in 2002, eleven of fifteen internal conflicts had clear spillovers – and three of the remaining cases were taking place on islands (Seybolt, 2002). Spillover may be indirect, such as a regional decline in economic activity (Murdoch and Sandler, 2002) or an upsurge of weapons and contraband trafficking. Rebellion next door may make a population anxious to rectify its own grievances (Marshall, 1999). Or spillover may be direct through trans-border movement of rebels or displaced population (Stedman and Tanner, 2003).

Neighborhood effects are one variable in the statistical literature on civil conflict that has drawn few criticisms from policy practitioners or field researchers. In fact, these results come as little surprise to those familiar with case specific dynamics in areas such as the Great Lakes region of Africa, the

Indochinese Peninsula, or Central Asia. A useful next direction of this line of research would be to concentrate on figuring out how developing societies can cheaply and effectively counter violence and criminal activity along their borders.

How much do macro studies explain?

Thus far, I have reviewed the findings of the quantitative literature on civil war, pointing out the ambiguities in these results and the further lines of research they suggest. In most cases, what seems to be needed is more precise, fully specified explanations for the correlations and non-correlations that appear repeatedly in statistical tests. For several reasons, we cannot expect to resolve the debates in the statistical literature solely through additional macro-level country-year statistics. First, it is difficult to overstate the problems of availability and reliability of relevant data on the global level. Many of the factors political scientists would like to test either have never been adequately measured (such as states' tax capacity) or cannot be perfectly quantified (such as democracy). Data for quantitative studies are usually limited to the post-World War II period, and some variables (especially economic data) are available for far fewer years. Second, some variables may powerfully influence civil conflict, but only in certain contexts or in contradictory ways. Such relationships can be investigated statistically, for example, by noting the simultaneous presence of multiple variables (e.g. the interaction of ethnic polarization and inequitable education policy), but a researcher seldom knows to look for such subtle patterns in her data unless she has been able to build a theory of civil conflict based on another mode of inquiry. Finally, few global statistical models have succeeded in correctly predicting even as much as 25 percent of the onset of civil war. Thus, macro models do not contain anything like a complete explanation of the origins of internal violence.

Resolving the ambiguities in the current statistical literature on civil war will require research designs that are tailored to grapple with the opaque nature of many of the correlations that have been uncovered thus far. For example, Miguel *et al.* (2004) have used drought measures to study the effect of economic shocks on civil peace; their research design captures only a certain kind of shock and considers only Africa, but it has the advantage that the authors can be more certain they are testing only the economic process of interest, avoiding the ambiguous measures and daunting endogeneity problems of cross-country regressions of GDP growth rates. Changing the unit of analysis is also a promising direction, as in the increasing use of survey research to answer questions about the individuals – soldiers and civilians – who experience civil war (Weinstein and Humphreys, 2006). Another example is the collection of event data (Uppsala Department of Peace and Conflict Research, 2005, Restrepo *et al.*, 2004) which may help researchers to distinguish when certain variables like regime instability played a role in increasing the risk of conflict as opposed to being epiphenomenal to the descent into conflict.

These suggestions for further research should not overshadow the contributions of the macro work on civil conflict to date. The role of global statistical studies should normally be to highlight broad commonalities in order to inform more targeted research design. And, importantly, global statistical models have already been able to debunk crudely primordial or fatalistic views of conflict. No intractable factor – such as culture, ethnic diversity, religious make-up, or terrain – dooms a society to violence. In fact, the importance of economic and political variables in predicting civil war is in many ways encouraging, because though it is difficult to generate economic development and stable governance, it can be done. No people or region is without potential for civic peace.

Note

1 Portions of this essay appeared in an article titled 'From Side Show to Centre Stage: Civil Conflict after the Cold War', *Security Dialogue*, 2004, 35(29), 191–205. The essay reflects insights into the quantitative literature on civil war gained at a conference hosted by the Centre for Human Security at the University of British Columbia on 'Mapping and Explaining Civil War: What to Do About Contested Datasets and Findings?', Oslo, 18–19 August 2003, and from the ECPR Joint Session of Workshops, Workshop 21 on 'Resources, Governance Structures, and Civil War', 14–18 April 2004, Uppsala, Sweden.

References

Bates, R. and Lien, D.H.D. (1985) 'A Note on Taxation, Development, and Representative Government', *Politics and Society* 14: 53–70.
Benson, M. and Kugler, J. (1998) 'Power Parity, Democracy, and the Severity of Internal Violence', *Journal of Conflict Resolution* 42: 196–209.
Berdal, M. and Malone, D.M. (eds) (2000) *Greed and Grievance: Economic Agendas in Civil Wars*. Boulder, CO: Lynne Rienner.
Collier, P. (2000) 'Rebellion as a Quasi-Criminal Activity', *Journal of Conflict Resolution* 44: 839–853.
Collier, P. and Hoeffler, A. (2001) 'Greed and Grievance in Civil War', World Bank Policy Research Working Paper 2355.
Collier, P. and Hoeffler, A. (2002) 'The Political Economy of Secession', Washington, DC: World Bank.
Collier, P., Elliott, L., Hegre, H., Hoeffler, A., Reynal-Querol, M., and Sambanis, N. (2003) *Breaking the Conflict Trap: Civil War and Development Policy*. Oxford: Oxford University Press.
Collier, P., Hoeffler, A., and Söderbom, M. (2004) 'On the Duration of Civil War', *Journal of Peace Research* 41: 253–273.
de Soysa, I. (2002) 'Paradise is a Bazaar? Greed, Creed, and Governance in Civil War, 1989–99', *Journal of Peace Research* 39: 395–416.
Elbadawi, I.A. and Sambanis, N. (2002) 'How Much War Will We See? Explaining the Prevalence of Civil War', *Journal of Conflict Resolution* 46: 307–334.

Ellingsen, T. (2000) 'Colorful Community or Ethnic Witches' Brew?' *Journal of Conflict Resolution* 44: 228–249.

Esty, D.C., Goldstone, J., Gurr, T.R., Surko, P.T., Unger, A.N., and Chen, R.S. (1998a) 'The State Failure Project: Early Warning Research for U.S. Foreign Policy Planning', in J.L. Davies and T.R. Gurr (eds) *Preventive Measures: Building Risk Assessment and Crisis Early Warning Systems.* Lanham, MD: Rowman & Littlefield.

Esty, D.C., Goldstone, J., Gurr, T.R., Surko, P.T., Unger, A.N., and Chen, R.S. (1998b) *The State Failure Report: Phase II Findings. Environmental Change and Security Project Report 5.* Washington, DC: Woodrow Wilson Center.

Fearon, J.D. (2004) 'Why Do Some Civil Wars Last So Much Longer than Others?' *Journal of Peace Research* 41: 275–301.

Fearon, J.D. (2005) 'Primary Commodity Exports and Civil War', *Journal of Conflict Resolution* 49: 483–507.

Fearon, J.D. and Laitin, D.D. (2003) 'Ethnicity, Insurgency, and Civil War', *American Political Science Review* 97: 75–90.

Gandhi, J. and Vreeland, J. (2004) 'Political Institutions and Civil War: Unpacking Anocracy', unpublished manuscript, Emory University and Yale University.

Gates, S. (2002) 'Empirically Assessing the Causes of Civil War', paper presented at 43rd annual convention of the International Studies Association, New Orleans, LA, 24–27 March.

Gates, S., Hegre, H., Jones, M., and Strand, H. (2006) 'Institutional Inconsistency and Political Instability: The Duration of Polities', *American Journal of Political Science* 50: 893–908.

Gleditsch, N.P., Wallensteen, P., Eriksson, M., Sollenberg, M., and Strand, H. (2002) 'Armed Conflict 1946–2001: A New Dataset', *Journal of Peace Research* 39: 615–637.

Gourevitch, P.A. (1979) 'The Reemergence of "Peripheral Nationalisms": Some Comparative Speculations on the Spatial Distribution of Political Leadership and Economic Growth', *Comparative Studies in Society and History* 21: 303–322.

Grossman, H.I. (1999) 'Kleptocracy and Revolution', *Oxford Economic Papers* 51: 267–283.

Gurr, T.R. (1993) *Minorities at Risk. A Global View of Ethnopolitical Conflicts.* Washington, DC: US Institute of Peace Press.

Hegre, H. (2003) 'Disentangling Democracy and Development as Determinants of Armed Conflict', paper presented at 44th annual convention of the International Studies Association, Portland, OR, 26 February–1 March.

Hegre, H., Ellingsen, T., Gleditsch, N.P., and Gates, S. (2001) 'Towards a Democratic Civil Peace?', *American Political Science Review* 95: 33–48.

Hegre, H., Gissinger, R., and Gleditsch, N.P. (2003) 'Globalization and Internal Conflict', in G. Schneider, K. Barbieri, and N.P. Gleditsch (eds) *Globalization and Armed Conflict.* Oxford: Rowman & Littlefield.

Horowitz, D.L. (1985) *Ethnic Groups in Conflict.* Berkeley, CA: University of California Press.

Keen, D. (1998) *The Economic Functions of Violence in Civil Wars.* London: International Institute for Strategic Studies.

King, C. (2001) 'The Benefits of Ethnic War: Understanding Eurasia's Unrecognized States', *World Politics* 53: 524–552.

Lacina, B. (2006) 'Explaining the Severity of Civil Wars', *Journal of Conflict Resolution* 50: 276–289.

Marshall, M.G. (1999) *Third World War: System, Process, and Conflict Dynamics*. Boulder, CO: Rowman & Littlefield.

Marshall, M.G. and Gurr, T.R. (2005) *Peace and Conflict 2005: A Global Survey of Armed Conflicts, Self-Determination Movements, and Democracy*. College Park, MD: Center for International Development and Conflict Management, University of Maryland.

Marshall, M.G. and Jaggers, K. (2003) *Polity IV Project*. College Park, MD: Center for International Development and Conflict Management at the University of Maryland.

Miguel, E., Satyanath, S., and Sergenti, E. (2004) 'Economic Shocks and Civil Conflict: An Instrumental Variables Approach', *Journal of Political Economy* 112: 725–753.

Montalvo, J.G. and Reynal-Querol, M. (2005) 'Ethnic Polarization, Potential Conflict, and Civil Wars', *American Economic Review* 95: 796–816.

Murdoch, J.C. and Sandler, T. (2002) 'Economic Growth, Civil Wars, and Spatial Spillovers', *Journal of Conflict Resolution* 46: 91–110.

Murshed, S.M. and Gates, S. (2003) 'Spatial-Horizontal Inequality and the Maoist Insurgency in Nepal', *Review of Development Economics* 9: 121–134.

Regan, P. (2002) 'Third Party Interventions and the Duration of Intrastate Conflict', *Journal of Conflict Resolution* 46: 55–73.

Regan, P.M. and Norton, D. (2005) 'Greed, Grievance and Mobilization in Civil Wars', *Journal of Conflict Resolution* 49: 319–336.

Restrepo, J., Spagat, M., and Vargas, J.F. (2004) 'The Dynamics of the Columbian Civil Conflict: A New Data Set', *Homo Oeconomicus* 21: 396–429.

Reynal-Querol, M. (2002) 'Ethnicity, Political Systems, and Civil Wars', *Journal of Conflict Resolution* 46: 29–54.

Richardson, L.F. (1960) *Statistics of Deadly Quarrels*. Pittsburgh, PA: Boxwood Press.

Ross, M. (2001) 'Does Oil Hinder Democracy?', *World Politics* 53: 326–361.

Ross, M. (2004a) 'How Do Natural Resources Influence Civil War? Evidence from Thirteen Cases', *International Organization* 58: 35–68.

Ross, M. (2004b) 'What Do We Know about Natural Resources and Civil War?', *Journal of Peace Research* 41: 337–356.

Salehyan, I. and Gleditsch, K.S. (2006) 'Refugees and the Spread of Civil War', *International Organization* 60: 335–361.

Sambanis, N. (2001) 'Do Ethnic and Nonethnic Civil Wars Have the Same Causes? A Theoretical and Empirical Inquiry (Part I)', *Journal of Conflict Resolution* 45: 259–282.

Sambanis, N. (2002) 'A Review of Recent Advances and Future Directions in the Quantitative Literature on Civil War', *Defence and Peace Economics* 13: 215–243.

Sambanis, N. (2004) 'What is a Civil War? Conceptual and Empirical Complexities of an Operational Definition', *Journal of Conflict Resolution* 48: 814–858.

Seybolt, T.B. (2002) 'Major Armed Conflicts', *SIPRI Yearbook 2002: World Armaments and Disarmament*. Oxford: Oxford University Press.

Stedman, S.J. and Tanner, F. (eds) (2003) *Refugee Manipulation: War, Politics, and the Abuse of Human Suffering*. Washington, DC: Brookings Institution.

Stewart, F. (2002) *Horizontal Inequalities: A Neglected Dimension of Development*. Oxford: Queen Elizabeth House, University of Oxford.

Uppsala Department of Peace and Conflict Research (2005) *Uppsala Conflict Database*. Uppsala: Uppsala University.

Weinstein, J. and Humphreys, M. (2006) 'Handling and Manhandling Civilians', *American Political Science Review* 100: 429–447.

Zakaria, F. (2003) *The Future of Freedom: Illiberal Democracy at Home and Abroad*. New York: W.W. Norton.

4 Civil wars and interstate disputes

Kristian Skrede Gleditsch and Idean Salehyan

Introduction

Although general theories should apply to all forms of armed conflict, a curious dichotomy has developed between empirical studies that analyze inter-state conflicts and those that deal with civil war or intra-state conflict. Whereas studies of civil war tend to look primarily at features within countries that are believed to affect the risk of war – such as weak government institutions or terrain that facilitates insurgencies – studies of interstate conflict generally look at attributes of relations between states, such as the extent of trade, power ratios, and geographic distance. In this chapter, we contend that the analytical separation between internal and external conflict is a false dichotomy, which masks strong linkages between conflict within states and conflict between governments. Just as international factors may influence the opportunity and willingness of domestic actors to challenge the state, what begin as 'internal' conflicts may become the subject of state-to-state militarized disputes.

In our previous work, we have considered various ways in which international or transnational factors can affect the risk of civil war (see Gleditsch 2007; Salehyan and Gleditsch 2006). In this chapter we look at another side of transnational conflict linkages and explore how issues originating from conflict within societies can threaten international security or lead to conflict between governments.[1] For instance, the NATO attack on Yugoslavia in spring of 1999 was an international dispute that emanated as a direct response to an internal conflict, namely the treatment and status of the Albanian population of the Kosovo province. Likewise, years of civil war in Afghanistan created conditions that allowed the fundamentalist Taliban regime to seize power and the Al-Qaeda network to set roots there. The Taliban regime's refusal to comply with US extradition requests in turn prompted a US invasion in the wake of the September 11 attacks on New York and Washington. Our principal claim in this chapter is that these examples are not isolated occurrences, and that civil wars are an important source of international conflict. We demonstrate empirically that the probability of disputes between state governments increases dramatically when at least one state is experiencing a civil war, and we identify a number of ways in which conflicts within countries can give rise to disputes between governments. We use the new narratives available from the Military Interstate Dispute (MID) data to show how a number of international crises are rooted in actors and events that arise from periods of internal conflict. These linkages strongly suggest that many common approaches to the study of interstate conflicts – emphasizing exclusively international or bilateral factors – fail to fully appreciate the triggers and origins of a large number of international disputes.

The domestic origins of interstate disputes

The separation of the study of violence between and within societies mirrors the traditional field separation within political science, where comparativists examine processes within nation-states and international relations scholars look to relations between states. The field of conflict studies emerged as a response to major international events such as the world wars and the confrontation between the nuclear superpowers, and was largely subsumed within the field of international relations.[2] As a result, international conflict studies has generally accepted the core tenets associated with the field of international relations – in particular, the assumption that relations between sovereign states in a system without a higher authority is somehow qualitatively different from politics within states. Traditional international relations theory has emphasized the inherent possibility of war under 'anarchy' – where states exist in a self-help world of power politics – which stands in stark contrast to the domestic rule of law. In the words of Waltz (1959: 232), 'war happens because there is nothing to prevent it'.

According to traditional international relations theory, 'hierarchy' characterizes politics within states, and states are authoritative bodies that can enforce compliance and domestic peace.

Whereas traditional international relations theory emphasized structural characteristics making war possible, modern studies generally view international conflict as the outcome of strategic interactions between states, where violence occurs when states fail to settle their disagreements over particular contentious issues (see, for example, Fearon 1995; Powell 1999). The prospects for violence or peaceful settlement are usually seen as a function of dyadic attributes or characteristics of the relations between states. Researchers have identified a number of features believed to be associated with a higher or lower likelihood of escalation to violence, including differences in power, the extent of economic integration and interdependence, and whether both states are democratic.

The alleged hierarchical nature of domestic politics is clearly often false. Waging violent conflict does not require a state, merely organized armies and the means to use force. A formally sovereign state is not a guarantee against violent conflict within its territory, and there are more instances of the organized use of violence *within* countries than *between* nation-states. Weak and inept states often lose control over their territory, leading to conditions that, to a greater or lesser degree, resemble international 'anarchy'. There is increasing recognition that applying a strict anarchy–hierarchy dichotomy to politics within and between states is both overstated and misleading, and that there is no reason why one should need different theories of conflict and cooperation for domestic versus international politics (see, for example, Lake 2003). Therefore in recent years, many conflict researchers have become interested in internal conflict and the possible insights from international relations theory that can be applied to civil war.

Although this theoretical synthesis between studies of civil and international war indeed is promising, considerable gaps remain between the two fields. In particular, we see remarkable differences between empirical studies of civil war versus interstate conflict. Even though what we call civil wars are composed of dyadic interactions between a government and an insurgent group(s), most empirical studies tend to be monadic and emphasize state or aggregate country characteristics such as political institutions or police capabilities, without looking in depth at attributes of rebel actors or strategic interactions between governments and insurgents. Moreover, most studies of civil war look only at conditions that influence the risk of civil war within the boundaries of the national state, thereby assuming that relations with other states or transnational actors are irrelevant. There are strong reasons to suspect that the closed-country model of civil war is overly restrictive and ignores important international linkages. Indeed, even a cursory examination of civil conflicts over the last several decades in areas such as Western Africa, Central America, and the Balkans suggests that transnational factors are prominent. In many cases, the actors themselves may be present in more than one state, and insurgents are often heavily dependent upon resources and support mobilized outside national boundaries. Several studies have demonstrated more systematically how international factors can influence civil war, including Gleditsch (2007), Salehyan and Gleditsch (2006), and Sambanis (2001).

If international factors and relations with other states can increase the risk of civil war, then we should also consider the possibility that conflict *within* societies may generate conflict *between* states. Civil wars can give rise to a number of issues that threaten the foreign relations of states, including border violations when states pursue rebels into the territory of neighboring countries; protests over the maltreatment of co-ethnics in states with internal conflicts; and disputes over responsibility for international externalities that arise from internal conflict such as refugee flows. Just as research on civil war has tended to ignore international factors, research on *interstate* conflict traditionally looks at relations between states and largely overlooks non-state actors or the potential for intergovernmental disputes to arise over conflict within states. Moreover, researchers have tended to focus on constraints on the use of force that make particular dyads less likely to experience violence, while ignoring the particular *issues* that states may come into conflict over (e.g. Morgenthau and Thompson 1985; Singer 1980). For instance, the extensive literature on the 'democratic peace' focuses on institutional and/or normative constraints on state behavior that makes violence less likely to erupt among democracies, but has little to say about the potential sources of international friction (see Bueno de Mesquita *et al.* 2003; Oneal and Russett 2001; Schultz 2001). Most of the existing literature on the importance of 'issues' in international conflict makes no mention of internal conflict as an issue area for disputes among states (e.g. Diehl 1992; Hensel 2002). The so-called diversionary theory of war does relate interstate conflict to domestic turmoil (see Levy 1989), but sees external conflicts merely as efforts to divert attention away from domestic woes rather than being linked directly to incompatibilities arising out of internal conflicts.

A growing body of work has explored how internal *ethnic* conflicts may give rise to interstate wars as state actors intervene to protect their kin in other countries (see, for example, Caprioli and Trumbore 2003; Cetinyan 2002; Moore and Davis 1998; Saideman 2001; Trumbore 2003; Woodwell 2004). Valuable as these contributions are, however, not all civil conflicts can be characterized as contests between governments and ethnic groups, and transnational ethnic relations is only one potential source of friction between states. In our view, there are many additional aspects related to civil conflict that can lead to international conflict that have been ignored in existing research.

For example, consider how the internal conflict in Colombia has influenced its relations with its neighbors in the region, particularly Venezuela. Fighting between the government of Colombia and various rebel forces – most notably the Revolutionary Armed Forces of Colombia (FARC) and the National Liberation Army (ELN) – has lead to events that have threatened Venezuela's security and has strained relations between these neighboring states. Although Colombia and Venezuela have not fought one another directly in a large-scale war, the internal conflict in Colombia has generated severe bilateral disputes and sources of tensions that carry a risk of violent confrontation. To cite but a few incidents, in February of 1995, between 150 and 200 Colombian rebels crossed the border into Venezuela and attacked a naval post in Cararabo, killing eight soldiers. Venezuela strongly protested the attack, and the two neighbors began bilateral talks aimed at policing their common border. However, in February of 1997, ELN rebels again attacked Venezuelan troops, wounding three, and prompting pursuit into Colombia by Venezuelan forces. During the pursuit across the border, the Venezuelan troops fired on a boat suspected of carrying Colombian rebels, but instead killed a three-year-old boy and wounded five civilians. Colombia strongly protested the action, and filed a legal suit in the Inter-American Court of Human Rights.[3] The Venezuelan Foreign ministry responded by blaming the Colombian government for not protecting their border, and declared that 'time is running out to resolve diplomatically with the Colombian government the security problem on our common border'.[4]

Concerned with drug-trafficking in the region, Venezuela again launched attacks on Colombian territory on October 15, 2000 to destroy a coca plantation, which may have been used to finance rebel activities. During the operation, several troops, accompanied by two Venezuelan helicopters and an airplane, launched an attack on several farms and houses in the region of Tres Bocas.[5] The foray across the border lasted several hours and destroyed Colombian homes, livestock, and property. Relations between Colombia and Venezuela further deteriorated after Hugo Chavez, seen by many in Colombia as a radical leftist, assumed the presidency of Venezuela. The most severe crisis in recent times occurred in December of 2004, when Colombian authorities bribed a Venezuelan National Guardsman to arrest and return Rodrigo Granda, a leading operative of the FARC, who had been residing in Caracas. Venezuela strongly protested the maneuver; President Hugo Chavez stated '[a] crime was committed here, and Venezuela's sovereignty was violated'.[6] A major diplomatic rift between the neighboring countries ensued as Venezuela temporarily recalled its ambassador in Bogotá and suspended commercial relations.

The impact of the Colombian conflict on Colombia–Venezuela relations illustrates a more general trend that civil wars often lead to contentious disputes between states. In this chapter, we demonstrate that internal conflict is a frequent and important source of interstate disputes that has generally been ignored in conceptions of conflict that focus exclusively on interstate relations or international factors. Although the Colombia–Venezuela example does not amount to a full scale war, major violent international incidents have followed civil conflicts, as, for example, when Israel invaded Lebanon in pursuit of PLO forces operating from that country's territory, leading to a protracted and very contentious occupation of southern Lebanon (see, for example, Timerman 1982). Similarly, repeated international disputes can give rise to protracted crises and international rivalries that heighten hostility between states and carry the potential to escalate into more severe events (see, for example, Diehl and Goertz 2000).

In this chapter, we wish to more systematically explore the consequences of civil conflict for interstate disputes. Since the value of theorizing is greater if people accept that there is a common phenomenon to explain, we start by offering some preliminary evidence that countries undergoing civil war indeed are more likely to experience interstate disputes with other countries. After demonstrating that such linkages can be found empirically at the aggregate level, we then proceed to show that these events do not merely coincide in time, but are causally linked in the sense that issues related to civil conflicts in many instances serve as triggers that give rise to interstate disputes. We identify a series of potential mechanisms by which civil conflict may give rise to conflict between states, and we provide examples of these mechanisms using the new narratives for the Militarized Interstate Dispute data. We conclude by discussing the implications for theories and empirical studies of conflict.

Evidence linking civil wars to international disputes

To support our claim that international conflicts often result out of issues arising from civil wars we first conduct a statistical analysis of these linkages. If we are correct that interstate disputes often are linked to civil wars, then countries experiencing civil conflicts should also be more likely to experience international disputes with other states.[7] We conduct both a monadic and a dyadic analysis to test our main hypothesis. We expect international disputes to be more common for states involved in a civil conflict, and these differences should be observable both at the monadic and the dyadic level. For the monadic test, we analyze all country-years from 1950 to 2001, giving us nearly 6,000 observations. Our dependent variable for this analysis is state involvement in any MID during the year in question.[8] For the dyadic analysis, we replicate Russett and Oneal's well-known model for the likelihood of disputes for all dyad-years from 1945 to 1992, adding the presence of civil conflict as an additional right-hand-side variable.[9] Our key measure of the presence of civil conflict is based upon the Uppsala/PRIO armed conflict data on internal violent conflicts.[10] For our main independent variable in the monadic analysis, we include a dichotomous variable coded 1 if the country is involved in a civil war; for the dyadic analysis, we include a similar variable coded 1 if either country (or both) in the dyad is involved in a civil war.

Table 4.1 reports the relative frequency of MIDs for annual country observations where there was a civil conflict versus cases where there was no conflict. As can be seen, in a majority (56 percent) of the country-years where there was civil war, that country also experienced militarized interstate disputes with other states. The observed frequency of MIDs is 1.6 times higher in states that experience a civil conflict than states without violent domestic conflict.

Although Table 4.1 is suggestive of a link between internal conflict and interstate disputes, it is possible that many state characteristics believed to make international conflict more likely – such as autocratic institutions and low deterrent capacity – also may be related to civil conflict. In Table 4.2, we present results for a more complete monadic model, where we include several controls for other factors that may plausibly influence the risk of civil war and also be associated with a higher likelihood of interstate disputes.[11]

Table 4.1 Interstate conflict (MID) and civil conflict

		Interstate conflict		
		No	Yes	Total
Civil conflict	No	4,153 (65%)	2,247 (35%)	6,400 (100%)
	Yes	507 (44%)	639 (56%)	1,146 (100%)
	Total	4,660	2,886	7,546

Table 4.2 Logit of likelihood of MID, monadic data

	Coefficient	Standard error	z
Civil conflict	0.645	0.088	7.310
CINC	5.695	1.583	3.600
Democracy	−0.013	0.006	−2.190
Log GDP per capita	−0.099	0.041	−2.390
Log population	0.180	0.029	6.290
Peaceyears	−0.849	0.042	−20.000
Spline 1	0.000	0.000	0.020
Spline 2	−0.024	0.002	−11.930
Spline 3	0.006	0.001	9.790
Constant	−0.654	0.440	−1.490

Notes
N = 5835, LR χ^2 (df = 9) = 1941.48.

First, we consider a state's military capabilities, as more powerful countries are more likely to become involved in international disputes, reflecting their greater ability to project force. Second, we control for the level of democracy, wealth, and population, as previous research suggests that wealthier countries and democratic states are less likely to be involved in disputes and that more populous countries are more likely to experience conflict. Third, since subsequent years of war and peace are unlikely to be independent of one another, we take into account the pacifying impact of consecutive years that a country has remained at peace, using the non-parametric approach suggested by Beck et al. (1998) to allow for a possible non-linear relationship.

The results in Table 4.2 indicate that countries undergoing civil conflict are far more likely to experience international disputes, even after controlling for other factors believed to be associated with interstate conflict. Indeed, the coefficient estimate implies that everything else held constant, the odds of international conflict is nearly twice as high in countries experiencing internal violence. We can demonstrate this substantive effect by comparing predicted probabilities for a hypothetical case with and without a civil conflict. For a baseline case where a country has mean levels of GDP per capita, population, and capabilities, a Polity score of 0, and 5 years of prior peace, the estimates of the model imply a 7.5 percent probability of a MID in the absence of a civil conflict. The presence of a civil conflict, holding other factors constant, increases the predicted probability of an international dispute to 13.3 percent, or a 77 percent increase over the baseline risk.

In Table 4.3 we insert our measure of civil conflict into Oneal and Russett's dyadic model of interstate disputes, including covariates such as dyadic democracy, trade interdependence, joint membership in intergovernmental organizations, the ratio of power capabilities, presence of an alliance, measures of joint contiguity and distance, and finally, minor power status.[12]

Table 4.3 Replication of Oneal and Russett (2001), including civil conflict

	Coefficient	Standard error.	z
Civil conflict	0.273	0.114	2.390
Democracy	−0.049	0.012	−4.100
Trade	−40.400	21.661	−1.870
IGO membership	−0.022	0.006	−3.810
Capability ratio	−0.337	0.061	−5.480
Allies	−0.735	0.190	−3.880
Non contiguous	−1.190	0.251	−4.730
Distance	−0.447	0.084	−5.300
Minor power	−0.889	0.272	−3.260
Constant	0.527	0.690	0.760

Notes
N = 28,229, Wald χ^2 (df = 9) = 185.59.

Table 4.3 again shows that even when controlling for other factors known to be important for international conflict, countries that undergo civil conflicts are much more likely to become involved in disputes with other states. For a baseline scenario with a non-allied, contiguous dyad, where both countries are minor powers, and all other variables are set to their means, the presence of a civil conflict in at least one state would raise the probability of conflict in the dyad from 0.9 percent to 1.2 percent, or by about one-third.

Identifying internal-to-international conflict linkages

The aggregate analysis reported in the previous section clearly shows that cases where countries are involved in civil conflict are associated with a higher incidence of militarized interstate disputes, consistent with our argument that behavior in civil conflicts can give rise to disputes with other states. However, although suggestive, these aggregate results cannot by themselves tell us what it is about civil conflicts that can lead to international disputes or whether the correlations are in fact causally linked. In this section, we outline more systematically five possible ways in which disputes between states may arise as a response to civil conflict within a state. We highlight how disputes may arise out of violations of the territorial sovereignty of another country; actual or alleged outside support to insurgents and intrusion in internal affairs; conflict over responsibilities for potentially unintended spillovers of conflict; conflict over human rights abuses and treatment of minorities; as well as responses to irregular government changes. We illustrate the different varieties of linkages or mechanisms using examples from the conflict narratives available for the 1993–2001 period in the new version of the MID data.[13]

We see these categories as common ways in which aspects of internal conflict gives rise to disputes between states. We do not claim to provide an exhaustive list of internal-to-external conflict linkages, or that these categories are mutually exclusive in the sense that only one may apply in a given case. However, analyzing these categories separately, we believe, provides a useful way to think about possible causal links, which can inform future research. We will return to the issue of how these insights can be incorporated in empirical studies of interstate conflict in the conclusion, after discussing each of the suggested civil conflict to interstate conflict linkages.

Violations of sovereignty and attacks on neighboring state territory

The first type of international conflict that may emerge out of civil war pertains to protests and frictions over border violations and attacks on neighboring state territory that occur as a result of government conduct during counter-insurgency operations. Previous research has shown that civil wars are more likely to occur in the vicinity of a state's borders (Buhaug and Gates 2002). Insurgents may operate in border areas for a variety of reasons. On the one hand, conflict zones may be likely to involve border areas, since borders are often drawn in areas with natural physical boundaries such as mountains and dense forests, and these geographic features may provide hiding grounds for insurgents.[14] However, beyond terrain or infrastructure features, international borders may by their nature provide certain advantages for insurgents. Many international borders are porous, and rebels often maintain bases across national boundaries in order to find a degree of protection from government repression (see Salehyan 2006). Operating from other states can provide some safety to rebels, in the sense that it is more difficult for the government in the conflict country to target rebels on the territory of another sovereign state, removed from territory under its own control. Additionally, the rebels may be tacitly or deliberately provided with safe havens in neighboring countries by governments hostile to the government in the conflict country. Finally, even when neighboring states do not wish to let rebels from other states operate on their territory, they may not have the capacity to prevent them from doing so.

Although international borders limit the use of force by state agents, governments still frequently violate the sovereign territory of others in pursuit of rebels. Cross-border strikes against rebels on foreign soil are one example of how the conduct of a country during counter-insurgency operations can provoke disputes between states. In some cases, governments have even occupied areas of neighboring states in order to deny insurgents and rebels the opportunity to use their territory. Israel, for example, invaded southern Lebanon in 1982 in order to oust the PLO. Rwanda similarly invaded Zaire/DRC in pursuit of Hutu rebels following the 1994 genocide. Incidents when states pursue rebels into neighboring territories or occupy outside territories are likely to lead to protests and possible retaliation from the states whose sovereignty has been violated.

Turning to the MID narratives, Southeast Asia provides a number of examples of disputes originating as a response to border violations. MID 4001, for example, refers to a dispute between Thailand and Cambodia. The MID narratives describe the event as starting with Cambodian troops engaging Khmer Rouge forces in 1994, shelling Thai territory in the process, which unleashed return shelling from Thai forces and subsequent hostile interactions until the end of the dispute in 1996. Similarly, MID 4003 pertains to an incident where Burmese forces came to occupy territory claimed by Thailand, following a peace agreement with Shan warlord Khun Sa in which the contested territory was given to Burma. As another example, in MID 4113, on November 6, 1994, Iran fired Scud missiles at a rebel base in Iraq, leading to protests from Iraq, which claimed that its security had been threatened. MID 4083 between Uganda and Kenya provides an interesting example of a dispute involving alleged foreign sanctuaries and support for rebels. Relations between Uganda and Kenya had initially become tense as Uganda refused to hand over the alleged leader of a Kenyan rebel organization, and a police post in western Kenya was raided by rebels operating from Uganda. Following alleged intrusions of Kenyan security forces into its territory, Uganda moved to build up its troops along the border with Kenya.

Interventions and support to armed factions

Another common type of intra-to-interstate dispute linkage pertains to instances where foreign governments either intervene directly or are alleged to support participants in an internal conflict. Other states often have strong preferences about the outcome of civil wars, and may take steps to provide aid or support to one of the sides in an ongoing conflict. Although it is widely acknowledged in the literature that civil war can become internationalized through direct military intervention,[15] existing research has paid less attention to cases where foreign governments back rebel factions through less direct forms of support (but see Regan 2000). Civil wars can become interstate conflicts if states intervene militarily in support of insurgents, as in the case of NATO intervention in the Kosovo conflict (MID 4137). However, international conflict is not limited to cases where external governments provide direct military support to organized rebel factions. Governments often use less intrusive ways of providing support to insurgents and dissidents, including providing them funding, diplomatic recognition, or intelligence. Any such alleged forms of intervention by other states are likely to provide reaction from governments in conflict countries. In addition, private citizens in other countries may provide support to dissident or rebel groups, which can also provoke international tensions as targeted states view such actions as violation of its sovereignty.

Sudan's relations with its neighbors provides many examples of disputes emanating from alleged support to insurgencies (e.g. MIDs 4078, 4079,

4081, 4124, and 4130). Sudan has engaged in militarized disputes with Ethiopia, Eritrea, and Uganda over these countries' support to insurgent groups in the south, and in turn, these governments have protested Sudan's alleged support of militant Islamism in the region. Eritrea even broke diplomatic relations with Sudan, following alleged Sudanese support of the Islamic Jihad opposition group. In a similar manner, governments in western and central Africa have often clashed over allegations and counter-allegations of neighbors supporting insurgents (MIDs 4085, 4116, 4122, 4252, and 4253). Again, such disputes may arise even when the government in intervening states denies any responsibility, and the extent of foreign support for rebels is frequently unclear.

As previously mentioned, disputes against alleged interference may follow actions by private parties rather than government agents. Albania, for example, initiated a dispute with Greece over border violations committed by Greek citizens rather than military troops. MID 4041 emerged after Greek nationalists attacked an ethnically Greek region of Albania. The government of Albania subsequently issued a complaint to Greece, alleging that Greek authorities had supported the invaders, even though the Greek government denied any involvement in the incident.

Conflict over externalities

The first two types of conflict linkages we have discussed so far stem from cases where states intentionally violate the sovereignty of other states either by intruding on their territory or by interfering in civil conflicts in other states. However, conflicts may also arise when civil conflicts create unanticipated consequences for other states. It is well established that civil wars often entail negative externalities for other states in the region. For example, Sandler and Murdoch (2004) show that civil wars tend to depress rates of economic growth in neighboring states (see also Easterly and Levine 1998). Moreover, civil conflicts often generate flights of refugees or forced migrants, which can place a heavy burden on neighboring states (Moore and Shellman 2004; Salehyan and Gleditsch 2006). Finally, internal conflicts often generate casualties in other states as a result of accidental bombs or shelling of other states' territory. Unlike the linkages that we discussed above, these consequences arise as unintended byproducts of the conduct of internal conflict rather than deliberate decisions or disregard for the sovereignty of other states.[16] However, regardless of whether harm was intended or not, affected states may hold the country of origin responsible, and disputes may arise when states issue military threats combined with demands for action or some form of compensation.

The 1993–2001 period witnessed several events where conflict emerged over unintended consequences of conflict. With regard to misplaced bombings, MID 4085 pertains to a dispute between Nigeria and Cote d'Ivoire after Nigerian planes struck a bridge between Cote d'Ivoire and Liberia as part of the ECOWAS involvement in Liberia. Nigeria later characterized the bombing as a 'mistake' and apologized for the incident. Similarly, MID 4071 stems from an Angolan aircraft accidentally bombing a Zairean military base. Although Angola apologized immediately, citing bad weather as the cause, Zaire sent troops to the border in response to the incident. Concerns over refugees also prompted military action in several instances. India and Bangladesh have experienced several disputes where India deployed its troops to the border region to prevent the entry of refugees (e.g. MIDs 4006 and 4313). Similarly, in MID 4159, Iran fortified and closed its border with Afghanistan over concerns about refugees, and in MID 4066, Ghana militarized its borders to prevent refugees from Togo from entering the country.

Conflict over human rights violations or treatment of minorities

Counter-insurgency operations can often be severely destructive and threaten civilian populations. Other states may become concerned about atrocities carried out during civil wars and the humanitarian effects of conflict. States may protest against human rights violations committed by the government; for instance, there was near universal condemnation of the Racak massacre in Kosovo in January 1999, when Yugoslav security forces shelled and raided an Albania village believed to be a stronghold for the Kosovo Liberation Army. But the use of direct military force for humanitarian reasons alone is rare, and humanitarian motives are often coupled with strategic interests. In some cases, states have strong links to particular groups that are involved in conflicts elsewhere. Ethnic groups involved in conflict with a government are often present in more than one state, which serves to heighten attention to human rights conditions affecting such groups. In some cases, a peripheral group in one state may be politically dominant in another state. In these cases with transnational kinship ties, government repression is likely to lead to diplomatic protests from other states, sometimes accompanied by military threats.

The Balkans in the 1980s and 1990s provide several examples of protests concerning human rights abuses and minority group treatment. Towards the end of the Cold War and into the 1990s, there was considerable concern across Europe that a war could arise over the harsh treatment of the Hungarian minority in Romania. Even though Hungary and Romania were formally allies in the Warsaw Pact, the Romanian policy of forced resettlement of largely ethnic Hungarian villages to new planned communities created severe strains in the bilateral relations between the two countries as well as Romania's relations with other countries in western Europe (see, for example, Linden 2000). Concern over atrocities in the former Yugoslavia partly explains military intervention there. More recently, the treatment of the Albanian population in the province of Kosovo created a number of disputes between Yugoslavia and other countries. The suppression of the Albanian population initially led to a series of disputes between Yugoslavia and Albania, which had ethnic ties to the province (e.g. MIDs 4043, 4045, and 4136). Although Albania was not in a position to militarily challenge Yugoslavia, NATO countries became involved in the dispute and demanded an end to the repression of the Kosovars, threatening military action if Yugoslavia did not comply (MID 4137). NATO attacked with air-strikes and later sent in ground forces, essentially seizing control over the province under the auspices of the Kosovo Force (KFOR). This has in turn led to a number of new disputes with Yugoslavia over the status of the region (MIDs 4186 and 4295).

Responses to irregular government change

States often come into conflict with one another after regime changes, which disrupt the status quo. Irregular seizures of power, for example, popular revolutions and coups, significantly (or completely) change the composition of the government and its established policies. Other countries often become concerned that the newly empowered government will change its policies in such a way as to negatively affect their interests, such as nationalizing foreign assets or taking a more belligerent foreign policy stance. Irregular changes in government may also be viewed as illegitimate, and can provoke international censure. In some instances, states may take military action as a result of the new regime's anticipated policies. Likewise, other governments may try to capitalize on coups or revolutions and launch an attack while the new regime is still weak. For example, Iraq invaded Iran shortly after the Iranian revolution while the new government was still consolidating power. But foreign adventures may also be beneficial to the new government as it provides a means to consolidate power at home. Iran may have prolonged conflict with Iraq as an opportunity to suppress domestic dissent.

Several MIDs over the 1993–2001 period emerge as a response to coups. The perhaps best-known event over the period is the response to the coup against Haitian president Aristide (MID 4016), where the Clinton administration, along with a number of other countries, demanded the immediate reinstatement of Aristide. The refugee exodus from Haiti also contributed to the USA's involvement. The US-led coalition first responded with a naval blockade and ultimately landed troops on the island after military leaders ceded power. Likewise, in the context of the ongoing Kashmir crisis between India and Pakistan (MID 4223), India called a military alert after General Pervez Musharraf deposed Pakistani Prime Minister Nawaz Sharif. In Sierra Leone, Nigeria intervened militarily under the auspices of the Economic Community of West African States (ECOWAS) to reinstate the previous government ousted by the rebels on May 25, 1997 (MID 4251), and fighting over control for political power dragged on for several months afterwards. Sometimes, the new government moves to preemptively protect itself from outside aggression. In MID 4293, the government of Qatar placed its forces on high alert after a bloodless coup, fearing that Saudi Arabia might try to take advantage of the coup to seize disputed territory.

Implications for the study of international conflict

We argued at the outset of this chapter that countries that undergo civil conflicts are more likely to become involved in disputes with other states. Events that are seen as 'internal' conflicts often have important implications for other states, and can heighten international tensions. Through a statistical analysis, we have shown that countries that experience civil war are substantially more likely to become engaged in international disputes. Our review of the narratives provided by the new MID dataset demonstrates that interstate disputes often originate out of internal conflicts, and we have listed a number of internal-to-external conflict linkages. In this section we comment on the broader implications of our analysis for the study of international conflict, as well as areas that deserve greater attention in future research.

Since the early 1990s, a large number of articles have developed statistical models of international conflict using the MID dataset (see, for example, Bremer 1992; Bremer and Cusack 1995; Oneal and Russett 2001). It is well known that the predictive ability of these models are rather disappointing and that these studies have not been very successful in identifying conflict areas (see Beck *et al.* 2000; Ward and Gleditsch 2002). Researchers have pointed to data inadequacies, overly strict model assumptions, and inherent uncertainty in bargaining situations as possible explanations for why quantitative studies of international conflict have not been more successful in a predictive sense (see, for example, Beck *et al.* 2000; Gartzke 1999; Gleditsch and Ward 2000). In addition, our analysis suggests that many models may perform poorly because they rely exclusively on bilateral or international features, and do not pay greater attention to the issues underlying conflicts. Many recent international conflicts such as the interventions in Kosovo and Afghanistan, or the war in the Democratic Republic of Congo, provide strong evidence that many wars originate in conflict within countries. Looking at the proximate issues that can motivate resort to violence, rather than less direct background conditions such as power ratios and trade interdependence that may affect the cost of conflict, is likely to be fruitful and improve upon our predictive abilities.[17]

We believe that the linkages we have identified can help scholars to start thinking about how to better specify models of international war. A great deal of useful information can be gathered by a theoretically informed examination of internal conflicts. First, data on the geographic dimensions of civil war can be integrated into studies of international war. Internal conflicts where fighting takes place near international borders and/or cases where rebels have bases in neighboring countries may provoke international disputes over conflict externalities, cross-border strikes, and external support to opposition groups. We have collected information about these characteristics for the internal conflicts listed in the Uppsala conflict data (see Cunningham *et al.* 2006). Second, information about refugee flows between countries can be incorporated into models of international conflict. Third, collecting data on the ethnic affiliation of rebel groups can help to identify cases where other countries, especially those with ethnic ties to combatants, are likely to intervene. Fourth, data on external funding and support to rebel groups can help to identify cases that are likely to erupt into international violence. Finally, beyond a simple listing of coups or revolutions, data collection on the *direction* of regime change and ensuing policy shifts can help to identify countries that are likely to become involved in international disputes (see Gleditsch and Choung 2006). For instance, democracies may be more likely to intervene in cases where coup leaders overthrow a democratic government.

In closing, from a policy perspective, our analysis strongly suggests that civil conflicts can give rise to potentially serious interstate crises and violence, and as such should become a matter of common concern in the international community. International governance, on a broad multi-lateral level or regionally, may be able to mitigate some of the intergovernmental tensions that can arise in the context of civil conflict. For example, if states can cooperate to monitor their common borders against cross-border security threats, they may be able to prevent conflict from escalating within neighboring states and creating costly externalities for neighbors. Moreover, better global strategies for development assistance and institution building can serve to prevent civil wars in states at risk. In this sense, efforts to prevent tensions within countries from escalating to violence are not simply acts of altruism, but are potentially important means to prevent future international security threats.

Notes

1 In this chapter, we use the terms 'conflict' and 'dispute' broadly to imply mutual antagonism over issue incompatibilities, which may or may not result in violence. We use the term 'war' to refer to violent incidents, but we do not necessarily imply a minimum deaths threshold such as 1,000.
2 For decades, the comparative study of violence *within* societies (e.g., DeNardo 1985; Gurr 1970; Tilly 1978) has largely ignored insights from international relations, with the important exception of Skocpol (1979) who sees 'international turmoil' as an important condition for successful social revolutions. Even prominent recent studies of civil conflict treat international factors as secondary to domestic politics (e.g. Collier and Hoeffler 2004; Fearon and Laitin 2003).
3 Agence France Presse, February 8, 1997. *Colombian town to sue Venezuela for boy's death in border skirmish.*
4 Quoted in the International Boundaries News Database: www.ibru.dur.ac.uk/resources/newsarchive.html.
5 British Broadcasting Corporation, October 19, 2000. *Colombian army 'confirms' Venezuelan cross-border raid.*
6 *New York Times*, January 23, 2005. *Capture of rebel divides Latin American neighbors.*
7 Many empirical data collection efforts – notably the Correlates of War project's

conflict data (see Sarkees 2000) – define interstate and intrastate conflict as mutually exclusive categories where a given conflict has to be either intrastate or interstate. This will, by construction, make it unlikely that civil and interstate conflicts could be recorded at the same time. The Vietnam War, for example, becomes an international war in the COW data once the US intervention is deemed to have made the conflict international, thereby 'ending' the previous civil war. In this paper, we use data on intrastate and interstate conflict coded independently of one another.

8 For details on the MID data, see Jones et al. (1996: 168). We retrieved the MID data as well as all other control variables from EUGene (version 3.03), see www.eugenesoftware.org and Bennett and Stam (2000) for details on the measures.

9 Russett and Oneal's analysis covers the period 1885 to 1992, however, as our civil war variable is only collected from 1945 on, we must restrict our analysis to the post World War II period.

10 For events to be included in this dataset as civil conflict there must be an identifiable incompatibility between a government and an insurgent group over either control of territory or the central government that generates at least 25 battle-related deaths within a given year. See Gleditsch et al. (2002) for details.

11 Our control variables are all from standard sources: We use the Correlates of War project's Composite Index of National Capabilities (CINC) as a measure of capabilities (see, for example, Singer et al. 1972), the Polity index as a measure of democracy (see Jaggers and Gurr 1995), and expanded population and income data from Gleditsch (2002b).

12 For a full description of the dataset, see Oneal and Russett (2001). To make our results comparable to theirs, we report population-averaged generalized estimating equations estimates with an autoregressive (AR1) component, and robust standard errors estimates, clustering on dyads.

13 These narratives are available from the MID project home page cow.la.psu.edu/COW2%20Data/MIDs/MID302.html. Unfortunately, the available MID narratives cover only for the 1993–2001 period, and narratives are not available for all of the recorded disputes over the period. Although we are hesitant to make any claims about the origin of disputes from such a small set, we find that that civil conflict was a trigger in a little over a third of the disputes where conflict narratives were available.

14 These are all features that previous research has argued tend to facilitate insurgences, see Fearon and Laitin (2003) or Buhaug and Rød (2006).

15 The Uppsala armed conflict data identify 'internationalized' civil wars as a separate category of conflict, and code about 5 percent of the internal conflicts for 1946–2003 as internationalized. The Correlates of War project's civil war data, which relies on a higher conflict threshold, indicates that about 25 percent of conflicts to include foreign interventions.

16 We recognize that refugee flows imposing burdens on other states in some cases may not be a clear case of an unintended externality, as governments and individuals in states with conflict often make more or less concerted efforts to get other ethnic groups to re-settle in particular countries perceived as their appropriate 'home' countries.

17 If international factors that are associated with conflict or propensity to disputes also influence the risk of civil war as we have argued elsewhere (see Gleditsch 2006; Salehyan and Gleditsch 2006), then there may be issues of endogeneity in the relationship between civil conflicts international tension that we have not taken into account in the preliminary analysis presented here. For one attempt to take into account the endogeneity between civil conflict and interstate crises, see Chiozza et al. (2006).

Bibliography

Beck, N., Katz, J.N., and Tucker, R.M. (1998) 'Taking Time Seriously: Time-Series Cross-Section Analysis With a Binary Dependent Variable', *American Journal of Political Science* 42 (4): 1260–88.

Beck, N., King, G., and Zeng, L. (2000) 'Improving Quantitative Studies of International Conflict: A Conjecture', *American Political Science Review* 94: 21–36.

Bennett, D.S. and Stam, A. (2000) 'EUGene: A Conceptual Manual', *International Interactions* 26: 179–204.

Bremer, S.A. (1992) 'Dangerous Dyads: Conditions Affecting the Likelihood of Interstate War, 1816–1965', *Journal of Conflict Resolution* 36 (2): 309–41.

Bremer, S.A. and Cusack, T.R. (1995) *The Process of War: Advancing the Scientific Study of War*, Luxembourg and Philadelphia, PA: Gordon and Breach.

Bueno de Mesquita, B., Smith, A., Siverson, R.M., and Morrow, J.D. (2003) *The Logic of Political Survival*, Cambridge, MA: MIT Press.

Buhaug, H. and Gates, S. (2002) 'The Geography of Civil War', *Journal of Peace Research* 39 (4): 417–33.

Buhaug, H. and Rød, J.K. (2006) 'Local Determinants of African Civil Wars, 1970–2001', *Political Geography* 25(3): 315–35.

Caprioli, M. and Trumbore, P.F. (2003) 'Ethnic Discrimination and Interstate Violence: Testing the International Impact of Domestic Behavior', *Journal of Peace Research* 40 (1): 5–23.

Cetinyan, R. (2002) 'Ethnic Bargaining in the Shadow of Third-Party Intervention', *International Organization* 56 (3): 645–77.

Chiozza, G., Gleditsch, K.S., and Goemans, H. (2006) Civil War, Tenure, and Interstate Insecurity. Typescript, University of California, Berkeley, University of Essex, and the University of Rochester.

Collier, P. and Hoeffler, A. (2004) 'Greed and Grievance in Civil War', *Oxford Economic Papers* 56 (4): 563–95.

Cunningham, D., Gleditsch, K.S., and Salehyan, I. (2006) Dyadic Interactions and Civil War Duration. Typescript, University of Essex.

DeNardo, J. (1985) *Power in Numbers*. Princeton NJ: Princeton University Press.

Diehl, P.F. (1992) 'What Are They Fighting For? The Importance of Issues in International Conflict Research', *Journal of Peace Research* 29: 333–44.

Diehl, P.F. and Goertz, G. (2000). *War and Peace in International Rivalry*. Ann Arbor, MI: University of Michigan Press.

Easterly, W. and Levine, R. (1998) 'Troubles with the Neighbours: Africa's Problem, Africa's Opportunity', *Journal of African Economies* 7 (1): 120–42.

Fearon, J.D. (1995) 'Rationalist Explanations for War', *International Organization* 49 (3): 379–414.

Fearon, J.D. and Laitin, D.D. (2003) 'Ethnicity, Insurgency, and Civil War', *American Political Science Review* 97 (1): 75–90.

Gartzke, E.A. (1999) 'War is in the Error Term', *International Organization* 53 (3): 567–87.

Gleditsch, K.S. (2002a) *All International Politics is Local: The Diffusion of Conflict, Integration, and Democratization*, Ann Arbor, MI: University of Michigan Press.

Gleditsch, K.S. (2002b) 'Expanded Dyadic Trade and GDP Data, 1946–92', *Journal of Conflict Resolution* 46 (5): 712–24.

Gleditsch, K.S. (2004) 'A Revised List of Wars Between and Within Independent States, 1816–2002', *International Interactions* 30: 231–62.
Gleditsch, K.S. (2007) 'Transnational Dimensions of Civil War', *Journal of Peace Research* 44 (3): 293–309.
Gleditsch, K.S. and Choung, J.L. (2006) Autocratic Transitions and Democratization. Typescript, University of Essex.
Gleditsch, K.S. and Ward, M.D. (2000) 'War and Peace in Time and Space: The Role of Democratization', *International Studies Quarterly* 44 (1): 1–29.
Gleditsch, N.P, Wallensteen, P., Eriksson, M., Sollenberg, M., and Strand, H. (2002) 'Armed Conflict 1946–2001: A New Dataset', *Journal of Peace Research* 39 (5): 615–37.
Goemans, H., Gleditsch, K.S., and Chiozza, G. (2006) Archigos: A Database on Political Leaders. Typescript, University of Rochester and University of Essex, URL: mail.rochester.edu/~hgoemans/data.htm.
Gurr, T.R. (1970) *Why Men Rebel*. Princeton, NJ: Princeton University Press.
Hensel, P.R. (2002) General Codebook: Issue Correlates of War (ICOW) Project. Department of Political Science, Florida State University.
Jaggers, K. and Gurr, T.R. (1995) 'Tracking Democracy's Third Wave with the Polity III Data', *Journal of Peace Research* 32 (4): 469–82.
Jones, D.M., Bremer, S.A., and Singer, D.J (1996) 'Militarized Interstate Disputes, 1816–1992: Rationale, Coding Rules, and Empirical Applications', *Conflict Management and Peace Science* 15 (2): 163–213.
Lake, D.A. (2003) 'International Relations Theory and Internal Conflict: Insights from the Interstices', *International Studies Review* 5 (4): 81–9.
Lake, D.A. and Morgan, P. (eds) (1997) *Regional Orders: Building Security in a New World*, State College, PA: Pennsylvania State University Press.
Levy, J.S. (1989) 'The Diversionary Theory of War: A Critique'. In Midlarsky, I.M. (ed.) *Handbook of War Studies*. Ann Arbor, MI: University of Michigan Press.
Linden, R.H. (2000) 'Putting on Their Sunday Best: Romania, Hungary, and the Puzzle of Peace', *International Studies Quarterly* 44 (1): 121–45.
Moore, W.H. and Davis, D.R. (1998) 'Ties That Bind? Domestic and International Conflict Behavior in Zaire', *Comparative Political Studies* 31 (1): 45–71.
Moore, W.H. and Shellman, S.M. (2004) 'Fear of Persecution: A Global Study of Forced Migration, 1952–1995', *Journal of Conflict Resolution* 40 (5): 723–45.
Morgenthau, H.J. and Thompson, K.W. (1985) *Politics Among Nations: The Struggle for Power and Peace*, New York: McGraw Hill.
Oneal, J. and Russett, B.M. (2001) *Triangulating Peace: Democracy, Interdependence, and International Organizations*, New York: Norton.
Powell, R. (1993) 'Guns, Butter, and Anarchy', *American Political Science Review* 87 (1): 115–32.
Powell, R. (1999) *In the Shadow of Power: States and Strategies in International Politics*, Princeton, NJ: Princeton University Press.
Regan, P.M. (2000) *Civil Wars and Foreign Powers: Interventions and Intrastate Conflict*, Ann Arbor, MI: University of Michigan Press.
Saideman, S.M. (2001) *The Ties That Divide: Ethnic Politics, Foreign Policy, and International Conflict*, New York: Columbia University Press.
Salehyan, I. (2006) 'Rebels Without Borders: State Boundaries, Transnational Opposition, and Civil Conflict', PhD dissertation, Department of Political Science, University of California, San Diego.

Salehyan, I. and Gleditsch, K.S. (2006) 'Refugee Flows and the Spread of Civil War', *International Organization* 60 (2): 335–66.

Sambanis, N. (2001) 'Do Ethnic and Non-Ethnic Civil Wars Have the Same Causes? A Theoretical and Empirical Inquiry (Part 1)', *Journal of Conflict Resolution* 45 (3): 259–82.

Sandler, T. and Murdoch, J. (2004) 'Civil War and Economic Growth: Spatial Dispersion', *American Journal of Political Science* 48 (1): 138–51.

Sarkees, M. (2000) 'The Correlates of War Data on War: An Update to 1997', *Conflict Management and Peace Science* 18 (1): 123–44.

Schultz, K.A. (2001) *Democracy and Coercive Diplomacy*, Cambridge: Cambridge University Press.

Singer, D.J. (1980) 'Introduction', in Singer, J.D. (ed.) *The Correlates of War II: Testing Some Realpolitik Models*, New York: Free Press.

Singer, D.J, Bremer, S., and Stuckey, J. (1972) 'Capability Distribution, Uncertainty, and Major Power War'. In Russet, B.M. (ed.) *Peace, War, and Numbers*, Beverly Hills, CA: Sage.

Skocpol, T. (1979) *States and Social Revolutions: A Comparative Analysis of France, Russia and China*, New York: Cambridge University Press.

Thompson, W.R. (1995) 'Principal Rivalries', *Journal of Conflict Resolution* 39: 195–223.

Tilly, C. (1978) *From Mobilization to Revolution*. Reading, MA: Addison-Wesley.

Timerman, J. (1982) *The Longest War*. New York: Alfred Knopf.

Trumbore, P.F. (2003) 'Victims or Aggressors? Ethno-political Rebellion and Use of Force in Militarized Interstate Disputes', *International Studies Quarterly* 47 (2): 183–201.

Wagner, R.H. (2004) War and the State: An Introduction to the Study of International Politics. Draft Book Manuscript, University of Texas, Austin.

Waltz, K.N. (1959) *Man, the State and War: A Theoretical Analysis*. New York: Columbia University Press.

Ward, M.D. and Gleditsch, K.S. (2002) 'Location, Location, Location: An MCMC Approach to Modeling the Spatial Context of War and Peace', *Political Analysis* 10: 244–60.

Woodwell, D. (2004) 'Unwelcome Neighbors: Shared Ethnicity and International Conflict During the Cold War', *International Studies Quarterly* 48 (1): 197–223.

5 Robin Hood or Al Capone?

Natural resources and conflict in India's Naxalite insurgency

William Noël Ivey

Introduction

On October 1, 2002, an Indian insurgent organization, the People's War Group or 'PWG', posted a death warrant on the internet for chief ministers of three states in India:

> Death Warrant By the Suppressive actions of the comprador State Governments of Andhra Pradesh, Jharkhand, West Bengal, Bihar, MP, ChattisGarh [*sic*] the respective comprador Governments [*sic*] have virtually signed their own Death Warrants. Buddhadeb Bhattacharyya, Chandrababu Naidu, Babulal Marandi shall perish. Peoples' War gives a call to all revolutionaries to take up arms and join the struggle for emancipation. Death to Buddhadeb Bhattacharyya, Chandrababu Naidu, Babulal Marandi. Long live revolution. Inquilab Zindabad.
> (CPIMLPWG 2002)

This was no hollow threat, and on October 1, 2003, the PWG attempted to kill Andhra Pradesh chief minister Chandrababu Naidu. Naidu survived, but thousands have died in a decades old insurgency regarded as one of India's main national security threats.

Since the late 1970s, the PWG and other Maoist insurgent groups – often called 'Naxalites' – have been involved in conflicts over contested forest areas and agricultural land, but not over mineral resources. The conflicting parties are numerous and overlapping, but the dominant pattern of conflict is between Naxalites who have mobilized lower-caste, 'untouchable', and indigenous communities that rely on natural resources for their income and subsistence against those who have deprived them of those resources or supported such deprivation: higher caste landlords, forestry companies, private militias, police, politicians, and others.

Since the Cold War's end, research on relationships between natural resources and civil conflict has gained substantial academic and policy attention, and two bodies of work have become prominent. One body of research contends that in poor societies in which the majority of the population depends upon renewable natural resources for their subsistence and income, various forms of resource scarcity may cause or aggravate social, economic, and political problems that in turn may lead to civil conflicts between groups contending for access to resources. Other research argues that in countries where natural resources account for a significant portion of export income (around 25 to 33 percent), civil conflict is the result of insurgents' efforts to capture those resources' financial benefits and render rebellion financially viable.

These ideas are often depicted as almost mutually exclusive assessments of links between natural resources and civil conflict – sometimes portrayed as, respectively, grievance or greed – yet Naxalites act in ways that are explained by both of these supposedly opposite theories. For example, in 'Robin Hood' fashion, Naxalites have used armed force to help indigenes regain access to forests from which they were excluded by government policies and commercial interests, but Naxalites have also been accused of acting as 'Al Capone' mafia thugs that illegally market forest products, extort businesses, and kill to settle personal rivalries rather than to address injustices.

However, various other aspects of the Naxalite insurgency are not clearly explained by previous research on natural resources and civil conflict. Why does Naxalite violence not occur in regions with lucrative mineral resources or in areas with resources controlled by landlords who control substantial landholdings and economically and socially exploit thousands existing at the knife-edge of survival? Why are Naxalites active in two areas that are non-contiguous? Why have they been active for decades in a flat plains region with some of India's most productive cropland without deriving any tactical benefit from the land or any direct financial benefits from the rice, wheat, and other commodities that it produces?

Based on analysis of the Naxalite insurgent, this chapter argues that in economies where the majority of the population directly depends upon natural resources for their income and subsistence, variations in the duration and geographic scope of civil conflict are influenced by the manner in which the distribution of natural resources between antagonists affects the balance of coercive means that conflicting actors can mobilize in their contention for control over the distribution of and access to natural resources. Naxalites have attempted to mobilize armed struggles to redistribute natural resources, but in several regions these attempts were localized to a few areas, brief (six months or less) and episodic (often less than one or two conflict events in a month) in areas with highly skewed distributions of natural resources that rendered poor, socially-discriminated groups incapable of engaging in long-term, organized conflict against the elites that control those resources. However, Naxalite incidents and casualties have been far higher and have endured for decades in regions that experienced moderate land reforms that weakened the economic, social, and political influence of the elites who traditionally controlled that land and thus contributed to an 'opportunity structure' amenable to enduring conflict.

This chapter does not attempt to falsify existing theories of natural resources and civil conflict, but to test and build upon them with additional analysis. Indeed, the findings herein suggest that the explanatory power of prominent theories of natural resources and civil conflict are enhanced when they are essentially combined on the basis of their shared characteristics. Somewhat like Sartori's 'ladder of abstraction' theories of natural resources and civil conflict can be generalized to a greater number of cases when their broad similarities are emphasized. The analysis herein is largely qualitative, and the unit and level of analysis are the regions of eastern India in which Naxalites are active. Furthermore, this research is essentially one step in an on-going research project, and subsequent analyses will continue to examine other aspects of natural resources and the Naxalite insurgency.

This chapter will first examine existing research on the relationships between natural resources and conflict and how these theories relate to other theories of civil conflict. The chapter will then examine how the Naxalites support and challenge existing research on natural resources and civil conflict and ultimately how the Naxalites suggest that resources and conflict may be related in ways not specifically addressed by such research. Subsequently, this chapter will examine how one state in India has emerged from Naxalite violence through policies that have helped prevent that violence from recurring. Finally, the conclusion will provide an assessment of what this article does and does not add to existing research and suggest what needs to be done in future research on this subject.

But before proceeding further, some terms used in this chapter need to be clarified. Revolutions, insurgencies, riots, and numerous other 'contentious' events generally occurring within countries have been denoted by various terms, but this chapter will refer to both the range of events and particular incidents as 'civil conflict'. In addition, several Indian terms are used herein. The term *dalits* refers to persons born as non-casted Hindus, sometimes called 'untouchables' or 'scheduled castes' by the Indian government. *Adivasis* are indigenous persons often called 'tribals' or often officially designated as 'scheduled tribes'. Chhattisgarh and Jharkhand are states formed from regions that were part of the states of Madhya Pradesh and Bihar, respectively. But unless otherwise noted, Bihar refers to both Bihar and Jharkhand, and 'Madhya Pradesh' includes both Madhya Pradesh and Chhattisgarh since much of what is discussed occurred prior to the creation of Jharkhand and Chhattisgarh in November 2000.

Natural resources and civil conflict: grievance or greed?

Among the research on natural resources and civil conflict, two related but debated bodies of work have captured much scholarly and policy attention. One body of research contends that scarcities of renewable natural resources may cause civil conflicts if those scarcities create or aggravate social and economic problems that are not sufficiently addressed by government intervention or social adaptation. 'Scarcity' itself is defined as a declining per capita amount of resources resulting from resource degradation, population growth, skewed distributions of resources along identifiable social boundaries, or combinations of these processes. These conflicts are generally between those whose incomes and subsistence suffer from discriminated access to the natural resources upon which their livelihoods depend and those who gain disproportionate economic and social benefits from their substantial influence on the distribution of and access to those resources (Baechler 1999; Homer-Dixon 1999). While this work includes different theories of natural resources and civil conflict, for brevity's sake this general body of work will be collectively referred to as 'resource scarcity'.

Another body of research claims civil conflicts related to natural resources occur in countries with weak and poorly diversified economies in which primary commodity exports account for a high proportion of GDP (usually 25 to 33 percent). Lured by individual material gains from natural resources such as illicit drugs, diamonds, and timber, insurgents use civil conflict as the requisite coercion to tax or traffic these resources while creating negative externalities for societies, such as perpetual violence, further weakened economies, and reductions in government tax revenues. Thus, civil conflicts may be forms of violent entrepreneurialism in which insurgents utilize existing grievances as public relations cover for their self-serving actions. The same is not expected to occur in countries in which primary commodity exports account for a higher proportion of GDP because governments are expected to earn such substantial revenues that they are too strong to be challenged by insurgents (Berdal and Malone 2000; Collier 2000; Collier and Hoeffler 2001; de Soysa 2000, 2002a, 2002b). This body of work will be collectively referred to as 'resource abundance'.

These bodies of work are often posed as different explanations of civil conflict related to natural resources, and their theoretical differences supposedly hinge on the motivations of insurgent actors – 'grievance or greed' – rather than the structures of resource scarcity or abundance in which insurgents act. However, works emphasizing resource scarcity cite cases in which state and societal actors used violent repression to maintain skewed distributions of natural resources for their benefit, such as Rwanda and South Africa (Baechler 1999, 162–163; Homer-Dixon 1999: 96–98). Furthermore, research accentuating abundant, financially beneficial resources has suggested that inequalities in resource ownership have been an important factor in some civil conflicts, such as Colombia, but not in others (Collier 2000: 840, 2003: 40).

Yet analyzing these works by focusing on the motives is problematic for many of the same reasons as emphasizing motives as a crucial causal factor in civil conflicts of any category. For one, actors in conflict are not always sure why they participate in it, and the reasons why people believe they are in conflict are not necessarily identical to the actual reasons for the conflict (Roy 1994; Vick 1998; Kaufman 2002). Furthermore, research emphasizing motivations or inequality as causes of civil conflict has been inconclusive as to how these factors vary with the absence and occurrence of conflict (Davies 1962; Gurr 1970; Lichbach 1989). Thus, using motivations as a basis of comparison for research on natural resources and civil conflict emphasizes factors that are neither the central foci of these bodies of work nor does such an analysis reveal much about the causes of these or other types of conflicts.

Indeed, grievance, greed, and other motives are far more common and enduring than conflict, often because motivations to engage in conflict are not synonymous with the capacity to do so. Insurgencies, civil wars, and other forms of large-scale conflict are inherently between opposing groups rather than individuals, and the duration, geographic scope, and casualties reflect the collective capacities of groups rather than individuals. Research on the capacities of groups to pursue their collective interests generally treats individuals' motivations as axiomatic and examines groups – be they corporations, unions, or insurgents – as organizations requiring systematic inputs of money, personnel, and other resources to pursue their interests. Thus, changes in the inputs that groups can mobilize are strongly associated with which groups can pursue their interests as well as various characteristics of their activities, such as location, scale, type, commencement, frequency, and duration (Zald and McCarthy 1977; Tilly 1978).

Yet groups' mobilization of resources is not necessarily manifest in successful or enduring group activity. Theories of 'collective action' suggest this is because individuals commonly pursue their interests in seemingly paradoxical manner. In theory, individuals' decisions reflect attempts to maximize the 'relative benefits' of their choices, that is, to maximize personal gains and minimize personal losses. Though people may join groups (such as unions) to gain benefits (such as pay increases), they gain the greatest relative benefits when they do not personally bear the costs of acquiring those benefits (not going on strike) and 'free ride' on the efforts of other members that do so (engaging in strike activities that risk arrest or loss of employment). Groups may not achieve any collective benefits at all if some sufficient number of members 'free ride'. To overcome 'collective action problems', groups may attempt to render participation relatively more beneficial than free-riding by punishing free-riding in some way or offering short-term and long-term selective incentives (often material incentives) to encourage continual participation (Olson 1971; Popkin 1979; Lichbach 1998).

For insurgent leaders attempting to mobilize people for potentially violent conflict, collective action problems can be acute: death is indeed a low payoff that can make free-riding seem more prudent than selfish. Furthermore, if organizers are mobilizing poor and discriminated communities, then collective action problems can be pervasive, even for non-violent action. Those communities may have a collective interest in regime change or ending economic and social discrimination, but the potential short-term costs of acting to achieve those objectives – beatings, imprisonment, or loss of a single day's wages – may exceed almost any selective incentive that organizers may be able to provide. Additionally, in spite of selective incentives that organizers can offer, potential activists can be daunted by far more powerful opponents.

Another reason why groups' mobilization of organizational inputs is not sufficient for enduring group engagement in rebellious activities is because groups' engagement in contentious activities is a function of their internal resources and their 'opportunities' for using those resources. Whereas 'mobilizing resources' refers to the factors *internal* to mobilizing groups that enable them to realize their collective goals, 'political opportunity structure' generally refers to factors *external* to groups that affect the balance of mobilization resources between mobilizing groups and their opponents and thus influence groups' relative costs and benefits of engaging in collective action to realize their collective interests. Opportunities result from reductions in the balance of coercive powers between challengers and opponents that reduce the costs of contentious action for challengers. 'Constraints' on opportunity result from large or increasing balances of coercive powers that increase the cost of contention. Constraints include alliances among opponents, effective domestic security forces, and strong popular support for governments. Opportunities include divisions between opponents, weakened military and police, economic depressions, and prior success by other mobilizing groups. Opportunities and constraints may materialize and disappear over time, and it is not a given that mobilizing groups will necessarily perceive such changes when they exist (Eisinger 1973; Jenkins and Perrow 1977; Piven and Cloward 1977; Tarrow 1989).

Clearly, the resources that groups are able to mobilize for their goals and the structural environments in which they may be active should not be seen as completely separate variables, but as dynamic and interacting variables that affect changes in groups' strategies (McAdam 1985; Koopmans 1993).

Examinations of natural resources and civil conflict often treat mobilizing resources and opportunities that suggest more important similarities in these bodies of work than may be apparent from analyzing them on the basis of motivations. Resource abundance literature contends that the selective benefits, organizational resources, and opportunities for insurgency may be a function of natural resource availability. In poorly-diversified economies, with low rates of growth, and in which a significant portion of export earnings come from natural resources that can be accessed with simple tools and little or no formal training, the costs of rebellion are low and its benefits high. Rebels' costs may be low because persons with low incomes and little formal education can gain greater economic benefits from coercive control of valuable natural resources than legitimate forms of employment. The costs of rebellion are also low if little capital is needed to extract resources and weaponry can be obtained inexpensively. Thus, rebels may be economically motivated to coercively control access to and distribution of natural resources accessed with little capital or expertise, and rebel groups can use income from resources for organizational finance and for selective incentives to entice active participation. Opportunities for insurgency arise if governments' coercive capacities are limited by factors that render policing inefficient and costly, such as geographically-dispersed populations or mountainous terrain (Berdal and Malone 2000; Collier 2000; Collier and Hoeffler 2001; de Soysa 2000, 2002a, 2002b).

Resource scarcity literature is generally less explicit about insurgents' organizational resources and selective incentives, but clearly acknowledges the importance of these variables for the realization of insurgency. Indeed, these factors are generally treated as axiomatic, but the use of natural resources as organizational inputs is not. Resource scarcity literature suggests that natural resource scarcities may indirectly weaken the coercive capacities of states and societal actors if resource scarcity causes or intensifies competition among elites, declining finances, increased demand for state services, and declining popular legitimacy. Furthermore, the selective material incentives of insurgency – such as seized cropland – may generate support for and participation in insurgency and may reduce the economic and social influence of resource controllers (Baechler 1999; Homer-Dixon 1999).

Thus these ostensibly opposite theories both contend that natural resources are linked to insurgency by affecting the opportunities for it. Both argue that civil conflicts may be contention for access to resources, particularly in weak and poorly-diversified economies in which the productivity of natural resources are the chief means for providing livelihoods and thus hoarding these resources can be extremely beneficial. Resource abundance literature tends to focus on how insurgents use coercion to hoard resources for their financial benefit, and resource scarcity literature points out how societal elites, governments, mafias, and others may use coercive means to create and maintain skewed distributions of resources that insurgents seek to redress.

In both resource abundance and scarcity research, the opportunities for conflict arise when shifts in the benefits that natural resources provide to societal actors or states lead to reductions in the balance of economic and coercive power between insurgents and their state or societal opponents. Whether natural resources directly enhance the coercive capacity of insurgents or indirectly reduce the coercive capacity of states and societal elites, changes in the economic benefits of natural resources undermine the political and social forms of control that were based on previous distributions of natural resources' economic benefits. Thus if insurgents capture the economic benefits of diamonds or forest products, they gain a newfound form of coercive influence that challenges states' capacities to police them, particularly if insurgents' economic gains are economic losses for the state. Similarly, losses in the economic benefits that societal elites derive from cropland can reduce the economic, political, and social influence they previously enjoyed relative to other social groups and thus weaken their coercive capacities relative to those other social groups. Civil conflicts continue as insurgents effectively maintain or increase these diminished power differentials and as they perpetuate conflict in order to continue accruing individual benefits (Baechler 1999; Grossman 1999; Homer-Dixon 1999; Collier 2000; de Soysa 2000, 2002a, 2002b; Collier and Hoeffler 2001; Skaperdas 2002).

This reasoning is based partly on analysis of existing literature but also on empirical analysis of the very complex Naxalite insurgency in India. The following section summarizes the Naxalites' history and activities up to 2005, and evidence suggests that where Naxalites are active – and where they are not – is at least partly influenced by the ways in which shifts in the benefits of natural resource productivity have affected the opportunities for Naxalites to engage in enduring insurgent activity. As would be expected from resource scarcity literature, Naxalites are active in areas where some form of resource scarcity has had various deleterious economic consequences for at least some significant portion of the population and also weakened the coercive capacity of government institutions, societal elites, or both. As would be expected from resource abundance literature, Naxalites are active in areas with valuable natural resources that can be easily accessed and distributed or marketed by insurgents. However, the following will show that Naxalites activity has endured in ways that are related to natural resources and in a manner that is something of a combination of prominent research on natural resources and civil conflict.

The Naxalite movement: Robin Hoods or Al Capones?

The Naxalite insurgency has received little Western press coverage, but it has lasted longer than the more publicized violence in the Kashmir and estimated casualties exceed those of conflicts in the Kashmir, Northern Ireland, and Israel/Palestine (Sahni 2000; Mahapatra et al. 200: 30). The Naxalites are not a single insurgent organization, but dozens of independent groups that share some similarities in ideology and tactics, but which have also factionalized, fragmented, fought between themselves, and even combined into the same organizational structure (Roy 1975; OPDR 1978: 53; Sen 1982: 221–222; Duyker 1987: 77–79). Indeed, the two largest Naxalite organizations, the People's War Group and the Maoist Communist Centre ('MCC'), were occasional rivals but joined to become the Communist Party of India (Maoist) in September 2004.

The event often credited as triggering the insurgency occurred on May 24, 1967, in Naxalbari, West Bengal, the place from which the term 'Naxalite' is derived. Allegedly, indigenous 'adivasi' sharecroppers and an upper-caste landlord had a disagreement over payment of rent in kind for leased agricultural land. A subsequent adivasi protest prompted police involvement, and ensuing violence would become legendary among activists. Months prior to this incident, local activists with the Communist Party of India (Marxist) had actively promoted forcible land seizures, and they quickly utilized the violence to mobilize peasants in a rebellion that would become much-publicized in India.

The conflict in the Siliguri area around Naxalbari lasted about two months – until July 1967 – but many activists and leaders involved in this short rebellion remained active in rural and urban activities until 1972. Indeed, it seems that the importance of Naxalbari is not what occurred there, but what that rebellion seems to have influenced elsewhere. The events in Siliguri are believed to have inspired short-lived insurgent activity after May 1967 and during the early 1970s in other areas of West Bengal as well as in the states of Kerala, Maharashtra, Punjab, Tamil Nadu, and Uttar Pradesh. Little information is publicly available about Naxalites in these areas, but it appears that violence was typically sporadic, often around ten events or less over a period of less than one year, and generally localized to a few areas within two to three districts in these states. However, in West Bengal's Midnapore and Birbhum regions episodes of violence were relatively more numerous and frequent, and endured over a one-and-a-half year period. Movement leaders were often college students or political activists from urban areas that had little, if any, military training, and state- and national-level politicians were seriously concerned about the possibility of new 'Naxalbaris'. Thus, many groups were crushed by heavy police and military pressure, and by 1972 Naxalites were largely inactive in these states. Naxalite activists did re-emerge in Uttar Pradesh and West Bengal, but episodes of violence have been few and infrequent (Roy 1975; Sen 1982; Singh 1995; Duyker 1987; Mehra 2000; Ministry of Home Affairs 2003, 2005).[1]

However, one of the two regions in which Naxalites did establish an enduring base of activity was the Bhojpur region of southwestern Bihar. In June 1967 – just one month after the beginning of events in Naxalbari – activists from Bihar and neighboring West Bengal attempted to mobilize insurgent activity in numerous areas in Bihar, usually in the state's northern and eastern districts. These attempts, however, were consistently undermined by poor organizational resources, populations with high opportunity costs, and repression from both police and landlords. By 1972 Naxalites became active in the southwestern region of Bhojpur, and after the end of nationwide martial law in 1977 Naxalite activities became progressively more frequent in several districts comprising the Bhojpur region. By the late 1980s, Naxalites were active to a lesser degree in the regions of south Bihar that eventually became the state of Jharkhand, and after Jharkhand's statehood Naxalite incidents have exceeded those in Bihar. Moreover, quite a lot of violence in Bhojpur has been perpetrated by landlord-funded militias called 'senas' that target both Naxalites and members of social groups that have actively or tacitly supported Naxalites, particularly lower castes and dalits. Thus, the violence in Bihar is notorious for its overwhelming caste orientation and the questionable capacity of the Bihar state government to stop it (Roy 1975: 251–252; Mukherjee and Yadav 1980; PUDR 1981; Sen

1982: 226–227; Singh 1995; Louis 2002; Prasad 2002; interviews with anonymous persons in 2003 and 2005).

The other region in which Naxalites have established an enduring base of activity is the Telengana region in the northwestern portion of Andhra Pradesh as well as some contiguous districts in the neighboring states of Maharashtra, Orissa, and portions of Madhya Pradesh that later became part of the state of Chhattisgarh. The Naxalites began in 1967 in two regions of Andhra Pradesh, Srikakulam and Telengana. Like Naxalites elsewhere, Naxalite leaders in these regions were from the regions and were already attempting to mobilize indigenous, dalits, and others before the events in Naxalbari apparently inspired them to attempt to form a larger movement. It is unknown how many incidents of violence occurred in the early years of these insurgencies, but the violence in Srikakulam and Telengana ceased in 1973 (Sinha 1989; Singh 1995).

However, the re-emergence of activists in Telengana in the late 1970s eventually led to possibly the most carefully organized Naxalite group in India, the People's War Group. Through the 1980s and 1990s, the Andhra Pradesh government would have a relationship alternatively characterized by outright support of the PWG and outright repression of the group. However, the PWG grew in financial and popular support, and by November 2004 a public rally of support for the PWG in the state capital, Hyderabad, drew an estimated 150,000 supporters. The PWG and other Naxalite organizations are believed to be active in many areas of Andhra Pradesh, but violence has generally occurred in the Telengana region, although violence has been increasing in Srikakulam since 2002. Since the early 1980s, incidents of violence have occurred in forested, contiguous districts in neighboring states, and while violence has been increasing in frequency and casualties in these regions it remains far below the amount of violence in the Telengana region (Sinha 1989; Singh 1995).

Table 5.1 provides the number of Naxalite incidents and deaths from those incidents from 2000 to 2004 according to the Indian government.

Analyses of Naxalites have focused on the motivations for insurgency, and the general consensus is that the insurgency was started to address various economic and social injustices related to highly skewed distributions of cropland but later became heavily corrupted as Naxalites used extortion, robbery, and other criminal methods to financially maintain the insurgency and to benefit from it. These analyses also often utilize state level indicators to explain these injustices. For example, analyses of the Naxalites in Bhojpur focus on Bihar's poor social and economic indicators, and indeed a litany of depressing statistics illustrate the state's almost medieval living standards. For example, the state's 2001 Human Development Index is India's lowest at 0.367, and if Bihar were a country – and its population of over 80,000,000 surpasses that of most European countries – its HDI would rank 167 out of 176 countries (Pathak 1993; Singh 1995; GOI 2001; Prasad 2002; Louis 2002).

Table 5.1 The number of Naxalite incidents and deaths, 2000–2004

	Incidents						Deaths					
	2000	2001	2002	2003	2004	Total	2000	2001	2002	2003	2004	Total
Andhra Pradesh	425	461	346	577	310	2,119	113	180	96	140	74	603
Bihar	278	169	239	250	323	1,259	170	111	117	128	171	697
West Bengal	4	9	17	6	11	47	2	4	7	1	15	29
Orissa	15	30	68	49	35	197	3	11	11	15	8	48
Maharashtra	35	34	83	75	84	311	11	7	29	31	15	93
Madhya Pradesh	7	21	17	13	13	71	4	2	3	1	4	14
Chhattisgarh	79	105	304	256	352	1,096	48	37	55	74	83	297
Jharkhand	318	355	353	342	379	1,747	193	200	157	117	169	836
Uttar Pradesh	4	22	20	13	15	74	4	12	6	8	26	56
Other states	14	2	18	16	11	61	2	0	1	0	1	4
India	1,179	1,208	1,465	1,597	1,533	6,982	550	564	482	515	566	2,677

Source: Ministry of Home Affairs 2003 and 2005.

However, examining the insurgency on the basis of motivations or state level indicators does not explain why the Naxalite activities have historically clustered in particular regions of states rather than occurring statewide. Indeed, it is unclear in these analyses why Naxalites have been mostly active in the Bhojpur region, whose social and agricultural indicators generally rank above the state average. While northern Bihar has naturally better rainfall and soil productivity, Bhojpur's far better irrigation infrastructure has enabled many of the region's farmers to utilize Green Revolution agricultural technologies that have dramatically increased the region's agricultural productivity (Sengupta 1978a: 1–2). Thus, Bhojpur appears to be the least likely region of Bihar to have insurgency, but other details suggest that the region is distinctive from the rest of Bihar in the manner in which changes in the distribution of benefits of natural resource productivity have created structural opportunities for enduring Naxalite activity. A very similar process occurred in Andhra Pradesh, although in a slightly different manner.

In both Bihar and Andhra Pradesh, regional changes in the distribution of agricultural land and state funding of agricultural inputs along caste lines altered the positions of castes in regional economic hierarchies and political influence in the state itself. Present forms of land tenure in farming vary between and within states, but generally the forms of land tenure are broadly similar to colonial land tenure forms. During the colonial era in northern India the 'zamindari' system of land tenure prevailed, and in much of southern and western India the 'ryotwari' system of land tenure prevailed. These land tenure systems were not created by the British; rather the British took over their administration from previous rulers and modified them in various ways so that the colonial administration was the top-most – but not necessarily the greatest – financial beneficiary. In colonial Telengana, a system of land tenure quite similar to the zamindari system was maintained by the relatively autonomous Hyderabad Presidency. Hence, land tenure systems vary across India as do their social and economic effects (Gadgil and Guha 1994).

The zamindari system was prevalent in what are now the states of Bihar, Orissa, central and eastern Uttar Pradesh, and West Bengal. This form of land tenure is an essentially feudal land tenure system in which upper-caste 'zamindar' land owners possess large agricultural landholdings of 50 hectares or more that are cultivated by lower castes, dalits, and adivasis employed as wage laborers who are paid in kind daily, or sharecroppers that pay rents in kind, cash, or varying combinations of the two. Sharecropper rents are often well over half of the harvested crop output. This is generally a continuation of the colonial zamindar land tenure system in which land rents were collected on behalf of the colonial administration by zamindars intermediaries who collected rents from the actual cultivators, paid some portion to the colonial administration, and retained the balance as profit. There was often a hierarchy of zamindars, each retaining some portion of land rents, and the number of intermediaries in these hierarchies varied across localities (Henningham 1982; Zagoria 1971; Jannuzi 1974; Sengupta 1978a).

Alterations in land tenure systems were often due to contentious events in particular regions, and after zamindari challenges to colonial rule in Bihar and West Bengal in 1793 the colonial administration fixed in perpetuity the amount zamindars paid to the administration in perpetuity. This enabled zamindars to increase their profits to such a degree that the provincial government saw the landlords as exercising a degree of control over rural areas that rivaled and sometimes exceeded the colonial administration's power over those areas. Zamindars' income was not derived by investing in agricultural productivity but from maximum extraction of agricultural produce by those that provided the labor for producing it. Subsequently, the zamindars and their caste kin essentially dominated Bihar state policies until the late 1960s (Henningham 198: 17–19; Government of Great Britain 1930; Nair 1979).

Just as threats to colonial control led to alterations in the zamindar system, one of the bloodiest uprisings in nineteenth-century India led the British to significantly alter land tenure in the Chota Nagpur region of southern Bihar, which is now part of Jharkhand. To obviate further unrest among indigenous peoples in the region, the British passed the Chota Nagpur Tenancy Act, which protected indigenes from land speculators and landlords by limiting maximum landholding size and interest on agricultural loans and by restricting land transfers from indigenes to nonindigenes. The policy is believed to have had lasting effects on the region, and landlessness is believed to be relatively far less frequent than other regions of Bihar (National Labour Institute 1989: 25; Weiner 1978).

The other prominent system of land tenure under colonialism was the ryotwari system and was found mainly in western and southern areas of India that came under British administration later than areas of east India, such as Punjab, Haryana, western Uttar Pradesh, Tamil Nadu, and coastal Andhra Pradesh. Under the ryotwari land tenure system, peasant proprietorship was common, tenants had inheritable rights to the land they cultivated, and there were few intermediaries. Therefore, in contrast to the zamindari system, the ryotwari system was far more conducive to personal initiative and entrepreneurship (Misra 1991; Viegas 1991).

What is distinctive about Naxalite regions of activity (Bhojpur and Telengana) is that unlike other areas of the states in which they are active, Naxalites regions have been affected by minimal land redistribution, 'Green Revolution' agricultural inputs, or some combination of both. Under pressure from peasant organizations, the Bihar state government passed land reform legislation in 1962 that redistributed little land, although the land that was redistributed went mostly to the lower-caste Koeris, Kurmis, and Yadavs that were most active in those peasant organizations. A subsequent food crisis in Bihar during 1966 and 1967 in the Bhojpur and Santal Parganas region led the World Bank and national government to provide Green

Revolution technologies to the Bhojpur region because its irrigation infrastructure provided relatively better agricultural growth potential, and these agricultural inputs were largely utilized by the aforementioned lower castes who did not share the upper castes' ritual aversion to agricultural labor. These changes helped the lower castes in Bhojpur to challenge the economic and political dominance of the upper castes that were the traditionally powerful landowning castes.

A similar process occurred in Andhra Pradesh, though in a slightly different manner. Like Bhojpur in Bihar, the Srikakulam region in northeast Andhra Pradesh has the state's best irrigation and was also targeted for Green Revolution agricultural inputs in the late 1960s. The Srikakulam landlords are predominantly from the Kamma caste, and have had longstanding political rivalries with the dominant landlord caste in Telengana, the Reddys. The Reddys dominated Andhra state politics until the late 1960s and early 1970s, when the Kammas were able to utilize advanced agricultural inputs to become an emerging economic force in the state and thus challenge the Reddy's traditional economic and political power. Subsequently, the Andhra Pradesh government pursued various social development policies in Srikakulam (the northeast of the state) that drew support away from the Naxalites, but offered nothing similar to adivasis in Telengana (the state's northwest region) and opted to establish a strong police presence there in order to prevent subsequent conflict. Furthermore, Naxalite leaders that were active in the Srikakulam region were generally killed in police actions, whereas the Telengana leaders were jailed and, in fact, released at the end of martial law in 1977. These factors help explain why the Naxalite activity in Srikakulam was practically eliminated in the early 1970s (Seshadri 1983: 163–165; Kohli 1990; Yogandhar *et al.* 1993; Singh 1995: 37).

The same was not true in northern Bihar, Orissa, and eastern Uttar Pradesh where upper-caste landlords have continued to maintain extremely skewed distribution of agricultural land. Nor is the same in the southern regions that became Jharkhand because agriculture plays a much smaller role in those regions' economies. In those regions, mineral production comprised almost 40 percent of Bihar's state revenues, and the creation of Jharkhand thus cut Bihar's state revenues by nearly half (Jannuzi 1974: 244–247; Sengupta 1978b: 79; Mukherjee and Yadav 1980: 34; Henningham 1982: 71; Brass 1986: 246; GOI 2000).[2]

Thus, when various Naxalite organizers in Bihar and Andhra Pradesh attempted to mobilize agricultural laborers and sharecroppers, they were essentially joining the existing fray of conflicts between upper and lower castes and doing so in regions where there was a tremendous challenge to the hierarchical social system that traditionally regulated behaviors and expectations and that substantiated the disproportionate distribution of economic resources. To put it differently, Naxalites attempting to organize insurgencies in north Bihar, eastern Uttar Pradesh, Orissa, and West Bengal were doing so in areas where the balance of natural resources and the benefits of those resources significantly benefited large landlords over impoverished laborers and sharecroppers. However, in the Bhojpur region of Bihar and the Telengana region of Andhra Pradesh, the economic and political power of traditionally powerful landlords was significantly reduced by challenges from castes that were able to shift the distribution of cropland and its productive benefits to their advantage. Hence, there was an opportunity structure for enduring Naxalite activity in Bhojpur and Telengana, and structural constraints contributed to short-lived Naxalite activity elsewhere.

A similar process has occurred in forested areas. In the early 1950s, the governments of Andhra Pradesh, Madhya Pradesh, and Orissa attempted to benefit from the forests' commercial potential by allowing greater access to commercial contractors and limiting indigenous access. Occasional protests and a generally uncooperative indigenous population complicated these initial efforts, but during a period of martial law from 1975 to 1977, these states classified over half their forested areas as 'protected forest reserves' and largely limited the harvesting of forest products to state-licensed commercial contractors. The state governments' enforced limitations on forest access undercut indigenes' household consumption by limiting their access to forest products they consumed and by limiting the amount of land that could be used for shifting cultivation. Furthermore, in spite of legal measures against transfers of indigenous lands, non-indigenous migrants have acquired a substantial amount of agricultural land quite cheaply through various means. Thus, many adivasis became engaged in casual and seasonal employment in forestry, agriculture, mining, and construction. Furthermore, contractors in many areas are the sole brokers of forest products and often pay indigenes below subsistence prices for harvested forest material. In these heavily forested areas, Naxalite cadres are largely indigenous adivasis, and their targets are those whom they regard as limiting their capacity to obtain their livelihoods, such as government forest officials, commercial forest contractors, and other non-indigenous business persons, particularly money lenders. The PWG is believed to have utilized the forests as a mobilization resource: they have 'taxed' forest contractors' access to the forest, brokered sales of forest products, and used access to the forests as a selective incentive for adivasi support. Moreover, the cost of rebellion is reduced by terrain that is difficult to access by police and conventional military forces (OPDR 1978; Sen 1982: 222–225; Patel 1986; Srivastava 1990; Singh 1995: 40–46; Gregory 1997: 90, 101; Sahni 2000).

Thus, the economic and tactical benefits of forested areas have certainly been helpful for the insurgents, but these factors are not entirely responsible for their presence and endurance in this region. Indeed, the escalation of conflict in Dandakaryana is not only associated with changes in the motivations of insurgents, but also with the willingness of the Andhra Pradesh government to police them. For reasons that remain debated, two competing political parties ostensibly sought the support of the PWG during closely contested state elections in 1982 and 1989, and interestingly the party seeking such support won the election and subsequently released Naxalites from jail and relaxed, or virtually eliminated, security forces' pressure on the insurgents. Evidently, the PWG in particular took advantage of those opportunities to expand their mobilization efforts (Patel 1986; Gregory 1997: 113–114; Sahni 2000; Mahapatra et al. 2001).

It is unclear whether the easing of government pressure enabled the expansion of PWG activities, if PWG expansion led to conciliatory, even supportive, gestures by state actors, or what the interaction of these developments might have been. However, it seems unlikely that two competing political parties would seek the support of rural insurgents in two different elections if they calculated that those insurgents were incapable of providing desired electoral support. Similarly, it is unclear why state governments would increase developmental funds for the Telengana region during periods of high Naxalite activity and conversely reduce such efforts during periods of waning Naxalite activity (Sahni 2000). Indeed, these matters suggest that while the state of Andhra Pradesh has at times had the upper hand in terms of coercive power, the Naxalites' coercive power has at times challenged governing capacities – and the Naxalites' coercive capacities in the Telengana region are heavily influenced by the manner in which they have affected changes in the distribution of natural resources economic benefits.

One obvious question that arises is why Naxalites have mobilized in these areas and not in other forested areas of India. The Dandakaryana region has India's highest concentration of both forest area and people that depend upon the forest. Andhra Pradesh, Bihar, Gujarat, Madhya Pradesh, Maharashtra, and Orissa have almost 65 percent of India's total forest area and 62.76 percent of India's 'scheduled tribe' population, which tend to live in upland forest areas (GOI 1999). India's seven northeast states also have a high concentration of indigenes and forested area, and the northeast has numerous separatist insurgent organizations, such as the United Liberation Front of Assam ('ULFA'). Thus, a number of insurgent groups are already active in the forested regions of the northeast provide stiff competition for the Naxalites. Furthermore, the western state of Gujarat does not demonstrate nearly the degree of weak state capacity as states with Naxalite activity, nor has any particular social group experienced resource discrimination in a manner similar to indigenes in Telengana. Thus, in Bhojpur and Telengana, in both cases, the opportunity costs of rebellion are reduced when there is significantly reduced capacity to resist rebellion by states and private actors.

This may also help explain why Naxalites have substantially increased their presence in Jharkhand soon after it was established as a state. Jharkhand does have valuable mineral deposits and hilly, forested terrain that is tactically advantageous to insurgents. However, criminal gangs and large corporations control the minerals industry, therefore maintaining substantial economic power, which creates large economic differences between themselves and potential Naxalite challengers. Furthermore, Naxalites may have become capable of dramatically escalating their activities in the hilly, forested areas of Jharkhand only after the establishment of the state because this newly forming state has not established meaningful government control in rural areas.

The comparisons may be helpful in understanding how natural resources are linked to conflict and the spatial variations in such conflicts. However, these are comparisons of areas that have not experienced the Naxalite insurgency with areas in which Naxalites have continually been active. It is also instructive to make comparisons with areas in which Naxalites were active but have not returned, as this may suggest how governments can address insurgencies and their related problems.

Neither Robin Hood nor Al Capone? Naxalites and West Bengal

It is somewhat ironic that so much of what has been written about the Naxalites pertains to their initial activities in West Bengal, because the state may better illustrate why the insurgency did not continue rather than why it started there.

In many ways, West Bengal and Bihar were quite similar during the onset of their respective Naxalite insurgencies. Both had very small landholdings, near-feudal agrarian systems, and both had areas using Green Revolution technologies. Like Bihar and other states with Naxalite activity, West Bengal initially used heavy police pressure to subdue the initial Naxalite insurgency.

But unlike Bihar and other states experiencing Naxalite activity, West Bengal has adopted various policies that seem to have severely reduced the possibility of insurgents returning to the state. Interestingly, this has not been accomplished through *redistributive* land reform, but by ameliorating many of the common problems often associated with land maldistribution and advanced Green Revolution agricultural inputs. Examples of such common problems are differences in access to capital and credit that can reduce input prices for large landholders but increase them for small and medium landholders. Moreover, the state has done so by enhancing the productive capacities of many sectors of the population rather than improving the livelihood of one portion of the population at some expense to another portion.

In many areas of West Bengal, land distribution reflected physical constraints such as high rural population density, fragmented landholdings, and lack of assured irrigation. Socio-economic constraints also influenced land distribution of substantial expropriation of surplus productivity created by agricultural laborers and land-poor sharecroppers. Much like the landless and land-poor in Bihar, these constraints limited peasants' agricultural productivity and often forced them to be economically dependent on medium and large landowners (those owning 4–10 hectares and more than ten hectares, respectively; Webster 1989).

The state's land reforms have been regarded as the most successful in India in terms of the amount of land acquired for redistribution, the number of sharecroppers that have been accorded legal protection from eviction, and the number of recipients of redistributed land. Still, West Bengal has actually redistributed very little land, but it has increased the productivity of the little land to which the rural poor has access through expanded irrigation and promotion of summer rice cultivation. The summer rice cultivation and various seasonal employment schemes have enhanced both the diets incomes of many rural poor (Webster 1989; Ghosh 2000).

Furthermore, the establishment of rural banks and village co-operatives enabled sharecroppers and owners of marginal landholdings to have access to credit with different interest rates and also to access inputs such as seeds and pesticides. These changes had the effect of reducing dependency on village moneylenders and their usually usurious interest rates and enhancing the agricultural capacity of many rural poor. These changes have not eliminated the bias in credit access and advanced inputs enjoyed by owners of medium and large landholding, but they have reduced the dependency of the rural poor on the aforementioned category of landowners (Webster 1989).

However, the most remarkable change has been the way in which the government of West Bengal has improved governance by enhancing local government structures. When the 'United Front' government returned to power in 1978, it set about establishing village level government structures called panchayats. These structures have effectively implemented state government policies at the local level and informally regulated various aspects of sharecropper and landowner relationships (such as divisions of crops). Therefore, people in rural areas no longer need to resort to non-governmental actors, such as insurgents, to resolve local disputes. The development of the *panchayats* has also had the effect of improving tenure security for sharecroppers and weakening their economic dependency on landowners. The officials that implement these policies are locally elected, thus their loyalties lie with the local electorate rather than state-level administration (Webster 1989).

This suggests that West Bengal has *not* reduced social problems associated with an iniquitous agrarian structure through significant land reform or weakening of exploitative structures of social dependency. Instead, social problems have been reduced somewhat by avoiding programs that depended upon one social group improving their livelihood at the cost of another.

Just as importantly, the case of West Bengal suggests the ways in which governments can positively intervene in conflict-prone situations. In many ways, land scarcity in West Bengal is much like Bihar, yet the manner in which West Bengal has addressed the problems resulting from scarcity suggests that the real concern with natural resources is not necessarily their distribution among people that are dependent upon them. Rather, the basic concern is whether or not people are able to provide for their livelihoods.

In Naxalite areas, governments have essentially failed to address problems related to resources' productive output, and thus the principle way people secure or improve their livelihoods is to treat those resources as zero-sum. In other words, when their livelihoods can only be maintained or improved through acquiring more resources rather than making those resources more productive, then those resources can be perceived as zero-sum, as can livelihoods – one will only do better at the expense of another. However, in West Bengal livelihoods can be maintained or improved by acquiring inputs that make land more productive rather than simply acquiring more land. Thus, those resources are not as likely to be perceived as zero-sum since livelihoods can be improved without redistributing land.

Al Capone, Robin Hood, or both

Naxalite violence is partly due to circumstantial issues, as detailed investigations of particular Naxalite incidents often trace their immediate causes to rapes, personal rivalries, and other anecdotal matters.[3] However, these issues are found all over India, but insurgency is not. Furthermore, Naxalite activities are the results of numerous human calculations to achieve various objectives: from revenging personal affronts to promoting nationwide revolution, from providing subsistence to gaining wealth and social prestige. Yet various Naxalite organizations have failed and others have succeeded well beyond their founders' original plans – both unintended consequences of similar decisions.

Unquestionably, circumstantial issues, human calculations, and various social divisions are causes of particular Naxalite incidents and of the insurgencies in general. Yet what appears to be more strongly related with the presence of Naxalite activity are the structural characteristics of the areas in which the circumstances, decisions, and social differences are manifest. More specifically, differentials in control of access to natural resources influence actors' actual and potential mobilization resources and opportunities because those natural resources are the most important influence in actors' economic and social standings.

In every state in which Naxalites are active – and for that matter, in every state in India – over half of the population depends upon local sources of natural resources for their daily livelihoods for most of the year. But what distinguishes areas of Naxalite activity from areas without the insurgency are reduced differentials in the control of natural resources that enhance the insurgents' mobilization resources, reduce their opponents' resistance capacities, and thus create opportunities to sustain insurgency. In areas of very stratified resource distributions, Naxalites have failed in spite of circumstances, motivations, and social tensions; in areas with reduced resource maldistributions, Naxalites have endured in spite of periodic wanes in movement growth. This is quite similar to international relations research in which war between countries is more likely when the distribution of power among rival states approaches parity than when one rival holds a preponderance of power (Organski and Kugler 1980; Geller 2000; Singer 2000).

However, the structural effects of natural resource distributions alone do not explain why insurgencies endure, as the actions of insurgents themselves clearly influence conflict duration. While the Naxalites were initially organized to address natural resource scarcities, over time they have settled into a veritable market niche in which organization resources and perceived legitimacy are derived from acting as informal authorities that 'tax' commercial entities' access to resources and that act as veritable police and judges addressing problems associated with resource scarcities, particularly the social transgressions perpetrated by actors benefiting from highly skewed distributions of resources. In other words, their mobilizing resources and popular support are derived from addressing the symptoms of resource scarcities rather than the causes.

In Bihar, the Naxalites have failed to expand their areas of operation and to redistribute land, but these shortcomings have not limited the organizations' appeal and support. They are able to continue operating in Bihar not because they provide 'goods' in the form of redistributed land, but because they have reduced the social and economic 'bads' that result from maldistributed land. In Naxalite areas of control, they act as both police and courts, and upper-caste landlords can no longer rape lower-caste and dalit women with impunity nor can they engage in previously common forms of wage exploitation. Therefore, Naxalites have reduced the 'bads' resulting from disproportionate control of natural resources, and because they have done so lower castes and dalits often tolerate and support the Naxalites.

Of course, the insurgents have only been able to act as informal authorities in areas where the distribution of natural resources has favorably influenced their mobilization capacities and opportunities relative to their opponents. The insurgents have not endured in areas in which economies are characterized by severe stratification between powerful resource holders and the resource deprived, such as between the large landlords and landless laborers found so often in northern and southeastern Bihar. They have endured in areas in which the economic and social stratification between resource holders and resource deprived has been substantially diminished by factors such as land reforms that have shifted arable land away from landlords. They have also endured in areas in which they were able to use the topographic and financial benefits of resources – particularly forested areas – as tactical and financial gains for themselves and corresponding obstacles for opponents. In both situations, Naxalites have endured much longer in areas where resource distribution approaches parity than in areas with highly-skewed resource distribution.

Notes

1 According to data from India's Ministry of Home Affairs, from 2000 to 2004 there were 74 Naxalite incidents in Uttar Pradesh and 56 deaths from those incidents as well as 47 Naxalite episodes in West Bengal and 29 deaths from those incidents. See Ministry of Home Affairs 2003 and 2005.
2 The region also has lucrative mineral deposits, so lucrative that the central colonial administration assumed direct control of the revenues. In exchange, Bihar was the only province exempted from revenue payments to the central government, though the stipulation was that Bihar received no funds from the central government. With fixed land revenues and no income from its most valuable asset, by 1930 the provincial government described itself as being in a state of 'financial embarrassment' with few options to rectify the situation. The province's revenues and expenditures were the lowest in India, which created substantial difficulties for the provincial government, particularly since its districts were heavily populated and often twice as large as those in other provinces. For example, policing was particularly problematic for financially-strapped Bihar which had the lowest number of police per 1,000 persons in India, yet the numerous peasant protests against landlords are believed to have become gradually less sporadic and more organized over time (Government of Great Britain 1930: volume XII, pp. 372–380).
3 Various Indian human rights organizations have published rich, detailed studies of particular Naxalite and *sena* events. Probably the best known are the People's Union for Civil Liberties (PUCL) and the People's Union for Democratic Rights (PUDR), and some of their reports can be found on-line at www.pucl.org.

References

Baechler, G. (1999) *Violence Through Environmental Discrimination*, Dordrecht: Kluwer Academic Publishers.
Berdal, M. and Malone, D.M. (eds) (2000) *Greed and Grievance: Economic Agendas in Civil Wars*, Boulder, CO: Lynne Rienner.
Brass, P.R. (1986) 'The Political Uses of Crisis: The Bihar Famine of 1966–1967', *The Journal of Asian Studies* 45(2): 245–267.
Collier, P. (2000) 'Rebellion as a Quasi-Criminal Activity', *Journal of Conflict Resolution* 44(6): 839–853.
Collier, P. (2003) 'The Market for Civil War', *Foreign Policy* 136: 38–45.
Collier, P. and Hoeffler, A. (2001) 'Greed and Grievance in Civil War', World Bank Paper, Washington, DC: World Bank.
Communist Party of India Marxist-Leninist People's War Group (CPIMLPWG) (2002) 'Repression'. Place of publication unknown: Communist Party of India Marxist–Leninist People's War Group. On-line document at www.geocities.com/cpimlpwg/repression.html.
Davies, J.C. (1962) 'Toward a Theory of Revolution', *American Sociological Review* 27(1): 5–19.
de Soysa, I. (2000) 'The Resource Curse: Are Civil Wars Driven by Rapacity or Paucity?'. In M. Berdal and D. Malone (eds) *Greed and Grievance: Economic Agendas in Civil War*, Boulder, CO: Lynne Rienner.
de Soysa, I. (2002a) 'Paradise Is a Bazaar? Greed, Creed, and Governance in Civil War, 1989–99', *Journal of Peace Research* 39(4): 395–416.
de Soysa, I. (2002b) 'Ecoviolence: Shrinking Pie, or Honey Pot?', *Global Environmental Politics* 2(4): 1–34.

Duyker, E. (1987) *Tribal Guerrillas: The Santals of West Bengal and the Naxalite Movement*, Delhi: Oxford University Press.

Eisinger, P.K. (1973) 'The Conditions of Protest Behavior in American Cities', *American Political Science Review* 67 (1):11–28.

Geller, D.S. (2000) 'Material Capabilities: Power and International Conflict. In J.A. Vasquez (ed.) *What Do We Know About War?*, Lanham, MD: Rowman & Littlefield.

Gadgil, M and Guha, R. (1994) 'Ecological Conflicts and the Environmental Movement in India', *Development and Change* 25 (1): 101–136.

Ghosh, B. (2000) 'Land Reforms: Lessons from West Bengal'. In B.K. Sinha and Pushpendra (eds) *Land Reforms in India: An Unfinished Agenda*, New Delhi: Sage.

Government of Great Britain (1930) *Indian Statutory Commission, Volume XII*, London: Government of Great Britain.

Government of India (GOI) (1999) *State of Forest Report 1999: Forest Survey of India*, New Delhi: Government of India, Ministry of Environment and Forests.

Government of India (GOI) (2000) 'Jharkhand State', New Delhi: Government of India, Ministry of Information, Research, Reference, and Training Division., Online document at rrtd.nic.in/Jharkhand.html.

Government of India (GOI) (2001) *National Human Development Report 2001*, New Delhi: Government of India, Planning Commission.

Gregory, C.A. (1997) *Savage Money: The Anthropology and Politics of Commodity Exchange*, Amsterdam: Harwood Academic Publishers.

Grossman, H.I. (1999) 'Kleptocracy and Revolutions', *Oxford Economic Papers* 51:267–283.

Gurr, T.R. (1970) *Why Men Rebel*, Princeton, NJ: Princeton University Press.

Henningham, S. (1982) *Peasant Movements in Colonial India: North Bihar 1917–1942*, Australia National University Monographs on South Asia No. 9. Canberra: Australia National University, South Asian History Section.

Homer-Dixon, T.F. (1999) *Environment, Scarcity, and Violence*, Princeton, NJ: Princeton University Press.

Jannuzi, F.T. (1974) *Agrarian Crisis in India: The Case of Bihar*, Austin, TX: University of Texas Press.

Jenkins, J.C. and Perrow, C. (1977) 'Insurgency of the Powerless: Farms Workers Movements (1946–1972)', *American Sociological Review* 42: 249–268.

Kaufmann, M.T. (2002) 'Jonas Savimbi, 67, Rebel of Charisma and Tenacity', *New York Times* February 23: A1.

Kohli, A. (1990) *Democracy and Discontent: India's Growing Crisis of Governability*, Cambridge: Cambridge University Press.

Koopmans, R. (1993) 'The Dynamics of Protest Waves: West Germany, 1965–1989', *American Sociological Review* 58(5): 637–658.

Lichbach, M.I. (1989) 'An Evaluation of "Does Economic Inequality Breed Political Conflict?" Studies', *World Politics* 41(4): 431–470.

Lichbach, M.I. (1998) *The Rebel's Dilemma*, Ann Arbor, MI: University of Michigan Press.

Louis, P. (2002) *People Power: The Naxalite Movement in Central Bihar*, New Delhi: Wordsmiths.

McAdams, D. (1985) *Political Processes and the Development of Black Insurgency* Chicago, IL: Chicago University Press.

Mahapatra, R., Das, B. and Verma, P. (2001) 'Forest War', *Down to Earth* December 31: 28–35.

Mehra, A.K. (2000) 'Naxalism in India: Revolution or Terror?', *Terrorism and Political Violence* 12 (2):37–66.
Ministry of Home Affairs (2003) *Annual Report*, New Delhi: Ministry of Home Affairs.
Ministry of Home Affairs (2005) *Annual Report*, New Delhi: Ministry of Home Affairs.
Misra, S. (1991) *Politico-Peasantry Conflict in India*, New Delhi: Mittal Publications.
Mukherjee, K. and Yadav, R.S. (1980) *Bhojpur: Naxalism in the Plains of Bihar*, New Delhi: Radha Krishna.
Nair, K. (1979) *In Defense of the Irrational Peasant: Indian Agriculture After the Green Revolution*, Chicago, IL: University of Chicago Press.
National Labour Institute (1989) *Agrarian Change, Agrarian Tensions, Peasant Movements and Organisation in Bihar*, New Delhi: National Labour Institute.
Olson, M. (1971) *The Logic of Collective Action: Public Goods and the Theory of Groups*, Cambridge, MA: Harvard University Press.
Organization for the Protection of Democratic Rights (OPDR) (1978) *Srikakulam Movement: A Report to the Nation*, Secunderabad: Organization for the Protection of Democratic Rights.
Organski, A.F.K. and Kugler, J. (1980) *The War Ledger*, Chicago, IL: University of Chicago Press.
Patel, V.P. (1986) *Studies in Development Anthropology*, Bhubaneswar: Society for Anthropological and Archaeological Studies.
Pathak, B. (1993) *Rural Violence in Bihar*, New Delhi: Concept Publishing Company.
Piven, F.F. and Cloward, R.A. (1977) *Poor Peoples Movements: Why They Succeed, How They Fail*, New York: Pantheon Press.
Popkin, S.L. (1979) *The Rational Peasant: The Political Economy of Rural Society in Vietnam*, Berkeley, CA: University of California Press.
Prasad, B.N. (2002) *Radicalism and Violence in Agrarian Structure: The Maoist Movement in Bihar*, New Delhi: Manak.
People's Union for Democratic Rights (PUDR) (1981) *Agrarian Unrest in Patna: An Investigation into Recent Repression*, New Delhi: People's Union for Democratic Rights.
Roy, A.K. (1975) *The Spring Thunder and After: A Survey of Maoist and Ultra-Leftist Movements in India*, Columbia, MO: South Asia Books.
Roy, B. (1994) *Some Trouble with Cows: Making Sense of Social Conflict*, Berkeley, CA: University of California Press.
Sahni, A (2000) '"Naxalism" The Retreat of Civil Governance', *Faultlines* 5: 79–103.
Sen, S. (1982) *Peasant Movements in India: Mid-nineteenth and Twentieth Century*, Calcutta: K.P. Bagchi.
Sengupta, N. (1978a) 'The People of Bihar'. In National Labour Institute, *Agrarian Change, Agrarian Tensions, Peasant Movements and Organisation in Bihar*, New Delhi: National Labour Institute, pp. 1–38.
Sengupta, N. (1978b) 'The Setting: Post Independence'. In National Labour Institute, *Agrarian Change, Agrarian Tensions, Peasant Movements and Organisation in Bihar*, New Delhi: National Labour Institute, pp. 79–116.
Seshadri, K. (1983) *Rural Unrest in India*, New Delhi: Intellectual Publishing House.

Singer, J.D. (2000) 'The Etiology of Interstate War: A Natural History Approach'. In J.A. Vasquez (ed.) *What Do We Know about War?*, Lanham, MD: Rowman & Littlefield.

Singh, P. (1995) *The Naxalite Movement in India*, New Delhi: Rupa and Company.

Sinha, S. (1989) *Maoists in Andhra Pradesh*, New Delhi: Gian Publishing House.

Skaperdas, S. (2002) 'Warlord Competition', *Journal of Peace Research* 39(4): 435–446.

Srivastava, A.R.N. (1990) *Tribal Encounter with Industry: A Case Study from Central India*, New Delhi: Reliance Publishing House.

Tarrow, S. (1989) *Democracy and Disorder: Protest and Politics in Italy 1965–1975*, Oxford: Clarendon Press.

Tilly, C. (1978) *From Mobilization to Revolution*, New York: McGraw Hill.

Vick, M. (1998) 'Old Friends at War', *Washington Post* June 18: Section A.

Viegas, P. (1991) *Encroached and Enslaved: Alienation of Tribal Lands and Its Dynamics*, New Delhi: Indian Social Institute.

Webster, N. (1989) *Agrarian Relations in Burdwan District, West Bengal: From the Economics of Green Revolution to the Politics of Panchayati Raj*, Centre for Development Research Working Paper 89.2. Copenhagen: Centre for Development Research.

Weiner, M. (1978) *Sons of the Soil: Migration and Ethnic Conflict in India*, Princeton, NJ: Princeton University Press.

Yogandhar, B.N., Gopal Iyer, K. and Datta, P.S. (eds) (1993) *Land Reforms in India*, volume 3, New Delhi: Sage Publications.

Zagoria, D.S. (1971) 'The Ecology of Peasant Communism in India', *American Political Science Review* 65(1): 144–160.

Zald, M.N. and McCarthy, J.D. (1977) *The Dynamics of Social Movements: Resource Mobilization, Social Control, and Tactics*, Cambridge, MA: Winthrop Publishers.

6 Government restructuring and reallocation of resources in the face of ethno-nationalist insurgency in the Basque Country (1979–2005)

Enric Martínez-Herrera

Introduction

The ethno-nationalist conflict in the Basque Country has been the target of a wide array of constitutional and legislative initiatives. These comprise a substantial restructuring of governance structures and reallocation of public resources that can be covered by the concept of 'responsive policies'. This chapter considers the history of political murders produced by the organisation *Euskadi ta Askatasuna* (ETA, Basque Country and Freedom) and elaborates an account based on the main responsive governmental initiatives with regard to the Basque conflict, which is tested with a multivariate research design. It focuses, in particular, on the effects of two major changes in political structures that have also entailed a massive reallocation of public resources: political decentralisation and democratisation. However, it shows that while political decentralisation has made a major contribution to the appeasement of Basque insurgency, democratisation has not had a direct effect on this development.

Ethno-nationalist violence in the Basque Country provides exceptionally rich data and a wide variation in both independent and dependent variables. Since the late 1970s, the Spanish political system has generated a wide array of repressive policies and responsive policies concerning that conflict. Repression has ranged from a rather indiscriminate repression towards Basque nationalism to the selective incrimination of terrorist activists. Similarly, rejection of the Basque cultural, social and political differences has changed into constitutional recognition of the Basque 'nationality', which has provided the Basques with an unprecedented amount of political autonomy. The relationship between terrorism and counter-terrorism is a non-recursive and strategic one – i.e. policy-makers and terrorists react to the actions of one another (Hoffman and Morrison-Taw 1999). Yet, here, I confine myself to account only for one part of the process, focusing on the impact of public policies on insurgent violence, aiming at evaluating and, eventually, inspiring policy.

To better understand the outcomes of the different policies, I conduct a statistical multivariate evaluation of the consistency of a number of theoretical hypotheses in the literature. Although conventional wisdom – even more sophisticated thought – suggests possible answers to conflict, these seldom are univocal: some advise a good deal of repression; others suggest satisfying as much as possible those struggling violently, in as much as their cause is regarded as legitimate. Hence, there is still a need for research on the optimal combination of measures to be adopted into different socio-political settings. Here, on the basis of the available data and different research techniques, I put forward that the appeasement of Basque nationalist insurgency is best explained through a combination of efficacious but democratically inspired repressive policies, together with a substantial restructuring of government and the subsequent reallocation of public resources. In particular, given the ethno-nationalist nature of the Basque conflict, the decentralisation of political power has been the key responsive policy to appease insurgency, rather than democratisation.

Responsive approaches in the face of insurgency and political extremism

The study of governmental responses to insurgency tends to be confined into two bodies of literature that are virtually separate and hardly communicate with each other. Though, with exceptions, most analyses and prescriptions still tend to focus either on repressive policies or on responsive policies vis-à-vis rebellious groups.[1] Nevertheless, here, they will be considered as two different but compatible dimensions. The view that authority and force are intrinsic to the nature of government predominates in the former. In contrast, the latter corresponds to integrative views of public power where authority is conceived as sensitive to social needs and demands, and where communication, attention to the material and cultural bases of conflicts, as well as the quest of mutual compromises, are regarded as useful instruments. Even though a comparison of the effectiveness of each of these two frames in reducing insurgency and political extremism could be attempted, one might suspect that the correct depiction of the problem is not a disjunction but a more complex dialectics. It is plausible that a strategy combining sanctions and rewards, with a reinforcing effect, tends to be the most efficacious.

I consider the case of Basque nationalist insurgency within the broader concept of 'political extremism'. This term refers to a perception of political conflict in a war-like manner, in which extremists practice, advocate, or at least accept the use of violent means to reach their goals – the extremists do not necessarily carry out violent behaviour, but at least show a supportive attitude to it. From a historical comparative perspective, the most usual policies towards any sort of rebellion have been those of 'repression' (Gurr 1993; Gurr and Moore 1997). They develop an intrinsic attribute of the modern state, namely, that its authority is supported by violence. By regarding force as its main resource of power, the predomination of a hierarchic and coactive logic of imposition of values on the social environment is an ideal-typical trait of these policies. Within the subject under study here, authority and force materialise in coercion and eradication of violent anti-system political behaviour. Another trait defining the repressive approach is the perception of conflict in terms of its symptoms. The objective of those policies – be they reactive or preventive – is to eliminate the threatening *effects* of conflict rather than to face its deep causes (Martínez-Herrera 2002b).[2] Albeit not being the primary focus of this chapter, a set of variables involving repressive policies has been taken into account as control variables.

In turn, the term 'responsive policies' refers to those interventions aimed at coping with the social and political causes that lie in the background of political extremism as well as reducing their effects. The approach that predominates is the inclusiveness, which is typical for the pluralist democratic approach and, more generally, for regimes that are sensitive to the needs and demands of every social group. In the face of the eruption or risk of insurgency, the authorities pay attention to its structural and cultural social bases. The rulers are ready to consider the demands of the unsatisfied groups and to engage in a dialogue with them, and may also be ready to negotiate and cooperate in pursuit of mutual benefit.

Thus, their instruments, rather than force, are: (a) the recognition – not necessarily formal – of either material or perceived conflicts; (b) reciprocal communication and compromise; and (c) a disposition to share, to some extent, material resources, prestige positions and even power. It should be stressed that responsiveness does not necessarily entail weakness and unilateral concessions. Therefore, it does not need to satisfy any claim. Nor does this approach have to be the result of certain ultimate principles or values either, since it may also be developed for simply instrumental reasons. Moreover, responsiveness does not need to entail a zero-sum game where improvement for some implies harm for others, but it can supply all the involved actors with a general improvement. As for the sectors, levels and manners of action, these policies can be extremely heterogeneous, involving, in accordance to the roots of the conflict, many different policy fields (e.g. culture, religion, education and labour), as well as the very distribution of public power. As to their degree of institutionalisation, they can be enforced in the form of constitutional engineering policies, as ordinary legislation, or even as simple administrative decisions (cf. Gurr 1993; Hoffman and Morrison-Taw 1999).

My previous research has highlighted the effects that some major responsive policies have had to mitigate substantially Basque nationalist extremism and insurgency. However, it did not distinguish at the operational level between the effects of two major responsive factors involved, namely: political decentralisation and democratisation (Martínez-Herrera 2002a, 2002b). This chapter puts forward an effort to enhance this distinction. From positive political science, the most outstanding example of a responsive approach to interethnic or nationalist conflicts is the 'consociational' model of Arend

Lijphart (1984, 1999). He analyses institutions that induce the protection, and possibility of expression and decision of organised minorities in plural societies. These institutions are also directed towards enabling their elites to participate in power and, thus, enhancing the integration of political systems that otherwise tend to break up and/or to underperform. However, the concept 'responsiveness' is broader than those of 'consociativism' and 'accommodation' since political integration is not always based on an institutionalisation of minorities' rights and power. Other opportunities rest on pluralist policies (Dahl 1971) and on attempts at co-optation seeking the assimilation of minorities into the majority in exchange for economic and prestigious advantages – less theorised but often put into practice (see Bloom 1990; Gurr 1993; Hoffman and Morrison-Taw 1999; cf. Saideman et al. 2002).[3]

One of the most salient political arrangements to integrate multinational polities is federalism, which tends to reduce the levels of ethnic violence (Horowitz 1985; Stepan 2001; Saideman et al. 2002). However, some scholars have also warned about possible risks of federalism, which could induce an escalation of ethnic conflict. As a matter of fact, some argue that some plurinational states – namely, Czechoslovakia, Yugoslavia and the Soviet Union – disintegrated because of their federal design, which fostered the framing of conflict in terms of ethno-nationality while providing the groups with state organisation resources to organise large scale rebellion (Linz 1993; Roeder 1999; Skalnik-Leff 1999; Snyder 2000; Saideman et al. 2002). Thus, this is still an open empirical question. However, rather than the term 'federalism', I prefer to use the term 'political decentralisation', which comprises federalism tout court, as well as other forms of transference of political decision-making power from the centre to the periphery – including 'devolution' – that do not fulfil all the requirements of the former concept.

In any case, many other policies fall into the analytical category of responsiveness. Some policies are directly aimed at the allocation of resources among social groups. They comprise the distribution of wealth, opportunities of education, access to health, social positions praised in terms of status or social prestige and resources for the preservation of certain kinds of socially-valued cultural heritage such as language and religion. One allocation of resources between groups that can satisfy their needs and claims can be achieved without giving to the groups the power of allocation nor formal quotas or guarantees. However, like the example of federalism, steps in this direction usually involve formal guarantees of political inclusion that may give rise to structural reforms. In fact, besides the redistribution of resources, responsive policies in the face of interethnic and/or nationalist conflict typically involve a government restructuring that may even reach the formalised shape of constitutional engineering. Political restructuring measures comprise such developments as federalist arrangements, proportional representation and several types of power-sharing institutions, such as group quotas in public and private jobs (Horowitz 1985; Stepan 1998). Having said this, another salient but more controversial responsive policy consists of the democratisation, which restructures the very nature of the political regime.

Dankwart A. Rustow (1970), Robert Dahl (1971), Juan J. Linz (1978) and more recently other authors, have alluded to the difficulties that a feeling of alienation with regard to the political community involves the instauration and persistence of democracies. Rustow contended that 'national unity' is the 'single background condition' for a transition to democracy. Among other things, his 'political unity' entailed that the existing political community was not challenged by alternatives among its members. Other authors have further developed some of his arguments. Certain measures of 'national unity' could be necessary, in the first place, because, for existing freedom of speech and association, a disposition to coexistence is indispensable. Secondly, because ethnic differences may easily be politicised and sharpened, since they constitute an accessible and profitable resource of political mobilisation to win elections (Horowitz 1985; Skalnik-Leff 1999; Saideman et al. 2002). The combination of intolerance, the 'winner takes all' formula (majoritarian electoral system) and the existence of structural ethnic political majorities is likely to lead to protest, rebellion, civil war and secession (Lijphart 1984).

In spite of the importance of conflicts about the political community in many scenarios around the world the mainstream literature on transitions to democracy overlooked them until democratisation reached Eastern Europe.[4] What is more, some authors suggest that democracy could be the most appropriate regime to settle conflicts within contested political communities, contending that if the challenger groups obtain access to channels of representation and accountability enabling them to express their demands, they will have fewer incentives to resort to force, and thus the negotiation of compromises will be easier (Saward 1998). However, this view has recently been challenged by authors that argue that democratisation of multiethnic or plurinational polities tends to exacerbate ethnic conflicts (Roeder 1999; Skalnick-Leff 1999; Snyder 2000). In effect, implementing a multivariate research design, Saideman and his colleagues (2002) found that democracy tends to be more prone to both ethnic protest and rebellion than autocracy.[5] Thus, in this chapter, besides testing the effects of political decentralisation on the Basque conflict, I shall examine whether the effects of democratisation have been of increasing or decreasing the conflict.

Ethno-nationalist insurgency in the Basque Country

The most prominent materialisation of political extremism and political violence in the Basque Country is terrorism carried out by ETA. This is one of the most long-lived terrorist organisations in the Western world, with more than forty years of existence, more than thirty years of personal attacks, and more than eight hundred cases of murder and assassination (Domínguez-Iribarren 1999; Jaime-Jiménez and Reinares 1999).

Still, expressions and consequences of extremism on a polity do not confine themselves to terrorism, however implacable and persistent this can be. Extremism must be observed from a broader perspective: to begin with, because its repertoire of actions are able to destabilise the political system is broader than terrorism; and then because, if one wants to give an account, specifically, of armed struggle, one should try to understand the conditions in which it is formed and sustained. First of all, not all violence is 'terrorist', in the sense that it intimidates a social group beyond its direct victims (Reinares 1998). Second, the extremism gives rise to varieties of contentious non-conventional, although non-violent, types of political behaviour – e.g. general strike, petty sabotage and civil disobedience (Tarrow 1994; Dalton 1996) – which are equally destabilising for the political system. Third, extremism can obstruct institutional performance and destabilise the system from within, by means of behaviour that formally respects the law but is actually contrary to the principles of the polity. Finally, and more generally, the presence of impenetrable political subcultures, strongly structured internally and antagonistic, makes cooperation and coordination in favour of the whole society exceedingly difficult (Almond and Verba 1963; Boix and Posner 1998) – this being particularly true where there is an inclination to justify, promote or practice violence. As a matter of fact, all these types of behaviour can be observed in the recent history of the Basque Country.

On the other hand, ETA's origin and persistence could not be understood without its exchanges with the broader environment. Like other organisations, its own internal dynamics explain, to a large extent, its persistence and autonomy (organisational culture, opportunity costs for its members and internal incentives and sanctions). Yet its interaction with the broader social context becomes crucial. Its obvious aspect is the success or failure of the security forces in arresting ETA activists and in the protection of ETA targets. Nonetheless, the inputs that favour ETA are no less important. ETA reproduction, for decades, has required, above all, regular generational replacement of its commandos. In the same way, the role of the environment in the provision of information, ammunition, infrastructure and moral support cannot be neglected (Funes 1998; Reinares 1998).

In this sense, in the case of ETA at least, it is possible to consider a system of concentric circles, which are hierarchically related (cf. Mata 1993). In the centre, there are the terrorist organisations. In a broader circle, there is a network of interconnected support organisations, including political parties, trade unions, associations, mass media and firms, which, on the whole, are often called the Basque National Liberation Movement (MLNV). Next, there are the voters for those parties. The external ring corresponds to those who share ideas of rejection towards Spain, independence for the Basque Country, *and* accept violence as a means. At the basis of Basque nationalist extremist behaviour lies a system of beliefs that constitutes a clear example of political subculture. It is a structured, consistent and stable system of attitudes of rejection (even hatred) towards Spain, while adhering to a Basque national identification, preferences for secession and an understanding appraisal of violence (Linz *et al.* 1986; Llera 1994; Reinares 2001). In this text, however, I shall focus on the more salient activity flowing from the core of these concentric circles, namely, political murdering.

Actual violence is the most obvious dimension of extremism. All the more so when, by taking the form of terrorism, the perpetration of assassination and murder results from the desire for public impact, and when terrorist organisations exert an outstanding leverage over the extremist movement at large. An annual number of murders denotes, to a large extent, the operability of the Basque nationalist terrorist organisations and, especially, their capability of psychologically influencing great numbers of people.[6] I refer basically to ETA, but also to its several factional splinter groups, such as the ETA-m ('military'), ETA-pm ('political-military') and the Anti-capitalist Autonomous Commandos.

As a measurement, this turns out somewhat unsatisfactory, since, in terms of propaganda, the impact of every victim – a prime minister or an ordinary member of the public – is not identical, and, in operative terms, a massive attack with a car bomb, which is relatively safe for the perpetrator, produces many more victims than one directed to a protected public personality, which is much more risky. However, these are the best available data for both their validity and time extension.[7] In addition, for the period 1968–2004, there is a strong correlation between mortality and frequency of attacks with victims (Pearson's $r = 0.95$), which means that the variation in murder techniques (small weapons *vis-à-vis* car bombs) hardly changes lethality in the long run.

Thus, in this chapter, I aim to assess the contribution of the main responsive policies towards the Basque conflict to explain changes in time-series of the number of ETA homicides from the late 1970s.[8] The maximum activity took place between 1978 and 1980, during the delicate period of the twofold transition to democracy and self-government, and the trend since then has been decreasing, though with many short-term variations (see Figure 6.1). The task is to account for these developments by paying attention to the possible impact of the different state policies while controlling by other relevant yet theoretically exogenous factors.

Responsive and repressive policies in the Basque Country

As argued above, the repertoire of state policies is extremely wide. Nevertheless, within this mixture, responsive policies and repressive policies stand as the two most relevant dimensions. In the following pages, I shall describe the main policies in both domains, although with a particular stress on responsive policies, especially on the restructuring of the political system and the reallocation of resources within.

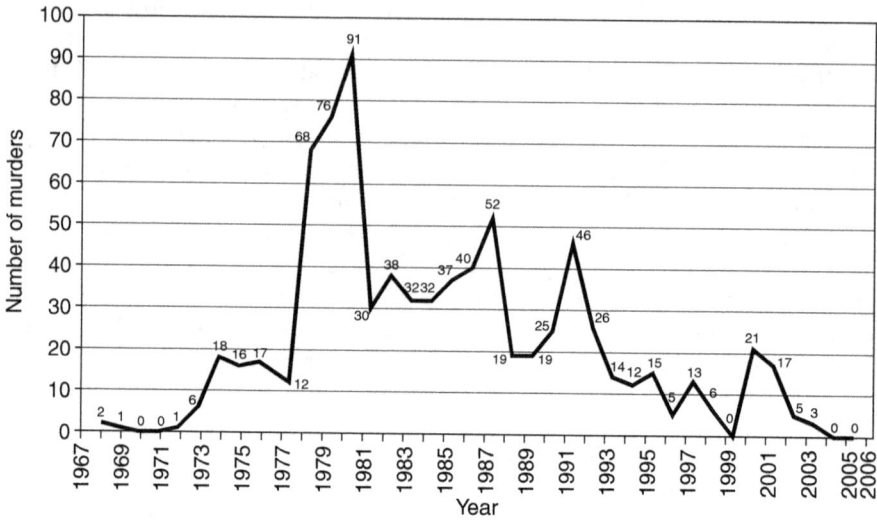

Figure 6.1 Murders of ETA, 1968–2005 (source: Author's elaboration of police data).

Responsive policies

As far as the social background of Basque nationalist extremism is concerned, an historical dynamic of political decentralisation and re-centralisation synthesises and articulates most of the policies. After the Spanish Civil War (1936–39), the Spanish nationalist winning side dismantled most Basque self-government institutions, minimising the responsive approach. Contrary to this, the Spanish Constitution of 1978 and the Basque Autonomy Law (with the rank of constitutional law) of 1979 enacted an unprecedented political autonomy. This juridical frame establishes a Basque parliament and a Basque executive chosen by universal suffrage. The matters over which they have jurisdiction comprise education, health, culture and social services, as well as the collection of the most important taxes, a part of which is then passed on to the central state, after mutual agreement (Aja 1999). Moreover, they also command a regional police force that has largely taken over from that of the state (Jar-Couselo 1995; Jaime-Jiménez 2002). The current Constitution also bears an important symbolic intention, since it recognises the existence of 'nationalities' within the 'nation' (Spain) and establishes the protection and fostering of minority languages and cultures as a doctrinal fundamental principle of law.

As a consequence, the administration of the regional self-government institutions has achieved a great volume of staff, physical assets and financial resources, thus implying a massive reallocation of resources. In order to get an overall indicator of the amount of resources administrated by the Basque self-governing regional institutions, I have elaborated data on their budget.

The Ministry for Public Administrations has produced an indicator expressing the share of the overall statewide public spending that has been yearly administrated by the regional institutions at large (MAP 1997, 2002; Moreno 2001). However, they are not detailed per region and the speed of budgetary transfers has been different from one region to another. In order to attain a good measure for the Basque Country, I have weighted the proportion of total regional public spending by a ratio that divides the proportion of the Basque regional budget upon the total regional budgets by the average proportion of Basque population out of the Spanish total population.[9] The results of these calculations are displayed in Figure 6.2. In the Basque Country, regional public spending has attained, on average, a share of around 35 per cent of the overall public spending corresponding to the region, and that this share was immediately attained once regional self-government was established.

The reallocation of resources has also involved other relevant consequences. In this sense, it has often been claimed that most good jobs depending on the regional government, are taken up by Basque nationalists, and the regional government allocates many resources by means of subventions that favour associations and cooperatives led by Basque nationalists (Mansvelt-Beck 2005). Moreover, the Basque language and folklore has been resolutely fostered by means of both staff and financial resources, the Basque language is compulsory in the schools, and it enjoys an action of positive measures in university – such as quotas for lecturers teaching in the vernacular. In order to operationalise political decentralisation in the multivariate

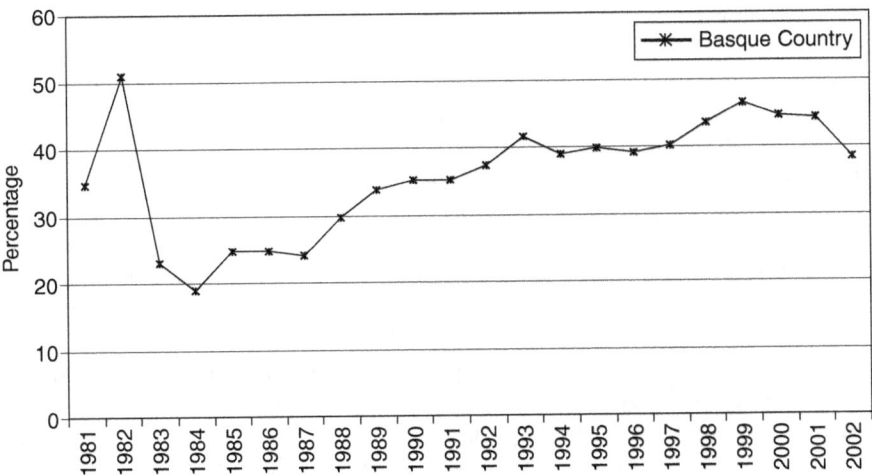

Figure 6.2 Rate of regional public spending out of the total public spending corresponding to the Basque Country, 1981–2002 (source: Author's elaboration of data from the Ministry of Public Administrations and the Ministry of Economy and Finance).

analyses, I have devised the rate of regional public spending out of the total public spending corresponding to the Basque Country. This is an optimal proxy indicator of the resources available for the regional institutions, which expresses, to a large extent, their relative power as compared to the central and local layers of government.

Responsiveness, however, also stands up in other domains. Another factor is the type of political regime. One of the motives that originated nationalist extremism was the dictatorial context, which, in the collective imaginary, associated the idea of 'Spain' with the idea of oligarchic domination (cf. Pérez-Díaz 1993). It could thus be possible that the achievement of a democracy in Spain contributed to attenuate the rejection towards the Spanish political community among one segment of the Basque population. Even so, that type of regime entails theoretically a certain paradox, since in each one of the considered dimensions – responsiveness and repression – it would influence in an opposed direction: whereas autocracy has more 'operability' in the administration of force, it tends to provoke rejection in terms of legitimacy. The opposite, in both dimensions, seems to happen in a democracy (Reinares 1998). As argued above, nevertheless, there are also reasons to expect that democracy could exacerbate further the ethno-nationalist conflict. In order to operationalise democratisation, I have chosen three different indicators that are used alternatively. The first one is the Freedom House index of political freedoms, which is widely used in the literature on democratisation.[10] The second measure is the Polity2 index of democracy, which has been elaborated by the Center for International Development and Conflict Management (CIDCM).[11] The third one is a dummy variable representing democratisation as a change produced, in an abrupt permanent manner, in 1979, and remaining constant since.

In addition, the electoral system established along with democratisation, which combines proportional representation with small electoral districts, eases, especially, the representation of minorities that are territorially concentrated. Hence, during several legislatures, the parties ruling at the Spanish level – either social-democrats, centre-right or conservative parties – but lacking an absolute majority in Parliament have reached agreements on investiture, even on legislature, with the Basque Nationalist Party (PNV). There have also been many coalition governments in the autonomous community between this party and the Spanish-wide social-democrats. In turn, both types of inter-partisan agreements have eased multilevel government collaboration (Aja 1999). These factors, however, have not been considered in the multivariate analyses.

Moreover, the quest of some Basque nationalist governments of an agreement with the organised extremist movement which could integrate the latter into the political system and thus diminishing its inclination to violence is also noteworthy. There have been dialogue round tables, meetings and some agreements. The most important accord reached was the so-called Pact of Lizarra of 1999, which comprised the institutional collaboration between Euskal Herritarrok (the political branch of ETA), the Basque Nationalist Party and Eusko Alkartasuna (the two nationalist parties that had governed the region till then) and, in particular, the investiture of the regional president. The pact was announced shortly after the 'military' ETA had announced a cease-fire at about the end of 1998, represented as inspired by the Ulster agreement and driven by a will to negotiate. This cease-fire is the single variable able to account for the absence of deaths in 1999.[12] However, the persistence of ETA's truce for almost a year seems, to a large extent, to be due to the *rapprochement* between nationalist parties.

Prospects about an association between responsive policies and ETA murders can be briefly expressed as a negative hypothetical causal relation, save for the Freedom House index, in which high values mean more autocracy. It is possible to expect that every government action satisfying a need (articulated or not as a demand) or making up for a motive of reactivity in different domains (culture, self-government, economy) of the social bases of Basque extremism and the extremists themselves, will contribute to reduce insurgent violence. However, to disentangle the effects of these policies, it is necessary to take also into account the simultaneous effects of factors stemming from the repressive side. Table 6.1 summarises the main variables in the analysis as well as their hypothetical relations to the number of ETA murders.

Table 6.1 Variables utilised in the modelling of the number of murders

	Observed period	*Expected relationship*
Dependent variable		
Number of victims of ETA	1968–2004	
Responsiveness variables		
Political decentralisation	1968–2004	Negative
Autocracy (Freedom House)	1968–2004	Positive
Democracy (Polity2)	1968–2004	Negative
Democracy dummy	Dummy	Negative
Repression variables		
Number of arrested in Spain	1977–2004	Negative
Bidart operation (1992)	Dummy	Negative
Number of reinserted fighters	1982–90	Negative
Algiers negotiations (1989)	Dummy	Negative
Number of murders of GAL-BVE	1978–87	Positive/Negative
Exogenous variables		
Coup d'État (1981)	Dummy	Negative
ETA truce (1998/9)	Dummy	Positive
September 11 context (2001/4)	Dummy	Negative

Repressive policies and other control variables

In general terms, it can be put forward the hypothesis that the more efficacious – for example, in the number of imprisonments – the repression of extremism, the more likely extremist behaviour will decrease. Throughout history, this hypothesis has often been, in practice, taken by political rulers as an unquestioned assumption, from which a prohibition of any expression and organisation, even peaceful, of extremist views has followed. Supposedly, repression would produce a loss of influence of the core group of extremists over their social environment, and consequently the reduction of extremism among the population. This proposition, however, can be substantially amended if one considers that the efficaciousness of the whole policy will be greater in so far as the violence of the state is considered legitimate in the relevant contexts, such as in the social milieu where force is applied and an international environment where human rights and political freedoms are highly valued. This involves aspects related to the public image of the policy, such as the accuracy in the application of force and the respect of human rights. At any rate, repressive policies are expected to diminish violence, directly, by removing active violent actors and, indirectly, by increasing the subjective cost of those actions.

The repressive approach includes the development of policing and judiciary policies. All of these have varied greatly in relation to Basque nationalist extremism. The better quantified repression variables, which I have considered in my analysis here, are: (a) the number of arrests of alleged ETA members; (b) the amount of reintegrated terrorists;[13] (c) direct negotiations with ETA with a governmental disposition to penal concessions; and (d) state terrorism against ETA and its environment.

The most prominent aspect of repression are arrests. In the case of ETA, this factor is contemporarily correlated to the number of victims as, understandably, police activity increases every time that a terrorist attack occurs. However, it seems more useful to know the reverse impact of arrests on attacks. The foreseen relation should be negative and its effect should have, at least, a delay of one year, since the substitution of commands needs some time. This relation does not show up at first glance. However, an effect of the measurement method could bias the results. In an organisation with a hierarchical structure, the arrest of a leader should have a greater impact than, say, the arrest of a militant in charge of logistics. Thus, a dummy variable representing the detention of major ETA leaders in Bidart (French Basque Country) at the beginning of 1992 has also been computed.[14] This intervention was the result of international cooperation, as French police implemented it after an investigation by the Spanish *Guardia Civil*. The Bidart operation caused, for ETA, the loss of its most experienced leaders and important infrastructures, and allowed security agencies to obtain very useful information to struggle against it in the following years (Reinares 1996; Sánchez-Cuenca 2001).

Another device employed early by democratic rulers was the social reintegration of fighters. By the 1980s, the government thus supplied an outlet for almost 150 activists, most of them from the 'political-military' ETA splinter group, which had unilaterally renounced its armed struggle in 1982. Eighty-six amnesties were added between 1982 and 1990 (Domínguez-Iribarren 1999; Jaime-Jiménez and Reinares 1999).[15] In this manner sanctions derived from past actions were removed, hence important opportunity costs that could have caused them to persist were avoided. This policy could produce, moreover, three other delayed effects: (a) an interruption of active recruitment by this faction; (b) a modification, among 'military' ETA members, of the perception of their opportunities structure; and (c) a lower probability of new recruits, owing to an effect of fall of the critical mass of armed collective action.

Nonetheless, during the democratic period, murders of alleged ETA members or supporters were carried out from the structures of the state, too. The so-called 'dirty war' almost always took place in the French Basque Country and was aimed at eliminating ETA's refuge there. Two periods can be distinguished. From 1978 to 1980, while the centre-right *Unión del Centro Democrático* was in office, seemingly uncontrolled members of the security forces who gave themselves the names of *Batallón Vasco Español* (BVE) and Triple A committed ten murders. From 1983 to 1987, under social-democratic rule, the newly arrived *Grupos Antiterroristas de Liberación* (GAL) added 28 homicides more. These later caused several policemen and politicians – including one former Minister of the Interior – to be imprisoned (Domínguez-Iribarren 1999). On this issue two competing hypotheses exist: on the one hand, the responsible policemen and politicians could have thought that the illegal violent campaign would restrain ETA, forcing it to be much more cautious in its French 'sanctuary'. On the other hand, it has been argued that this actually provided new arguments to ETA when its social legitimacy was in crisis (Unzueta 1994; Reinares 1996).[16]

Another hypothetical factor consists of attempts of communication with ETA to negotiate reintegration of its members, a reduction of their sentences, or the attenuation of other consequences (particularly, transferring convicts to prisons near their social milieu), in exchange for a renunciation to violence. The most important meeting between government and ETA representatives occurred in Algiers in 1989, while holding a truce that stood three months.[17]

Finally, a couple of theoretically exogenous factors have been considered in the models. In previous analyses, I observed a pronounced temporary drop in 1981. My *ex post* interpretation was that this could be due to the failed coup d'état attempt of that year (Martínez-Herrera 2002b). In fact, during the transition to democracy, ETA had been seeking polarisation, the coup being the most unequivocal expression at that time of its apparent success, and also an occasion for having a rest after a very long and intense terrorist offensive during the previous three years. It has even been argued that

ETA-m aimed at a returning of the dictatorship (Unzueta 1994).[18] At the same time, however, many activists, especially those of ETA-pm, could take stock of the situation and ask themselves whether a return to dictatorship was what they actually wanted. The second theoretically exogenous factor is the international atmosphere after the terrorist attacks in New York and Washington in September 2001. The attacks prompted a substantial widening and intensification of collaboration between national governments in the field of security and counter-terrorism. For this reason, ETA could have tactically attempted to go temporarily unnoticed in the international scene.

Empirical analysis

I present a multivariate analysis modelling the yearly variation of terrorist attacks of ETA. Its multivariate character is aimed at rejecting spurious causal relations and unveiling hidden relations. The analysis affords the possibility of studying the change both diachronically and with a quasi-experimental multivariate approach. The methodology is deductive, seeking to falsify the theoretical hypotheses formulated beforehand. As independent variables, the models incorporate indicators that operationalise the different theoretical explanatory factors. The independent variables that do not yield statistically significant effects on the dependent variables are progressively dropped from the models until a parsimonious model that only contains those variables that yield significant effects is achieved.[19]

However, both the character of the hypotheses and, by and large, the time-series approach entail some inductive traits as well. Social theories do not usually specify the amount of time between causes and effects. Because of this, according to the very philosophy of time-series analysis, the amount of the lag between cause and effect is identified by means of exploration, selecting the lag that yields a relationship with the expected direction and better magnitude. In other words, this methodology allows us to find out a detail omitted by theory. Yet, once these parameters have been identified, the applied method is confirmatory again, rejecting those factors whose effects are not statistically significant or are theoretically inconsistent when controlling by the effects of the remaining variables. The process of identification of the lags has followed the recommendations of McCleary and Hay (1980: chap. 5). After making sure, to begin with, that the series are stationary (differentiating them if necessary), a Cross Correlation Function (CCF) has been estimated to identify the lags attaining a stronger and theoretically consistent association in every expected bivariate relation – this is of crucial importance for avoiding arbitrary results. Then, the models have been conducted with event count data analysis and specify the lagged effects as previously identified.

The yearly level of ETA murders has been estimated using a negative binomial event-count model. Since these events always take positive integer values and tend to be rare, the distribution is discrete and skewed, resulting in errors that are not normally distributed. This could generate inefficiency of the statistical signification tests in classical regression (OLS). Thus, in this situation, event-count models are preferred, which fit the number of occurrences of an event using maximum likelihood estimators. Moreover, since the data examined here are over-dispersed (variance greater than the mean), negative binomial regression is more appropriate than the standard Poisson regression.[20]

I aim to explain changes in the level time-series of the number of ETA murders from 1979 to 2004. Because of the lack of information about some essential factors till the mid-1970s, variations prior to 1979 are excluded from the analysis, though. As stated above, the yearly number of murders has undergone a declining trend, with short-term irregular fluctuations around it. The task is to account for all these variations by attending to the possible impact of the different state policies. The models in Table 6.2 assess the effects of the different explanatory factors as claimed by the theoretical hypotheses laid out above.

To begin with, the models evaluate the effects of factors stemming from a repressive approach to conflict resolution. Some models do not yield statistically significant coefficients for the impact of political decentralisation on ETA murders. However, once the models are free of other non-significant independent variables, decentralisation attains, as expected, a significant negative effect, which is lagged three years with respect to variations in the independent variable (see Models 4, 6 and 7).

In turn, democratisation has been operationalised by means of three alternative indicators. However, neither the Freedom House nor the Polity2 indices (Models 1 to 4) nor the dummy representing democratisation (Model 5) yield statistically significant effects. However, as will be argued below, this is not to deny that democratisation may have impinged on the declining of violence through indirect mechanisms.

In turn, the models also consider the claimed effects of a set of repressive policies. The most prominent aspect of repression is the arrests, which are measured as both ordinary arrests and the extraordinary arrest of the leadership of ETA that happened in Bidart in 1992. The outcome of the Bidart operation was a drastic decrease in fatalities, apparently definitive, seemingly due to the organisational problems for ETA and the information obtained by security agencies. In turn, ordinary detentions show a statistically significant negative effect with a delay of two years.

Another policy instrument was the social reintegration of fighters, which was implemented during the 1980s. Besides removing opportunity costs that could cause them to persist, this could produce other delayed effects on recruitment by the insurgent organisation. The analysis lends further credence to this hypothesis, as all models yield a statistically significant negative effect, with a delay of six years. The length of the lag makes theoretical sense as the alluded mechanism of undermining recruitment and training entails a long process. The killing by ETA of a reinserted prominent former

Table 6.2 Negative binomial event count regression of ETA murders

	Lag	Model 1 coefficient	Model 2 coefficient	Model 3 coefficient	Model 4 coefficient	Model 5 coefficient	Model 6 coefficient	Model 7 coefficient
C	–	4.694***	4.310***	4.571***	4.507***	4.621***	4.608***	4.622***
Arrested	–2	–0.001***	–0.001***	–0.001***	–0.002***	–0.001***	–0.001***	–0.001***
Bidart Operation	–1	–1.553***	–1.421***	–1.508***	–1.643***	–1.508***	–1.486***	–1.518***
Decentralisation	–3	–0.006^{ns}	–0.005^{ns}	–0.006^{ns}	–0.011**	–0.006^{ns}	–0.007*	–0.006*
Autocracy (Freedom House)	–3	–0.029^{ns}	0.144^{ns}	0.025^{ns}	–	–	–	–
Democracy (Polity2)	–3	–	–	–	0.044^{ns}	–	–	–
Democracy (Dummy)	–2	–	–	–	–	–0.025^{ns}	–	–
Reinserted	–6	–0.035***	–0.029***	–0.032***	–0.038***	–0.032***	–0.031***	–0.033***
GAL-BE	–2	–	0.016^{ns}	–	–	–	0.013^{ns}	–
Coup d'État	–	–0.649**	–0.556**	–0.624***	–0.764***	–0.624***	–0.632***	–0.637***
Algiers	–	0.200^{ns}	–	–	–	–	–	–
ETA Truce	–	–4.914***	–4.892***	–4.896***	–4.905***	–4.896***	–4.898***	–4.898***
September 11	–	–1.281***	–1.287***	–1.280***	–1.241***	–1.280***	–1.272***	–1.277***
Sample	–	79–04	79–04	79–04	79–04	79–04	79–04	79–04
N	–	26	26	26	26	26	26	26
R^2	–	0.94	0.95	0.94	0.96	0.94	0.95	0.94
Adj. R^2	–	0.90	0.92	0.91	0.93	0.91	0.92	0.91
Log likelihood	–	–74.77	–74.39	–74.98	–73.73	–74.98	–74.55	–74.99
AIC	–	6.60	6.57	6.54	6.44	6.54	6.50	6.46
LR index (Pseudo-R^2)	–	0.74	0.74	0.74	0.74	0.74	0.74	0.74

Notes
Significant: *** 0.01; ** 0.05; * 0.10; ns not significant.

leader (Yoyes) in 1986, however, seems to be the main motive for the government to terminate this policy (Domínguez-Iribarren 1999).

However, murders of alleged ETA members and sympathisers were carried out from the structures of the state, too. There are two rival hypotheses on this issue: on the one hand, state terrorism ought to restrain ETA; on the other, these illegal murders actually provided new arguments for ETA legitimising itself in its social milieu. The tests, however, reject both hypotheses as far as murders are concerned, since no statistically significant coefficients are obtained (see Models 2 and 6).

Another hypothetical explanatory factor consists of attempts of communication with ETA to negotiate penal matters in exchange for a renunciation to violence. The most important meeting between the government and ETA occurred in Algiers in 1989. However, the statistical effect of these negotiations is not significant (Model 1). Even though the number of victims that year was comparatively low, this seems to be due to a period of insurgent weakness, since there were an equal number of victims in 1988.[21]

Furthermore, late in 1998 and until the middle of 1999, ETA proclaimed a unilateral truce. Although the trend in the previous years could suggest another period of operative weakness, its coefficient is significant in all models. Actually, the cease-fire is the single variable able to account for the decrease in 1999. Police pressure and massive mobilisation in favour of peace occurring by the end of 1998 must be regarded at the background of that decision, but also there were some factors of a political nature.[22] This is because, immediately after the cease-fire announcement, the Pact of Lizarra, which involved important agreements of institutional collaboration between the political branch of ETA and the governing nationalist parties, was reached. To a large extent, the persistence of the truce for almost one year seems to be explained by this collaboration.

Finally, a couple of theoretically exogenous factors have been considered. Both the failed *coup d'état* of 1981 and the conjuncture of international collaboration against terrorism following September 2001 account for statistically significant decreases in murders in their respective periods.

Discussion and concluding remarks

Basque nationalist extremism has declined dramatically during the last 25 years. By relying on a theoretically-driven multivariate statistical approach of the available data, the analysis has sought to account for the decline of terrorist murders. The analysis has shown that the appeasement of the Basque conflict has been, to a large extent, the product of a substantial transfer of political power towards the Basque territory and the reallocation of resources stemming from this restructuring of government. The establishment of a Basque Autonomous Community, together with a perseverant law-ruled repression policy, materialised in the policing efficacy and the reintegration of combatants, emerged as the main causes of this mitigation.

In effect, the evidence supplied here is consistent with an explanation that accounts for the variations in the yearly number of ETA murders on the basis of a combination of responsiveness and repression. Another factor is ETA's cease-fire, which can either be considered as a consequence of political factors or – in a somehow tautological but plausible manner – as a consequence of those very police actions. The failed *coup d'état* in 1981 (as a theoretically exogenous variable) and the international atmosphere after the attacks in New York add to these factors as theoretically exogenous factors.

Therefore, this chapter argues that the combination of the satisfaction of demands of the extremist movement's social milieu with effective policing seems to explain the decrease of violence. However, the impact of democratisation on ethnic conflict is not as expected by the comparative literature on democratisation. This is because, contrary to the expected by many authors, democracy, operationalised by means of three different operational constructs, has not shown any statistically significant effects – neither positive nor negative – on political murders. This lack of direct effects, however, does not preclude the possibility that democratisation has impinged indirectly on violence. The most obvious path of indirect influence is that political decentralisation – which *does* show direct effects on nationalist violence – is a product of democratisation. Another plausible path is the rationale that the renunciation of the ETA-pm faction to violence happened after the failed putsch, which was perceived as an indication of the risk of a regression towards autocracy. This faction of ETA considered the struggle for democracy – not only nationalist goals – to be all-important.

One of the last developments in the struggle against violence in the Basque Country has been a series of measures against the array of groups that provide resources to ETA. For instance, a few hundred members of the political branch – including elected representatives – of the organisation were sentenced for collaborating with it. A major political decision was adopted in 2002, when the Spanish parliament passed a new legislation on political parties, which allows the executive to demand judicial procedures to outlaw political groups either maintaining links with a terrorist organisation or showing unwillingness to condemn terrorism. Shortly before the bill was passed, judge Baltasar Garzón had already suspended *Batasuna* on the basis of strong indications of its organisational links with ETA. Then, once the bill was enacted, the government asked the Supreme Court to make the political branch of ETA-m illegal, which finally happened in 2003.

These initiatives prompted a controversy in the Basque Country, and their outcomes on nationalist terrorism are an open empirical question. Albeit the number of murders has dropped from 2002 to 2005 – what can also be a consequence of the international scenario of the War against Terror – the unknown concerns what will occur in the middle and long run. On the one hand, the dismantling of the satellite structures of ETA might accelerate further the decline of ETA, which would find it exceedingly difficult to sustain its recruitment and financing. Opinion surveys show that support for

ETA among Basque citizens is, from 2001, weaker than ever before, which lends credence to this prediction. On the other hand, however, ETA might regain popular support upon the discourse that radical nationalism is oppressed, as it already did in the past. In this sense, rejection of Spanish identification undergoes an increase from 2004 and, in the 2005 regional election, a list supported by the extremist movement attained great success.[23] Thus, hitherto, evidence is ambivalent and insufficient to clarify this conundrum. In any event, in May 2005 the parliament authorised the executive to initiate negotiations with ETA with a view to reaching a permanent peace. Next, in March 2006, ETA proclaimed a unilateral permanent cease-fire in order to initiate talks. However, in December 2006 ETA resumed its attacks with two new murders.

Appendix

Nonstationarity and a replication with a forecasting approach

Most of the variables – both dependent and independent – in the analysis are nonstationary, which is a potential source of spuriousness. However, Studenmund points out that it is possible that both X and Y are 'nonstationary to the same degree; that is, suppose that ΔX_t and ΔY_t are both stationary. In such a situation there's a reasonable possibility that the nonstationarity in the two variables will "cancel each other out", leaving [the equation] free of nonstationarity'. Thus, an estimate of the association between them is not necessarily spurious. To assure this result, Studenmund advises us to apply the Adjusted Dickey-Fuller (ADF) test to the residuals in order to reject the hypothesis of unit root: 'If the residuals are stationary, then we have evidence that the nonstationary variables [...] are in the same wavelength and the first differences are not necessary' (Studenmund 1997: 491–2). In this manner, the double trouble that a use of first differences – the usual remedy in time-series analysis – may entail is avoided, namely conceptual change of the variables and the overlooking of the long-term tendencies. The ADF has rejected the hypothesis of unit root in the residuals of all the models (signification level = 0.05).

Additionally, this procedure avoids some problems stemming from introducing a lagged dependent variable or autoregressive (AR) operators in the right-hand side of the regression equation. These are typical procedures in financial research, which is primarily concerned about producing forecasts rather than explanations. By contrast, following the mainstream tradition of social science, I believe that causality is to be found somewhere else rather than in the dependent variable itself. As an example in point, I cannot see how last year killings by ETA could *explain* current killings by ETA. Having said this, in order to reassure the followers of the forecasting tradition, I have also conducted a replication of some models in the chapter by including a lagged dependent variable among the explanatory variables (see the Table 6.A-1).

These models show that the number of arrests and the number of combatants reinserted resists the inclusion of the dependent variable in all cases. Concerning political decentralisation, in the first place, its coefficient loses its statistical signification if the number of arrests is excluded from the equation (Model 9). However, this operation would entail the omission of a relevant variable and, hence, a problem of misspecification of the model. Second, if lagged murders, political decentralisation and the index of political freedoms of the Freedom House are evaluated simultaneously into the model, none of them attains a significant effect because of co-linearity (Model 10). At last, the single interesting difference between the forecasting approach and the explanatory approach is that the former yields a statistically significant effect of the Polity2 index of democratisation while keeping political decentralisation significant (Model 11). Thus, in general terms, this replication shows the robustness of most of the results attained in the main text.

Table 6.A-1 Negative binomial event count regression of ETA murders with a forecasting approach

	Lag	Model 8 coefficient	Model 9 coefficient	Model 10 coefficient	Model 11 coefficient
c	–	4.180***	3.575***	4.662***	3.987***
Murders	–1	0.006**	0.010**	0.007^{ns}	0.007*
Arrested	–2	–0.001***	–	–0.001***	–0.001***
Bidart Operation	–	–1.427***	–0.753***	–1.436***	–1.515***
Decentralisation	–3	–	–0.00^{ns}	–0.005^{ns}	–0.008*
Autocracy (Freedom House)	–	–	–	–0.271^{ns}	–
Democracy (Polity2)	–3	–	–	–	0.060**
Reinserted	–6	–0.029***	–0.019**	–0.031***	–0.034***
Coup d'État	–	–0.832***	–4.913***	–4.781***	–4.793***
ETA Truce	–	–4.813***	–4.913***	–4.781***	–4.793***
September 11	–	–1.285***	–1.335***	–1.234***	–1.219***
Sample	–	79–04	77–04	79–04	79–04
N	–	26	26	26	26
R^2	–	0.948	0.775	0.953	0.974
Adj. R^2	–	0.923	0.680	0.921	0.956
Log likelihood	–	–74.628	–96.344	–73.898	–72.174
AIC	–	6.433	7.525	6.531	6.398
LR index (Pseudo-R^2)	–	0.742	0.701	0.744	0.750

Notes
Significant: *** 0.01; ** 0.05; * 0.10; ns not significant.

Notes

1 For a conspicuous exception, see Gurr (1993).
2 Apart from that, repressive policies show broad heterogeneity (see Reinares 1998: chap. 4; Hoffman and Morrison-Taw 1999).
3 Although my term 'responsiveness' is similar to Gurr's (1993) 'accommodation', the latter ought not to be confused with Lijphart's term.
4 See, for instance, the influential collection directed by O'Donell and Schmitter (1986), which gave birth to the 'transitologist' school; a conspicuous exception is the production of Linz (especially 1978). It is ironic that, having Spain been a favourite or 'flagship case' of those studies, the question of its national integration has been overlooked (in this vein, see also Stepan 1998; Skalnik-Leff 1999).
5 In addition, Saideman et al. (2002) found a sort of honeymoon effect by which younger democracies are less prone to ethnic conflict than the older ones. However, Hegre et al. (2001) found the opposite effect, in which transitions to democracy are prone to violence. This agrees with Reinares (1996) and Snyder (2000), who argue that strategies of provocation are particularly likely to occur in newly democratising but institutionally weak regimes.
6 Some authors prefer to count the frequency of terrorist activity (usually, attacks). By and large, however, mass psychological impact of a murder is much more intense than other actions within the terrorist repertoire.
7 Apart from that, any attempt at weighing qualitatively the murders could turn out controversial (cf. Sánchez-Cuenca 2001: 180–1). The data on victims draw from police sources.
8 According to former social-democrat Spanish minister Professor Ernest Lluch, the first homicide occurred in 1961, when a baby died in an explosion of a device placed at a train stop. ETA, who shows off the death of a tortured policeman in 1969 as their first intentional murder, has not confirmed that information. Two policemen died in 1968 as a result of a non-planned skirmish.
9 The algorithm is as follows: (Average Basque Regional Proportion of Public Spending × [(Regional Budget × 100)/Total Regional Budgets])/Proportion of Basque Population upon Spanish Population. I have drawn the figures of public spending of the Basque Autonomous Community from the yearly calculations of the Ministry of Economy and Finance (MEH 1980–2001). I am grateful to Professor José-María Mella and to Librarian Mrs Manuela Gómez, from the Universidad Autónoma de Madrid, for helping me to access this data.
10 The Freedom House index of political freedoms ranges from 1 (high political freedom) to 7 (low political freedom).
11 The Polity2 index ranges from −10 (high autocracy) to +10 (high democracy).
12 The cease-fire in 1998 and 1999 has been operationalised with scores 0.25 and 0.75, respectively.
13 I consider social reintegration within the repression dimension since it corresponds to the administration of force – however, in this case, a moderation of its use could also be interpreted as a responsive policy. The data on detentions, imprisonments and social reintegration draw from Domínguez-Iribarren (1999; personal communication for updating), except for detentions since 2001, which are taken from the newspaper El País.
14 The dummy Bidart scores 0 till 1991 and 1 since 1992, hence modelling an 'abrupt-permanent' effect (McCleary and Hay 1980: chap. 4).
15 The handled data series on social reintegration comprises 102 reinsertions, plus ten amnesties conceded in 1990, as I do not have the data for when the remaining reinsertions and amnesties were produced. For an alternative view on the effect of reinsertion, cf. Sánchez-Cuenca (2001).

16 However, Reinares (1996, 1998; Jaime-Jiménez and Reinares 1999) has also suggested that the main goal of the GAL was indeed 'pressing the French authorities to put an end to the sanctuary', what actually happened after a few years of their activity.
17 Indeed, there were many contacts during 1987 and 1988 as well, but accompanied with both murders and arrests (Sánchez-Cuenca 2001). The dummy variable scores 1 in 1989.
18 But cf. Sánchez-Cuenca (2001).
19 It should be clear, though, that this is not stepwise analysis.
20 The same models were also tested with Ordinary Least Squares regression, which yielded robust results.
21 The fact that many murders of 1987 were done by means of car bombs lends further credence to the hypothesis that the decrease of murders in 1989 was produced by insurgent weakness rather than by the talks of Algiers.
22 Peaceful mobilisation against terrorism tends to be useful in several ways. In some contexts, however, these actions can be useless, or even counterproductive. In a society divided into hermetic blocks, mobilisation of an opposed group can plausibly encourage insistence on and entrenchment of their own positions to counterbalance that mobilisation. Despite this, I agree that collective action increases the costs for those attracted to extremism, while helping organise the collective action, both coordinative and cooperative, of those harmed by violence and its many consequences.
23 For the attitudes, see Euskobarómetro (2006).

References

Aja, E. (1999) *El Estado autonómico: federalismo y hechos diferenciales*, Madrid: Alianza Editorial.

Almond, G.A. and Verba, S. (1963) *The Civic Culture*, Princeton, NJ: Princeton University Press.

Bloom, W. (1990) *Personal Identity, National Identity and International Relations* Cambridge: Cambridge University Press.

Boix, C. and Posner, D.N. (1998) 'Social capital: explaining its origins and effects on government performance', *British Journal of Political Science* 28: 686–93.

Dahl, R.A. (1971) *Polyarchy: Participation and Opposition*, New Haven, CN: Yale University.

Dalton, R.J. (1996) *Citizen Politics in Western Democracies: Public Opinion and Political Parties*, Chatham, NJ: Chatham House.

Domínguez-Iribarren, F. (1999) *¿El final de ETA? De la negociación a la tregua*, Madrid: Taurus.

Euskobarómetro (2006) www.ehu.es/cpvweb/pags_directas/euskobarometroFR.html (last access, 12 June 2006).

Funes, M.-J. (1998) 'Social responses to political violence in the Basque Country: peace movements and their audience', *The Journal of Conflict Resolution* 42(4): 493–510.

Gurr, T.R. (1993) *Minorities At Risk: A Global View of Ethnopolitical Conflicts*, Washington, DC: US Institute of Peace.

Gurr, T.R. and Moore, W.H. (1997) 'Ethnopolitical rebellion: a cross-sectional analysis of the 1980s with risk assessments for the 1990s', *American Journal of Political Science* 41(4): 1079–103.

Hegre, H., Ellingsen, T., Gates, S. and Gleditsch, N.P. (2001) 'Toward a democratic civil peace? Democracy, political change, and civil war, 1816–1992, *American Political Science Review* 95(1): 33–48.
Hoffman, B. and Morrison-Taw, J. (1999) 'A strategic framework for countering terrorism', in F. Reinares (ed.) *European Democracies Against Terrorism: Governmental Policies and Intergovernmental Cooperation*, Aldershot: Asghate.
Horowitz, D.D. (1985) *Ethnic Groups in Conflict*, Berkeley, CA: University of California Press.
Jaime-Jiménez, O. (2002) *Policía, terrorismo y cambio político en España, 1976–1996*. Valencia: Tirant lo Blanch.
Jaime-Jiménez, O. and Reinares, F. (1999) 'Countering terrorism in a new democracy: the case of Spain', in F. Reinares (ed.) *European Democracies Against Terrorism: Governmental Policies and Intergovernmental Cooperation*, Aldershot: Ashgate.
Jar-Couselo, G. (1995) *Modelo policial español y policías autónomas*, Madrid: Dykinson.
Lijphart, A. (1984) *Democracies: Patterns of Majoritarian and Consensus Government in Twenty-one Countries*, New Haven, CN: Yale University Press.
Lijphart, A. (1999) *Patterns of Democracy: Government Forms and Performance in Thirty-six Countries*, New Haven, CN: Yale University Press.
Linz, J.J. (1978) *Breakdown of Democratic Regimes*, Baltimore, MD: Johns Hopkins University.
Linz, J.J. (1993) 'State building and nation building', *European Review* I(4): 355–69.
Linz, J.J., Gómez-Reino, M., Orizo, F. and Vila, D. (1986) *Conflicto en Euskadi*, Madrid: Espasa Calpe.
Llera, F.J. (1994) *Los vascos y la política*, Bilbao: Universidad del País Vasco.
Mansvelt-Beck, J. (2005) *Territory and Terror: Conflicting Nationalisms in the Basque Country*, London: Routledge.
MAP (1997) Estudio sobre reparto del gasto público en 1997 entre los distintos niveles de administración, Madrid: Ministerio de Administraciones Públicas. Typescript (November).
MAP (2002) Estimación del reparto del gasto público entre los subsectores de administraciones públicas (1982–2002), Madrid: Ministerio de Administraciones Públicas. Typescript (September).
Martínez-Herrera, E. (2002a) 'From nation-building to building identification with political communities. Consequences of political decentralisation in Spain, the Basque Country, Catalonia and Galicia, 1978–2001', *European Journal of Political Research* 41(4): 421–53.
Martínez-Herrera, E. (2002b) 'Nationalist extremism and outcomes of state policies in the Basque Country, 1969–2001', *International Journal on Multicultural Societies* 4(1): 17–41 www.unesco.org/most/vl4n1martinez.pdf.
Mata, J.M. (1993) *El nacionalismo vasco radical. Discurso, organización y expresiones*, Bilbao: Universidad del País Vasco.
McCleary, R. and Hay, R.A. (1980) *Applied Time Series Analysis for the Social Sciences*, Beverly Hills, CA: Sage.
MEH (1980–2001) *Cuentas de las administraciones públicas* (21 vols), Madrid: Intervención General de la Administración del Estado (Ministerio de Economía y Hacienda).
Moreno, L. (2001) *The Federalisation of Spain*, London: Frank Cass.
O'Donnell, G. and Schmitter, P.C. (eds) (1986) *Transitions from Authoritarian Rule* (4 vols) Baltimore, MD: Johns Hopkins University.

Pérez-Díaz, V. (1993) *La primacía de la sociedad civil*, Madrid: Alianza Editorial.
Reinares, F. (1996) 'The political conditioning of collective violence: regime change and insurgent terrorism in Spain', *Research on Democracy and Society*, Vol. 3: 297–326.
Reinares, F. (1998) *Terrorismo y antiterrorismo*, Barcelona: Paidós.
Reinares, F. (2001) *Patriotas de la muerte. Quiénes han militado en ETA y por qué*, Madrid: Taurus.
Roeder, P. (1999) 'Peoples and states after 1989: the political costs of incomplete national revolutions', *Slavic Review* 58: (4) 854–83.
Rustow, D.A. (1970) 'Transitions to democracy. Toward a dynamic model', *Comparative Politics* 2: (3) 337–63.
Saideman, S.M., Lanoue, D.J., Campenni, M. and Stanton, S. (2002) 'Democratization, political institutions, and ethnic conflict. A pooled time-series analysis, 1985–1998', *Comparative Political Studies* 35(1): 103–29.
Sánchez-Cuenca, I. (2001) *ETA contra el Estado. Las estrategias del terrorismo*. Barcelona: Tusquets.
Saward, M. (1998) *The Terms of Democracy*, Cambridge and Oxford: Polity Press.
Skalnik-Leff, C. (1999) 'Democratization and disintegration in multinational states. The breakup of the communist federations', *World Politics* 51: 205–35.
Snyder, J.L. (2000) *From Voting to Violence: Democratization and Nationalist Conflict*, New York: Norton.
Stepan, A. (1998) 'Modern multinational democracies: transcending a Gellnerian oxymoron', in J. Hall (ed.) *The State of the Nation: Ernest Gellner and the Theory of Nationalism*, Cambridge: Cambridge University Press, pp. 219–39.
Stepan, A. (2001) 'Toward a new comparative politics of federalism, (multi)nationalism, and democracy: beyond Rikerian federalism', in A. Stepan, *Arguing Comparative Politics*, Oxford: Oxford University Press, pp. 315–61.
Studenmund, A.H. (1997) *Using Econometrics: A Practical Guide*, Reading, MA: Addison-Wesley.
Tarrow, S. (1994) *Power in Movement*, Cambridge: Cambridge University Press.
Unzueta, P. (1994) 'Las tres provocaciones de ETA', in J. Aranzadi, J. Juarista and P. Unzueta (eds) *Auto de terminación*, Madrid: El País-Aguilar, pp. 245–9.

7 Political marginalization and economic exclusion in the making of insurgencies in Sudan

Aleksi Ylönen

Introduction

War in Sudan is often portrayed as a conflict between the Arab Muslim north, and the African Christian and Animist south. However, although this might provide politicians rhetoric for the social justification of violence, it does not adequately explain the role of political and economic factors contributing to the emergence of insurgencies. When attempting to discover the causes of civil war in Sudan, it is essential that we consider the roots of culturally and regionally imposed political marginalization and its economic consequences leading to periphery grievances.

Much of the recent scholarship on civil conflict has been influenced by the work of Paul Collier and Anke Hoeffler, who argue that the emergence of civil wars is due to economic agendas and in particular finds rebel economic opportunity an essential factor leading to civil war. On the other hand, Collier and Hoeffler argue that objective grievances, such as inequality, political rights, ethnic polarization and religious fractionalization have only marginal explanatory power (Collier and Hoeffler, 2001).

The Collier–Hoeffler thesis is often applied to Africa in order to explain the causes of insurgencies in states such as Angola, Liberia or Sierra Leone (Collier, 2003). However, in the case of Sudan, it lacks explanatory power for two principal reasons, which are both related to its conceptual emphasis. First, Collier and Hoeffler disregard the economic implications of the concentration of political power to one group, which is common in Africa. Particularly in the case of Sudan, the Collier–Hoeffler framework's shortcomings arise from its inability to explain the culturally defined political marginalization and economic exclusion or dispossession that has group-based and regional economic effects. Second, by concentrating on rebel opportunity and therefore placing the responsibility for the insurgencies with the anti-state actors, the Collier–Hoeffler framework disregards the government's role in the emergence of civil violence, which in the case of Sudan is essential in explaining the emergence of conflict. As a result, Collier and Hoeffler's way of interpreting insurgencies through rebel economic opportunity overrides other factors that may be appropriate in explaining civil wars.

In this chapter I suggest that rather than attempting to understand the origins of Sudanese insurgencies through the Collier–Hoeffler framework, the three major rebellions in the Sudan's periphery should be explained through an analysis that centers on culturally defined political marginalization and its economic effects in the peripheral regions. I further argue that principally it has been the national governments' repressive policies rather than the rebel opportunity that has resulted in violent responses.

The chapter is organized in the following manner. The next section reviews the basic Collier–Hoeffler literature and some of its shortcomings. The section after that introduces the theoretical basis used in this chapter to understand the Sudanese insurgencies. The three following sections deal with the emergence of conflict in the south in the 1950s, again in the 1980s, and the escalation of conflict in Darfur, respectively. Finally, the last section concludes.

The Collier–Hoeffler framework: economic agendas and civil war

An increasing emphasis in the literature on civil wars on economic agendas as causes of internal conflict has resulted in a polarization of the study along the greed-versus-grievance debate. This emerged as a result of the inability of the prevailing classic arguments, such as ancient hatreds or failed states, to adequately explain economic imperatives that are considered increasingly important to the formation and evolution of contemporary internal conflicts (Kaldor, 1999). Although the overwhelming prevalence of the emphasis on economic agendas' in today's civil war literature seems novel, Collier and Hoeffler do in fact have precursors in the literature. Tilly (1990) has demonstrated the historical importance of economic incentives to wage war and Grossman (1991, 1999) has described rebellion as rational behavior that generates profits from looting. Yet, the importance of openly economic motivations in today's civil wars has reinforced the focus on economic agendas, and the political economy perspective on civil conflict has emerged as a popular approach.

The foundation for the greed-versus-grievance debate was laid by a number of influential articles by Paul Collier and Anke Hoeffler on economic causes of civil conflict. In their first significant study of civil conflict in 99 countries, Collier and Hoeffler (1998) concluded that higher per capita income reduces the risk of civil war due to the high opportunity cost of rebellion. They also found that the existence of natural resources in low-income states together with a large and dually polarized population increases the risk of civil war. The conclusions in Collier (2000a) added that the arguments regarding civil war onset that are founded on grievances lack explanatory power. Thus, individual inequality has no significant effect on the onset of civil war, political repression gives only confusing results, and ethnic and religious divisions lower the risk for civil war. Therefore, Collier and

Hoeffler argue that financial viability of rebel organizations through lootable primary commodities and diaspora funding are the most important determinants of the emergence of civil war.

These arguments have not gone uncontested. Reno suggests that 'Collier and Hoeffler's claim that ethnic and religious diversity and tensions "play surprisingly unimportant" roles in causing conflicts is more controversial' and suggests that 'greed and grievance can play variable role in this process ... [while] ... Explaining these variations requires an analytical framework that has some contact with the world of politics and can deal with complexity' (2004: 4, 22). Indeed, some authors have found grievances more significant in the civil war onset than Collier and Hoeffler (Nafziger and Auvinen, 2002; Reynal-Querol, 2002; Easterly, 2002). In addition, the Collier–Hoeffler framework has provoked a growing body of literature that has criticized its methodology, proxies, and the greed-versus-grievance dichotomy (Gomes Porto, 2002; Humphreys, 2003; Keen, 2001).

Collier and Hoeffler have since made an effort to modify their hypothesis in order to better incorporate grievances to the framework. Collier presented an initial moderation of his position by suggesting that greed may be complemented by grievance:

> greed may need to incite grievance. Thus, grievance and greed may be necessary for sustained rebellion: grievance may enable rebel organization to grow to the point at which it is viable as a predator; greed may sustain the organization once it has reached this point.
>
> (Collier 2000b: 852)

Finally in 2001, the Collier and Hoeffler emphasis evolved from greed to rebel opportunity. According to their study of civil wars over the 1960–1999 period, economic opportunity is vital in explaining the emergence and sustenance of rebel organizations seeking or not seeking profit. However, the authors recognize that rebel grievances have a role to play even if they 'may be substantially disconnected from the large social concerns of inequality, political rights, and ethnic or religious identity', which Collier and Hoeffler consider the main indicators of grievances (Collier and Hoeffler, 2001: 17).

Overall, the Collier–Hoeffler tradition portrays civil war formation as an economic process with grievances playing only minimal or insignificant role. In addition, it attributes the emergence of conflict to the rebel opportunity. This, I argue, obscures the responsibility of the government in provoking violent response. In Sudan, for example, repressive government policies, rather than rebel economic opportunity, seem to have played a principal role in promoting conflict. Hence, the Collier–Hoeffler thesis does not provide adequate tools to explain the formation of insurgencies in Sudan. In contrast, the following section introduces a framework founded upon historical narrative that considers the political and economic factors in an attempt to explain the emergence of rebellion in Sudan's periphery.

Theoretical framework: political power, economic exclusion, and internal conflict

Mainstream economic theory has difficulty explaining civil conflict. The main reason is that this body of theory was never intended to be used for this purpose. Therefore, an interdisciplinary investigation that includes explanations from political and historical spheres may enrich the economic analysis of civil wars. In the case of Sudan, the Collier–Hoeffler framework, designed to point out the causes of civil conflict, suffers from two principal shortcomings: its disregard of political power relationships and its neglect of opportunism and provocation on the part of the government.

First, in order to examine the origin of conflicts in Sudan it is essential to understand the relationship between the concentration of political power exclusively to one societal group and its economic consequences. Evidence for this is found mainly in historical narratives that point out both the center-periphery relationship based on violent extraction of resources in the nineteenth century and the handing over of political power exclusively to the northern elite at the end of British colonialism. The concentration of political power in one group (associated with the North) has enabled it to impose itself over the periphery and ensured the continuing political marginalization of the local populations. It has been largely justified through the two building blocks of the Arab–Muslim national identity that has enabled the northern elite to politically and economically exclude the peripheral groups that do not fulfill these two prerequisites. According to Keen (1997) this means that they are 'fair game' for violence, exploitation, and expropriation.

As a result of political marginalization, the peripheral populations have been excluded from the prospects of regional economic development and personal enrichment through political positions. This has created the preconditions for violence in the face of the economic prosperity of the northern riverain Sudan, which has long enjoyed the wealth extracted from the periphery through oppressive and at times violent government policies.

Second, due to its focus on the rebels' economic incentives to make war, the Collier–Hoeffler framework disregards the opportunism by which the government could oppress the periphery in order to exploit its natural resources. Historically, this has in Sudan resulted in violent response and resistance in the periphery, and, as this chapter argues, two southern rebellions and the current insurgency in Darfur. Hence, the combination of the continued oppression of the periphery that has laid preconditions for violent response, and the short-term events that have triggered it, has critically contributed to the insurgencies in Sudan. Therefore, rather than exclusively being manifested in rebel economic opportunity, the main motivation for the insurgencies in Sudan lies largely in attempts to escape the state's oppressive policies that have resulted in culturally and regionally imposed political marginalization. In other words, the loss of hope of economic well-being caused by the government's oppressive policies is principally behind the violent response in the Sudanese periphery.

As suggested above, both long-term continuities and short-term events need to be considered when we examine the onset of civil conflict in Sudan. For instance, it is essential to understand the violent history of northern domination and the fears of its resumption, while it is equally important to consider the Sudanese political environment and its relation to the oppressive government policies. Finally, we also need to examine the immediate factors that led to the outbreak of violent resistance.

Towards the first southern rebellion

Historical domination of the south

Among the most intensive periods of violent exploitation of the south took place during the Turco-Egyptian imperial rule in the nineteenth century, when the region's resources were extracted in order to feed the Egyptian economy and the northern riverain Sudan, the latter of which developed as the administrative and economic center of the colony (Hassan, 2000). Among the most important products extracted from the south were slaves, ivory, and livestock (Hassan, 2000; Sconyers, 1976). However, it was the slave raiding and the establishment of the Arab–Muslim dominated social hierarchy in which black Africans occupy the lowest societal position that had the most severe impact on ethnic relations in post-colonial Sudan. For instance, Deng argues that

> Northern prejudices against the South are pervasive and easily revealed in their collective identification of the Negro as an inferior race, the traditional source for the slave. While the Arabs have had the power to assert their political dominance and material superiority, southerners deeply despise them and look down on them. This mutual disdain, coupled with geographical and territorial separation, makes coexistence extremely difficult.
>
> (Deng 1995: 488)

Johnson further suggests that, 'Following a pattern first begun in the nineteenth century, religion and race are increasingly determining who has access to the greatest economic opportunities through financing, government leases and concessions, and use and control of the work force' (2002: 3). It is therefore necessary to view the emergence of the southern rebellion in the context of a history of violent exploitation and the establishment of the social hierarchy that leads to the political and economic marginalization of the southerners.

Political marginalization in the 1940s and its economic implications

In a number of African states the elite's control of national politics is essential for its economic prosperity. Sudan is no exception since the political power is highly concentrated in the northern Arab–Muslim elite, which enables this group to dominate the national political economy (Woodward, 2002). This is directly linked to the impoverishment of other populations and regions that are largely economically excluded. As a result, relative regional differences in economic development have emerged between the center and the periphery. For instance, during the Anglo-Egyptian Condominium the northern riverain Sudan enjoyed larger-scale economic and educational development than the south (Johnson, 2003; Sconyers, 1976).

The British colonial authorities separated northern and southern Sudan in the 1920s through 'Closed Door Ordinances', aspiring to annex the south later to British East Africa (Sconyers, 1976: 59). Hence, diverging development and educational policies were adopted. However, after the emergence of northern nationalism, the educated Arab–Muslim elite increasingly pressured the British to annex the south to the future independent Sudan. As a result, the British became gradually more convinced that Sudan should be unified and administered from the northern riverain region that they had endowed with the greatest agricultural and educational development. The initiation of the unification process had largely to do with doubts about the economic and political ability of the south to stand on its own and with Arabic criticism of the 'Closed Door' policy.

The British initiated the process of transformation of Sudan toward self-rule according to the 1946 Sudan Administrative Conference (SAC) decision that led to formal administrative unification of the north and the south without southern consent (de Chand, 2000). Consequently, they began replacing the colonial officials and civil servants with Sudanese citizens. However, in the process, the northerners were overwhelmingly favored over the peripheral groups. Taisier and Matthews (1999) point out that out of 800 administrative posts opened up, the British granted only six junior level positions to the southerners, arguing that the northerners held better educational competency along with their Arabic language advantage.

The SAC reopened the south to northern influence and dominance as the better educated northerners were able to serve as officials in the south and the northern merchants were able to return to the south due to the abolition of restrictions on trade and migration (Markakis, 1998). In addition, the official administrative language of the south was changed from English into Arabic, thereby facilitating access for northerners to official positions in the south (de Chand, 2000).

The southern leaders questioned the unification process and voiced their fears of renewed northern domination. As a result, the 1947 Juba Conference was organized to hear their concerns. In Juba the southern representatives were guaranteed that the northern domination would not resume within unified Sudan. Although they accepted the unification that was already in progress due to the SAC decision, which was taken without southern participation, the southern leaders argued that the salary gap between the north and the south was unjustifiable and divided the communities, while religious discrimination should be stopped and southern rights secured (Marwood, 1947; de Chand, 2000).

In 1948, the Sudan National Legislative Assembly (NLA) was established in order to guide the unified Sudan to self-rule. Similarly to the political marginalization of the southerners in the local level, the 'Sudanization' process resulted in insignificant southern political participation nationally. Thirteen southerners were picked to symbolically represent the region in the NLA, although control of the assembly was placed firmly in the hands of the northern elite. This, of course, led to the political exclusion of the south and the demise of hopes for individual prosperity and regional economic development.

Finally, the 1953 Cairo Conference set the timetable for independence again without southern consent (de Chand, 2000). Rather, the representatives of the northern elite negotiated with the British and the Egyptians, concluding that Sudan was to achieve self-determination within a three-year transitional period during which 'Sudanization' of the public administration was to be completed and foreign troops withdrawn.

The outbreak of the first rebellion

The first southern rebellion against this pattern of northern domination broke out in 1955. The specific short-term effects that led to the violent response and the escalation of hostilities included the first parliamentary elections that gave control of the Sudanese government to the northern elite, the mutiny of the southern troops, and the violent government response to put down the revolt.

The first parliamentary elections in 1954 resulted in an overwhelming victory of the northern political parties. The elections handed complete control of the political scene to the northern elite, which has dominated national government and Sudanese politics ever since. In contrast, the southerners perceived themselves deprived from effective political representation at both the local and the national level. In addition, they found the new language policy threatening because the replacement of English with Arabic as the administrative language of the south reflected an effort to ensure the northern domination. Johnson (2003) points out that,

> There was thus widespread discontent in the South as a result of the outcome of the 1954 elections and the Sudanization process. The rapid increase of Northerners in the South as administrators, senior officers in the army and police, teachers in government schools and as merchants, increased Southern fears of Northern domination and colonization.

The violence sparked in August 1955 in the southern city of Torit, where the army's Southern Equatoria Corps (SEC) mutinied because of rumors that they would be disarmed or transferred to the north under the leadership of northern officers (Markakis, 1998; ICG, 2002). Government forces experienced difficulty suppressing the revolt and in the confrontations between the army and the rebellious troops at least 300 people were killed, of whom 261 were northerners (Markakis, 1998; O'Ballance, 1977). However, when the British assured they would arbitrate the trials and reconsider the order to be transferred to the north, some mutineers laid down their arms, and were either instantly executed for sedition or imprisoned for life (de Chand, 2000). Although the government was able to end the mutiny in this way, many of the remaining mutineers escaped to the bush and organized military and political opposition against the government. Finally, they found sanctuary in the southern borderlands and later in neighboring Ethiopia and Uganda, which grew sympathetic to the rebel cause.

Political marginalization in the making of the first southern rebellion

It is essential to recognize the link between political control and economic prosperity in the emergence of Sudan's first civil war. The political marginalization of the south in the preparation of Sudan for self-rule led to the shattering of hope for increasing prosperity and regional economic development. Instead, it encouraged fears of renewed northern domination that had traditionally resulted in the violent extraction of southern resources. The repression also had a cultural dimension, which specifically targeted periphery populations that did not consider themselves Arab–Muslim. According to Deng, 'For the South ... independence was to prove merely a change of outside masters, with the northerners taking over from the British and defining the nation in accordance with the symbols of their Arabic-Islamic identity' (Deng, 1995: 484).

This culturally and regionally oriented political marginalization largely excluded the southerners from local and national politics. As a result, the south's educated elite along with the general population was almost entirely excluded from the economic benefits of the administrative positions, often considered a way to political influence, financial wealth, and status. Since there was no effective southern representation at the national level that could compete with the northern interests, it was not possible to divert national resources to promote economic development in the south. Rather, according to the northern interests the south was to adhere to its traditional role as the region that provided resources to fuel the northern economy. In practice, the region was condemned to enduring poverty.

The fears of renewed northern domination and the shattering of the southern elite's dream of economic development and personal enrichment created the preconditions for the first rebellion. In 1954, they were linked to short-term events such as the parliamentary elections, the end of the 'Sudanization' process, and the implementation of Arabic as the official administrative language in the south. All these measures further angered the southerners. Finally, it was the SEC mutiny that triggered the violence. Although a moderate government response to end the revolt might have prevented the insurgency, it was the violence used to end the mutiny that forced the remnants of the mutineers to flee to the bush. Also, the violent policies of the later governments inspired further resistance and contributed to the increased support for the rebellion (O'Ballance, 1977).

There is no evidence that the post-colonial conflict in Sudan materialized exclusively due to rebel economic opportunity to loot natural resources or due to Diaspora financing. Instead, the political marginalization within the unified Sudan and the shattered dream of economic development, linked with the resumed Arab–Muslim domination, are essential in explaining the emergence of the first southern rebellion. It is also plausible to argue that the rebellion took place in circumstances of poverty and deprivation, feeding on the perceived differences between south and north. This was manifested not only in the differences in cultural characteristics but also in a distinct socioeconomic and political group status (Ylönen, 2004).

The emergence of the second southern insurgency

Government economic opportunism and political exclusion of the south

The origins of the second large-scale insurgency in the south are principally attributed to the Nimeiri regime's effort to sustain its political power. This was undertaken through the renewed political marginalization of the south to deprive it from its natural resources for the benefit of the government.

Due to the poor results of the socialist economy experimentation and the failed attempt to convert Sudan into a regional 'breadbasket', the Nimeiri regime found itself in deep economic problems that got worse as the 1970s wore on (Kontos, 1991). The discovery of oil in the south in the late 1970s suddenly provided an opportunity to escape the economic downturn and the resulting popular discontent (Melvill, 2002). Still, there was a problem in accessing the oil fields since they were located in the south, which had been granted a limited autonomy as part of the Addis Ababa Peace Agreement in 1972, which had ended the first rebellion.

The location of the oil fields near to the northern border of the south added to the government incentive to violate the Addis Ababa conditions in order to gain control of the oil territory. However, since the agreement gave the south some financial autonomy and the right to collect all taxes due to the central government from industrial, commercial and agricultural ventures in the south, the government would not have had the freedom to exploit the oil (Alier, 1990).

In an attempt to gain unrestricted access to the southern petroleum reserves, the Nimeiri regime designed policies to politically marginalize the south and deprive it of the prospects of oil revenue. This was undertaken in three principal manners. First, Nimeiri intervened politically by suspending the southern regional assembly several times in the late 1970s and early 1980s while gradually pushing southern representation out of the central government (Markakis, 1998). Second, the regime began replacing southern troops near the oil fields with northern army units in order to take territorial control of the region. Third, it redrew the provincial boundaries in order to carve out the oil region from the southern territory, and established a new Unity Province in an effort to remove the jurisdiction of the petroleum fields from the south (Melvill, 2002).

Once the first oil licensing contracts were signed, Nimeiri pocketed the resulting revenues rather than handing them over to the southern regional government, which was legitimately to administer them. In addition, the regime initiated plans to build a pipeline from the oil fields to Port Sudan, in order to facilitate exportation of the crude oil. Other plans were made to construct an oil refinery. The location of the future refinery became an important issue because of its impact on regional development. The southerners argued that it made sense to build it in proximity to the oil fields, while the government preferred to concentrate all economic ventures in the Nile River valley. In the end, the refinery was built in the north and the southerners felt that they had again been economically deprived (Johnson, 2003).

Finally, in order to secure the extraction of resources from the south through further political reforms, in June 1983 Nimeiri partitioned the region along ethnic lines so as to diminish its resistance and political power. As a result, the south was divided into its three original provinces that had been established during the colonial period in an attempt to reduce the regional political influence of the south's largest Dinka ethnic group (Lesch, 1998; Markakis, 1998).

Although it was principally the oil reserves that fueled the regime's aspirations to violate the Addis Ababa peace conditions, another controversial project to divert southern water resources was planned in the early 1970s. Propelled by Nimeiri's attempt to improve relations with Egypt, the construction of the Jonglei canal faced some resistance especially among the southern population (Lesch, 1991; Johnson, 2003). Although the southern regional government hesitantly accepted the project, some perceived it as yet another effort to extract southern resources for northern development without recompense (Alier, 1990; Garang, 1987).

Northern political maneuvering and its impact on the south

The Nimeiri regime faced increasing opposition during the 1970s not only due to its poor management of the national economy, but also because of the discontent of the northern political opposition and especially the Islamists that were growing in political influence. The opposition was critical of the Addis Ababa peace agreement, which was viewed negatively in conservative circles and considered a government defeat. However, soon after the peace treaty, Nimeiri put forward a program to appease the dissatisfied northern groups by reaffirming Islam's central position in Sudan, recognizing Islamic law, *Sharia*, as the source of all legislation, offering conservative Islamists high posts in the state apparatus, and releasing political prisoners and members of the Islamic religious orders (Johnson, 2003).

Despite his tenacious efforts to save the regime, it soon became apparent that Nimeiri was unable to appease the northern factions through concessions. As a result, the elements of the northern elite that had been sidelined after the 1969 Nimeiri coup organized in exile. In July 1976, backed by Libya and a year after another failed coup, they unsuccessfully attempted to overthrow the Nimeiri regime (Johnson, 2003).

After surviving both attempts by nothern forces to depose him, Nimeiri became convinced of the need to secure his political support and preserve political power by courting the northern opposition factions. Largely for this reason, the regime entered a period of 'National Reconciliation', which led to concessions to the northern opposition through the appointment of several opposition leaders to government positions (ICG, 2002). As a result, the political scene began to turn increasingly Islamist, leading in the late 1970s to the sidelining of the small southern representation in the national government.

Gradually the growing power of the Islamist opposition resulted in demands for the regime to review security, border trade, language, culture, and the religious provisions of the Addis Ababa agreement (Alier, 1990). In order to appease the opposition, Nimeiri allowed the first elections for the People's Assembly under his regime to take place in order to demonstrate that the regime enjoyed popular support. According to the 'National Reconciliation' policy, the northern Umma, the Democratic Unionist Party, and the Muslim Brotherhood were the only recognized non-government parties allowed to nominate candidates.

The 1978 elections resulted in the independents gaining almost half the parliamentary seats, while the political forces of the regime won a small majority. The poor election results demonstrated the increasingly corrupt regime's declining ability to support official candidates and the popular discontent it faced. With the regime's political power gradually weakening due to corruption and the growing support of the opposition, Nimeiri adopted an absolutist leadership position. He gave the State Security Organization, the secret police force, a free hand to imprison thousands of opponents and made sure to remove and replace any minister or military officer who was suspected of building a personal power base (LOC, 1991).

After initial concessions to the Islamic organizations, and due to their growing power, Nimeiri felt obligated to appoint Muslim Brotherhood leader Hassan Turabi as Attorney General in 1983. This reflected the crystallization of the infiltration of the Muslim Brothers in the state apparatus and the military, which Turabi had organized through recruitment of young men from civil service, universities, and the military to service the organization that later converted to the National Islamic Front (NIF) (Melvill, 2002). The Muslim Brothers also gained growing influence in the Sudanese banking sector, securing an economic base and widening their influence (Woodward, 2002).

Finally, after assuming the position of Attorney General, Turabi imposed Islamic law as the basis of state law, marginalizing the peripheral populations that did not identify with Islam. This was particularly the case of the predominantly Animist and Christian south, which perceived the imposition of *Sharia* not only as a form of renewed northern domination but also as a violation of the Addis Ababa conditions that were to protect the south against Islamization.

Mutiny and the second southern insurgency

Despite the Addis Ababa peace treaty that had ended the major hostilities in the south in 1972, some residual guerilla activity still took place in the south due to some southerners' refusal to accept its conditions (Johnson, 2003). However, after Nimeiri deprived the south of its oil licensing revenue and began tampering with the terms of the Addis Ababa agreement, discontent spread widely among the southern population. While the southern grievances were growing, the possibility of a renewed rebellion became reality. According to the International Crisis Group (2002: 13), 'In January 1983, southern troops of the 105th battalion refused orders to abandon their weapons and be transferred north'. Since Sudanese units had been deployed in Iraq to fight Iran, a fear existed among the southern troops about a possible transfer to the Middle East; in order to leave the south increasingly vulnerable for northern domination (Johnson and Prunier, 1993). First government reaction to end the mutiny was through negotiations but when the half-hearted effort failed, the regime launched an attack to end it.

The government ordered Colonel John Garang, a southerner from the Dinka ethnic group, to put down the mutiny. Garang, however, was unhappy about the resumed northern domination in the form of economic exploitation of southern oil and water resources, as well as in the increasingly Islamic zeal of the Nimeiri government that politically marginalized the south nationally (Garang, 1987). He was also a member of a southern elite that may have been planning violent resistance in the event that northern oppression resumed. Hence, Garang took leadership of the rebellion, aided the mutineers to safety, and inspired other revolts and desertions in the south throughout the rest of the year (Johnson and Prunier, 1993).

Finally, he led the rebels to Ethiopia, where they found a sanctuary and support base. While in Ethiopia, Garang organized the rebels into the Sudan

People's Liberation Army (SPLA) and its political wing the Sudan People's Liberation Movement (SPLM), which denounced Islamic law and hit the government oil installations and the Jonglei canal scheme as their first targets (Garang, 1987).

Political marginalization, economic dispossession, and violent response

As demonstrated by the narrative above, the violent response in the south emerged largely due to the Nimeiri regime's economic opportunism and attempts to preserve its political power. Both infringed on the southern political autonomy dictated by the 1972 Addis Ababa peace agreement. Hence, in the onset of the second Sudanese civil war, government economic and political agendas were overtly related to the oppression of the south and the provocation of violent response. While it is impossible to know if Garang was principally motivated by greed, grievance, or both when taking the leadership of the revolt, the government rather than the insurgents is the principal actor driven by the economic opportunity to illegally dispossess the south of its oil and water resources.

The regime attempts to preserve political power resulting in concessions to the Islamists, followed by political oppression of the south, which also contributed to the insurgency. As a result, culturally and regionally imposed political marginalization was again an important factor. This time it resulted in the loss of hope for southern economic development and prosperity through the dispossession of prospective oil revenues, and in social repression through the imposition of the Islamic law.

In the end, the mutiny triggered the violence. Similarly to the first rebellion, the government again reacted violently to put down the revolt. However, unlike the first rebellion, a prominent figure sent to end the uprising took the leadership of the insurgency. Hence, based on the evidence above it seems that it was principally the mobilization along southern political and economic grievances, rather than the rebel economic opportunity, that led to the violent response and ultimately to the rebellion.

Violence in Darfur

Government regional interests and escalation of traditional conflicts

Violence between ethnic groups in Darfur has traditionally been the norm partly because for centuries between 36 and 90 ethnic groups have competed for basic land and water resources (Idriss, 1999). The population is ethnically composed of two main groups, Arabs and non-Arabs. While the non-Arabs are predominantly black Zurga, mainly sedentary Fur, some Masaleit and the nomadic Zaghawa, the Arabs are principally nomadic, Baggara.

The Baggara are the most recent group to arrive in Darfur in search of pastures on the western fringe lands. While they have at times faced the Zurga in disputes over land and water, most of the traditional struggles have occurred between the Arab communities (Harir, 1994).

The security situation in Darfur deteriorated in the late 1980s as a result of the economic descent of the northern Sudan, regional food scarcity, and the Chad–Libyan conflict, which spilled over to the region. Salih notes,

> The position worsened still further in March 1988 after Libyan troops in the 'Islamic Legion' crossed the Sudanese border and began to use Darfur Province as a base to attack military posts in eastern Chad. Their presence escalated the conflict and resulted in further penetration by Chadian troops into western Sudan.
>
> (Salih, 1990: 220–221)

As a result, the region experienced large-scale violence during which the sedentary, predominantly Zurga, civilian population suffered from armed robberies, killings, and destruction of property. This disrupted the lives of many Fur and resulted in the emergence of a Fur militia. The conflict escalated into an ethnic war through the polarization of identities in which nomadic populations came to be seen as Arabs fighting the sedentary Fur. While the Arab militia burned villages, killed civilians, and looted property, the Fur militia responded with similar actions in order to clear the land of Arab influence (Harir, 1994).

The erosion of traditional stability and the escalation of unprecedented violence rendered traditional methods insufficient to resolve the disputes. It took a great effort by the mediators to get the warring parties to the negotiation table in May 1989 with the two parties accusing each other of racism. After all, during the course of the conflict, the motivations for violence had included territorial conquest, racial prejudices, and political subjugation (Harir, 1994).

The Fur–Arab conflict left its scars on regional ethnic relations at least in the short term. Therefore, the Fur, in particular, have been sympathetic to the SPLA, and their tribal militias have occasionally joined forces with the main southern rebel group (ICG, 2004). The 1991–1992 SPLA–Fur offensive in Darfur resulted in the government counteroffensive that laid the basis for ongoing militia violence in the region throughout the 1990s. Similarly to the Fur–Arab conflict, the Arab militias have since been mobilized through supremacist propaganda and promises of economic benefits from looting the sedentary Zurga communities. Hence, although the Arab militias were created by earlier governments in the mid-1980s, their legacy has endured and the current regime has made the most of their use (HRW, 2004b).

Concerning the recent violence it is important to note that some Baggara, such as the Rezaiqat and the Missairia, served as the government militia, the

Murahaleen, in the 1980s in order to terrorize the southern Dinka populations in the north–south 'Transition Zone' (Salih and Harir, 1994: 193–196). The notorious Janjaweed militia members who are directly responsible for the latest violence in Darfur are predominantly recruited from these Arab communities with the government using the traditional conflicts and counter-insurgency rhetoric as a cover-up for its violent Arabization policy (HRW, 2004a; HRW, 2004b).

Moreover, the most recent escalation of violence in Darfur is intimately linked to the NIF (currently the National Congress Party (NCP)) government policies and its internal quarrels. Since its origins, the NCP has targeted the Sudanese periphery as a region to either be assimilated according to the 'National Salvation' ideology or to be politically and economically sidelined. Its policies have included systematic resource transfer from the periphery to the Arab–Muslim center in order to deprive the peripheral populations of their livelihoods and disrupting their economies in an attempt to control land and labor, or violently to extract goods such as livestock (Johnson, 2002). Furthermore, as the western periphery of Sudan, Darfur has been traditionally deprived of centrally induced economic development, while it has historically been a frontier land submitted to violent taxation (Hassan, 2000; Ylönen, 2004). Consequently, the regional leaders have often been critical of the NCP's exclusivist policies that have favored Darfur's enduring exclusion from national politics and economic development.

In 2000 yet another internal power struggle within the NCP had a politically destabilizing impact on Darfur. In his efforts to rally support to challenge the Bashir presidential hegemony, the Islamist leader Turabi founded the Popular National Congress (PNC) party that has based its support largely in Darfur. Since he found no support from the sidelined traditional northern parties, Turabi reached for the Sudan's African majority for support and claimed that the Islamic Brotherhood in power was deliberately obstructing representatives from the marginalized regions from gaining access to high government positions, while favoring the central riverain Sudanese (ICG, 2004).

Finally, it has become increasingly clear that one of the two main rebel movements that have emerged in Darfur since early 2003, the Justice and Equality Movement (JEM), has been linked to the Islamist movement splinter group, the PNC. Its founder, Khalil Ibrahim, who was a member of the northern elite and a friend of Hassan Turabi, returned to Sudan in 2003 to respond to the Janjaweed atrocities by mobilizing resistance in Darfur. As a result, the PNC, headed by Turabi, has repeatedly justified the rebel cause and sided with them, making the violence in Darfur not only a search for equality and political participation but also a manifestation of the internal power struggle within the Islamist elite that dominates Sudan (ICG, 2004).

Social justification for violence and the politico-economic control

Since an important factor in the promotion of NCP ideology is the Arab–Muslim identity and the supremacist rhetoric promoting Arabism over other ethnicities, its domination of the central government has had repercussions in peripheral regions including Darfur. Hence, similarly to other peripheral populations of Sudan, the African groups in Darfur have been deliberately politically weakened in the face of expanding Arab influence. The latest manifestation has been the escalation of Janjaweed violence against the African populations in order to promote displacement, followed by a settlement of Arab groups on the emptied lands (HRW, 2004b). This has been undertaken by dispossessing the local populations from their economic assets through burning, killing, looting, and enslaving civilians (HRW, 2004a, HRW, 2004c). As a result, some have described the situation in Darfur as genocidal (BBC, 2004).

However, rather than meaningless extermination, the violence in Darfur needs to be understood in the context of government aspirations to control the region politically and economically. Since Darfur, particularly during the current regime, has been a source of political instability in the northern Sudan by aligning itself with the south, supporting Turabi, and demanding political representation and economic development, the NCP government has seized the opportunity to attack the political opposition and intensify its efforts to dominate the region.

The attempts to weaken the 'African' Darfur by enforcing Arab influence in the region dates back to the Arab Gathering in October 1987, during which 23 Darfurian Arab leaders agreed upon the supremacist idea that Arab race created civilization in the region through governance, religion, and language (ICG, 2004). The government backing of the Arab Gathering in the 1980s was an attempt to polarize the ethnicities in Darfur in order to legitimize violence and gain broader political influence and control over productive resources. Since the 1989 coup, the current NCP government has continued the policy of arming Arab militias as part of its political project to advance the Arab–Muslim domination of Sudan (HRW, 2004b).

Periods of heavier violence

The traditional conflicts between nomads and sedentary populations in Darfur took place for the most part through the nomadic seasonal intrusions on the lands of the agriculturalists in order to find pastures for their cattle. However, due to desertification and population expansion, their presence in the area became increasingly permanent, with an influx of small arms in the region adding to the intensity of conflict. These factors contributed to the breakdown of the traditional reconciliation methods. However, it was principally the central government's policy of exploiting the traditional conflicts by political maneuvers and arming Arab militias that led to the escalation of ethnic conflict in Darfur during three particularly intense episodes.

First, the rise of ethnic conflict in Darfur in the 1980s materialized in a struggle for regional political power, and land and water resources between the dominant Fur Ethnic Group and the Arab nomads. This split the group mobilization along an Arab–African divide. It was driven by the Fur attempt to secure the fallow fertile land surrounding the cultivated areas, while the Arab nomads viewed the same land as legitimately available for cattle herding. This bloody episode ended in the accusations that the Fur marginalized Arabs in Darfur in an attempt to drive them out and promote African domination in the regional government, while the Fur accused the Arab groups of racial war that disrupted their livelihoods through looting, burning, and pillaging in an attempt to take over their land (Harir, 1994).

Second, after defeating the joint Fur–SPLA offensive of 1991–1992 in Darfur, the Khartoum regime intensified the armament of tribal militias in Darfur (ICG, 2003). In addition, in its efforts to politically deprive the Fur of their dominant political position and affirm the government power in the region, in 1994 the NCP regime split Darfur into three states dividing the Fur homeland (ICG, 2004). Furthermore, to capitalize on the momentum in the following year in an effort to transfer productive resources for its constituents, the regime redistributed the Masaleit traditional lands in Western Darfur into 13 principalities and allocated five of them to Arab groups, which laid the foundation for the bloody 1996–1997 Masaleit–Arab conflict (ICG, 2004).

Third, the most recent escalation of violence in Darfur materialized in response to the Janjaweed militia violence and the government's empty promises to appease the region. The Sudan Liberation Army (SLA) emerged as the first major rebel movement in February 2003 to respond to the Arab militia violence, demanding an end to political and economic marginalization and to the lack of development in Darfur, as well as a separation of church and state (ICG, 2004). These demands, strikingly similar to those of the SPLA, have later been specified as calls for equitable development, land rights, schools and clinics, and local democracy (de Waal, 2004). Although the SLA was initially founded upon the previously disarmed Fur tribal militia, in 2001 it received an influx of Zaghawa and Masaleit males who wanted an end to the violent repression of all Zurga groups in Darfur. As mentioned above, the JEM soon followed the SLA with similar political agenda, although its links to the Islamist elite are manifested in its leadership and its ambiguous stand on religion and state.

Political marginalization and the intensification of violence

Political marginalization is an essential factor in the escalation of conflict in Darfur in the 1980s and 1990s. Takana (1998) finds that the lack of development efforts, weak government administration and its deliberate destabilizing of traditional local administration systems in order to replace them with Arab dominated centralized administration have contributed to the regional political confusion. It is plausible to think that similar grievances have motivated the response to the violent oppression both in the south and in Darfur. Recently, oil has been found in Darfur, adding to the attraction of the territory not only as a pastureland but also as a highly profitable economic asset, which may have resulted in further government incentives to violently transfer land away from the local sedentary populations to government-controlled groups (Zaman, 2004).

Along with the rest of the Sudanese periphery, Darfur has been largely deprived of participation in national politics and of resources for regional economic development. This has resulted in grievances at the individual and the community level similar to the south. In addition, the government's willingness to use violence for political and economic ends has contributed to the increase of grievances and to the violent response in Darfur. Particularly since the 1989 NCP coup, the regime has attempted to subjugate the region politically and economically. The central government has historically enjoyed only trivial administrative authority in Darfur and the region has often supported the opposition to the national regimes. Since the internal quarrels within the Islamic Brotherhood, the growing instability of the Khartoum regime is partly related to the political scene in Darfur and the constituency it provides for Turabi's aspirations. Hence, the motives for violence have included the disruption of regional politics and advancing Arab interests in Darfur. Second, the NCP policy of systematically stripping peripheral populations of their economic assets, such as land, for the benefit of its constituents and the groups that principally form the Arab militias is partially an effort to extend Arab domination and control over the regional economy.

In sum, as the narrative above demonstrates, similarly to the south, the culturally and regionally imposed political marginalization in Darfur together with its economic consequences is at the heart of the violent opposition to government policies. The government attempt to politically secure itself against the Turabi opposition and its regional economic aspirations are largely behind the escalation of violent repression. As a result, the regional grievances together with the intensification of Arab militia violence triggered the violent response.

Concluding remarks

As in the case of a number of other African states, in Sudan the control of the central state apparatus and the highly concentrated political power guarantee economic prosperity of the groups related to the regime through domination over national resources. This contributes to the highly contested nature of the state and the multiple coups and insurgencies that have occurred in Sudan since its independence. It also provides evidence of the state promotion of violence in order to preserve its domination over the national politics and economic resources. Therefore, the Collier–Hoeffler argument, which claims that insurgencies take place due to rebel opportunity, does not sufficiently explain the emergence of civil conflict in Sudan. Rather, a suitable framework for investigating conflict in the Sudanese periphery should take the form of a historical analysis based on an understanding of political processes and how they are linked to economic incentives. Blaming rebel groups for the violence ignores the culturally imposed political marginalization and its economic consequences, which largely explain the emergence of violent resistance to government policies in Sudan's south and Darfur.

The first southern rebellion emerged in circumstances in which the British annexed the south to the northern Sudan in the preparation for independence. In the process, control of the national politics was handed over exclusively to the northern Arab–Muslim elite, while the southerners were also sidelined regionally. Southerners were deprived of effective political participation and of any hope of economic development and individual prosperity. The political marginalization and its economic effects were accompanied by fears of renewed northern domination and a repetition of the violent extraction of resources that had taken place for most of the nineteenth century. Finally, the violence and the broken promises in the aftermath of the SEC mutiny led to the first southern insurgency.

Government economic opportunism and its efforts to preserve its political power played an important part in the making of the second rebellion in the south. These contributed to the government's tampering with southern autonomy in an effort to politically marginalize the region. The dispossession of the oil and water resources of the south was partly undertaken in an attempt to save the regime from bankruptcy. In a similar vain, political concessions were given to the northern opposition parties in an attempt to water down their incentives for regime change. The impact of the repressive policies imposed on the south was political marginalization, economic dispossession, and cultural repression partly through the extension of the Islamic law to the region. In the end, similarly to the events of 1955, a mutiny in the south resulted in violent government response and a rebellion.

Thirdly, the violence in Darfur has evolved largely in response to persisting political marginalization of its population and government policies that have intentionally aggravated the traditional ethnic cleavages. Since the 1980s, the policies of the successive governments that largely excluded the region from national politics and economic development have resulted in increased grievances. However, it has been primarily the Arab militia devastation that has resulted in the violent response and the increased gap between the 'African' and the 'Arab' Darfurians. The repressive government policies in Darfur are largely due to the threat that Turabi poses to the NCP government. Finally, it may also be that the militia strategy of driving the sedentary groups off their land has not only been supported by the government because it wants to reward the Janjaweed, but because of its willingness to control the oil reserves discovered in the region. This would mean that the attempts to preserve its political power and economic opportunism are at the heart of the oppressive government policies in Darfur. Thus, in general, the main cause of violence in the Sudanese periphery lies in the national government's political and economic opportunism.

References

Alier, A. (1990) *Southern Sudan: Too Many Agreements Dishonoured*, Reading: Ithaca.
BBC (2004) 'US House calls Darfur "genocide"', British Broadcasting Company, July 23, 2004, online at news.bbc.co.uk/2/hi/africa/3918765.stm.
Collier, P. (2000a) 'Doing Well Out of War: An Economic Perspective', in M. Berdal and D.M. Malone (eds) *Greed and Grievance: Economic Agendas in Civil Wars*, Boulder, CO: Lynne Rienner.
Collier, P. (2000b) 'Rebellion as a Quasi-Criminal Activity', *Journal of Conflict Resolution*, 44: 839–853.
Collier, P. (2003) 'Market for Civil War', *Foreign Policy*, May/June.
Collier, P. and Hoeffler, A. (1998) 'On Economic Causes of Civil War', *Oxford Economic Papers*, 50: 563–573.
Collier, P. and Hoeffler, A. (2001) 'Greed and Grievance in Civil War', *World Bank Policy Research Paper*, Washington, DC: The World Bank.
de Chand, D. (2000) 'The Sources of Conflict Between the North and the South in Sudan'. Presented at the Fifth International Conference of Sudan Studies, University of Durham, August 30–September 1.
de Waal, A. (2004) 'Darfur's Deep Grievances Defy All Hopes for an Easy Solution', in *The Guardian Observer*, July 25, online at observer.guardian.co.uk/international/story/0,6903,1268647,00.html.
Deng, F. (1995) *War of Visions: Conflict Identities in the Sudan*, Washington, DC: The Brookings Institution.
Easterly, W. (2002) *The Elusive Quest for Growth: Economists' Adventures and Misadventures in the Tropics*, Cambridge, MA: MIT Press.
Garang, J. (1987) *John Garang Speaks*, London: KPI.
Gomes Porto, J. (2002) 'Contemporary Conflict Analysis in Perspective', in J. Lind and K. Sturman (eds) *Scarcity and Surfeit: The Ecology of Africa's Conflicts*, Pretoria: African Centre for Technology Studies and Institute for Security Studies.
Grossman, H. (1991) 'General Equilibrium Model of Insurrections', *American Economic Review*, 81: 912–921.
Grossman, H. (1999) 'Kleptocracy and Revolutions', *Oxford Economic Papers*, 51: 267–283.
Harir, S. (1994) '"Arab Belt" versus "African Belt": Ethno-Political Conflict in Dar Fur and the Regional Cultural Factors', in S. Harir and T. Tvedt (eds) *Short-Cut to Decay: The Case of The Sudan*, Uppsala: Nordic Africa Institute.
Hassan, A.I. (2000) 'The Strategy, Responses and Legacy of the First Imperialist Era in the Sudan 1820–1885.' Presented at the Fifth International Conference of Sudan Studies, University of Durham, August 30–September 1.
HRW (2004a) 'Darfur in Flames: Atrocities in Western Sudan', *Human Rights Watch Report*, Vol. 16, No. 5(A), April, online at www.hrw.org/reports/2004/sudan0404/.

HRW (2004b) 'Darfur Documents Confirm Government Policy of Militia Support', Human Rights Watch Briefing Paper, July 19, online at hrw.org/english/docs/2004/07/19/darfur9096.htm.

HRWc. (2004c) 'Sudan: Darfur Atrocities Spill into Chad', Human Rights Watch News, June 21, online at www.hrw.org/english/docs/2004/06/21/sudan8882.htm.

Humphreys, M. (2003) 'Economics and Violent Conflict', Harvard University February, online at www.preventconflict.org/portal/economics.

ICG (2002) 'God, Oil and Country: Changing the Logic of War in Sudan', *International Crisis Group Report* No. 39, Brussels, January 28, online at www.crisisgroup.org/home/index.cfm?id=1615&l=4.

ICG (2003) 'Sudan's Other Wars', *International Crisis Group Briefing*, Brussels, June 25, online at www.crisisgroup.org/home/index.cfm?id=1808&l=4.

ICG (2004) 'Darfur Rising: Sudan's New Crisis', *International Crisis Group Report* No. 76, Brussels, March 25, online at www.crisisweb.org/home/index.cfm?id=2550&l=1.

Idriss, S.A.-N. (1999) 'The History of Darfur', in *Darfur: Ethnic Composition, Armed Conflicts and Violations of Human Rights*, special issue of *Sudanese Human Rights Quarterly*, Sudan Human Rights Organization, Cairo, July.

Johnson, D. (2002) 'Food Aid, Land Tenure and the Survival of the Subsistence Economy', Presented at the Money Makes the War Go Round: Transforming the Economy of War in Sudan, Brussels, June 12–13.

Johnson, D. (2003) *The Root Causes of Sudan's Civil Wars*, Bloomington, IN: Indiana University Press.

Johnson, D. and Prunier, G. (1993) 'The Foundation and Expansion of the Sudan People's Liberation Army', in M.W. Daly and A.A. Sikainga (eds) *Civil War in the Sudan*, New York: St. Martin's.

Kaldor, M. (1999) *New and Old Wars: Organized Violence in a Global Era*, Cambridge: Polity Press.

Keen, D. (1997) 'A Rational Kind of Madness', *Oxford Development Studies*, 25: 67–76.

Keen, D. (2001) 'A Response to Paul Collier's "Doing Well Out of War" and Other Thoughts'. Presented at CODEP Conference, June 18–20, School of Oriental and African Studies, University of London.

Kontos, S. (1991) 'Farmers and the Failure of Agribusiness in Sudan', in J.O. Voll (ed.) *Sudan: State and Society in Crisis*, Bloomington, IN: Indiana University Press.

Lesch, A. (1991) 'Sudan's Foreign Policy: In Search of Arms, Aid, and Allies', in J.O. Voll (ed.) *Sudan: State and Society in Crisis*, Bloomington, IN: Indiana University Press.

Lesch, A. (1998) *The Sudan: Contested National Identities*. Bloomington, IN: Indiana University Press.

LOC (1991) *A Country Study: Sudan*, The Library of Congress, online at lcweb2.loc.gov/cgi-bin/query/r?frd/cstdy:@field(DOCID+sd0040).

Markakis, J. (1998) *Resource Conflict in the Horn of Africa*, London: Sage Publications.

Marwood, B.W. (1947) 'Juba Conference 1947', *Juba Conference Minutes by Governor of Equatoria*, EP/SCR/1.A.5/1, June 21, online at www.sudansupport.no/english_pages/juba_conference_1947.pdf.

Melvill, D. (2002) 'Restoring Peace and Democracy in Sudan: Limited Choices for African Leadership', occasional paper no. 34, Institute for Global Dialogue, Braamfontein, South Africa, November.

Nafziger, E.W. and Auvinen, J. (2002) 'Economic Development, Inequality, War, and State Violence', *World Development* 30(2): 153–163.

O'Ballance, E. (1977) *The Secret War in the Sudan: 1955–1972*, London: Faber and Faber.

Reno, W. (2004) 'The Empirical Challenge to Economic Analyses of Conflicts'. Presented at SSRC-sponsored Conference, Washington, DC, April 19–20.

Reynal-Querol, M. (2002) 'Ethnicity, Political Systems, and Civil Wars', *Journal of Conflict Resolution*, 46(1): 29–54.

Salih, K.O. (1990) 'The Sudan, 1985–9: The Fading Democracy', *Journal of Modern African Studies*, 28: 199–224.

Salih, M.A.M. and Harir, S. (1994) 'Tribal Militias: The Genesis of National Disintegration', in S. Hair and T. Tvedt (eds) *Short-Cut to Decay: The Case of the Sudan*, Uppsala: Nordic Africa Institute.

Sconyers, D. (1976) 'British Policy and Mission Education in the Southern Sudan, 1928–1946', unpublished PhD dissertation, University of Pennsylvania.

Takana, Y. (1998) 'Effects of Tribal Strife in Darfur', in A.A.-Z. Mohamed and A.-T.I. Weddai (eds) *Perspectives on Tribal Conflicts in Sudan*, Khartoum: University of Khartoum, Institute of Afro-Asian Studies.

Taisier, M.A and Matthews, R. (1999) *Civil Wars in Africa: Roots and Revolution*, London: McGill-Queen's University Press.

Tilly, C. (1990) *Coercion, Capital, and European States, A.D. 900–1992*, Oxford: Blackwell.

Woodward, P. (2002) 'Peace and Elite Non-Oil Economic Interests'. Presented at the Money Makes the War Go Round: Transforming the Economy of War in Sudan, Brussels, June 12–13.

Ylönen, A. (2004) 'The Shadow of History: Marginalisation, Identity Construction and Conflict in Sudan', drafted for IBACS Conference in Burgos, October 7–10.

Zaman (2004) 'Oil Underlies Darfur Tragedy', Zaman Newspaper Online, July 7, online www.sudan.net, accessed in July 10, 2004.

8 Military intervention, democratization, and post-conflict political stability

Scott Gates and Håvard Strand[1]

Introduction

Recent cases of military intervention in Iraq, Afghanistan, and Haiti have ignited a policy dispute as to whether democratic government can be imposed externally. Advocates of aggressive democratization point to the remarkable rehabilitation of Japan from the time of its surrender in 1945 to the restoration of sovereignty in 1952 when it emerged as a stable democracy.

> It was the victor's justice that drove the new monumental undertaking and powered the twin goals of demilitarization and democratization. The victors tinkered with the media, the educational system, and the textbooks. Those are some of the things that will have to be done if a military campaign in Iraq is to redeem itself in the process.
> (Ajami, 2003: 15)

Opponents of an aggressive democratization policy respond that the US no longer has the capacity or will to do what was done in Japan.

> Washington does not have the capacity for political follow-through across a broad spectrum of post-conflict or post-intervention requirements. As Afghanistan and Iraq illustrate, the U.S. government lacks the interagency mechanisms, institutional memory, doctrine, and committed personnel and budget resources necessary for rebuilding failed states and collapsed regimes.
> (Crocker, 2003: 41)

The recent record of military intervention is that it can serve as an effective policy tool for inducing regime change. Milosevic was removed from power in Yugoslavia shortly after the Kosovo War in 1999. The Taliban lost control of Afghanistan after the US intervened and shifted the balance of power in the Afghan Civil War. Saddam Hussein's regime too collapsed after the US invasion. Indeed, losing a war frequently leads to regime change, particularly in autocratic polities (Bueno de Mesquita and Siverson, 1995; Werner, 1996). As for military interventions, the results of panel (cross-temporal, cross-national) analyses indicate that they do have a positive effect on democratization in target states (Gleditsch *et al.*, 2004; Tures, 2003; Peceny, 1999a, 1999b, 1995; Hermann and Kegley, 1998, 1996; Kegley and Hermann, 1997; Meernik, 1996). Though the studies by Meernik and Peceny regard US military intervention only and the research by Herman and Kegley and Tures is limited to the Cold War period, the finding that military interventions can be a tool of aggressive democratization is robust. Gleditsch *et al.* (2004) offer a comprehensive overview of military intervention from 1960 to 1996, thus incorporating the Cold War and post-Cold War periods in their analysis. They concur with the others. Military intervention does promote democratization. One common problem with these analyses is that democratization regards any form of political transformation in the direction of some democratic ideal. This means that a political transformation from a strong autocracy to a regime that is neither a democracy nor an autocracy is considered to be equivalent to a shift from an autocracy to a genuine democracy.

We argue here that political transformations from autocracy to intermediate political types do not constitute democratizations. Indeed, the inbetween regime types are the ones most in danger of civil war and autocratization – this is hardly the goal of military intervention. If we are to evaluate the success of an aggressive democratization policy, we need to determine whether or not these regime changes induced by military intervention endure and the resulting regime was a genuine democracy. The post-World-War-II cases, Japan, Italy, and West Germany, serve as examples of successful regime change. All have been politically stable. (Yes, even Italy; while Italian governments always seem rather fragile, the political system has been stable.) The problem is that all of these cases involve military intervention in connection with interstate war; yet military interventions in civil wars have predominated in the post-Cold War period.

Von Hippel's book, *Democracy by Force: US Military Intervention in the Post-Cold War World* (2000) examines the efforts to reconstruct post-conflict states and to build the foundations for democratic development through four case studies, Panama in 1989, Somalia in 1992, Haiti in 1994, and Bosnia in 1995. None of these cases exhibit the type of success witnessed in Japan, West Germany, or Italy; and only Panama is the only unambiguous case of interstate intervention. Of these four cases, Panama continues to be plagued by political instability. Haiti as we witnessed in 2004, failed to develop a consolidated democracy. Somalia was and remains a catastrophe. Bosnia is the most successful case. It is politically stable, but hardly a ringing success. Can we generalize from these four case studies? What is the general record of military intervention as a method of democratization? Has aggressive democratization been successful? Are civil war interventions different than interstate war defeats?

Imposing democratization through the use of force sounds like a paradox. If we imagine a scenario where a transformation would be successful, it would be one where a dictator rules over a freedom-yearning population, much like some of the German-occupied polities of World War II. In this scenario, merely removing the dictatorship would unleash civil society's constructiveness and the democratic institutions would appear without further assistance from the intervening force. This corresponds to an idea of a 'liberating' intervention. But does this logic apply in the context of a civil war?

If political transformation is the goal of military intervention, internal order must take precedence. Obviously after defeat in war, infrastructures have to be rebuilt. Governmental institutions reformulated. The economy restored. But possibly most important of all, the occupying armies must be able to provide daily security to the broader populace. Insecurity and fear has traditionally sent the masses in search of a strongman rather than a reformer. Security and rule of law is also a basic condition for the economic development that can be a valuable ally in the transition process. Whether after a civil war or an interstate war, security must be guaranteed. The losing side must be disarmed, either through negotiated settlement or surrender.

North (1990) argues in his study of long-term economic growth that formal political institutions, such as free elections, are dependent on informal institutions, which he defines as the norms and values of a population. His argument is that a free market, both in the trade of goods and votes, is dependent on a strong inter-personal trust. Only in such a climate will people invest their money and political support for benefits far ahead in the future. These are the ingredients of political stability. In civil conflict, when war further estranges members of society, such informal institutions are sure to break down. The task of rebuilding a civil peace becomes an especially laborious task. In this regard, then, we expect to see a difference between the political stability of post-civil war and post-interstate war regimes.

Political transformation also demands that attention be given to the interaction of different political institutions. Gates et al. (2006) have shown that certain configurations of formal political institutions are re-enforcing. Free and contested elections with broad enfranchisement and participation, extensive constraints on executive authority, and open recruitment of the executive constitute a set of institutions that define democratic polities. Concentration of authority into the hands of a single dictator who is not elected, whose authority is not constrained, and where political participation is substantially limited constitutes an ideal autocracy. Gates et al. (2006) find that political systems characterized by such re-enforcing institutions tend to be much more durable than polities with mixed systems, those possessing some autocratic and some democratic features. What this tells us is that democratization alone does not guarantee political stability. Democratization must go 'all the way' instituting all aspects of democratic governance, not just some aspects.

This chapter examines the robustness of political regimes in the aftermath of military interventions. As such, our chapter is inductively driven.

Given the evidence that military intervention leads to democratization (Gleditsch et al., 2004; Tures, 2003; Peceny, 1999a, 1999b; Herman and Kegley, 1998; Kegley and Hermann, 1997; Meernik, 1996), we ask: How stable are these regimes?

Drawing on our previous work on political stability and comparative analysis of the duration of different political systems (Gates et al., 2006), we analyze the effect of military intervention, differentiating between civil war and post-interstate war intervention. To assess the stability of different polity types, we investigate differences in their survival times – the time between the polity changes that mark the start or end of a polity. To estimate the survival time ratios of different political systems we utilize a log-logistic hazard function, which captures the non-monotonic nature of political stability. Our chapter proceeds as follows. After a short overview of the statistical model used to conduct our event history analysis and the variables used in our analysis, we discuss the results. By examining the underlying cofactors associated with regime duration and political instability, we are to assess the robustness of regime changes induced by military intervention in civil and interstate wars.

The log-logistic model of duration

To assess the stability of regimes established after a military intervention, we investigate differences in the survival times of different polities – the time between the polity changes that mark the start or end of a polity. As we demonstrate elsewhere (Gates et al., 2006), the duration dependence of a political system is non-monotonic, such that the hazard of regime collapse initially increases and then as consolidation mechanisms come into play, the hazard declines. We therefore use the log-logistic distribution in our analyses.[2]

The hazard function of the log-logistic model is:

$$h(t) = \frac{\lambda^{\frac{1}{\gamma}} t^{\frac{1}{\gamma}-1}}{\gamma\left(1 + (\lambda t)^{\frac{1}{\gamma}}\right)},$$

Where $\lambda = e^{-x\beta}$ and the scale parameter γ is estimated from the data. If the estimate of gamma is less than one ($\gamma < 1$), the hazard function is non-monotonic – in our case, initially increasing and subsequently decreasing. This pattern is clearly evident in Figure 8.1, which shows the hazard function of the log-logistic regression.

The coefficients from a log-logistic model can be difficult to interpret. We report 'Time Ratio estimates' instead of the coefficients, which are much easier to understand. A Time Ratio gives us the expected ratio between two otherwise equal units which differ by one unit on the variable in question. We also produce some illustrative graphs to ease interpretation further.

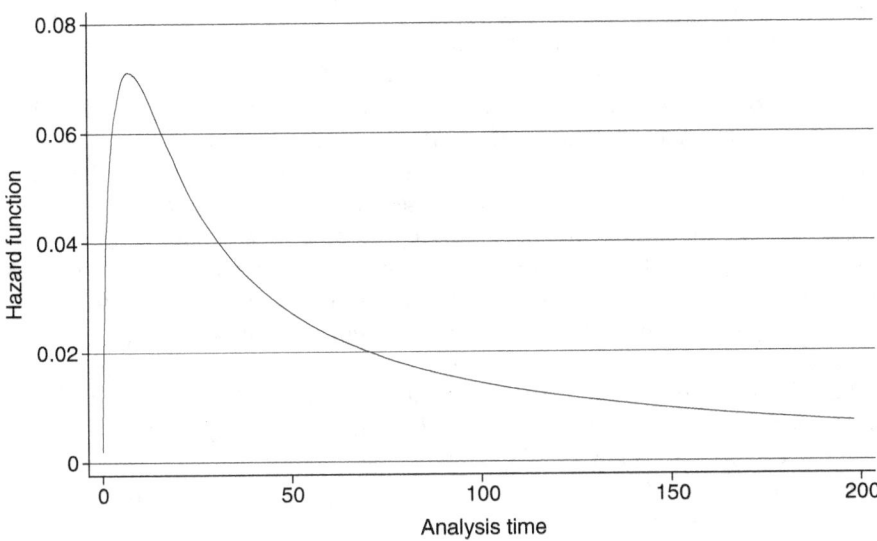

Figure 8.1 Hazard function of the log-logistic regression.

Variables and research design

Our dependent variable is the duration of a set of political institutions. Following Gates *et al.* (2006), we define a *polity* as a system which consists of institutions governing the recruitment of the executive officer; the constraints on the power of the executive officer; and the extent of popular participation in general elections.[3] When a country experiences a significant change in any of these dimensions, we define that as a regime change. The time period between these events defines the dependent variable. Our study is limited to the time period January 1, 1946–December 31, 1996. We censor all regimes that had not yet failed on the final day of this time period, in order to avoid an artificial set of failures.

In addition, all independent variables that do not describe the institutional setup of the polity vary over time. For example, it is not possible to describe the level of economic development of a long-lasting regime with one value. Therefore, we divide each polity into several observations, lasting no longer than a year each. These annual observations are all coded as censored, parallel to the censoring of the final observations. These one-year censored observations function as a control group, and allow us to compare regimes that fail within a couple of years after an intervention with regimes that either do not fail or do not experience interventions at all. The dataset is a version of what if often referred to as a single-failure, multiple-record dataset (Stata, 2003: 94ff).

A primary independent variable in this study is: regimes following a military intervention. We use Pickering's updated (1999) version of the Pearson *et al.* (1994) military intervention dataset. Pickering defines military intervention as 'the purposeful dispatch of national military personnel into other sovereign countries' (Pickering, 1999: 369). We use the data on military interventions to identify regimes that follow a military intervention. For this study, we choose to only include the intervention coded as being either in support of an anti-government organization or directed against the government itself. As mentioned, our research question is whether democratized regimes following interventions are durable, not whether interventions affect the regimes that are intervened against. Thus, we define our dependent variable as a dummy variable, where '1' is a regime which follows a regime change within two years of an intervention. All other regimes function as the control group, and are coded as '0'.

Civil War interventions arise when a Pickering (1999) case of military intervention occurs in a country defined to be experiencing armed civil conflict as defined by the Uppsala Armed Conflict database; i.e. whereby an armed conflict is defined as to occur between representatives of the state and another organized domestic party over a contested political incompatibility resulting in a number of casualties exceeding 25 battle casualties (Gleditsch *et al.*, 2002).

We also identify polities that follow defeat in an interstate war as coded by the Correlates of War project (Small and Singer, 1982). Similar to the coding of the 'following-an-intervention' variable, we code a regime change as resulting from a war loss if the change happens within two years from that loss. The loss in the Falkland War is usually given as the immediate cause of the junta's fall, but these two events occurred with more than a year between them. A two year window seems like an appropriate choice for capturing this effect. This variable is also a dummy, which is coded '1' if the regime was installed less than two years within a war loss, and '0' for all other regimes.

Examining recent incidents of military intervention highlights an important difference. When the US intervened in Haiti, it did so without any major military opposition. In contrast, both Mullah Omar and Saddam Hussein had to be removed by force. As both the Afghan and the Iraqi regimes can be said to have lost interstate wars at the same time as they were intervened against, we add another dummy variable measuring whether the intervention resulted in a war. This variable is an interaction between the 'regime-succeeding-an-intervention' variable and the 'regime-succeeding-a-lost-war' variable.

Since our regime data are based partially on the Polity dataset, we must take into account the coding of interregnums. If we were to regard an interregnum following a lost war or an intervention as a proper regime, our findings would be very misleading. These regimes are by default short-lived. We therefore disregard these periods and consider the first proper regime after the interregnum as the successor to the regime that experienced intervention or that lost a war.

The literature on both regime duration and military interventions argues that there has been a change after the cold war ended. What was named the 'new world order' emphasized less tolerance for human rights violators and other rogue regimes. We add a dummy variable for the Cold War, which we code as having ended in 1990.

Since the current discussion is focused on democratizing non-democratic regimes, it is interesting to see if it matters whether the new regime is significantly more or less democratic than its predecessor. We add two dummy variables to check this, one, coded '1' if the new regime is significantly more democratic than its predecessor, and another for significantly autocratized regimes. The reference category is no regime change.

Our control variables are all from Gates *et al.* (2006). We control for economic development with ln (GDP per capita), in constant 1995 dollars per capita. Przeworski *et al.* (2000) and Sanhueza (1999) demonstrate the role of economic development on political stability and democratization.[4] The economic development variable was lagged to reduce potential endogeneity bias. We also include a squared term as there is strong evidence of a curvilinear relationship between wealth and political stability.

In Gates *et al.* (2006) we find that different political systems exhibit considerable variation with respect to duration. Following the distinctions made by Gurr (1974), we identify four types of political system: Caesaristic; Autocratic; Democratic; and, Institutionally Inconsistent, which serves as the reference category. Caesaristic regimes are strong-men regimes with no institutionalized means of succession. Autocratic regimes include monarchies and dictatorships exhibiting a concentration of political authority. In the most extreme cases, power is vested in a single individual with few constraints if any. Democratic regimes are those that are characterized by democratic institutions along all three dimensions, such that the executive is held accountable to the general public. Institutionally inconsistent systems exhibit aspects of democratic and autocratic systems, but are neither. These are the least stable type of political system. To assess the robustness of post-intervention regimes, we control for the type of political system. Note also that to qualify as a 'democratization,' a regime must become a democracy.

We control for the impact of the political neighborhood by adding a variable measuring the average 'political distance' from each polity's location in the polity space (see Figure 8.1) and the polity locations of its neighbors (Gleditsch, 2002; Gleditsch and Ward, 2001; 2004).[5] A political neighborhood consists of all contiguous countries that have either a common border or less than 150 nautical miles between them. For countries without contiguous neighbors (i.e., isolated islands), we assign the average political distance from that country to all countries in the world as the value for the Political Neighborhood variable. The variable was normalized to range from 0 (completely similar) to 1 (completely different).

Table 8.1 Descriptive statistics

Variable	Observations	Mean	Standard deviation	Minimum	Maximum
First Regime after					
Lost war	7,329	0.0404	0.197	0	1
Intervention	7,329	0.109	0.312	0	1
Lost war and intervention	7,329	0.0045	0.067	0	1
Cold War period	7,329	0.767	0.423	0	1
Institutional variables					
Semi-democratic (reference category)					
Strongman	7,329	0.108	0.310	0	1
Autocratic	7,329	0.306	0.461	0	1
Democratic	7,329	0.370	0.483	0	1
Regime change variables					
No significant change (reference category)					
More democratic	7,329	0.287	0.453	0	1
More autocratic	7,329	0.509	0.500	0	1
Ln (GDP/cap)	7,329	0.025	1.47	−3.32	3.42
Ln (GDP/cap)^2	7,329	2.17	2.29	0.00	11.70
Neighborhood difference	7,329	0.351	0.210	−0.624	0.937

Analysis

The most easily interpretable analysis of the duration of intervention-born regimes is to compare the median duration of the regimes in question and the control group. A new regime established within two years of an intervention is part of the effect group. All other regimes compose the control group.

The numbers in Table 8.2 are the median survival times for each regime category, given in years. The numbers in parentheses are the number of polities that go into each group. The bivariate comparison indicates that a regime following an intervention should be just as stable as any other regime, *ceteris paribus*, while those regimes that follow a regime that fell due to a lost war are much less durable than other regimes. The combination of the two seems to be even more damaging than just losing a war.

Table 8.2 Comparing median duration of regimes across conflict experience

	Lost war	Intervention
Control Group	4.29 (843)	4.34 (738)
Effect Group	2.53 (19)	4.11 (124)
Sum	4.28 (862)	4.28 (862)

These numbers, however, do not tell us whether the regimes in the effect group have become more or less *democratic*. If we break up the control group into three categories, we can shed more light on the fate of different developments. The three categories are significant democratization, significant autocratization and a category for minor changes. In this comparison, we do not differentiate between lost wars and interventions as events that precede one another.

When looking at the 137 regimes that experience a change within two years of either an intervention or a loss in an interstate war, we see that 90 of them, or 66 percent, experience significant democratization. (Look at the Effect Group row in Table 8.3) This is in accordance with the findings of Gleditsch *et al.* (2004). However, we also see that the median survival times vary considerably. For a regime in our effect group, which is significantly more democratic than its predecessor, the median survival time is 2.69 years, compared to almost four years for regimes in the control group. This difference, however, is not significant at the 95 percent level of confidence. This difference adheres to what we already know about new democracies. The regimes democratized without interventions seem to last for just under four years, which makes sense since most election cycles are four years. The median survival time of our Effect Group indicates that these regimes tend to fail even before their first 'test' through an election held by a democratic government.

The median survival times for both minor change and movement toward autocracy are higher than the figures for democratization. Even though the differences might seem dramatic, neither is significant. This indicates that there is a fair amount of variance within each category. Based on the findings from Gates *et al.* (2004), it is reasonable to assume that this variance to a certain extent is due to the institutional characteristics of the new regimes. If democratization means movement from an institutionally consistent autocracy toward an institutionally inconsistent semi-democracy, it is not surprising that these new regimes are less stable. Indeed, Gleditsch *et al.* (2004) point out that many of the regimes they find to have democratized, have moved from autocracy to semi-democracy. In order to control for such factors, we must leave the bivariate analysis and consider multivariate duration analysis. As discussed above we estimated our models with a log-logistic hazard.

In Table 8.4, Model 1 indicates that without any control variables, military intervention does not affect political stability in post-conflict regimes at

Table 8.3 Comparing median regime duration across types of political change

	Democratization	Minor change	Autocratization
Control Group	3.96 (397)	6.04 (118)	4.38 (210)
Effect Group	2.69 (90)	20.93 (11)	7.64 (36)
Sum	3.69 (487)	7.18 (129)	4.87 (246)

Table 8.4 Log-logistic estimates of polity survival time ratios, 1945–1996

	Model 1	Model 2	Model 3	Model 4
First polity after intervention	1.27 (1.40)	1.32 (1.59)	1.28 (1.60)	1.25 (1.61)
First polity after lost war	2.58* (1.67)	2.53* (1.67)	1.96 (1.62)	1.71* (1.66)
First polity after lost war	0.19** (−2.56)	0.23** (−2.13)	0.25** (−1.96)	0.28** (−2.33)
Armed civil conflict	—	0.67*** (−2.67)	0.68*** (−2.66)	0.80** (−1.70)
Political Regimes				
Anocratic (institutionally inconsistent)	—	—	ref. cat.	ref. cat.
Strongman regime (Caesaristic)	—	—	1.67*** (3.58)	1.57*** (3.20)
Autocracy	—	—	2.47*** (6.95)	2.22*** (6.36)
Democracy	—	—	4.84*** (8.15)	4.23*** (8.96)
GDP/Cap	—	—	—	1.32*** (5.70)
GDP/Cap squared	—	—	—	1.17*** (5.47)
Economic growth	—	—	—	6.65** (2.49)
Average difference from neighbor	—	—	—	0.47*** (−4.94)
First polity	—	—	—	1.43** (2.03)
Gamma	0.80*** (−5.48)	0.80*** (−5.64)	0.72*** (−8.06)	0.66*** (−10.02)
Number of subjects	649	649	649	649
Number of failures	491	491	491	491
LL, constant only	−917.78	−917.78	−917.78	−917.78
LL, full model	−915.07	−911.27	−859.51	−817.47

Note
* = $p \leq 0.10$; ** = $p \leq 0.05$; *** = $p \leq 0.01$.

a statistically significant level. We do find that regimes arising after an interstate war loss are in fact more durable as is evident from the survival time ratio of 2.58. But in stark contrast, polities that are installed after an interstate war loss involving military intervention tend to be markedly less robust. The survival time ratio is 0.19, which means that these polities endure less than 20 percent as long as all other types of regimes. Model 2 adds civil war intervention. We find that political systems that follow civil war intervention are less durable than other types of regimes, lasting about 67 percent as long as the average political system. Nonetheless, post-civil war intervention leads to a regime that is nearly three times as stable as one installed after interstate war intervention. (In this model the survival time ratio for such polities is 0.23.) As seen in Model 3, these results hold when controlling for regime type. Though, it should be noted that the p-value for polities that experience defeat in civil war falls slightly below the conventional level of statistical significance ($p < 0.05$). Our results reported in Gates *et al.* (2006) also stand. Democracies are very stable. Autocracies relatively stable. Strongman regimes (defined by Gurr (1974) as Caesaristic) are slightly more stable than institutionally inconsistent regimes. With these controls we find that if an intervention involves military defeat, the post-conflict regime is much less likely to survive (only 28 percent as long as those regimes are not involved in war or intervention).

In Model 4 in Table 8.4 we add controls to account for economic development, economic growth, political neighborhood effects, and account for whether or not a polity is the first in a country or not. The curvilinear effects of economic development (whereby very poor and wealthy countries experience less instability than those moderately poor) are accounted for by GDP per capita and GDP per capita squared. Both relationships are statistically significant and are associated with slightly greater duration. All of these controls are statistically significant. These controls do not affect the results found in Models 1, 2, or 3.

Figure 8.2 shows the hazard function of the log-logistic regression comparing the political durability of democratized (regardless of the degree of democratization) and all other regimes. A 95 percent confidence interval of the median duration of a post-conflict democratized polity ranges from a time ratio of 0.61 to 1.15. This means that we can expect democratized regimes to be of shorter duration or approximately equal duration when compared to polities that did not shift from one category to another.[6] The problem is that all cases of democratization are lumped together. As our analysis presented in Table 8.4 demonstrates, political stability is associated with polities possessing all three dimensions of democratic governance. Institutionally inconsistent (or mixed) regimes are much less durable. Democratization that leads to an institutionally inconsistent regime is likely to fail much sooner than an institutionally consistent regime.

Figure 8.3 shows the different hazard functions of regimes that follow military defeat associated with military intervention compared to all other

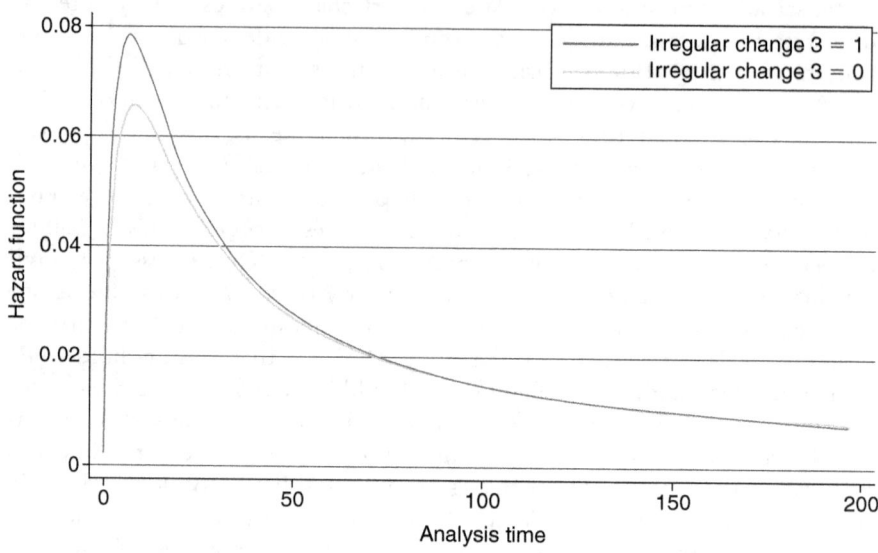

Figure 8.2 Hazard function of the log-logistic regression, comparing the duration of democratized polities to all other polities.

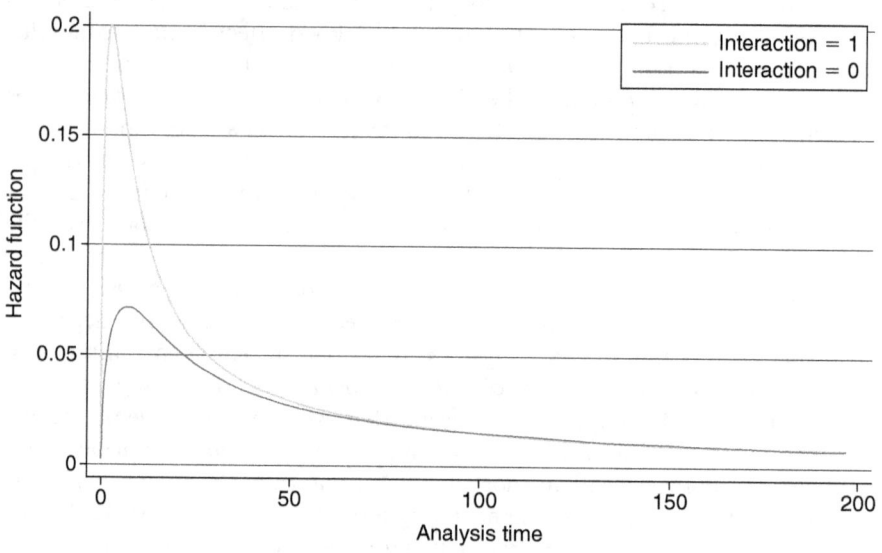

Figure 8.3 Hazard function of the log-logistic regression, comparing the duration of polities experiencing loss of war in an intervention to all other polities.

polities. Military defeat exhibits statistical significance and strong substantive effect on political stability. Such regimes are much less durable than others. This substantive effect is clearly evident in Figure 8.3.

Conclusions

The policy implications of our results are multifarious. The effect of military intervention alone on political stability is not significant. Intervening in a civil war to support the government serves neither to stabilize nor destabilize. One cannot say conclusively whether military intervention alone is politically stabilizing. However, if the military intervention entails installing a new regime after military defeat, the new regime is very likely to be short-lived. A super aggressive policy of democratization through conquest is not advised. Japan, in this regard, seems to be an exceptional case. Intervening in civil wars is also likely to lead to a short-lived regime. Polities that follow military intervention involving defeat or civil war intervention are likely to exhibit many of the same problems of re-establishing the informal institutions that support formal political and economic institutions. The forces of instability will be high in both situations.

Furthermore, if one is going to engage in a policy of aggressive democratization, our results indicate that the democratization must be thorough and complete. Partial democratization is de-stabilizing. For the most part, politically inconsistent regimes (democratized or not) are likely to be short-lived.

The debate about using military intervention as a tool for democratization is to a large extent a discussion about military intervention. Essentially the fight is about US foreign policy. During the Cold War, military intervention was nearly always justified as a means of protecting the world from communism. In the post-Cold War era, with the decline of the competing superpower, the realist–idealist debate has been re-invigorated. Idealist notions of democratization have become a primary objective of US foreign policy. With regard to policy, US military interventions in Panama in 1989, Somalia in 1992, Haiti in 1994, Bosnia in 1995, and Kosovo in 1999 kicked off a new debate between neo-realists and neo-liberals that echoed the debates from earlier in the twentieth century. The events of 9/11 have altered the nature of this debate.

Our results support the findings that military intervention can lead to democratization. This democratization, however, does not ensure a durable regime change. In terms of democratization, the long-term effect of aggressive democratization is negligible. If the goal of military intervention is to democratize, it is not an effective policy. Furthermore, if we are to consider costs in terms of lives lost and monies spent, military intervention must be justified in terms of other goals.

Notes

1 We thank Peter Burnell, Lene Siljeholm Christiansen, Nils Petter Gleditsch, Håvard Hegre, Patrick Regan, Ingrid Samset, Kaare Strøm, and Magnus Öberg for their valuable comments. A previous version of this chapter was presented as a paper at the WIDER Development Conference – 'Making Peace Work,' June 4–5, 2004. This paper is also part of the Polarization and Conflict Project (CIT–2–CT–2004–506048) funded by the European Commission – DG Research Sixth Framework Program. We also thank the Research Council of Norway for their support of the CSCW.
2 The models reported below were also estimated with several other distribution functions. The estimates are remarkably robust to the choice of distribution function. See Box-Steffensmeier and Zorn (2001), Collett (1994), and Cox (1972) for more information on hazard models.
3 Following Gates *et al.* (2006), we operationalize these dimensions with data from the Polity project (Jaggers and Gurr, 1995) and the Polyarchy project (Vanhanen, 2000).
4 GDP per capita data were drawn from Gates *et al.* (2004).
5 For instance, an ideal autocracy (0,0,0) with one neighbor that is an autocracy without any executive constraints (1,0,0) and another that is an ideal democracy (1,1,1) has a one unit distance from the inconsistent autocracy and $\sqrt{3}$ distance from the democracy (resulting in a normalized average of 0.79).
6 In stark contrast, Autocratization effects remain robust and very strong across estimations. Autocratization is unambiguously destabilizing.

Bibliography

Ajami, F. (2003) 'Iraq and the Arabs' Future,' *Foreign Affairs* 82(1), 2–18.
Box-Steffensmeier, J.M. and Zorn, C.J.W. (2001) 'Duration Models and Proportional Hazards in Political Science,' *American Journal of Political Science* 45(4), 951–67.
Bueno de Mesquita, B. and Siverson, R.M. (1995) 'War and the Survival of Political Leaders: A Comparative Study of Regime Types and Political Accountability,' *American Political Science Review* 89(4), 841–855.
Collett, D. (1994) *Modelling Survival Data in Medical Research*, London: Chapman, and Hall.
Cox, D.R. (1972) 'Regression Models and Life Tables (with Discussion),' *Journal of the Royal Statistical Society*, B74, 187–220.
Crocker, C.A. (2003) 'Engaging Failed States,' *Foreign Affairs* 82(5), 32–44.
Diamond, L. (1992) 'Promoting Democracy,' *Foreign Policy* 87(1), 25–44.
Gates, S., Hegre, H., Jones, M.P. and Strand, H. (2004) 'Democratic Waves? Global Patterns of Democratization, 1800–2000,' mimeo, Center for the Study of Civil War, PRIO, Oslo.
Gates, S., Hegre, H., Jones, M.P. and Strand, H. (2006) 'Institutional Inconsistency and Political Instability: The Duration of Polities,' *American Journal of Political Science* 50(4), 893–908.
Gleditsch, K.S. (2002) *All International Politics is Local: The Diffusion of Conflict, Integration, and Democratization*, Ann Arbor, MI: University of Michigan Press.
Gleditsch, K.S. and Ward, M.D. (2000) 'War and Peace in Space and Time: The Role of Democratization,' *International Studies Quarterly* 44(1), 1–29.
Gleditsch, K.S. and Ward, M.D. (2001) 'Measuring Space: A Minimum Distance

Database and Applications to International Studies,' *Journal of Peace Research* 38(6): 739–58.

Gleditsch, K.S. and Ward, M.D. (2004) 'Diffusion and the International Context of Democratization,' mimeo.

Gleditsch, N.P., Christiansen, L.S. and Hegre, H. (2004) 'Democratic Jihad? Military Intervention and Democracy,' paper prepared for the 45th Convention of the International Studies Association, March 17–20, 2004, Montreal.

Gleditsch, N.P., Strand, H., Eriksson, M., Sollenberg, M. and Wallensteen, P. (2002) 'Armed Conflict 1946–2001: A New Dataset,' *Journal of Peace Research* 39(5), 615–640.

Gurr, T.R. (1974) 'Persistence and Change in Political Systems, 1800–1971,' *American Political Science Review* 68(4), 1482–1504.

Hermann, M.G. and Kegley, C.W. Jr (1996) 'Ballots, a Barrier Against the Use of Bullets and Bombs: Democratization and Military Intervention,' *Journal of Conflict Resolution* 40(3), 436–460.

Hermann, M.G. and Kegley, C.W. Jr (1998) 'The U.S. Use of Military Intervention to Promote Democracy: Evaluating the Record,' *International Interactions* 24(2), 91–114.

Hook, S.W. (2002) 'Inconsistent U.S. Efforts to Promote Democracy Abroad,' in P.J. Schraeder (ed.) *Exporting Democracy: Rhetoric vs. Reality*, London and Boulder, CO: Lynne Rienner.

Jaggers, K. and Gurr, T.R. (1995) 'Tracking Democracy's Third Wave with the Polity III Data,' *Journal of Peace Research* 32(4), 469–482.

Kegley, C.W. Jr and Hermann, M.G. (1996) 'How Democracies Use Intervention: A Neglected Dimension in Studies of the Democratic Peace,' *Journal of Peace Research* 33(3), 309–322.

Kegley, C.W. Jr and Hermann, M.G. (1997) 'Putting Military Intervention into the Democratic Peace: A Research Note,' *Comparative Political Studies* 30(1), 78–107.

Meernik, J. (1996) 'United States Military Intervention and the Promotion of Democracy,' *Journal of Peace Research* 33(4), 391–401.

North, D.C. (1990) Institutions, *Institutional Change and Economic Performance*, Cambridge: Cambridge University Press.

Pearson, F.S. and Baumann, R.A. (1993–94) *International Military Intervention, 1946–88*. Ann Arbor, MI: Inter-university Consortium for Political and Social Research, Data Collection 6035.

Pearson, F.S., Baumann, R.A. and Pickering, J.J. (1994) 'Military Intervention and Realpolitik,' in F.W. Wayman and P.F. Diehl (eds) *Reconstructing Realpolitik*, Ann Arbor, MI: University of Michigan, pp. 205–225.

Peceny, M. (1995) 'Two Paths to the Promotion of Democracy during US Military Interventions,' *International Studies Quarterly* 39(3), 371–401.

Peceny, M. (1999a) *Democracy at the Point of Bayonets*, University Park, PA: Pennsylvania State University Press.

Peceny, M. (1999b) 'Forcing them to be Free,' *Political Research Quarterly* 52(3), 549–582.

Pickering, J.J. (1999) 'The Structural Shape of Force: Interstate Intervention in the Zones of Peace and Turmoil, 1946–1996,' *International Interaction* 25(4), 363–391.

Przeworski, A., Alvarez, M.E., Cheibub, J. and Limongi, F. (2000) *Democracy and*

Development. Political Institutions and Well-Being in the World, 1950–1990. Cambridge: Cambridge University Press.

Regan, P.M. (2000) *Civil Wars and Foreign Powers: Outside Intervention in Intrastate Conflict*, Ann Arbor, MI: University of Michigan Press.

Sanhueza, R. (1999) 'The Hazard Rate of Political Regimes,' *Public Choice* 98, 337–367.

Small, M. and Singer, J.D. (1982) *Resort to Arms: International and Civil Wars, 1816–1980*, Beverly Hills, CA: Sage.

Stata (2003), *Survival Analysis and Epidemiological Tables*. College Station TX: Stata Press.

Tures, J.A. (2001) 'Addressing Concerns About Applying the Democratic Peace Arguments to Interventions,' *Journal of Peace Research* 38(2), 247–249.

Tures, J.A. (2003) 'To Protect Democracy (Not Practice It): Explanations of Dyadic Democratic Intervention (DDI),' *OJPCR: The Online Journal of Peace and Conflict Resolution* 5(1), 32–55.

Vanhanen, T. (2000) 'A New Dataset for Measuring Democracy, 1800–1998,' *Journal of Peace Research* 37(2): 251–265.

Von Hippel, K. (2000) *Democracy by Force: US Military Intervention in the Post-Cold War World*, Cambridge: Cambridge University Press.

Werner, S. (1996) 'Absolute and Limited War: The Possibilities of Foreign Imposed Regime Change,' *International Interactions* 22(1), 67–88.

Part III
Termination and post-conflict stability

9 Enforcing alone

Collective action in ethnic conflicts settlement

Theodora-Ismene Gizelis[1]

Introduction

The specter of ethnic conflicts has ravaged both developed and developing countries and ethnic conflicts present a sustained challenge for theories on conflict management and resolution.[2] This chapter considers ethnic conflicts as a bargaining situation between ethnic groups and governments, where commitment problems may prevent the parties from reaching settlements and encourage the use of violence. When parties in a conflict are unable to reach an agreement by themselves, an external enforcer who can help the parties overcome credible commitment problems and bear the cost of providing the settlement may be necessary to reach an arrangement.[3] Since the inability to find settlement to violent ethnic conflicts can create severe regional security problems that can impose significant costs on external actors, external actors will often have incentives to facilitate a stable settlement in ethnic conflicts. However, if settlement is a collective good for more than one actor, then the actors may try to shirk and rely on others enforcing the settlement. In this chapter, I use the theory of public goods provision to identify when third party provision will be more or less likely. I illustrate the implications of the argument with case studies of Sri Lanka and Bosnia.

Ethnic conflict: violence, settlement, and enforcement

In this chapter, I use the term 'ethnic conflict' to denote conflict within a state involving communities which identify themselves as separate units with distinct cultural traits and historical experiences. In order for communities to become political actors they must be mobilized politically and develop a certain level of common identification as being somehow different. In this sense, ethnic conflicts are a subset of civil wars, which are not necessarily waged by distinct ethnic groups, but could also be based on ideological cleavages. The existence of multiple cultural communities does not by itself imply that conflict is inevitable, and conflictual relations between ethnic communities do not necessarily become violent. Indeed, despite examples of very violent conflict such as Bosnia, most relations between governments and ethnic groups see very limited if any violence (see, for example, Horowitz 1985; Shehadi 1993). My interest here lies in accounting for when violent civil conflicts can be formally settled short of the use of force, for example, by arrangements that permit ethnic groups to coexist within a single state, as in the case of Belgium or the divorce between the Czech and Slovak republics, or secede in ways that do undermine regional stability, as in the case of the former Yugoslavia.

Ethnic conflicts could in principle be settled without violence in the same ways as other forms of conflict. However, ethnic conflicts exhibit certain characteristics that make them quite different from conflicts between states. In an ethnic conflict, the ethnic communities that do not control the state apparatus often lack much by way of an organized military or political apparatus, and also lack the legal standing afforded to states under international law. These characteristics matter for the prospects for providing feasible settlements in important ways. In ethnic conflicts where one of the actors is not a state, it will often be more difficult to substitute negotiated or political strategies for the use of violence. The empirical record clearly shows that whereas interstate wars usually end in negotiations rather than the complete defeat of the other parties, ethnic conflicts are much less likely to end in negotiations (see, in particular, Walter 1997). Many researchers attribute the difficulty in establishing negotiated settlement to a commitment problem: since a government cannot credibly commit to refraining from cracking down on the rebels after peace agreements, rebels will be reluctant to decommission in the absence of guarantees. More generally, we have a commitment problem in that whatever guarantees that a socially and economically stronger group dominating the government makes to protect and respect the property rights of the minority ethnic group may not be fully credible (see, for example, Davies 1962; Lumsden 1973). This applies even in cases where animosities have not escalated to violence. As such, the credible commitment problems with respect to majority consent to the future protection of minority rights can feed and sustain pre-existing cultural and ethnic animosities (Lake and Rothchild 1998). However, the asymmetry in political status between governments and ethnic groups also makes it much more difficult for the international community to intervene in ways that are effective to provide settlements without generating criticism from the government for violating its sovereignty.

Whether the parties themselves to a conflict can reach a settlement depends on whether a state controlled by a majority ethnic group can credibly commit to offer future protection of the rights of a minority group. When conflicts become violent, as states cannot provide credible guarantees to protect the rights of minorities, external involvement can help establish stable settlements, for example, by establishing and monitoring cease-fire agreements and facilitate institutional arrangements that can improve the relationships between the majority and the minority ethnic groups.

External involvement and the settlement of ethnic conflicts

Why would external actors be willing to intervene in ethnic conflicts that occur in other states in the first place? An important reason stems from the fact that most ethnic conflicts are not isolated domestic events that affect only the state where the conflict occurs, but often affect neighboring states within a geographical-political region. Ethnic conflicts can spread or diffuse among states if the violence in one state directly expands to another state or the conflict creates externalities for other states through features such as refugee flows or adverse economic effects. Ethnic conflicts are particularly likely to diffuse when the neighboring states already experience related domestic ethnic tensions. A conflict in a neighboring country can then provide windows of opportunity and fertile strategic conditions for groups to pursue their goals by violent means. Ethnic conflict often becomes internationalized when other states in the area intervene on the side of one of the parties, as seen in the case of Bosnia-Herzegovina (e.g. Lake and Rothchild 1998). Such interventions can in turn generate counter interventions from other parties with ties to the other side of the conflict.

Ethnic conflicts can be destabilizing for other countries in a region, especially if groups have secessionist or irredentist claims, or neighboring countries have strong attachments to one of the parties or particular preferences over the terms of proposed settlements that may be incompatible with the views of other states.

Ethnic conflicts may also spread through a demonstration effect, where other ethnic groups observe the mobilization process and then try to imitate successful movements (e.g. Lake and Rothchild 1998). Successful ethnic conflicts elsewhere often lead actors to change their estimates of the probability of successful revolts and the costs of involvement. This implies that unsolved ethnic conflicts can create security dilemmas even for states and ethnic groups within the larger region who have no stake in the original conflict (Posen 1993). Moreover, an ethnic conflict creates problems of migration to the neighboring countries, and socio-economic instability in the region as well.

A stable settlement where parties refrain from violence would in this sense be a collective good for the region. Due to the commitment problem discussed above, the domestic parties to an ethnic conflict may be unable to implement negotiated settlements, and external actors can play an important role helping to enforce settlements. In the following section I expand on how external actors can help overcome the collective action problems in reaching a settlement to ethnic conflict.

Collective action, external enforcement, and the settlement of ethnic conflicts

When an ethnic conflict threatens to spread or create costly externalities neighboring countries have incentives in seeing a settlement to prevent further escalation. Under such circumstances, finding settlements to ethnic conflicts is akin to a public good for the surrounding countries in a region, to the extent that reaching a settlement benefits the national interests of all the neighboring countries, regardless of whether individual countries participate or not in providing peace.

The theory of public goods tell us that collective goods are likely to be underprovided since all actors will enjoy the benefit of the good regardless of whether or not they contribute to providing the good. Once the public good is provided, it cannot easily be withheld from actors who have not contributed. The immediate underprovision problem is further compounded by the long-term underprovision problem to sustain an agreement, since more than one actor is necessary to create a truce or a temporary ceasefire. The ultimate goal in the settlement of an ethnic conflict is not merely to end the political violence, but to eradicate the conditions that led to such a costly level of conflict. However, changing the bargaining power among a government and ethnic minority groups and creating incentives for all domestic actors to abide by the agreed settlement typically cannot be achieved, unless an external actor (or actors) is willing to actively commit to the process for the long run.

The settlement of an ethnic conflict requires a privileged actor or group of actors willing to bear the costs of enforcing a settlement by enacting policies that increase the cost of fighting for each participant; however, the benefits of such peace settlements cannot easily exclude states that do not contribute to facilitating or implementing a settlement. Potential external enforcers include both the major global powers as well as regional powers with more limited areas of national interest. Smaller regional powers tend to more actively intervene or to be involved in ethnic conflicts (Gleditsch and Beardsley 2004), but they are usually not willing or able to sustain the burden of long-term intervention in ethnic conflict. Smaller regional powers also lack the economic and military resources to enforce a settlement between fighting groups.

Intervention comes at a cost for enforcers. Due to the expected cost of the intervention and the security dilemma that ethnic conflicts create, major powers are more often than not reluctant to drastically alter the existing territorial structures (Heraclides 1990).[4] In addition, external actors often have difficulty in coordinating their policies and the settlement cannot be sustained or reached in the first place. Even in the post-Cold War system where the USA is the undisputed sole superpower, influential voices in the USA, such as Condoleezza Rice, argue that the USA cannot afford to intervene in every single secessionist ethnic conflict but must limit its position to a few key regions defined by the US national interest.

Lemke (2002) argues that major powers within regions or 'sub-hierarchies' behave locally in ways that are reminiscent of the major powers on the global stage. Even more important, a dominant country in the region that can bear higher costs than the rest of the countries might provide the settlement. However, if there are contenders for power with a region or sub-hierarchy, it will be extremely difficult for either one of them to assume the costs to support a given settlement without the consent of the remaining powers. Hence, the public good might not be provided or it is at best under-provided. By combining the model of settlements as a public good with Lemke's theory of 'sub-hierarchies', I can derive the conditions under which the external actors can provide and sustain the settlement of an ethnic conflict as a public good. I also examine the role of the global power and whether it is willing to act as a privileged actor to enforce the agreement when the regional powers fail to do so.

The following section presents the theoretical model of the settlement of ethnic conflicts as a collective action problem. The model analyzes the inherent problems of providing the collective good (in this case the settlement of the ethnic conflict). This model is applicable for either a major regional power or a major international power to intervene and settle an ethnic dispute. I then illustrate the insights from the model by contrasting the cases of Sri Lanka, where the regional power (India) did make an effort to play the role of an enforcer, and Bosnia, where the leading regional power (the European Union) came with feasible plans to settle the dispute (e.g. Carrington proposal) but failed to assume the cost of the enforcement.

The settlement of ethnic conflicts as a collective good

This model assumes a case of ethnic conflict where the international community or a major power is trying to press for negotiations and end the conflict. The settlement problem, which is modeled here, considers two actors, the leading country of the global hierarchy (i) and the dominant country of the sub-hierarchy (j). The purpose of the external intervention is to reach a settlement that reduces the domestic actors' discount factor for continuing violence in the future. For the settlement to be successful the majority group has to be pressured to offer a credible arrangement to the minority group(s).

The model is based on the public good game presented and analyzed in Fudenberg and Tirole (1995). Each player is aware of the benefits derived from the provision of the public good, but he(she) does not know what level of costs the other players can afford to provide the public good, in this case, to sustain a settlement in an ethnic conflict. Thus, the actors have to signal their level of commitment by the costs that they can carry to provide the public good. The actors have to update their beliefs, and the equilibrium outcome is a Perfect Bayesian Equilibrium (PBE) that satisfies all the conditions of incomplete-information games with independent types.

The key point in this chapter is that settlements require sustainable provision. In the case that the major neighboring countries or a major power of the local sub-hierarchy fails to bear the cost of providing the settlement, the enforcer of the last resort will be the global power, currently the United States. The preference to constrain the degree of disturbances in the international system depends on the position of the external actors in the international system and their strategic perceptions on how the emerging crisis may affect their interests. In the two examples, both India and the European Union experienced significant negative externalities from the respective ethnic conflicts in Sri Lanka and Bosnia-Herzegovina. These externalities motivated their interest to enforce a settlement that will put an end to the regional disturbance.

This game has two stages. Both players decide simultaneously whether they will move to a settlement or not at period $t = 0$ or period $t = 1$. The two time periods represent the two stages of the game. The actors' decision to contribute to the provision of the public good is a dichotomous choice. Either they bear the costs of providing the settlement or they refuse to enter any negotiation process and support a settlement. The payoffs in each period are clear: 1 if at least one of the players provides the public good and 0 if none does. Each player has a constant cost function – c_i for the global power and c_j for the leader of the local sub-hierarchy – where c_i and c_j are functions representing the cost of involvement for the external actors in terms of human lives, political, and economic resources. Their cost remains the same in both periods (stages). Although both players are aware of the benefits they derive from the provision of the public good, they are unaware of each other's cost function. Both players believe that their costs are drawn independently from the same continuous and strictly increasing distribution function $P(\cdot)$ on $[0, \tilde{c}]$, where $\tilde{c} > 1$.[5] The cost function represents the actor's type. Some actors are willing or able to sustain higher costs than others. The goal for each actor is to maximize the net benefits derived from the public good, irrespectively of who provides it. The actors choose strategies to maximize their expected benefits, given their cost function.

Given the actors' choice at the first stage of the game (i.e. whether they contribute to the settlement or not) the game has three possible scenarios for the second stage:

(1) Neither actor provides the public good in the first period: Both players then know that the cost of the other player exceeds their cutoff cost, $\hat{c}_i$ and $\hat{c}_j$ for the dominant country of the global hierarchy (i) and the dominant country in the local sub-hierarchy (j), respectively. If the cost for providing the settlement is lower than the cutoff cost, the probability that either actor will support the settlement changes in the second period. The actors will support the settlement in the second stage. This shows that the level of the cost, depending on the cutoff point for each player, determines the choices during the second stage on whether actors will support a settlement.

(2) Both players contribute during the first period: In the first period a type $\hat{c}$ that is willing to carry higher costs than the cutoff costs will signal its

ability to sustain higher costs in order to achieve and sustain a more favorable settlement and higher contributions by the other players.

(3) Only one player contributes: Suppose a situation where the dominant global power contributes resources to support the settlement in the first period, while in the local sub-hierarchy the major power(s) does not. The important element in this case is whether it is worth for the actors to reveal their type. Even if the global power is a type $\hat{c}$ or has a strong willingness to contribute exceeding the cut off costs of not providing the settlement, it will only support a settlement if the likelihood that the regional power provides the settlement is less than $1-P(\hat{c})$. Thus, there are two possibilities. Either, the global power is willing to support a settlement and bear the costs in the next stage; or the regional power(s) have low tolerance to casualties and other forms of cost and do not support a settlement in the second stage. In the latter case, it is better for the global power not to contribute in the first period and at the same time signal a high cost in the first period. By not contributing in the first period the global power will induce the regional power(s) to contribute in the second period. However, if the global power is willing to contribute in the first period and it is willing to compromise, regional actors will be more reluctant to contribute any resources to the settlement in the second period unless they are willing to bear high costs.

There are two main theoretical implications of this model. First, the critical aspect is the cost functions of the actors. The actors, either the global power or the local sub-hierarchy power(s), have to accept certain costs in order to provide the public good, in this case a settlement. Second, it is beneficial for the actors to signal that they have high costs and they are unwilling to contribute the collective good, in an effort to force other actors to compromise and contribute as well. The second proposition is controversial, as it suggests that in certain cases no external intervention will occur, regardless of how extreme the ethnic conflict may be (see Sudan or Congo). Moreover, it implies that the United States may be willing to have the major powers of the local sub-hierarchy act on their behalf rather than intervening directly. The role of the United States as a global power becomes critical in cases where the settlement is not provided or where the settlement is provided by an actor who has an interest to signal high costs in order to avoid total provision of the collective good in the second round.

Once, the global power decides to actively intervene, the game re-starts again. The public good game explains under what conditions the globally dominant power is going to make a pro-intervention choice. These conditions can be provided by the theory of the sub-hierarchies that delineate the interaction between the dominant power and the various local sub-hierarchies. First of all, if the United States perceives the situation as threatening to international stability, hence it is of high salience to intervene and facilitate the enforcement of a settlement.[6] Second, there are significant spillover effects from the continuation of the conflict that involves sub-hierarchies in which major allies of the United States are involved (e.g. the

Balkans). The third condition relates to the possibility of involvement in other sub-hierarchies (such as Africa and Central Asia). In that case the choice of the United States could be to work with the dominant country of that region or the major contender within that region, depending on its national interests. The implication of these conditions is that if they are not met, there are few reasons for the United States to intervene to facilitate the resolution of a conflict as the following cases illustrate.

Comparative case studies: Sri Lanka and Bosnia

In this section I will illustrate the model by contrasting the cases of Sri Lanka and Bosnia. Contemporary Sri Lanka has a Buddhist Sinhalese majority that constitutes 74 percent of the population and a Hindu Tamil minority of about 12 percent of the population, located mainly in the northern and eastern parts of the island. Sri Lanka is almost a textbook example of the commitment problem inducing violent ethnic conflict and the regional problems ethnic conflicts can create. The prior constitutional provisions by the British, the Soulbery Constitution of 1946, guaranteed the political and economic rights of the Sinhalese majority and the Tamil minority. During the 1970s the nationalism of the Sinhalese population rose. The Sinhala majority moved steadily toward reducing the socio-economic benefits of the Tamils, and decided to define the multiethnic society of Sri Lanka as a Sinhala-Buddhist state. Special privileges were assigned to both the language and the religion of the Sinhalese majority. Educational and employment quotas were institutionalized at the expense of the Tamils. When their demands for more democratic representation did not work out the Tamils requested autonomy and new political structures. The strife started soon after, leading to political violence against the Tamils in 1983 (see Jeyaratman, 1988).

The ethnic strife in Sri Lanka seriously affected the region. The migration of the 100,000 Tamil refugees to Tamil Nadu in South India created severe problems in Indian politics that eventually resulted in the assassination of Indian Prime Minister R. Gandhi in 1989. Moreover, there was extended fear in the region that the conflict in Sri Lanka could trigger ethnic movements in Bangladesh with the Chakma minority as well as in Nepal, which faced civil unrest by groups sympathetic to India. The involvement of India in 1987 led to the Provisional Councils Act and the Indo-Sri Lanka Agreement. These provided India with the leverage to deal with Sri Lanka on a bilateral basis, avoiding any interference from possible contenders like Pakistan. The external involvement to bring a peaceful settlement failed, however, because India was not able or willing to further commit to the proposed settlement of 1987. The failure of India to enforce such a settlement in 1987 is illustrative not only of the enormous costs that the enforcer has to suffer, but also of the difficulties involved in such an endeavor.

Whereas, in the case of Sri Lanka, it was India, the major regional power in southeast Asia, which assumed the burden to enforce the proposed settlement in 1987, in Bosnia-Herzegovina the role of the United States as the global dominant power became critical to provide the collective good of a settlement. In Bosnia, where the war was relentlessly continuing, the then UK Foreign Secretary Douglas Hurd went to Washington with the clear message for the United States to be involved in the resolution of the conflict. That movement brought the creation of the Contact Group. Although it is widely asserted that the aggressive deployment of NATO air-power against the Bosnian Serbs and the military ground offensive of Croats in August 1995 contributed to the final agreement at Dayton, Ohio, it cannot be ignored that the United States for the first time accepted a 51–49 percent geographical split and administrative autonomy for the Bosnian Serbs. The final agreement at Dayton, Ohio and the subsequent Treaty of Paris were the outcomes of coordination efforts both at the diplomatic and the military level led by the United States (Neville-Jones, 1996–1997). Contrary to the conflict in Sri Lanka, in Bosnia the enforced settlement, despite its limitations, addressed issues of constitutional autonomy and territorial division to the direction of the minority ethnic group, the Bosnian Serbs.[7]

After World War II, Bosnia's three national groups were more or less equally represented in Yugoslavia's decision-making structures. The economic and social decline of Yugoslavia after the death of Josip Broz Tito encouraged the rise of ethnic nationalism. In the 1990 elections nationalists gained power in the Yugoslav republics. Soon after the elections of the fall of 1991, military clashes erupted between the Yugoslav People's Army and forces controlled by Slovenia and Croatia. Following such clashes the United Nations and the European Community recognized the dissolution of Yugoslavia and also the independent republics as its successors. In the spring of 1992 the conflict spread to Bosnia, as the Bosnian Muslim government was trying to obtain control within the internationally accepted territory of Bosnia.[8] Bosnian Serbs became a majority within Yugoslavia and a minority within Bosnia. On the other hand, despite their minority status Bosnian Serbs controlled substantial amounts of socio-economic resources, while the Bosnian Muslims had the political control. This is the case of an ethnic conflict where both parties had to be forced to provide the collective good, nevertheless, the Bosnian Muslims were the ones, having the political control, to agree to a settlement that protects the future property and civil rights of the Bosnian Serbs.

During the early stages of the conflict, the Serbian forces were slightly stronger and far more homogenous, while the Bosnian Muslims had fewer resources to commit to the fight than the Bosnian Serbs. The rest of the actors, including the international actors, were weak, uncommitted, and/or scattered between the two extremes. The more committed Serbs could drive the bargaining region closer to their most preferred outcome. Nevertheless, for a brief period during 1994, there was small variability in the range of feasible outcomes. If an agreement had been adopted by the United States and the other international actors at that time, the Serbs would have been willing to accept settlements that have been closer to the preferences of the United States and the Bosnian government than the prevailing agreement. Thus, a stable and beneficial outcome for the Bosnian Muslims could have emerged (Friedman and Gizelis 1997, Economist 1994). From March 1994 to July 1995 the bargaining power of the Bosnian Serbs, who demanded half of the land and political autonomy, increased steadily.[9] Hence, up until 1994 the European Union with the Geneva talks and the ground UN forces (UNPROFOR) were struggling to reach an agreement between Bosnian Muslims, Serbs, and Croats. The negotiation process was at a stalemate, as the Bosnian Serbs rejected the international community's proposed settlements (e.g. the Vance and Owen plans).

The failure of the European Union as the major regional power to reach an agreement was not because of the lack of plans (plans Vance–Owen, Carrington), but because of its default to act as an enforcer and bear the necessary costs involved in a military and a diplomatic intervention to impose on all sides such a settlement. The negotiation process took a new turn when the international actors, primarily the United States, conceded to modifications of the status quo and committed more resources to enforce the proposed settlement.[10] Most external actors accepted an arrangement that would divide Bosnia into two regions of almost equal size between the Croat–Muslim coalition and the Serbs. Furthermore, each group would enjoy a certain degree of political autonomy. The peaceful settlement became feasible only when the United States committed more resources to support the negotiation process and it actively pressured the Serbs through bombing and sanctions on the Federal Yugoslav Republic (FYR) and exercised diplomatic pressure on Bosnian Muslims (see Neville-Jones, 1996–1997). The final settlement, established by the treaty signed in Paris on December 14, 1995, divided the territory of Bosnia equally between the Croat–Muslim federation and the Bosnian Serbs, and each community would maintain limited self-administrative privileges. A key component in the territorial division of the land was the guarantee of the Gorazde corridor in the north that unites the two parts of the Bosnian Serbs who feared being isolated from each other, hence weaker in case of a military emergency.

The importance of the Bosnian conflict for the region became significant, as the potential of a spillover effect was very strong in a region that suffers from the presence of ethnic minorities. Moreover, as a local hierarchy the Balkans were related to the vital national interests of the United States at that time.[11] The establishment of the political institutions, along with territorial arrangements (the Gorazde corridor), seemed at least temporarily to survive as long as there was the commitment of the United States to sustain them. Eventually, what was required was that the institutional arrangements could be self-enforced by the three ethnic groups, and primarily the majority of the Bosnian Muslims.

Concluding remarks

In the post-Cold War the trends in international relations have created even more regional sensitivities to ethnic groups. The spillover effects of migration, refugees, and the threat to the stability of different geographic regions are intensified in the post-Cold War era. For this reason the settlement of an ethnic conflict is treated as a public good, especially for each local regional hierarchy. The concept of public good allows for problems of collective action to be analyzed and it does not preclude the possible problems that emerge from lack of commitment from the external actors.

Settling an ethnic conflict requires commitment and willingness to bear the costs of the enforced settlement. This chapter presents a theoretical framework combining game theory with Lemke's theory of sub-hierarchies in international relations, which explores the conditions under which a settlement can be provided.

This chapter has also significant implications for international relations as it identifies the conditions under which the United States, as the major global power, or the local dominant power, if there is one, may be willing to intervene in an ethnic conflict. It offers also an explanation of why in some cases, such as Somalia or Sudan, the United States was a lukewarm participant at best, whereas in the case of Haiti or Bosnia the United States was directly and decisively involved.

This chapter points out that for a sustainable settlement to be reached the privileged actor needs to work along with the ethnic groups, whose future self-constraint will signal commitment in respecting the settlement. Without such a commitment the discount factor of the ethnic minority(ies) groups for a future settlement will be extremely small allowing for violence to become the preferred policy choice.

Notes

1 I am grateful for comments from Yi Feng, Gregorios Gizelis, Kristian Skrede Gleditsch, Jacek Kugler, and the editors of this volume. This research was started while I held the Theodore Lentz Post-doctoral Fellowship at the Center for International Studies and the University of Missouri, St Louis, and I am grateful for the financial support of the center.
2 Recent studies that examine the impact of ethnic conflicts on international relations include Heraclides (1990), Fearon (1998), Lake and Rothchild (1996), and Saideman (1997). Zartman (1985) was one of the first scholars who examined the settlement of secessionist conflicts as a problem of finding negotiated agreements. Earlier studies on ethnic conflicts include Suhrke and Noble (1977) and Shiel (1984).
3 For the significance of the external party as an enforcer see Walter (1997, 2002).
4 During the Cold War period, the Soviet Union and the United States were careful not to antagonize each other in the case of ethnic conflicts within each other's jurisdiction, although the United States had a more consistent record in that respect compared to the Soviet Union.
5 Cost in the case of a settlement consists of financial and military resources as well as political ones.

6 The lack of commitment by the United States in maintaining stability in Somalia gave the impression of a weak and uncommitted superpower. The leaders of Haiti inferred, from the prior failed engagement of the United States in Somalia, that the United States was not willing to assume any costs of involvement in Haiti, i.e. they miscalculated.
7 The Bosnian conflict also has elements of both a secessionist and an irredentist ethnic conflict. But only the first attribute is of primary interest in this chapter.
8 Warfare ensued as the Bosnian government, controlled by Bosnian Muslims, sought to re-establish control over its internationally recognized borders. During the early stages of the war the Bosnian Serbs gained control over approximately 70 percent of Bosnia. The remainder of the territory was divided between the Croats and the Muslims, who subsequently established a loose federation.
9 Although at the battlefield the Serbs experienced military defeats to the extent that the distribution of power was rather equal by 1995, in terms of bargaining power they were able to hold their positions. On the other hand, the Bosnian Muslims and the international community grew pessimistic and more flexible in their positions.
10 During the early stages of the conflict the United States, the most important external actor, insisted that Bosnia remain a unified state, under the internationally recognized government and borders. To attain a settlement the United States had to concede to some of the Bosnian Serbs' demands.
11 The international community, especially the United States, was initially unwilling to offer a settlement acceptable to the Bosnian Serbs. On multiple occasions, the European members of the 'contact group' were close to reaching an agreement between the Bosnian government and the Bosnian Serbs. Moreover, the Russians all along supported a rather moderate settlement similar to the final Dayton agreement, which could have been acceptable by the Bosnian Serbs. To all of these efforts US response was at best lukewarm. Thus, no agreement was reached over a relatively long period of time, while the conflict was prolonged. The international actors misperceived the resolve of the secessionist ethnic group (Boyd 1995; Glitman 1996–1997). Since 1995 there was a progressive shift in the United States' policies without any commitment to enforce any settlement.

References

Boyd, C.G. (1995) 'Making Peace With the Guilty: The Truth About Bosnia', *Foreign Affairs* 74(5): 22–38.

Davies, J.C. (1962) 'Towards a Theory of Revolution', *American Sociological Review*, 27: 5–19.

Economist, The (1994) 'The West Cries Enough', *Economist* February 12: 43–44.

Fearon, J.D. (1998) 'Commitment Problems and the Spread of Ethnic Conflict', in D.A. Lake and D. Rothchild (eds) *The International Spread of Ethnic Conflict*, Princeton, NJ: Princeton University Press.

Friedman, F. and Gizelis, I. (1997) 'Fighting in Bosnia: An Expected Utility Evaluation of Possible Settlements', *International Interactions* 23(3–4): 351–365.

Fudenberg, D. and Tirole, J. (1995) *Game Theory*, 4th edn, Cambridge, MA: MIT Press.

Gleditsch, K.S. and Beardsley, K. (2004) 'Nosy Neighbors: Third-Party Actors in Central American Conflicts', *Journal of Conflict Resolution* 48(3): 379–402.

Glitman, M. (1996–1997) 'US Policy in Bosnia: Rethinking a Flawed Approach', *Survival* 38(4): 69–70.

Heraclides, A. (1990) 'Majority Minorities and External Involvement', *International Organization* 44(3): 347–351.
Horowitz, D.L. (1985) *Ethnic Groups in Conflict*. Berkeley, CA: University of California Press.
Jeyaratman, W. (1988) *The Break-up of Sri Lanka: The Sinhalese-Tamil Conflict*, Honolulu, HI: University of Hawaii Press.
Lake, D.A. and Rothchild, D. (1996) 'Containing Fear: The Origins and Management of Ethnic Conflict', *International Security* 21(2): 41–75.
Lake, D.A. and Rothchild, D. (1998) 'Spreading Fear: The Genesis of Transnational Ethnic Conflict', in D.A. Lake and D. Rothchild (eds) *The International Spread of Ethnic Conflict*, Princeton, NJ: Princeton University Press:
Lemke, D. (2002) *Regions of War and Peace*, Cambridge: Cambridge University Press.
Lumsden, M. (1973) 'The Cyprus Conflict as a Prisoner's Dilemma', *Journal of Conflict Resolution* 17: 7–32.
Neville-Jones, P. (1996–1997) 'Dayton, IFOR and Alliance Relations in Bosnia', *Survival* 38(4): 45–65.
Posen, B.R. (1993) 'The Security Dilemma and Ethnic Conflict', in M.E. Brown (ed.) *Ethnic Conflict and International Community*, Princeton, NJ: Princeton, 105–119.
Saideman, S.M. (1997) 'Explaining the International Relations of Majority Conflicts. Vulnerability vs. Ethnic Ties', *International Organization* 51(4): 721–753.
Shehadi, K. (1993) *Ethnic Self-Determination and the Break-up of States*, London: International Institute for Strategic Studies, Adelphi Paper No. 283.
Shiel, F.L. (ed.) (1984) *Ethnic Separatism and World Politics*, Lanham, MD: University Press of America.
Suhrke, A. and Noble, L.G. (eds) (1977) *Ethnic Conflict and International Relations*, New York: Praeger.
Walter, B.F. (1997) 'The Critical Barrier to Civil War Settlement', *International Organizations* 51(3): 335–364.
Walter, B.F. (2002) *Committing to Peace: The Successful Resolution of Civil Wars*, Princeton, NJ: Princeton University Press.
Zartman, W. (1985) *Ripe for Resolution*, New York: Oxford University Press.

10 From bullets to ballots
Using the people as arbitrators to settle civil wars

Margareta Sollenberg

Introduction

At the height of civil war, cooperation and coexistence seem remote. With little respect for human life, warring armies are at the throat of each other – often for years – in order to capture the ultimate prize: the power over government and all its wealth, often including vast natural resources. As the war is raging, the role of the people is often only as victims. Yet bitter and protracted wars do end; a number of seemingly intractable civil wars have ended in recent years, sometimes with democratization. In Nicaragua in 1990, Mozambique in 1994, and in Liberia in 1997, elections were finally held which allowed ordinary citizens to decide who would hold power in the post-war society. The puzzle is then: *Why do warring elites sometimes hand over power to settle the war to the people – through competitive elections whose outcome is unknown – instead of simply dividing the spoils of war between them to ensure that they will at least receive a piece of the pie?*

Leonard Wantchekon provides a potential solution to this puzzle in his formal model on post-civil war democratization (Wantchekon and Neeman 2002; Wantchekon 2004). Given that a civil war[1] is inconclusive, that is, that both sides have come to realize that they cannot win the war, there will be incentives for warring parties to democratize even when the parties themselves do not normatively favor democracy. Wantchekon argues that as long as both parties stand a chance of winning elections (that is, that the outcome of elections is uncertain) and there are security guarantees for the loser, warring parties in an inconclusive civil war will choose to democratize rather than to continue the war. This is so because the benefits of the democratic system are greater than continuing the war.

In this particular situation of costly and inconclusive conflict, warring parties use competitive elections as a mechanism to arbitrate the dispute, thus democracy is treated in this study as a possible way out of war.[2] Consequently, the focus is not on democracy or democratization processes per se. The theoretical model does not deal with overall prospects for democracy or explaining how democratization processes come about. Even if the model may also have implications for the conditions under which democracy after war is sustained, it is not the object of this chapter, which solely focuses on the process leading up to and including the settlement of armed conflict. I am interested in democracy as a tool for settling armed conflict. Since this is the case, democracy is defined in a minimalist manner as 'a political system in which power is allocated by means of competitive elections whose outcome reflects citizens' preferences, and both the losing party and the winning party abide by the elections' (Wantchekon and Neeman 2002: 2).[3]

The purpose of this chapter is to investigate under what conditions civil war ends through competitive elections. This research question has not previously been empirically tested. In this chapter I empirically test some implications of the formal model presented by Wantchekon and Neeman (2002) and Wantchekon (2004) on a large-n dataset of armed conflicts 1989–2000.

Most research on armed conflict focuses on the conflict up to the point where it ends and peace agreements are implemented. Research on post-war democratization processes often take as their departure the point where the war ends. However, few have attempted to merge the two fields of research. We know that democracy is positively linked to peace in various ways, although the relationship is not as simple as to say that democracy necessarily brings peace or vice versa. Research has found that, for instance, democracies run a significantly lower risk of experiencing civil war than other types of government (e.g. Hegre *et al.* 2001). However, research on democracy and armed conflict has previously not focused on the link between internal armed conflict and its various aspects and the type of political system that follows. Wantchekon provides a theory that addresses the link between civil war and the post-war political system in which he connects the two fields of study using insights from both.

There is only one other previous empirical study that uses a similar dependent variable that this study does.[4] In their article on international peace building, Doyle and Sambanis investigate under which conditions international peace building operations are successful, that is, under which conditions they lead to peace (Doyle and Sambanis, 2000). They use two different versions of the dependent variable, peace, one of which is violence-focused whereas the second one defines peace in a wider sense including a minimum level of democracy in addition to the absence of violence. Their study deals with peace rather than democracy specifically, and they have a different theoretical starting point than this study. I will return to some of their main findings and how they relate to this study below.

In the following, I first present the main points of the theoretical model and place it in its theoretical context. I then go through some implications of the theory and formulate a number of empirically testable hypotheses. The following section discusses research design and data issues. Finally, I present my results and I end the chapter with some concluding remarks.

Theoretical framework

Wantchekon and Neeman (2002) and Wantchekon (2004) model the transition from political disorder (civil war) to political order (democracy).[5] They deal with political conflict where the rivals fight for power and seek to settle the conflict by some power-sharing contract involving an arbitrator. The situation can be seen as a classic prisoner's dilemma. Both parties want to see an end to the war since they no longer benefit from it or have lost the prospect of winning. However, if one party stops fighting and the other does not, the first party will lose. The only way out is if both of them choose to stop fighting and design some form of power-sharing contract.

The premises of the argument are (1) every political system is an arrangement to create political order; (2) such a contract requires a sovereign or an enforcer; and (3) the rule of the sovereign or enforcer depends on the consent of political actors which in turn depends on whether the sovereign is perceived as effective or neutral (Wantchekon and Neeman 2002). Another crucial premise of the model is that the parties' payoffs depend on the productive investments of the citizens (Wantchekon 2004).

Given that the armed conflict is inconclusive, there are three possible choices for the warring parties: (1) status quo, i.e. a continuation of the war, (2) external enforcement in the form of an invited foreign country (a 'Leviathan' using Wantchekon's terminology) who will decide who should run the country, and (3) internal arbitration, i.e. democracy.

In the situation of status quo, i.e. civil war, both warring parties expropriate freely. The situation is characterized by over expropriation of the citizens since the parties realize that whatever is not expropriated by one party may be expropriated by the other party. As expropriation increases, the level of the citizens' investments decreases. Simply put, citizens will tend to work less when more is taken from them. As a result, the whole economy shrinks. Thus, payoffs for the parties will also continuously decrease in a situation that resembles the 'tragedy of the commons'. This means that there will be incentives for the parties to find some way of regulating their expropriation to save the commons.

The second situation, under Leviathan, where an external enforcer (a foreign country) has been invited is characterized by less expropriation than under status quo but more expropriation than under democracy. Leviathan's role is to decide who will run the country and illegal expropriation will be eliminated in the process. It should be noted that the foreign country does this for some kind of reward, that is, a piece of the expropriation pie. Compared to the status quo, the party that loses out in the decision on which faction should rule the country would be worse off than during status quo since illegal expropriation is eliminated. Therefore, a party would only agree to invite an external enforcer if it receives a signal that it will be the party taking power. It is unlikely that they will receive this signal simultaneously, and even if they do, both parties realize that they cannot simultaneously be favored by the external actor. Since this is the case, they will not agree on inviting an external actor to decide who will take power.[6] If one party invites Leviathan against the will of the other, the resulting situation is a return to status quo, that is, a continuation of the war. Although Wantchekon does not make it explicit, this means that the war could cease being inconclusive. The change of dynamics could lead the inviting party to restore hope of being victorious in the war. (Obviously, all civil wars that are not inconclusive – for any reason – may also end in victory.)

In democracy, expropriation levels are lower than in both other situations. Under democracy, illegal expropriation is banned. Since the parties are dependent on the citizens for being elected and re-elected, once in power, there are incentives to lower the expropriation level to the party's level of expropriation when it was allowed to roam freely under civil war. This means that the total expropriation level is lower than under status quo where *both* parties expropriate on this level as well as under Leviathan when there is an additional actor competing about payoffs. As citizens make their investments, a positive externality – i.e. a growing economy – is created serving as payoffs for the warring factions and as such serving as a crucial incentive for the parties to democratize. Since there is less taxation in democracy this results in a surplus that benefits everybody; the ruling party as well as the regular citizens. The losing party will obviously earn less than when it was able to expropriate under anarchy (i.e. civil war), but it will also benefit from the positive spillover.

Theoretically, the warring factions cannot agree on an external enforcer for the reasons detailed above. Therefore, the choices remaining are status quo or democracy. If at least one party prefers status quo, status quo prevails but if both choose democracy, democracy prevails. Democracy will be chosen by the warring parties, if both of them perceive a chance of winning elections, i.e. the outcome of the elections cannot be anticipated in advance.

In order to keep the losing party in check, arrangements must be made before the elections (i.e. when the outcome of the elections is unknown), to make it costly to back down from the settlement. This means providing security guarantees for the loser to prevent it from backing down out of fear of the winning side as well as providing sanctions against any attempts to find a better deal through continued war. Since the people, who act as arbitrators, generally lack the means for enforcing the agreement, external enforcement is likely to be needed in the phase from the settlement to the holding and implementation of the elections. If either party suspects the enforcer of colluding with the other side, that party will back out of the agreement and ultimately revert to war. Therefore, the enforcer should be neutral and also be perceived as such by the warring parties. Note that this neutral external enforcer should not be confused with 'Leviathan', also an external enforcer. The former enforces a settlement arbitrated by the people, whereas the latter enforces an end to the conflict by choosing one of the warring parties as the winner.

To summarize Wantchekon's argument, democracy is possible if the warring parties believe they have a chance of winning the elections and citizens prefer democracy to status quo (civil war) because it provides order and protection against banditry.

The theoretical reasoning builds on ideas found in classical political economy on state-building as well as on ideas found in the democratization literature. First, it builds on the literature on state-building and endogenous property rights, e.g. the work by Mancur Olson on incentives for the transition from anarchy to order (the preference for 'stationary bandits' over 'roving bandits' using Olson's terminology). Once order is established through authoritarian rule, there are incentives for moving toward democracy and away from dictatorship. Olson concludes that the conditions necessary for the emergence of democracy are the same as those for securing property (Olson 1993). Whereas Olson's theory – as do most theories on the transition from anarchy to order (e.g. Huntington 1968) – assumes an intermediate authoritarian phase before making the final transition to democracy, the current model skips the intermediate phase altogether and proposes that it is possible to move directly from anarchy (war) to democracy. Second, Wantchekon also draws heavily on the democratization literature, notably on the work by Adam Przeworski on the uncertainties of democracy and the incentives for parties to accept election losses since by abiding to the democratic system they stand a chance of eventually realizing their interests. In other words, there are incentives to disregard temporary losses since it might lead them to achieve long-term successes (Przeworski 1991). To this work, Wantchekon adds the role of the citizenry and the issue of contract enforcement that he argues Przeworski overlooks (Wantchekon and Neeman 2002).

Implications of the theory

The purpose of the study is to investigate under which conditions civil wars are settled through competitive elections. Drawing on Wantchekon's model, I develop a number of hypotheses about when settlement through competitive elections might prevail over other possible outcomes.[7]

Presence of other sources of revenue than the citizens' productive investments

One of the central assumptions in Wantchekon's model is that the warring parties are dependent on the citizens' investments. The incentives associated with democracy are all based on what the parties can earn from taxation of the population in the country. When the parties' main income is derived instead from other sources than the citizens' productive investments, the incentives for moving toward democracy no longer apply. Examples of alternative sources of income that would violate the assumption of the model are natural resources, crime (e.g. drug trafficking), or support from foreign countries. Thus, we would not expect to see popular arbitration in these situations (Wantchekon 2004). Natural resources that should be relevant as an alternative source of revenue to the citizens' productive investments are lootable resources such as mineral assets (e.g. metals, gems, oil) rather than natural resources that require large-scale labor for extraction since this can be assumed to involve the citizens' productive investment. Since the warring parties have to agree to popular arbitration, it is enough if one of them derives its main income from alternative sources. This leads me to the formulation of the following hypotheses:[8]

> H1 *In inconclusive armed conflict, warring parties that lack access to lootable natural resources will be more likely to settle the conflict through competitive elections.*
>
> H2 *In inconclusive armed conflict, warring parties that do not have support from foreign countries will be more likely to settle the conflict through competitive elections.*

Heterogeneity of the electorate

Another implication of the theoretical model is that there must be uncertainty as to who will be victorious in the elections for elections to occur. This implies that a certain level of heterogeneity of the electorate is a precondition for internal arbitration (Wantchekon and Neeman, 2002). Heterogeneity may involve a number of different dividing lines, e.g. ethnicity, religion, or class. For instance, in ethnically fragmented societies, where parties may form various alliances, the outcome of elections is likely to be unknown beforehand. However, in societies where one ethnic group dominates over the other, the outcome of the elections is much easier to anticipate. Therefore, such societies would be less likely to see an end to war through competitive elections. A hypothesis derived from this theoretical implication is that:

> H3 *Inconclusive armed conflicts are more likely to end through competitive elections when there is a large number of ethnic groups in the country than when one ethnic group dominates or where there are only a few dividing lines.*

The neutral external enforcer

For the warring parties to agree to settling the war through competitive elections, their security before and after elections must be guaranteed.[9] A neutral external enforcer could play a crucial role providing security guarantees during post-war implementation of the settlement. If internal arbitration is chosen by the parties, i.e. if they invite the people to settle the conflict, it is a fact that the citizens rarely possess the resources to enforce that settlement. More specifically, since new governmental institutions including military and police forces have usually not yet been formed, the people generally do not have the means to provide security guarantees for the losing side. This is where the neutral external enforcer, typically the UN or any other neutral actor, comes in. However, there are reasons to expect that the nature of that involvement will affect the likelihood of competitive elections. As spelled out above, an external guarantor must not be suspected to collude with one party, i.e. it cannot support only one side. If it does, it will not be accepted as a guarantor by the other side. Even for neutral guarantees, it should be better if there is more than one state involved since the different states can function as checks on each other to make sure that the guarantees remain neutral. It should be noted that collusion does not have to take place; the fact that one of the parties suspects a guarantor of collusion is enough for him to back out of the negotiations or the settlement altogether (Wantchekon and Nickerson 1999). Thus, multilateral guarantees should not only make collusion less likely but also to be perceived as more trustworthy by the warring parties than unilateral guarantees. The discussion above leads me to the formulation of the following hypothesis:

> H4 *Neutral third party involvement in inconclusive armed conflict makes it more likely that the conflict will end through competitive elections.*[10]

Research design and data

I empirically test the hypotheses on what makes competitive elections after war more or less likely on a cross-sectional time-series dataset on all armed conflicts in the period 1989–2000.

This study uses annual observations of internal armed conflict over government. The unit of analysis is civil war year.[11] All years of governmental internal armed conflict in the period 1989–2000 are included in the study. Data on internal armed conflicts are taken from the Uppsala Conflict Data Program (UCDP) datasets on armed conflict (UCDP 2005).[12] The UCDP defines armed conflict as 'a contested incompatibility which concerns government and/or territory where the use of armed force between two parties, of which at least one is the government of a state, results in at least 25 battle-related deaths' (Wallensteen and Sollenberg 2001: 643).[13] One of the advantages of the UCDP data compared to other commonly used conflict datasets, e.g. Correlates of War (Singer and Small 1994), is that UCDP data covers low-intensity conflicts as well as high-intensity conflicts.

Only armed conflicts with governmental incompatibilities – that is, concerning the type of political system, or, the composition or replacement of central government (Wallensteen and Sollenberg 2001) – are included since it is assumed in the model that an end to war involves a settlement arrangement for the state as a whole. In an armed conflict over government, both parties strive for a solution within the same political unit, the state, whereas in territorial conflicts the parties strive for power in different political units;

one for maintaining power in the whole state and the other one for gaining power in a portion of it. It should be noted that there can only be one governmental armed conflict in a country at any given time. A new governmental armed conflict is coded if there is a complete change of actors on the rebel side from one year to another.[14]

All years from the first year the conflict was active in the period 1989–2000 to the last year of activity are included in the dataset including inactive years inbetween active years.

Dependent variable: conflict ending through competitive elections

The first component of the dependent variable, conflict ending, is rather straightforward. A civil war is considered to have ended if violence above the 25-threshold has terminated for the remainder of the period 1989–2000. It is coded as a dichotomous variable (civil war ending = 1, continued civil war = 0).

The second component of the dependent variable, competitive elections, deserves some elaboration. There is much discussion and much disagreement on what are valid indicators of the complex concept of democracy.[15] However important this discussion is, it is not of primary concern here since it all depends on what one tries to capture. The theoretical framework used in this chapter concerns elections as an arbitration mechanism to settle armed conflict. Whether one thinks competitive elections qualifies as democracy, or not, is outside the scope of this chapter.

In the theoretical model, competitive elections are used to arbitrate an end to civil war between the warring parties. If there is armed conflict this means that the warring parties are not using competitive elections to solve their dispute. If there is an end to armed conflict and there is democracy above a certain minimum threshold, I assume that the warring parties have decided to let the dispute be settled through competitive elections.[16] I am interested in whether the parties who fight for central power *use competitive elections for arbitrating their dispute*, and not in a shift in the level of democracy.[17] This means establishing whether there are competitive elections if the conflict has ended. Thus, I am looking for a level of democracy where competitive elections are held, that is, the passing of some threshold.

To measure competitive elections, I use Polyarchy data (Vanhanen 2000) which takes Dahl's notion of Polyarchy as its point of departure (Dahl 1971). Among the various datasets available on regime type and democracy specifically, I find Polyarchy data to have the most valid measure of the concept of competitive elections in the model as it deals directly with actual competition and participation.[18]

Vanhanen has coded two separate variables, Competition and Participation, which measure actual (percentage) levels of competition and participation in elections.[19] The two variables are then combined into a third variable, Index of Democratization (ID), where the two basic variables are multiplied and then divided by 100. The values of the ID variable range from 0 to 49.[20]

Which threshold to use for what constitutes a minimum level of democracy where competitive elections are held is a somewhat arbitrary matter. Vanhanen has coded Participation at 10 percent and Competition at 30 percent as minimum requirements of democracy. Following Vanhanen, I employ a cutoff point of 5.0 which is slightly higher than the combined value of the cutoff points for Competition and Participation which would be 3.0 (Vanhanen 2000). It should be noted that in none of my cases is the ID value below 5.0 when the Competition and Participation thresholds are met. I use the ID cutoff point in combination with cutoff points for Participation and Competition of 10 and 30 percent, respectively. Competitive elections are coded as having occurred if all three criteria are met.

When would we expect competitive elections to occur if they are used to end the armed conflict? Theoretically, the conflict ending is supposed to coincide with elections. In reality, however, it is reasonable to expect some time to pass before the agreement is implemented and elections are held. The holding of national elections is a huge and resource-demanding task and especially so for a country devastated by war. I measure the level of democracy the first year after the last year of active armed conflict (the highest value during a two-year period including the last year of active conflict), but also four years after the conflict ended (the highest value in a five-year period including the last year of activity).[21] The reason for including the last year of armed conflict is to allow for the possibility that parties manage to hold competitive elections immediately after the war which may have ended any time during the calendar year. The two versions of the dependent variable, *Competitive Elections (two-year)* and *Competitive Elections (five-year)*, are used in alternative regression models.

Inconclusive (H1, H2, H3, H4)

A central variable that needs to be operationalized is 'inconclusive'. How do we know when an armed conflict is inconclusive, that is, when the parties have reached a stalemate? It should be noted that the theory deals with situations that are not just inconclusive but where the parties are also seeking some kind of power sharing arrangement for which they need an arbitrator. It is very difficult to find an indicator that captures the aspect of inconclusiveness directly as it has to do with the perceptions of the warring parties. One could imagine that 'inconclusiveness' is a function of the duration of war or of the scale of destruction due to the war; human or material. However, since this varies a great deal between conflicts and there is little guidance as to what would be 'enough', it would be better to employ some other less arbitrary indicator.

I have chosen to use *negotiations* as the indicator for whether an armed conflict is inconclusive. This indicator directly focuses on whether the parties are actively seeking a settlement. Most armed conflicts that have reached the stage where the parties enter direct negotiations about settling the conflict can be assumed to be inconclusive. One could of course imagine other reasons than inconclusiveness for entering negotiations and where negotiations would serve as a well-needed break in the fighting for gathering new resources including anything from material means to recognition. Still, these cases are likely to be exceptions since negotiations with the adversary should in some respect also be costly to the actor although arguably less so for the rebels than for the government. It is more difficult to imagine civil wars without negotiations that are in reality inconclusive and where the parties strive for a power-sharing deal. However, it is reasonable to expect a time lag between the point in time when parties realize that the conflict is inconclusive and the actual holding of negotiations. Nevertheless, on the whole, negotiations should still be a fairly good proxy for 'inconclusive'.

Negotiations are defined as talks that are held between at least two of the warring parties in matters directly relating to the armed conflict, notably the incompatibility. Negotiations is coded on a yearly basis as negotiations 1, no negotiations 0. It is reasonable to assume that negotiations do not take place every single year in a conflict, without this necessarily implying that the conflict is no longer inconclusive. Therefore in addition to the first indicator (incidence of negotiations on a yearly basis), I have also coded a variable where all subsequent years after a year of negotiations are coded as inconclusive (i.e. 1). The latter variable, *Negotiations*, is used in the regression models presented in this chapter. Yearly data on negotiations is taken from the UCDP datasets (UCDP 2005).

Access to natural resources (H1)

I use a proxy for access to lootable natural resources in this chapter that is commonly used in the literature:[22] share of primary commodities exports in GDP which simply measures the ratio of primary commodities in total exports (World Bank 2004). It should be noted that this does not only include lootable resources but also various other natural resources. *Primary Commodity Exports* is lagged one year.

Support from foreign countries (H2)

To measure support from foreign countries I use two proxies. First, I include a variable on direct military support by foreign countries in the armed conflict (*Secondary Warring Parties*). Direct military support is taken to indicate other types of support that are difficult to capture directly and for which there is no data available.[23] Much of the support that is given in the context of war is assumed to be covert or at least extremely difficult to estimate. Secondary warring parties are defined as states that participate militarily in armed conflicts on the side of one of the primary warring parties. This variable is coded 1 for presence of secondary warring parties and 0 otherwise. Data is taken from the UCDP (UCDP 2005). Secondly, I use a variable on developmental assistance and aid (*Aid*) measured as the percentage share of aid of gross national income (GNI) as this is assumed to constitute a possible alternative source of income over taxation of the citizens and their productive investments. *Aid* is lagged one year. The data is taken from the World Bank (2004).

Ethnic heterogeneity (H3)

Ethnic heterogeneity is measured as ethnic fractionalization. Data on ethnic fractionalization is taken from Fearon (2003). The most commonly used data on ethnic fractionalization is the index on ethno linguistic fractionalization (ELF) which measures the probability that any two randomly selected people in a particular country speak a different language.[24] Fearon has constructed an alternative index that is similar to the ELF index in many respects with the crucial difference that it does not only take into account linguistic differences but is instead focused on how individuals view themselves, i.e. when they as well as fellow citizens in a country perceive the existence of an ethnic group. This means that the index takes into account various types of differences, notably race and religion, in addition to linguistic differences. In addition, the former includes some 160 countries whereas the latter includes only 112 (Fearon 2003). Most importantly, the Fearon index makes for a more valid indicator to test the hypothesis on ethnic heterogeneity since it is assumed in the hypothesis that individuals vote according to their identities.

The neutral external enforcer (H4)

In this study neutral third party military involvement is taken to equal United Nations peacekeeping operations (PKOs). PKOs are defined as third party interventions that involve the following: (1) deployment of military troops and/or military observers and/or civilian police; (2) a mandate for separating warring parties and to take responsibility for the security situation in relation to the warring parties; and (3) neutrality toward the warring parties, however, not necessarily implying impartiality toward their behavior (Heldt and Wallensteen 2004). Non-military third party operations that cannot provide the security guarantees proposed by the theory are not included in the study. It is not clear theoretically what their role would be, if any. It should also be noted that non-neutral military foreign involvement – that may sometimes be denoted 'PKOs' – are not included.[25]

The theory implies that multilateral third party involvement should be more conducive to the holding of competitive elections than unilateral involvement. Operations that involve a large number of states would generally be less prone to be biased or, equally important, to be *perceived* as biased. If there is only one state involved, the warring parties tend to be less trusting of that operation actually providing security guarantees for both sides. UN PKOs generally are multilateral and neutral in the sense described here. Most non-UN PKOs also include a number of states, but since the operations are often led by one dominant actor, usually a regional power, this would suggest that they would function as if they were unilateral and potentially biased. Prime examples are ECOMOG operations in West Africa that were dominated by Nigeria and CIS operations in Central Asia where Russia was a similarly dominating actor. Instead of coding which PKO is truly multilateral in nature and which ones function more as if they were unilateral, I have settled on treating all UN PKOs as neutral multilateral PKOs and all non-UN PKOs as potentially biased. This is obviously an oversimplification, but it should still make a fairly good proxy of the kind of neutral security guarantee that is hypothesized to be necessary for moving toward a settlement of the civil war through competitive elections. Presence of UN PKOs is coded 1 and all other instances including presence of non-UN PKOs are coded 0. Data is taken from Heldt and Wallensteen (2004).

Interaction terms

My theoretical expectation for the independent variables *(Primary Commodity Exports, Secondary Warring Parties, Aid, Ethnic Fractionalization* and *UN Peacekeeping Operations)* is that they have an effect in inconclusive civil wars. Therefore, these variables are included in the regression models as part of a number of interaction terms together with the central independent variable *Negotiations*, the indicator of inconclusiveness. I have no theoretical expectations as to the effect on the dependent variable of *Negotiations* by itself which means that it is not included in the regression models.

Since the calculation and interpretation of interaction (or multiplicative) effects is slightly less straightforward than the calculation and interpretation of additive effects, some elaboration is warranted.[26] By interaction effect is meant a moderating effect; the relationship between an independent variable and a dependent variable is moderated by a third variable. In contrast to an additive model where the coefficients of the independent variables are parameters that estimate a general relationship, the coefficients (and the standard errors) in an interactive model are conditional on the values taken by the other variable (or variables in the case of more complex interaction terms) in the interaction term.[27] Two types of coefficients result from a regression model where interaction terms are included. First, the coefficient for a component variable represents the effect of that independent variable on the dependent variable when the moderating variable, in my case *Negotiations*, takes the value 0. Second, the coefficient for an interaction term is the change in the dependent variable caused by the independent variable when moving one unit in the value of the moderating variable.[28] Since the moderating variable in this study is a dummy variable that can only take on two values (negotiations = 1, no negotiations = 0), this means that the coefficient for the interaction term represents the change in the dependent variable caused by the independent variable when the moderating variable, *Negotiations*, takes the value 1 instead of 0. The interaction effect is arrived at by adding up the two coefficients produced in the regression analysis. For this new coefficient a new standard error and *t*-value must be calculated in order to establish whether the interaction effect is statistically significant by itself.

In this study I am primarily interested in the interaction effects. Therefore, the presentation of regression results in the following section is focused on the interaction effects that can be calculated from the coefficients produced in the regression analysis. It might also be valuable to establish whether there is a statistically significant difference between the effect of an independent variable on the likelihood of war settlement through competitive elections in inconclusive civil wars, and, the effect of that same variable in civil wars that are not inconclusive. The purpose of this would be to evaluate the fruitfulness of separating the two situations theoretically. However, this is not the primary focus here and neither is the effect of the independent variables in wars that are not inconclusive, that is, the effect that can be read from the coefficients for the component variables. Nevertheless, I will comment on the two types of regression coefficients as well as the interaction effects themselves in the section on results.

Control variables

Control variables included in some of the models are the natural logarithm of GDP per capita (*ln GDP per capita*) and trade openness (*Trade*) measured as the share of trade in GDP. Both variables are lagged one year. Data is taken from the World Bank (World Bank 2004). Two control variables directly related to civil war are included: the duration of the conflict measured in years (*Duration of Conflict*) and if there was another armed conflict active at the same time in the country (*Other Conflict*). The latter is a dummy where the existence of another conflict is coded 1 and non-existence 0. For these two variables I employ UCDP data (UCDP 2005). Finally I have included a control for the yearly democracy level (*Democracy*). This variable is also lagged one year and data is taken from Vanhanen (2000).

Results and analysis

I employ logistic regression in the statistical analysis since the dependent variable is dichotomous. Standard errors are adjusted for clustering on conflict since the yearly observations for each armed conflict cannot be assumed to be independent from each other.[29]

Table 10.1 reports the results of logit estimates for the dependent variable, conflict ending through competitive elections proxied by a minimum level of democracy as measured by Vanhanen (2000). I present four models; a basic model including only the variables derived from implications of the

Table 10.1 Logit regression results

Independent variables	Model 1 (competitive elections 2-year)	Model 2 (competitive elections 2-year)	Model 3 (competitive elections 5-year)	Model 4 (competitive elections 5-year)
Primary Commodity Exports$_{t-1}$	10.32** (4.88)	0.72 (8.07)	20.28*** (7.28)	18.02* (13.87)
Aid$_{t-1}$	−0.13* (0.10)	0.08 (0.20)	−0.12* (0.08)	0.27** (0.13)
Ethnic Fractionalization	−2.28** (1.38)	1.52 (1.96)	−5.02** (2.27)	−2.56 (2.60)
UN Peacekeeping Operation	−14.87*** (0.92)	−17.24*** (1.51)	23.63*** (0.81)	20.01*** (3.05)
Negotiations*Primary Commodity Exports$_{t-1}$	−15.37*** (6.04)	−21.19*** (7.63)	−25.94*** (7.92)	−54.43*** (15.27)
Negotiations*Aid$_{t-1}$	0.10 (0.12)	−0.01 (0.20)	0.08 (0.11)	−0.20** (0.09)
Negotiations*Ethnic Fractionalization	2.74* (1.82)	6.27** (2.06)	5.30** (2.64)	13.77*** (3.59)
Negotiations*UN PKO	16.03 (.)[a]	22.35 (.)[a]	−22.00 (.)[a]	−11.76 (.)[a]
ln GDP per capita$_{t-1}$	–	3.31*** (0.90)	–	4.65*** (1.62)
Trade$_{t-1}$	–	0.03** (0.01)	–	0.07*** (0.02)
Duration of Conflict	–	−0.12*** (0.04)	–	−0.14*** (0.04)
Other Conflict	–	1.35 (1.99)	–	1.32 (2.37)
Democracy$_{t-1}$	–	0.02 (0.08)	–	0.04 (0.08)
Constant	−2.10*** (0.77)	−28.45*** (6.96)	−1.89** (0.85)	−40.60*** (13.91)
N	212	202	204	194
Pseudo R^2	0.11	0.50	0.24	0.65
Log likelihood	−45.97	−25.48	−42.39	−19.14

Notes
Robust standard errors in parenthesis (standard errors adjusted for clustering on conflict).
***$p < 0.01$, **$p < 0.05$, *$p < 0.10$ (one-tailed).
a No standard errors for these coefficients are produced in the regression analysis due to the high correlation (0.97) between this variable and the variable UNPKO.

Wantchekon model and where the dependent variable is measured during a two-year period including the last year of armed conflict (Model 1) and one expanded model where relevant control variables are included (Model 2) using the same time period for measuring the dependent variable as in Model 1. I also include an alternative version of each of these two models where competitive elections are measured for a five-year period. The basic model for the five-year period is Model 3 and the expanded model for the same period is Model 4. For a list of all war endings and their corresponding value on the dependent variable, see Appendix (Table 10.1A).

H1 that concerns access to lootable natural resources, receives strong support in Models 2 and 4 where the control variables are included. In these two models, the effect of *Primary Commodity Exports* moderated by *Negotiations* is negative ($0.72 + (-21.19) = -20.48$ and $18.02 + (-54.43) = -36.42$, respectively) and statistically significant ($p > 0.01$, one-tailed).[30] It is negative also in Models 1 and 3 and is just outside being statistically significant at the $p > 0.10$ level in Model 3. Although the finding is not fully robust across the four models presented here, the results from models 2 and 4 are robust across other time periods and specifications of the expanded model (not reported here).

In line with the theoretical model, this finding suggests that in situations of inconclusive civil war and where there is an abundance of natural resources, the warring parties are less likely to look to the democratic system for settling the war. This is consistent with findings by Doyle and Sambanis in their study on international peacebuilding where they test a set of hypotheses relating to the conditions under which international peacebuilding operations lead to peace and a minimum level of democracy (Doyle and Sambanis, 2000).[31]

H2 on support from foreign countries is slightly more difficult to interpret. First and foremost, the hypothesis receives no support regarding *Aid* moderated by *Negotiations*. The interaction effect is not significant in any of the models. *Aid* is, however, arguably a problematic indicator of support from foreign countries. The amount of developmental assistance and aid to a country fluctuates greatly over time and consequently, it might not be a source of income that the parties could rely on. Examples of major fluctuations are Burundi and Congo-Brazzaville where the share of aid of GNI shifts from about a third of the total income to a few percent in only a couple of years' time. Theoretically, for access to income from the outside (rather than from production within the country) to matter, that is, for the parties to disregard internal sources of income and thus also disregard incentives for moving toward democracy, we must assume a certain continuity of that external income. Developmental assistance and aid may not provide that kind of continuity.[32] However, although aid may not provide the kind of resource that would lead the warring parties to disregard citizen-based economic incentives for settling the conflict through democratic means, we can reasonably assume that it could provide an additional resource for the parties which in turn would postpone this process. The interaction term including *Secondary Warring Parties* (i.e. foreign states intervening with troops on the side of one of the main warring parties) which is the second proxy for support from foreign countries, is problematic too but in a more technical way than the interaction term including *Aid*. Including *Secondary Warring Parties* in the regression models creates a zero cell count problem. Therefore, *Secondary Warring Parties* is not included in the models reported in Table 10.2. It should be noted, however, that secondary warring parties are almost never present when an inconclusive civil war ends in competitive elections. As can be seen when cross-tabulating the interaction term on *Negotiations* and *Secondary Warring Parties* and *Competitive Elections (two-year)* there is only one instance of secondary warring party involvement when *Competitive Elections (two-year)* takes on the value 1 and 0 for the five-year version.[33]

Although *Secondary Warring Parties* is not included in the models, this would still suggest, as proposed in H2, that support from foreign countries does have a negative effect on the likelihood of settling the war through competitive elections. Both indicators on foreign support are problematic, nevertheless, the findings still suggest the hypothesized relationship; that foreign support is negatively related to competitive elections.

The hypothesis on ethnic fractionalization (H3) receives support in Models 2 and 4, that is, the same models in which the hypothesis on access to lootable resources is supported. In both models, the interaction effect is positive as expected (1.52 + 6.27 = 7.79 and −2.56 + 13.77 = 11.21, respectively) and statistically significant ($p > 0.01$, one-tailed). This finding is robust for alternative time periods and specifications of the expanded model, but not for Models 1 and 3 where no control variables are included. However, although the effects in the latter models are not statistically significant, the sign remains the same also in these models. Overall, the regression results still suggest that ethnic fractionalization in inconclusive armed conflicts is positively correlated to the holding of competitive elections. It can be contrasted with the finding by Doyle and Sambanis that ethnic heterogeneity has no effect on the prospects for peace defined to also include a minimum level of democracy (Doyle and Sambanis 2000).[34]

Table 10.2 Cross-tabulation of negotiations* secondary party and competitive elections

Negotiations* secondary warring parties	Competitive elections 2-year (5-year in parenthesis)		Total
	0	1	
0	237 (226)	15 (19)	252 (245)
1	18 (17)	1 (0)	19 (17)
Total	255 (243)	16 (19)	271 (262)

H4 receives no support. The fact that *UN Peacekeeping Operations* and the interaction term with *UN Peacekeeping Operations* and *Negotiations* are so highly correlated (0.97), results in a computational problem; the standard errors for the respective variables cannot be isolated.[35] Judging from the new coefficients in the four models that give the interaction effects (1.16, 5.11, 1.63, and 8.25, respectively) they are so low that standard errors for the coefficients for the interaction terms would have to be very small for the new coefficients to be statistically significant. Thus, even if standard errors could be calculated for the coefficients for the interaction terms, there may still be no statistically significant interaction effects. This can be contrasted with the finding by Doyle and Sambanis that UN PKOs are positively correlated with peace defined as absence of war and a minimum level of democracy (Doyle and Sambanis 2000).[36]

The coefficients for the interaction terms in the four models may be used to establish whether there is indeed a difference between effects in inconclusive civil wars that the theoretical framework in this study deals with, and civil wars that are not inconclusive. If there are significant differences, this would provide support for modeling inconclusive civil wars separately. Coefficients for the interaction term where *Primary Commodity Exports* is moderated by *Negotiations* are negative and statistically significant in all four models which indicates that *Primary Commodity Exports* has different effects in the two situations. Access to lootable natural resources seems to have a stronger negative effect in inconclusive civil wars than in civil wars that are not inconclusive. The same clear difference between the two types of civil wars can be seen when looking at coefficients for the interaction term involving *Ethnic Fractionalization*. The coefficients for the interaction term are positive and statistically significant in all models. Ethnic heterogeneity therefore seems to be more positively related to settlement through popular arbitration in inconclusive civil wars than in wars that are not inconclusive. Regarding the coefficients for the interaction term involving *Aid*, only the coefficient in Model 4 is statistically significant on any conventional level ($p > 0.05$, one-tailed). It is negative indicating that there may be a difference between the two types of civil wars where aid and developmental assistance may be more negatively related to war settlement through competitive elections in inconclusive civil wars than in wars that are not inconclusive. However, this finding is not robust across other model specifications. Coefficients for the interaction term involving *UN Peacekeeping Operations* cannot be used to draw any conclusions due to computational problems. Nevertheless, based on the results above, I conclude that modeling inconclusive civil wars separately is a meaningful exercise.

Although I have no theoretical expectations regarding effects of the independent variables in wars that are not inconclusive, the regression analysis exhibits some interesting results also regarding these effects. The effect of *Primary Commodity Exports* in situations where there are no negotiations is positive and significant in three of the models. In other words, given that the civil war is not inconclusive, access to lootable natural resources increases, rather than decreases, the likelihood for settlement through competitive elections. The effect of *Ethnic Fractionalization* on the dependent variable when there are no negotiations is negative and significant in two of the models. This suggests that ethnic heterogeneity may decrease the likelihood of settlement through competitive elections in wars that are not inconclusive. Interestingly, the effect of *UN Peacekeeping Operation* in situations where there are no negotiations is significant in all four models but differ between the short-term models, where it is negative, and the long-term models, where it is positive. In other words, the presence of UN PKOs seems to be conducive to settlement through competitive elections in the long run but may be counterproductive in the short-term perspective. *Aid* has no effect on the dependent variable for wars that are not inconclusive.

Regarding the control variables, *ln GDP per capita* is consistently significant and found to be positively correlated to competitive elections in the reported models as well as in alternative specifications. The richer the country, the more likely it will experience conflict settlement through competitive elections. *Duration of Conflict* is statistically significant as well and is found to be negatively correlated to the dependent variable. In other words, the longer the conflict, the less likely it will end in competitive elections. *Trade* is positive and statistically significant in the reported models and in alternative specifications indicating that the larger the share of trade of GNI in a country, the more likely the war in that country will end through popular arbitration. *Other Conflict*, which measures whether there was another active armed conflict in the country at the same time as the civil war, and the lagged *Democracy* variable are never significant. This holds also for alternative model specifications.[37]

Concluding remarks

Patterns in the data suggest support for the three out of four hypotheses tested in this study. This implies that the theoretical model developed by Leonard Wantchekon on the conditions that would lead to civil war settlement through competitive elections (Wantchekon and Neeman 2002; Wantchekon 2004) has some merit.

The theoretical model is based on the assumption that the warring parties are dependent on the citizen's productive investments. Only when this is the case will the parties benefit economically from moving away from war toward democracy. When the parties' main source of income is derived elsewhere, for example, from lootable natural resources and from support from foreign countries, these incentives no longer apply. The hypothesis on access to lootable natural resources as a disincentive for ending the conflict through the democratic system (H1) is supported in the empirical analysis. The second hypothesis (H2) which proposes that support from foreign countries would be negatively related to the settlement of war through competitive elections is supported but with some reservations. Although the empirical testing of this hypothesis encountered problems in my study, the results still hint to support for the hypothesis.

For popular arbitration to occur there must be uncertainty as to the outcome of the elections. The theoretical model has it that the election winner will be better off under democracy than under civil war. If both warring parties perceive that they have a chance of winning the elections, they will choose the option of internal popular arbitration since this could potentially provide them with all the benefits of the democratic system. The third hypothesis tested in my study which deals with uncertainty of election outcomes states that ethnic heterogeneity should be positively related to popular arbitration (H3). This hypothesis is also supported.

The model suggests that the warring parties will only take the chance of competitive elections if they believe that their security can be guaranteed during the transition to democracy. Only when external security guarantees can be trusted to be neutral would the warring parties agree to settle the conflict through the democratic system. The fourth hypothesis (H4) tested in this study deals with security guarantees and proposes that neutral third party involvement should have a positive effect on the chances for a democratic solution of the civil war. There is no support in the empirical analysis for the hypothesis suggesting that neutral security guarantees are a crucial component of the process outlined here.

In sum, the results from the hypothesis testing in this study suggest that the theoretical model developed by Wantchekon may provide an explanation for why some civil wars end in competitive elections and others do not. Wantchekon's formal model provides the only theoretical framework developed to address the issue of conflict settlement through democracy and there has been no previous empirical testing of this particular research question. My study is a first attempt to empirically assess which conditions make internal popular arbitration more likely. The results from the empirical analysis are promising. Moreover, they show that modeling inconclusive civil wars separately from other civil wars is a meaningful exercise.

There are a number of ways to go from here. First of all, the implications of the theory and corresponding hypotheses could be developed further and insights from other literature should be taken into account. Second, some of the indicators used in this study are admittedly crude. Therefore, finding more precise indicators would be an obvious way ahead.[38] Third, the time series could be expanded. Although this would require additional coding concerning some indicators (for example, negotiations, which have only been coded from 1989 onwards) the benefits of having more observations should outweigh the coding efforts. There are relatively few observations in this study compared to the number of variables. However, this should further strengthen the confidence in the conclusions drawn in this chapter.

Appendices

Table 10.1A List of all war endings, 1989–2000

Country	Opposition organization	Last active year	Competitive elections (2-year period)	Competitive elections (5-year period)
Algeria	vs. Takfir wa-Hijra	1991	0	1
Azerbaijan	vs. Husseinov military faction	1993	0	0
Azerbaijan	vs. OPON forces	1995	0	1
Burma	vs. ABSDF	1994	0	0
Burundi	vs. Palipehutu	1992	0	0
Cambodia	vs. Khmer Rouge	1998	0	n.a.
Chad	vs. Various groups	1990	0	0
Chad	vs. MDD, FARF	1998	0	n.a.
Comoros	vs. Presidential guard	1989	1	1
Djibouti	vs. FRUD	1994	0	0
Djibouti	vs. FRUD faction	1999	0	0
Egypt	vs. Al-Gama'a al-Islamiyya	1998	0	n.a.
El Salvador	vs. FMLN	1991	1	1
Ethiopia	vs. EPRP, EPRDF	1991	0	0
Georgia	vs. Zviadists	1993	1	1
Guatemala	vs. URNG	1995	1	1
Guinea Bissau	vs. Military faction	1999	1	n.a.
Haiti	vs. Leopard Corps	1989	0	0
Haiti	vs. Tonton Macoute, Engine Lourd	1991	0	0
Laos	vs. LRM	1990	0	0
Lebanon	vs. Leb. Army, Leb. Forces, Syria	1990	0	1
Lesotho	vs. Military faction	1998	0	n.a.
Liberia	vs. NPFL	1995	0	0
Mexico	vs. EZLN	1994	1	1
Mexico	vs. EPR	1996	1	1
Mozambique	vs. Renamo	1992	0	1
Nicaragua	vs. FDN/Contras	1989	1	1
Pakistan	vs. MQM	1996	1	1
Panama	vs. Military faction	1989	1	1
Paraguay	vs. Military faction	1989	0	1
Peru	vs. Sendero Luminoso	1999	1	n.a.
Romania	vs. National Salvation Front	1989	0	1
Russia	vs. Parliamentary forces	1993	1	1
Rwanda	vs. FPR	1994	0	0
Sierra Leone	vs. RUF	2000	n.a.	n.a.
Somalia	vs. USC-Aideed faction	1996	0	0
Sri Lanka	vs. JVP	1990	1	1
Tajikistan	vs. UTO	1996	0	0

continued

198　*M. Sollenberg*

Table 10.1A Continued

Country	Opposition organization	Last active year	Competitive elections (2-year period)	Competitive elections (5-year period)
Tajikistan	vs. MPT	1998	0	n.a.
Togo	vs. Military faction	1991	0	0
Trinidad and Tobago	vs. Jama'at al-Muslimeen	1990	1	1
Turkey	vs. Devrimci sol	1992	1	1
Uzbekistan	vs. IMU	2000	n.a.	n.a.
Venezuela	vs. Military faction	1992	1	1
Zaire (D.R.C.)	vs. AFDL, Rwanda, Uganda, Angola	1997	0	0

Source: UCDP 2005.

Note
n.a.: not applicable since the war had not been ended for a sufficient number of years.

Table 10.2A Summary statistics

Variable	Number of observations	Mean	Standard deviation	Minimum	Maximum
Conflict Ending	273	0.168	0.375	0	1
Competitive Elections (two-year)	271	0.059	0.236	0	1
Competitive Elections (five-year)	262	0.073	0.260	0	1
Negotiations	273	0.546	0.499	0	1
Primary Commodity Exports$_{t-1}$	256	0.125	0.128	0.003	0.508
Aid$_{t-1}$	228	9.210	11.009	0.003	59.110
Secondary Warring Parties	273	0.099	0.299	0	1
Ethnic Fractionalization	273	0.584	0.248	0	0.933
UN Peacekeeping Operations	273	0.132	0.339	0	1
Negotiations*Primary Commodity Exports$_{t-1}$	256	0.085	0.137	0	0.508
Negotiations*Aid$_{t-1}$	228	4.943	8.870	0	50.052
Negotiations*Seecondary Warring Parties	273	0.073	0.261	0	1
Negotiations*Ethnic Fractionalization	273	0.327	0.356	0	0.933
Negotiations*UN PKOs	273	0.125	0.331	0	1

continued

Table 10.2A Continued

Variable	Number of observations	Mean	Standard deviation	Minimum	Maximum
ln GDP per capita$_{t-1}$	237	6.314	0.972	3.968	8.305
Trade$_{t-1}$	230	52.384	32.822	3.591	180.639
Duration of Conflict	273	10.802	9.123	1	36
Other Conflict	273	0.172	0.378	0	1
Democracy$_{t-1}$	273	6.082	7.538	0	29.830

Notes

1 By civil war I mean internal armed conflicts fought over governmental issues. I use civil war and armed conflict interchangeably in this chapter and they always refer to internal armed conflicts over government as opposed to internal armed conflicts over territory (e.g. separatist armed conflicts).

2 There could be other reasons for settlement through competitive elections than that the warring parties voluntarily hand over power to the citizens for popular arbitration. The settlement could be imposed on the parties by military or otherwise superior powers. However, empirically, settlement through competitive elections (e.g. El Salvador, Nicaragua, Guatemala, Mozambique) do not typically involve imposed settlements but are rather examples of the voluntary choice dealt with in the theoretical model.

3 Typical features of a more inclusive definition of democracy, such as political rights and civil liberties are not the focus in this particular context. It should be stressed that this has nothing to do with what are important or relevant aspects of democracy, only that they are not relevant for explaining the particular process through which some wars end through arbitration by the people.

4 There is also an unpublished paper in which Wantchekon and Nickerson (1999) makes an empirical study on foreign intervention and democracy. Their 1999 study takes as its point of departure an earlier version of the theory presented in this chapter.

5 The model is a two-stage game where the first stage models the two warring parties deciding on the form of government and the second stage models the citizens investing and realizing the return on investment (Wantchekon and Neeman 2002). For the formal expression of the game, see Wantchekon and Neeman (2002).

6 Wantchekon points out that even if Leviathan decides to go for some kind of power-sharing deal, expropriation levels will still remain higher than under democracy without Leviathan, since Leviathan also takes a piece of the pie (Wantchekon 2004).

7 It should be possible to test Wantchekon's model as such which would include a test of implications regarding all possible outcomes in Wantchekon's theoretical model. However, my purpose is to investigate the particular research question posed in this study rather than to test Wantchekon's model.

8 For now, I will leave out the implication regarding drug trafficking since there is little available data on drugs. However, data on drug cultivation – which could serve as an indicator of drug trafficking – has recently been collected in a research project at the Norwegian University of Science and Technology. This data could be employed to test the implication on drug trafficking in the future.

9 There is plenty of research on the critical role of third party security guarantees in successful war settlement, for example, Walter (2002) and Werner (1999).
10 In an unpublished study, Wantchekon and Nickerson test the effects of intervention on the level of post-war democracy (Wantchekon and Nickerson, 1999). Their study is a test of an implication of an earlier version of the Wantchekon model and their main finding is that multilateral foreign intervention increases the level of post-war democracy. However, the study does not differentiate between second and third party intervention which means that the results are difficult to interpret. There are other limitations to their study notably regarding the measure of the dependent variable. Wantchekon and Nickerson measure the relative change in the level of democracy using Polity III data. The problem is that the theory (also in the 1999 version) is not about the relative change in the level of democracy but about crossing a minimum threshold of democracy, i.e. corresponding to the holding of competitive elections. This is not captured in their measure. There are additional problems in the study, notably that of failing to operationalize 'inconclusive'.
11 Note that civil war is used interchangeably with governmental internal armed conflict in this chapter. 'War' in civil war is not meant to indicate a certain level of intensity of the conflict (i.e. war usually denotes an armed conflict with more than 1,000 deaths per year (see, among others, UCDP 2005; Singer and Small 1994)). Instead, civil war should just be seen as a more commonly used term for what UCDP calls internal armed conflict concerning government.
12 All armed conflicts in the UCDP database are included. This differs from the data in the most recent UCDP article in *Journal of Peace Research* (Eriksson and Wallensteen 2004) and the UCDP/PRIO dataset on armed conflicts 1946–2003 (Gleditsch *et al.* 2002) in that the governmental conflict in the USA (Govt of USA vs. al-Qaeda, active 2001–2002) has been excluded. This case is currently under investigation in the UCDP.
13 For the full definition see Wallensteen and Sollenberg (2001) or www.ucdp.uu.se.
14 This is to avoid the problem of governmental armed conflicts running indefinitely.
15 See, for instance, the debate among some of the leading collectors of democracy data in *Comparative Political Studies* (35: 1).
16 As pointed out in note 2, there could be other reasons for settlement through competitive elections than that the warring parties voluntarily choose popular arbitration. However, empirically, settlement through competitive elections (e.g. El Salvador, Nicaragua, Guatemala, Mozambique) typically involve settlements that are examples of the voluntary choice dealt with here.
17 Countries may or may not be democracies during civil war, but what is key here is that the warring parties end their war through democratic means, that is, competitive elections. In several datasets (e.g. Polyarchy (Vanhanen 2000), Polity (Marshall and Jaggers 2005)), conflicts are often coded as democracies even during active civil war. Although it is reasonable to assume that civil war, especially large-scale civil war, paralyzes the democratic system thereby making democracy (e.g. competitive elections) in the country more or less impossible, this is not the case in all civil wars. There are several examples of countries at war where the democratic system is upheld at least to some degree (e.g. Colombia) and thus they will have been coded as democracies. It should be noted that large-scale civil wars are often coded as no democracy in the abovementioned datasets.
18 This can be compared to the most commonly used dataset on democracy, Polity (Marshall and Jaggers 2005), which is focused on the structure of the political system rather than that it actually performs according to that structure. The Polity variables that could be used in this context, Competitiveness of Executive

Recruitment, Openness of Executive Recruitment and Competitive Participation, would be indicators of a political system that *allows for* competitive elections, not for a political system where competitive elections are held.

19 Competition is calculated by subtracting the share of the largest party from 100. In other words, the value of the indicator is the share of votes won by all other parties than the largest party. Participation is simply the share of the population that voted in the elections. It should be noted that the percentage for participation is calculated from the total population rather than from the population entitled to vote. Vanhanen argues that although the latter would be a better measure, data on the age structure of the population is missing in a number of countries whereas data on the total population is generally available (Vanhanen 2000). For further discussion of the indicators and their respective strengths and weaknesses, see Vanhanen (2000).

20 The maximum value is 49 since Vanhanen sets a limit at 70 percent for both Competition and Participation. He argues that any percentages greater than that would indicate an undemocratic system (Vanhanen 2000).

21 Four years should be enough for competitive elections to be held. On the other hand, it might leave too much room for other events to occur in the country. It would make sense to control for outbreaks of war or any other major disruptive events occurring in the period during which democracy is measured. Such events can be assumed to affect the process of implementing the civil war settlement, if nothing else, simply by making the holding of elections impossible from a practical perspective. I have not controlled for such events in this chapter, but it would make sense to do so in the future.

22 See, for instance, Collier and Hoeffler (2004) and Doyle and Sambanis (2000).

23 Secondary non-military involvement, for instance, financial, military (short of regular troops), and logistic support from foreign states has been coded in the UCDP. However, the quality of the data varies greatly across conflicts, therefore, although it would be a better proxy for foreign support than the two proxies used here, this data is not employed in this study.

24 The ELF data was initially taken from Department of Geodesy and Cartography of the State Geological Committee of the USSR, Moscow (1964) and Taylor and Hudson (1972).

25 A good example is the SADC operation in Lesotho in 1998 involving troops from South Africa and Botswana. Although claimed to be a peacekeeping operation, the participating countries should rather be seen as secondary warring parties on the side of the government.

26 For an overview of the calculation and interpretation of interaction effects, see Friedrich (1982), Jaccard *et al.* (1990) and Jaccard (2001).

27 Note that not only the coefficients for the interaction terms but also the coefficients of the component variables represent conditional relationships with the dependent variable. The latter should therefore not be interpreted the same way as coefficients in an additive model where they represent general relationships, that is, that they are constant across all values of other independent variables. The fact that the coefficient for a particular independent variable may change when an interaction term is entered into a model does not indicate that these coefficients are not stable or reliable but it is rather a consequence of the conditional nature of the relationship (Friedrich 1982). The effects of control variables that are not part of any interaction terms in a regression model are interpreted as usual, that is, as representing general relationships across all values of the other independent variables.

28 Note that the p-value for the interaction term tells us whether this *change* is statistically significant, not whether the interaction effect is statistically significant.

29 I considered using splines to control for temporal dependence but since the time series is so short (12 years) it is not clear whether this would actually benefit the analysis. Beck *et al.* (1998) suggest the usage of splines for time series longer than 20 years. Therefore I simply included a variable measuring the duration of armed conflict.
30 Note that the new coefficients, standard errors and *t*-values are not reported in Table 10.1.
31 As mentioned in the introduction one version of their dependent variable includes a minimum level of democracy in addition to the absence of violence. One of their hypotheses concerns the effects of natural resource dependence and they find that, in line with the findings here, it decreases the likelihood of peace as well as democracy. It is important to note that the dependent variable is not identical in the Doyle and Sambanis study and in my study. Doyle and Sambanis focus on the success of peace. Although peace is defined to include also a minimum level of democracy, their dependent variable deals with whether there is recurrence of war or not. In my case, I am concerned with the settlement of conflict and whether it is settled through competitive elections or not. My focus is on conflicts that have actually ended; recurrence of war is not covered by this study since that would simply indicate that the conflicts have not ended. The difference in the dependent variable also means that Doyle and Sambanis link their results theoretically to research on the causes of war and the role of easily lootable resources as incentives for *new wars*, rather than as disincentives for *ending the war through competitive elections* as suggested by the theoretical framework used here. Although we arrive at similar results regarding the role of lootable natural resources, that is, that it is negatively correlated with peace and democracy, the dependent variable is not identical. Therefore, the theoretical explanation for why the role of natural resources has a negative effect on peace and democracy may also be different.
32 In some extreme cases, aid constitutes a huge portion of a country's gross national income. The importance of lagging this variable is very clear when looking at a case like Rwanda where aid in the last year of the first war (1991–94) constituted over 95 percent of GNI. This enormous flow of aid surely began after the war had ended – and after the genocide – mid-1994, but this fact is obscured due to the use of yearly observations. The lagging prevents those situations from being picked up in the analysis.
33 The one observation, Guinea-Bissau 1999, is dropped due to missing information on other independent variables.
34 The difference between the dependent variable in the Doyle and Sambanis study and my dependent variable that I discuss in note 31 should be noted.
35 This is not so much a substantial problem as multicollinearity between an interaction term and its component parts generally does not affect the value of the coefficients and their standard errors, as it is a practical problem. Nevertheless, it is still not possible to estimate the standard errors for both coefficients. See further Jaccard *et al.* (1990).
36 Again, note the different dependent variables employed in the Doyle and Sambanis study and my study.
37 Removing these two control variables from the analysis does not change any of the regression results.
38 For example, ethnic heterogeneity covers only part of the concept of heterogeneity which proxies uncertainty of election outcomes. Since uncertainty of election outcomes is a crucial component of the theory employed here, it would make sense to use other indicators on heterogeneity as well, for example religious, social and cultural fractionalization. Fearon (2004) has produced an index on cultural fractionalization that would be relevant as a measure of heterogeneity in

the context of my research project. Indexes on religious fractionalization also exist, e.g. Fearon and Laitin (2003) and Alesina *et al.* (2003). Collier and Hoeffler use an index on social fractionalization that is calculated as the product of the ethno linguistic fractionalization (ELF) index and a religious fractionalization index constructed by the same authors (Collier and Hoeffler 2004).

References

Alesina, A., Devleeschauwer, A., Easterly, W., Kurlat, S. and Wacziarg, R. (2003) 'Fractionalization', *Journal of Economic Growth*, 8(2): 155–194.
Beck, N., Katz, J.N., and Tucker, R. (1998) 'Taking Time Seriously: Time-Series–Cross-Section Analysis with a Binary Dependent Variable', *American Journal of Political Science*, 42(4): 1260–1288.
Collier, P. and Hoeffler, A. (2004) 'Greed and Grievance in Civil War', *Oxford Economic Papers*, 56(4): 563–595.
Dahl, R.A. (1971) *Polyarchy: Participation and Opposition*, New Haven and London: Yale University Press.
Department of Geodesy and Cartography of the State Geological Committee of the USSR (1964) *Atlas Narodov Mira*, Moscow: Department of Geodesy and Cartography of the State Geological Committee of the USSR.
Doyle, M.W. and Sambanis, N. (2000) 'International Peacebuilding: A Theoretical and Quantitative Analysis', *American Political Science Review*, 94(4): 779–801.
Eriksson, M. and Wallensteen, P. (2004) 'Armed Conflict, 1989–2003', *Journal of Peace Research*, 41(5): 625–636.
Fearon, J.D. (2003) 'Ethnic and Cultural Diversity by Country', *Journal of Economic Growth*, 8(2): 195–222.
Fearon, J.D. and Laitin, D. (2003) 'Ethnicity, Insurgency, and Civil War', *American Political Science Review*, 97: 75–90
Friedrich, R.J. (1982) 'In Defense of Multiplicative Terms in Multiple Regression Equations', *American Journal of Political Science*, 26(4): 797–833.
Gleditsch, N.P., Wallensteen, P., Eriksson, M., Sollenberg, M., and Strand, H. (2002) 'Armed Conflict 1946–2001: A New Dataset', *Journal of Peace Research*, 39(5): 615–637. (Data for 1946–2003 available at www.prio.no/jpr/datasets.asp and www.ucdp.uu.se.)
Hegre, H., Gates, S., Gleditsch, N.P., and Ellingsen, T. (2001) 'Toward a Democratic Civil Peace?', *American Political Science Review*, 95(1): 33–48.
Heldt, B. and Wallensteen, P. (2004) *Peacekeeping Operations: Global Patterns of Intervention and Success, 1948–2000*, Sandöverken, Sweden: Folke Bernadotte Academy Publications.
Huntington, S. (1968) *Political Order in Changing Societies*, New Haven, CT: Yale University Press.
Jaccard, J. (2001) *Interaction Effects in Logistic Regression*, Thousand Oaks, CA and London: Sage Publications.
Jaccard, J., Turrisi, R., and Wan, C.K. (1990) *Interaction Effects in Multiple Regression*, Thousand Oaks, CA and London: Sage Publications.
Marshall, M.G. and Jaggers, K. (2005) *Polity IV Project. Political Regime Characteristics and Transitions 1800–2002*, College Park, MD: Center for International Development and Conflict Management, University of Maryland. (Available at www.cidcm.umd.edu/inscr/polity/index.htm.)

Olson, M. (1993) 'Dictatorship, Democracy, and Development', *American Political Science Review*, 87(3): 567–576.

Przeworski, A. (1991) *Democracy and the Market. Political and Economic Reforms in Eastern Europe and Latin America*, Cambridge: Cambridge University Press.

Singer, J.D. and Small, M. (1994) *Correlates of War Project: International and Civil War Data, 1816–1992*, ICPSR 9905, Ann Arbor, MI: ICPSR. (Available at www.icpsr.umich.edu or www.umich.edu/~cowproj.)

Taylor, C.L. and Hudson, M.C. (1972) *World Handbook of Political and Social Indicators*, Ann Arbor, MI: ICPSR.

Uppsala Conflict Data Program (UCDP) (2005) *Uppsala Conflict Database*, Uppsala: Dept of Peace and Conflict Research, Uppsala University. (Available at www.ucdp.uu.se.)

Vanhanen, T. (2000) 'A New Dataset for Measuring Democracy, 1810–1998', *Journal of Peace Research*, 37(2): 251–265. (Available at www.prio.no/jpr/datasets.asp.)

Wallensteen, P. and Sollenberg, M. (2001) 'Armed Conflict, 1989–2000', *Journal of Peace Research*, 38(5): 629–644.

Walter, B.F. (2002) *Committing to Peace. The Successful Settlement of Civil Wars*, Princeton, NJ and Oxford: Princeton University Press.

Wantchekon, L. (2004) 'The Paradox of "Warlord" Democracy: A Theoretical Investigation', *American Political Science Review*, 98 (1): 17–33.

Wantchekon, L. and Neeman, Z. (2002) 'A Theory of Post-Civil War Democratization', *Journal of Theoretical Politics*, 14(4): 439–464.

Wantchekon, L. and Nickerson, D. (1999) 'Multilateral Intervention Facilitates Post Civil War Democratization', Working Paper, Yale University.

Werner, S. (1999) 'The Precarious Nature of Peace: Resolving the Issues, Enforcing the Settlement, and Renegotiating the Terms', *American Journal of Political Science*, 43: 912–934.

World Bank (2004) *World Development Indicators 2004*, Washington DC: World Bank.

11 Democracy after war

Causes and consequences of the 1948 Civil War in Costa Rica

Fernando F. Sánchez[1]

Introduction

Costa Rica ranks as Latin America's oldest uninterrupted democracy (Knight, 2001; Seligson, 2001b; Peeler, 1985). Among developing countries, the longevity of its democratic rule is only matched by India. Ruled by a presidential government, the country has enjoyed periodical democratic elections with widespread popular participation for over 50 years – since the Civil War of 1948. General elections were held in 1953, 1958, and every four years thereafter. In each election Costa Ricans choose their president, two vice-presidents, 57 members of congress, and municipal authorities. Surveys indicate 77 per cent of Costa Ricans prefer democracy over any other kind of government, 70 per cent claim to participate in transparent electoral processes, and almost 87 per cent think that it is important to vote in national elections (Latinobarómetro, 1996–2003; Rodríguez *et al.*, April 2002). Indeed, Forrest Colburn has grounds to describe Costa Rica as 'arguably the region's most successful democracy' (Colburn, September/October 2002: 11).

Central to Costa Rica's political regime has been the strength of its institutions, most notably, the electoral processes, the parliament, and its well-institutionalised party system (Mainwaring and Scully, 1995). The origins of Costa Rica's liberal democracy and the identity of its contemporary political parties have roots dating to the end of the nineteenth century, but, as argued by John Booth, 'the regime consolidated itself only in the aftermath of the 1948 Civil War' (Booth, 1999: 460). No other event has had as much influence in the way academics study the development of this country's democratic institutions (Lehoucq, 1998). The civil war is responsible for the common division of the political history of Costa Rica into two phases: the 'First Republic' (1889–1948) and the 'Second Republic' (1948–to date).

The causes and outcomes of the 1948 conflict are the key to understand how this nation developed into the region's most stable democracy. This study assesses, first, the main reasons that drove a political crisis to escalate into a civil war. Subsequently, it analyses the major institutional reforms undertaken after the armed conflict. These reforms are largely responsible for the development of a democratic political culture, respected electoral institutions, well-institutionalised political parties, and a balanced distribution of power. As it will be demonstrated in this study, Costa Rica did not 'adopt' democracy, but rather developed it.

Before the war

The 1940s were a critical decade in Costa Rican politics. The governing oligarchy's control over the electoral arena and state resources was finally challenged. Division within the elite and progressive social reforms, compounded with serious political and economic flaws by the government (corruption, electoral frauds, political persecution, and fiscal mismanagement), created an 'explosive' political ambience. This environment precipitated a scramble for political allies that ultimately produced two contending groups racing to obtain political control.

The group in office was headed by the Partido Republicano (PRep), whose leader was reform-oriented President Rafael Ángel Calderón-Guardia (1940–1944). It also included the Communist Party under the name of Partido Vanguardia Popular (PVP) – headed by Manuel Mora – as well as the Church, represented by Monsignor Víctor Manuel Sanabria. The opposition alliance merged the new Partido Social Demócrata (PSD), whose central figure was José Figueres-Ferrer, with the most conservative members of the oligarchy (bankers, entrepreneurs, coffee producers) represented by the Partido Demócrata (PD) and the Partido Unión Nacional (PUN).

These coalitions were about common enemies, rather than shared social, economic, or political objectives. Costa Rican politics during the 1940s were characterised by the disputes of political groups trying to retain or win power, not by antagonistic class projects (Lehoucq, 1998). In fact, there was a more substantial conflict between the social-democratic programme of the PSD and the anti-statist stance of the PUN (its coalition partner), than between the PSD's ideas and the social christian/socialist project of the government alliance. However, the urge to oppose a shared electoral enemy that was trying to monopolise power masked the conflicting agendas in the opposition alliance. Not surprisingly, once the civil war ended, the Social-Democrats and the conservatives became political adversaries.

After two consecutive PRep's governments, known as the 'eight-year regime' (Calderón-Guardia (1940–1944) and Picado (1944–1948)), the opposition alliance candidate, Otilio Ulate, won the 1948 election with 55.3 per cent of the votes, against 44.7 obtained by Calderón-Guardia – who was looking for a second term in office (Thibaut, 1993). However, the Republican–Communist coalition retained the majority in congress. Both sides charged fraud. The Electoral Tribunal declared Ulate the winner, but later, due to significant irregularities, the new congress nullified the presidential election. After the failure of several attempts to reach an agreement by the

Electoral Tribunal, Monsignor Sanabria, and PRep and PUN members, the civil war started. Claiming to fight in order to re-establish the country's democratic tradition, Figueres and his Ejército de Liberación Nacional (ELN) – consisting of approximately 600 men – engaged in an armed confrontation with the government. Following six weeks of warfare and around 2000 deaths, Figueres' army overthrew the regime.

The civil war of 1948: causes for the conflict

The causes of the civil war include: economic mismanagement, corruption and political repression by the government, a class conflict due to the eight-year regime's progressive social reforms influenced by the Left, and, most importantly, the electoral fraud in 1948 (Cerdas-Cruz, 1992; Schifter, 1981). These elements were enough of a reason for a political opposition to emerge, and even for the civil war to begin. Nevertheless, the armed confrontation could have been prevented or stopped, had the contending bands not been divided – particularly the opposition group – while trying to reach an agreement after the election. Other factors such as, Figueres' conviction that warfare was the only way to end the eight-year regime, as well as the position taken by international actors (especially the US Government) and the feebleness of the military, added the necessary elements for the political crisis to develop into a civil war.

Economic mismanagement and corruption

A persuasive explanation for the mounting popular discontent against the government was its economic failures, and the constant corruption and nepotism charges levelled against Calderón, his colleagues, and friends. As revealed by Aguilar-Bulgarelli, instead of undertaking the promised fiscal reform, Calderón's government had no restraints on public spending, and used it to benefit his supporters (Aguilar-Bulgarelli, 1993). Corruption charges included a series of contracts for public works (construction of roads, schools, governmental buildings, etc.) granted to companies owned by Calderón's friends without public auction processes, and the government's direct financing of the PRep's candidate during the 1948 election. Commentators have even defined the eight-year regime as a failed attempt to establish a corrupt dictatorship (Cañas, 1982).

Furthermore, the eight-year regime was censored for having no economic answer to the recession that the country endured due to the Second World War, for its growing budget deficit, and for its failure to develop new products in order to diminish the country's dependency on coffee exports. Finally, businessmen were very irritated by governmental inefficiency in controlling illegal trafficking of all sorts of goods (Aguilar-Bulgarelli, 1993; Salazar, 1981). In Aguilar-Bulgarelli's words, 'the country was suffering a real economic crisis' (Aguilar-Bulgarelli, 1993: 125).

Class division political repression

A so-called 'class division' prompted by the government's progressive reforms, PRep's alliance with a communist party, and the repression against members of the oligarchy (especially those of German, Italian, or Spanish descent), is regarded as another element that motivated the war (Rojas-Bolaños, 1979). This materialistic explanation of the armed conflict understands the political crisis as a class struggle in which the government and the Left, bolstered by urban and rural working classes, confronted an opposition alliance supported by members of repressed foreign communities, by international and local 'owners of capital' disgruntled by social reforms and leftist influence in the government's policies, and by a growing middle class, frustrated by the insufficient economic development of the country (Schifter, 1982). The social and economic contradictions of these contending bands, and the systematic repression of the government against its opponents, would have made it impossible for the 1948 political crisis to find a peaceful resolution.

Most members of the oligarchy did oppose the government in one way or another, and the PRep was indeed supported by many members of the working class. As demonstrated by Jacobo Schifter, during the electoral processes in 1946 (mid-term legislative elections) and 1948, the PRep got the majority of its support in San José (the capital, where most of the urban working class lived), and in the poor rural coastal provinces (holding the country's banana plantations). In contrast, the opposition alliance received most of its support in Heredia, Alajuela, and Cartago, provinces prominent for their coffee plantations and the corresponding oligarchy (Schifter, 1981). The 1940s should be regarded, in fact, not only as a time of political reform and crisis, but also as a social turning point, marked by the massive incorporation of the working class into the political system.

However, it would be misleading to consider the 1948 cleavage solely as a war of class-conflict. Members of the 'dominant class' did not show a decisive opposition to the government, as their interests were both positively and negatively affected by its policies (Lehoucq, 1998). The oligarchy's disagreement with the social reforms and a new progressive tax policy, by no means a generalised position in the sector, was surely mollified by governmental decisions to guarantee a minimum price for coffee and eliminate the tax on coffee exports. At the same time, local entrepreneurs were certainly satisfied with Calderón's decision to pass a law protecting new local industry from international competition. Moreover, the contending bands cannot be regarded as pure class movements because members of different 'classes' could be found fighting for both sides. In Schifter's words:

> It is inadequate to regard the civil war as a product of class polarisation.... The working class and the middle–high class were certainly polarised during the battle. However, they were not categorically divided. Members of different classes could be found in both sides.
>
> (Schifter, 1981: 109)

Costa Rica's central cleavage was basically political in nature. Its civil war was not a social revolution, but a struggle between two groups which battled over control of the political apparatus (Jonas-Bodenheimer, 1984). Endorsing this conclusion, veteran Omar Zumbado says, 'we fought for political reasons, not for ideological or social differences' (Zumbado, 22 January 2002). The 1948 Civil War divided the country between *calderonistas* and *figueristas* or *ulatistas*, not between 'capitalists' and 'the proletariat'.

Electoral fraud

Another important catalyst to the civil war was the significant irregularities in the 1948 election. Bruce Wilson asserts that the central causes of the war were the violence and the rampant fraud surrounding the election (Wilson, 1998). The opposition claimed fraud both during the presidential election in 1944 and the mid-term legislative election in 1946. Even the Left's leader, Manuel Mora, admitted that 'a real school of fraud had been established in Costa Rica' (Aguilar-Bulgarelli, 1993: 142). However, contrary to what had happened before, the electoral fraud in 1948 was not tolerated.

The denounced fraud in 1944 and 1946 led the opposition group to organise a commercial 'lockout' general strike ('Huelga de los Brazos Caídos') in 1947, in order to demand that Picado's administration guarantee a fraud-free electoral process in the coming year. Picado ended accepting their demands. Without the support of the Left, the government and the opposition signed a pact which stated that: (1) both sides would accept the decision of the Electoral Tribunal (the final declaration still remained a congressional prerogative), (2) they would share the responsibility for the fairness of the election (the opposition appointed the three members of the Electoral Tribunal and the president of the National Registry, while the government stayed in control of the police and the armed forces), and (3) the armed forces would be under the control of the winning candidate twenty-four hours after the Electoral Tribunal had announced its decision (Schifter, 1981). Such a disadvantageous agreement reveals the government's systematic loss of popularity, and the strength of the opposition alliance.

On 28 February 1948 (two days after law-stipulated date) the Electoral Tribunal declared Otilio Ulate, the PUN/PSD coalition candidate, winner of an election riddled with irregularities. The PRep members, having renounced control over the electoral institutions, were very suspicious of the low turnout, which declined from 78 per cent in 1940 and 1944, to 56 per cent in 1948. Moreover, they were unwilling to accept that the highest levels of absenteeism in 1948 were registered in provinces they had won in 1946 (Schifter, 1981).

Additionally, the *calderonistas* accused the National Registry of delaying the issue of identification documents to its supporters and speedily granting them to Ulate's followers. They also strongly questioned the Electoral Tribunal, as it based its resolution – arguing time restrictions – on the results of telegrams sent by its delegates around the country, instead of counting all the votes. When one of the members of the Electoral Tribunal openly expressed his disagreement with Ulate's victory, the government-controlled congress nullified the presidential election.

The congressional decision produced an immediate reaction from the opposition, which accused the government of not honouring the 1947 pact. Furthermore, the *ulatistas* blamed Calderón's supporters for a mysterious fire that destroyed part of the votes in mid-February, and denounced systematic repression and constant intimidation by the police and armed forces against its supporters and leaders (Güell, 23 January 2002). Ulate himself was imprisoned, and Dr Carlos Luis Valverde, one of the most prominent opposition supporters, assassinated (Aguilar-Bulgarelli, 1993; Schifter, 1981). Commentators have argued that, even though electoral fraud existed, it only affected the margin by which Ulate won and not the final result (Aguilar-Bulgarelli, 1993). By now, however, the government would not respect the electoral result, nor would the opposition accept the congressional resolution. The possibility of resolving the 1948 political crisis via elections vanished.

Internal division and failed negotiation

This was more than enough for a strong political opposition to form and even to initiate the hostilities, as indeed happened. However, as acknowledged by several authors, both the PRep and the PUN tried to negotiate a peaceful way out of the ongoing armed conflict (Lehoucq, 1998; Aguilar-Bulgarelli, 1993). In fact, at the end of March 1948, with the war already underway, Calderón and Ulate reached an agreement to end the hostilities. Exhorted by Monsignor Sanabria, they accorded that the congress would appoint an honourable and mutually accepted person, Dr Julio César Ovares – a Calderón supporter – to govern as an interim president for two years. After that, a new electoral process would have been organised.

The Left did not have major objections to this arrangement as they were satisfied with their majority in congress and were even ready to admit electoral defeat in order to prevent the imminent war (Aguilar-Bulgarelli, 1993). However, this was not the case of Figueres, the PSD, and his ELN, the ones actually fighting to end the eight-year regime. They rejected the pact and continued the hostilities.

The agreement's failure pointed out the division in the opposition alliance. The PUN's pact with the government clearly did not consider the PSD's position, for which any possibility of the continuation of the existing regime was unacceptable. The pact would jeopardise their idea of a complete transformation of Costa Rican society through a social-democratic programme. Moreover, winning an armed confrontation would allow them to govern without interference from the conservative PUN. Figueres' intentions were later made clear when, as the leader of the victorious ELN, he stated, 'Don't think that I will hand over the presidency to Ulate or to any corrupt politician. I came to transform this country' (Acuña, 1974). Figueres did hand power over to Ulate, but only after laying the foundations for his political project during an eighteen-month de facto government.

Some scholars argue that the electoral chaos was just the excuse Figueres needed to start his 'revolution' (Aguilar-Bulgarelli, 1993; Schifter, 1981). Civil war was truly catalysed by the electoral fraud of 1948. Nonetheless, it could have been prevented, or at least quickly ended, had the contending parties been able to negotiate a solution acceptable to the different groups. Figueres' conviction that war was the only way to end the existing regime, in conjunction with favourable internal and international conditions to carry out his plan, generated the setting needed to start the hostilities.

The Legión Caribe

Figueres had long been planning an armed rebellion to depose the eight-year regime, believing this was the only way to do it. Since 1942, when he was expelled from the country by Calderón's administration, Figueres launched several initiatives to acquire money and weapons (Figueres-Ferrer, 1987). While in Mexico, he signed the Pacto del Caribe (Caribbean Pact) with other Central American 'revolutionaries'. The signers, leaders of the so-called Legión Caribe (Caribbean Legion), vowed to free the region from its dictatorships through an armed struggle. Costa Rica was regarded as the best place to start the liberation process, due to its weak military forces and the existence of more civil liberties, in comparison with other countries such as Nicaragua, Honduras, or Panama. The reformist Guatemalan President Juan José Arévalo strongly supported the Legión Caribe by allowing them to use Guatemala as an *entrepôt* for men, weapons, ammunition, and fuel destined for the ELN. Backed by the Legión Caribe, Figueres was ready for war. It has been claimed that without the support of the Legión Caribe, Figueres would never have been able to organise a successful revolution (Bell, 1979).

The US government and a weak military

Figueres' crusade was fuelled with a rising popular unrest that characterised Costa Rica throughout the 1948 electoral process, especially after the annulment of the election. The restlessness in the country is well illustrated by the comments of an anonymous ELN soldier, 'The country was ready to follow the first one who fired a weapon' (Figueres-Ferrer, 1987: 114). Additionally, Figueres' movement benefited from the US government's position, as well as by the weakness of the Costa Rican army.

The American Embassy's position bolstered decisively the 'revolutionary' movement. At a time when the Cold War was gathering momentum, the United States was uncomfortable with the influence attained by the Left in the Costa Rican government and took several actions in order to eliminate this influence and prevent Costa Rica from becoming 'the Czechoslovakia of the Western Hemisphere' (Cerdas-Cruz, 1992: 293–294; Schifter, 1981: 133). First, they decided to appoint Nathaniel Davis as the new American Ambassador in the country. Mr Davis came to San José from the US Embassy in Moscow and was considered an expert on communism. Davis adopted an energetically anti-communist posture, hostile to Picado's government and favourable to the opposition.

Second, the Department of State demanded that Nicaraguan dictator, Anastasio Somoza, stop his interference in Costa Rica's internal affairs. Somoza had sent, with Picado's approval, his National Guard into Costa Rica in order to support the government. The Nicaraguan dictator feared a victory of the revolutionary movement, as he could have believed that his regime would be the next target of the Legión Caribe with Figueres in power. Finally, the United States not only did not obstruct the military aid received by the ELN, but also blocked the Costa Rican government's efforts to acquire military provisions (Schifter, 1982). As explained by Teodoro Picado in a letter communicating his resignation of the presidency to Mora and Calderón, 'incontestable forces are absolutely determined to make us lose the battle' (Aguilar-Bulgarelli, 1993: 383). The US was eager to clear the way for a revolutionary movement seeking to unseat a coalition government with leftist participation (Booth, 1998).

Figueres's movement also benefited from the vulnerability and the internal division of the armed forces. The Costa Rican army had progressively weakened since the end of the First World War, possibly as a reaction against the armed forces following the downfall of the Tinoco brothers' violent military dictatorship in 1919. In 1922 the US Department of State reported that a civilian police was gradually substituting the country's army. By 1931, American authorities in Costa Rica indicated that the nation's army was practically non-existent (Cerdas-Cruz, 1997).

The government forces were not unified, but divided into three distinct groups. The elite Unidad Móvil (Mobile Unit) responded to Picado's orders, the civil police was loyal to Calderón, and those known as the Brigadas de Choque (Hit Brigades) or the '*linieros*' were led by Manuel Mora and the Communist Party. This last group, mainly integrated by banana plantation workers, presented the greatest resistance to Figueres' ELN. Furthermore, there is evidence that the government did not fully trust the armed Left. Mora accused Picado of refusing to supply them with weapons, while the ELN captured munitions still in their original boxes stored in various government quarters (Aguilar-Bulgarelli, 1993; Schifter, 1982). The weakness and internal division among the government's armed forces should be considered, not only as a factor that eased the ELN victory, but also as an element that encouraged rather than deterred Figueres in the first place.

The political setting in Costa Rica on the eve of the civil war was characterised by a presidency built upon a controversial coalition, a non-independent parliament, 'fluid' parties forming unstable alliances, a feeble and divided military, ineffective electoral institutions, and increasing US intervention. This political configuration showed total inefficiency in controlling tensions, safeguarding constitutional guarantees, and preventing an armed confrontation after the fraudulent 1948 election. Finally, the mutual hatred of the two leaders of the contending coalitions (Calderón and Figueres) made war virtually inevitable.

The civil war outcomes: political reforms and party families

Figueres's ELN finally ousted the government, terminating the eight-year regime. The losing alliance successfully negotiated the preservation of their social reforms. The PUN supporters wanted Ulate to be declared president at once, fearing a Figueres dictatorship. But PSD members were ready to take advantage of the war's outcome and eager to get into office and start implementing their social-democratic project. This general post-war uncertainty ended with a Figueres–Ulate pact in 1948. It appointed Figueres to head a *de facto* Governing Junta for at least eighteen months, and stated that afterwards Ulate would assume office. Eighteen months later, after having called for a Constituent Assembly – dominated mainly by PUN members – Figueres kept his word.

The fact that Figueres signed and respected the pact when he had complete military control of the country shows not only the veracity of his democratic principles (Peeler, 1996), but also the significance of other contextual factors and political pressures that surely influenced his decision, including: (1) the logical contradiction of leading a dictatorship after claiming to fight to rescue democracy, (2) the fact that most of his supporters were indeed Ulate's followers, later recruited by the ELN to fight against the fraud, and (3) US pressures demanding Figueres not to continue with the Legión Caribe's plan to get rid of other dictatorships in the region. Ceding power to Ulate would have been a strategic move not to involve Costa Rica in this enterprise.

Anyway, at that moment the country presented every ingredient needed for the establishment of a military dictatorship. This, however, did not happen. On the contrary, one of the most important democratic precedents of Costa Rica's political history was settled when the winning candidate of the 1948 election assumed office in 1949. The door was opened for a succession of reforms that created the institutional framework needed for the consolidation of democracy in Costa Rica.

Political reforms

The post-war period was a time of reform. The country's political setting was mainly influenced by four of these reforms: (1) the weakening of the presidency and strengthening of the assembly, (2) the abolition of the army,

(3) the implementation of major electoral reforms – including a reinforced electoral tribunal, and (4) the banning of communist parties from electoral activities.

In the first place, the 1949 Constituent Assembly weakened the powers of the presidency and strengthened the legislative branch. This contrasts with the cases of most Latin American countries and can be explained as a constituents' reaction against the presidential power abuses (particularly electoral manipulation) characteristic of pre-1948 Costa Rican politics (Yashar, 1995; Wilson, 1998; Molina and Lehoucq, 1999). As John Booth wrote, 'The 1949 Constitution grants the Legislative Assembly powers that makes it one of the strongest legislatures in Latin America' (Booth, 1998: 59).

The weakening of the presidency and the strengthening of the congress bolstered party organisations, as a single capable leader was no longer enough to rule. A coherent and efficient party caucus in parliament became crucial. This led to the reinforcement of parties' cadres and resulted in stronger, more participatory parties, where it was not so common – as used to happen – for individual politicians to gain complete control. Politics thus became more a collegiate rather than a personalistic business.

Second, the Governing Junta headed by Figueres abolished the armed forces – his own ELN (Figueres-Ferrer, 1987). Later, the 1949 Constitution prohibited a standing army. The proscription of the armed forces distinguishes Costa Rica from most of Latin American countries, as no military groups may develop into political actors (Urcuyo-Fournier, 1990). The absence of an army not only has limited the struggle for political power to civilian groups through parties via democratic elections, but also has deepened the national democratic culture (Booth and Seligson, 1993; Seligson, 2001a; PEN, 2001).

In the third place, major electoral reforms were promptly approved. The mid-term legislative elections were eliminated, concentrating the presidential, legislative, and municipal contests into one single process, thus increasing the presidential candidate and his party's influence over the legislative and municipal elections results. This 'electoral concurrence' (Shugart and Carey, 1992) not only produced a stronger party discipline in congress, but also has become a central element reinforcing the formation of a two-party system in Costa Rica (Sánchez, 2001).

The Costa Rican electorate was also expanded in 1949. The few remaining voting restrictions – gender and race – were eliminated. The voting age was set at twenty – further lowered to eighteen in 1971 (Lehoucq, 1998). A broader and more geographically dispersed electorate forced parties to create stronger internal organisations, and to start a process of decentralisation and important logistic efforts which would permit the mobilisation of voters throughout the whole national territory. The political 'inclusiveness' achieved by the electoral reforms eventually led to a more representative government (Dahl, 2000).

Figure 11.1 depicts the increasing trend in citizens' electoral participa-

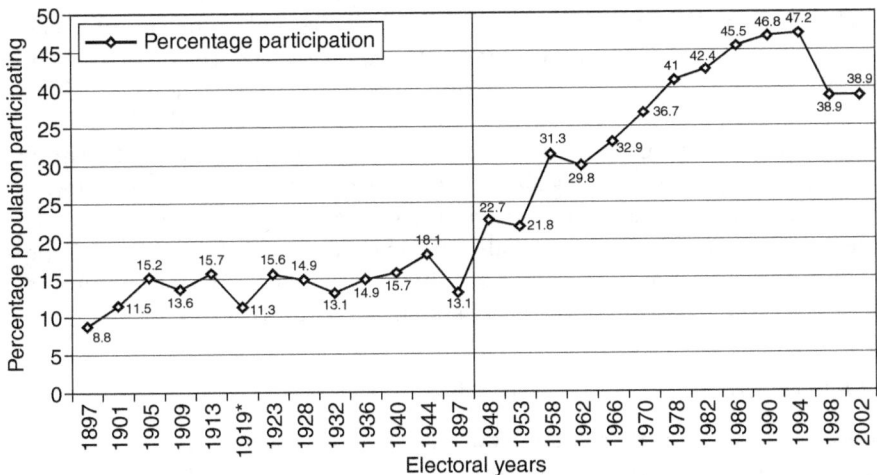

Figure 11.1 Voter participation in Costa Rican elections, 1897–2002 (sources: TSE, 2002; INEC, 2002; Stone, 1975: 236; Thibaut, 1993: 183–209).

tion resulting from these reforms in the post-war period (marked with a black line).

Another electoral reform took place when the 1949 Constitution reconstituted the Electoral Tribunal, creating the Tribunal Supremo de Elecciones ((TSE) Supreme Electoral Tribunal). This entity, defined as 'the real novelty of Costa Rica's political institutions' (Yashar, 1995: 93), received exclusive responsibility and absolute political and financial independence for the organisation, direction, and vigilance of acts relating to suffrage. The TSE magistrates are appointed by the Supreme Court of Justice.

The TSE may investigate charges of political partiality by public employees, file criminal charges against persons violating electoral laws, scrutinise and validate electoral results, and control the police forces during electoral periods. Furthermore, it regulates campaign organisations' compliance with the electoral law, monitors executive branch campaign neutrality, and disburses public campaign subsidies.

The TSE operates the Civil Registry, the other key electoral entity in Costa Rica – also reconstituted in 1949. The Civil Registry keeps and updates the general citizens registry, elaborates the electoral roll, and issues a mandatory national identity card that serves as the identification document during elections (Constitución Política de la República de Costa Rica, 1999: Articles 99–104).

This institutional engineering has proven highly efficient for organising transparent electoral processes in the country. The TSE's effectiveness in conducting elections has virtually eradicated the incidence of fraud, and accounts for the globally reputed fairness and honesty of Costa Rican elections.

An efficient, trustworthy, and independent electoral institution generates stability for political parties. Stability in the rules and nature of inter-party competition is the most important condition for the institutionalisation of a democratic party system (Mainwaring and Scully, 1995: 4–5). Regularly organised, pristine elections with clear and generally accepted rules dissuade party leaders from investing time in searching for ways to manipulate or circumvent the processes. They also motivate parties to generate longer-termed political strategies and institutions capable of accomplishing them. The electoral reforms of 1949 (especially the TSE) have played a central role providing the conditions for electoral stability and, therefore, for the progressive institutionalisation of the party system in Costa Rica.

Party families

Besides these reforms, the civil war also left the country divided into two conflicting political bands. This division, acknowledged by Oscar Fernández as the 'foundational conflict' of the Costa Rican party system (Fernández, 1996: 155), was later transformed into popular support for distinctive parties or party coalitions. Mitchell Seligson observes that:

> Despite numerous studies attempting to discover the socio-economic correlates that explain party votes, historical party loyalties, most likely dating from the civil war of 1948, remain the most important factor.
> (Seligson, 1987: 173)

Similarly, Deborah Yashar has highlighted the influence that the central figures of the 1948 events have on political parties (Yashar, 1995). Indeed, Costa Rica's main post-war parties developed around the leading figures of the 1948 battle, Calderón and Figueres.

So strong has been the political influence of these two leaders that both of their sons recently occupied the presidency – Rafael Ángel Calderón-Fournier (1990–1994) and José María Figueres-Olsen (1994–1998). Some argue that their parties (the Partido Unidad Social Cristina (PUSC) and the Partido Liberación Nacional (PLN), respectively) are administering an electoral machinery based on 'inherited charismas'. (Fernández, 1992: 36). Even though they constitute one of the better institutionalised party systems in Latin America, the historical origins of Costa Rican parties do not escape their share of personalism.

Partido Liberación Nacional

The first important party family to emerge during this period was the social-democratic one, blended in the PLN. Having its historical roots in the PSD, the PLN was formed in 1951 under Figueres' leadership. The PLN is the oldest party in Costa Rican politics. It was conceived as a social-democratic movement, advocating state-led economic growth, social welfare guarantees, and redistributive economic policies. This well-organised, permanent party controlled the country's politics from the 1950s to the mid-1980s. The profound influence of the PLN in Costa Rican politics has induced analysts to argue that since 1953 the country's political dynamics have been defined by a struggle between *liberacionistas* and *anti-liberacionistas* (Rovira-Mas, 1998; Wilson, 1998). Its pre-eminence from 1953 to 1986 led academics to characterise Costa Rica's party system during this period in several ways (Vega-Carballo, 1989; Mcdonald, 1971), and more precisely, as a 'bipolar system with one strong party and a series of shifting ad hoc opposition coalitions' (Peeler, 1998: 174).

Ideologically speaking, these opposition coalitions (composed by PRep and PUN members) had a conservative orientation, but initially lacked the internal cohesion to pose an alternative ideological project to that of the PLN. Therefore, from the 1950s until the beginning of the 1980s Costa Rica's political situation was characterised, if not by an ideological affinity, by the inability of the opposition to seriously challenge the social-democratic model. The PLN's hegemony allowed them to develop a project that defined the country's socio-economic evolution during the second half of the twentieth century. Some even name the post-war politics the 'Social-Democratic Republic' (Vega-Carballo, 1992: 204).

After 1986 the PLN continues to be regarded – not undisputedly – as a centre-left party. Despite the fact that its last two administrations (1986–1990 and 1994–1998) have been more receptive to neoliberal reforms, the PLN succeeded in incorporating members of diverse ideological backgrounds. An amalgam of ideological positions going from hardcore social-democrats to non-doctrinary neoliberals, are represented in a party showing an astounding ideological flexibility. As stressed by former Vice-President and PLN member Alberto Fait:

> Ideologically speaking, the only social-democratic belief that we all share in this party is that the economy should be at the service of society and not the other way around. We are all looking for ways to generate a better distribution of wealth, but no one is doing it by defending a dogmatic position.
>
> (Fait, 20 May 1992)

This phenomenon, typical of 'catch-all' parties (Kirchheimer, 1966), has surely hampered Costa Rica's moderate Left electoral performances, and permitted the PLN to go through a rather smooth ideological transition towards the centre of the ideological spectrum since the mid-1980s.

The PLN has participated in the fourteen national elections that have taken place since 1953, winning the presidency on eight occasions (including 2006). Furthermore, it has obtained at least relative legislative majority in ten elections, two of them (1958 and 1966) even after losing the presidency. Until 1982 all the PLN's national presidents were at the same time founding members of the party, showing the importance that the civil war and its outcomes had on the definition of the party's leadership. In fact, as revealed by Alberto Cañas (one of the founders of the party) the PLN's strongest leader – Figueres senior – retained his power for almost 30 years after the armed conflict (Cañas, 17 May 1992).

The social-democrats had an overwhelming electoral dominance in Costa Rican politics until the mid-1980s. This electoral dominance was followed by a period of alternation in power with the PUSC, which lasted until 1998. The 1998 elections marked the beginning of evident erosion in the PLN's electoral support. This phenomenon was confirmed in the 2002 process, when they not only lost the presidency for the first time ever after being in opposition, but also obtained the lowest support in history. After this fiasco, PLN members made a large effort to turn things around, becoming victors in 2006.

The 'Conservative Alliance' (CA)

PLN's post-war political opposition constituted the second of the party families. Ironically, previous electoral and war enemies, Calderón's PRep and Ulate's PUN joined forces after the PLN's overwhelming victory in 1953. This alliance was possible, first, because the PUN distanced itself from the PLN and the PRep from the Left, and second, due to their common opposition against the PLN. The two parties remained personalistic organisations, revolving around the leadership of Calderón and Ulate until their deaths. With this alliance, Calderón's social-christian orientation and his followers' strong loyalty, blended with PUN's old elite support and their conservative and anti-state interventionist ideological credo.

The two parties gathered around the Social-Democrats' opposition in the 1953 elections, the PD, and allied for the 1958 presidential election when they managed to beat the PLN. Their electoral defeat in 1962, after the PRep and the PUN decided to participate separately, convinced them that the only way to successfully confront the PLN was to coalesce. Hence, they created a stable coalition – Unificación Nacional (UN) – that succeeded in 1966. The UN was later substituted by the Coalición Unidad (CU), integrated by four parties, that won the 1978 election. Finally, in 1983, led by Rafael Ángel Calderón-Fournier, and under a political agreement with PLN's President Monge (Pérez-Brignoli, 1999), the CU members integrated into a permanent and coherent party, the PUSC.

The PUSC quickly became the other important political party in Costa Rican politics. In fact, its first electoral appearance in 1986 marked the beginning of what Jorge Rovira-Mas has named the 'two-party era'. From then on the Costa Rican party system undoubtedly took a bipartisan configuration (Rovira-Mas, January–June 1998: 10–14). Contrasting with the CA's previous electoral alliances, the PUSC promptly grew into a nationally organised and stable political group. Furthermore, it efficiently positioned itself as a centre-right party, keen to implement neoliberal reforms. However, the PUSC does not fully assume neoliberalism as a doctrine. In fact, a political setting dominated by two parties with no major ideological differences – PLN at the centre-left and PUSC at the centre-right – is one of the leading characteristics of Costa Rica's party system since 1983, and one reason for the country's democratic stability.

Prior to 2006, the PUSC accomplished steady electoral gains. In 1990 it won the presidential election for the first time, acquiring also a legislative majority, a feat only enjoyed by the PLN since 1953. Its second electoral victory came in 1998, obtaining a relative majority in congress; and its third in 2002, with similar results in the Legislative Assembly. As indicated, the alternation in power between the PLN and the PUSC between 1986 and 1998 (Peeler, 1998) was broken in 2002 when the PUSC was able to re-elect itself in office for the first time in the history of PLN opponents (Sánchez, 2003). Nevertheless, the PUSC collapsed bitterly in 2006 and was displaced by the newer Partido Acción Ciudadana (PAC) as the main opponent of the PLN.

The Left

The Left composes the last of the party families. Its origins must be traced back to 1923, when Jorge Volio formed and led the Partido Reformista. Afterwards, in 1931, the Partido Comunista de Costa Rica (PCCR) was organised under the leadership of Manuel Mora. Before the 1940s, leftist groups had limited influence on governmental policy. As shown, this changed dramatically between 1942 and 1948 after the Left – renamed Partido Vanguardia Popular (PVP) – coalesced with Calderón's PRep.

Even though it became an official party well before the armed conflict, the Left reached a major turning point after the civil war. Deviating from the other post-war democratic reforms, the 1949 Constituent Assembly banned communist movements from electoral politics. Along with the proscription of the Left came the closure of many of its supporting worker unions. In fact, from 1948 to 1953 the number of unions registered with the Ministry of Labour fell from 204 to 74 (Yashar, 1995). This prohibition lasted until 1975. The abrupt hindrance of an ascendant political party which played a central role in governmental policy during the 1940s, hampered the consolidation of what could have been a third strong party, easing the ideological debate in the country. Ironically, this undemocratic reform benefited the development of one of the pillars of Costa Rica's democratic stability: a strong, ideologically moderated two-party system.

Excluded from official participation, the Left ran candidates under different party names in order to circumvent the prohibition. It succeeded in electing one deputy in 1962 with the Partido Acción Democrática Popular (PADP). Absent in the 1966 elections, the Left participated again in 1970 with the Partido Acción Socialista (PAS), and in 1974 with the PAS and another party. The PAS elected two deputies in each election. From 1978 onwards – once the constitutional ban was lifted – the PVP restored its old name and implemented a series of electoral coalitions with other leftist parties that emerged in the 1970s. The Coalición Pueblo Unido (CPU) was formed and participated in the 1978 elections along with other two left-wing movements, and as the only leftist representative in the 1982 elections. It was during this period that the Left achieved its best electoral performance since 1948, obtaining four deputies in both elections.

However, in 1986 the CPU divided into two different coalitions, Pueblo Unido and Alianza Popular (AP), and their performance worsened thereafter. Each one got a single deputy in that election, and only the CPU was able to attain a lawmaker in 1990. Other smaller parties also participated in that year, namely, the Partido del Progreso (PP) and the Partido Revolucionario de los Trabajadores en Lucha (PRTL). In 1994 the PVP offered a Left wing option; while in 1998 the Partido Pueblo Unido (PPU) – no longer a coalition – and the Nuevo Partido Democrático (NPD) entered the electoral race. In those same elections (1994 and 1998) the newly formed Partido Fuerza Democrática (PFD) elected two and three representatives, respectively (TSE, 2002).

The PFD did not present itself as a leftist movement, but members from different sectors of this tradition made up the party. Although it started to show some signs of stability, it was seriously weakened by internal disputes, and by the emergence of other more appealing third parties – most notably the centre-left PAC (Sánchez, 2003), which also hindered the electoral performances of the other two racing leftist parties. As a result, the Left finished with no congressional representation at all after the 2002 electoral process, for the first time since 1966 (when no leftist party participated). The Left's disappointing results in 2002 seem to be the expected outcome of a long-standing tradition of internal conflicts and fragmentation. However, it managed to get one lawmaker in 2006, through the Partido Frente Amplio (PFA).

Generally, the Costa Rican Left – PFD and PFA included – has proposed a moderate, reformist agenda instead of revolutionary goals. Among the factors that have contributed to its unimpressive electoral performance are: the political repression suffered after 1948, the lack of ideological and organisational unity, a highly anti-communist press, and constant tensions between Costa Rica and Revolutionary Nicaragua during the 1980s (Chalker, 1995; Booth, 1999). Other factors hampering the Left's electoral results surely include Duverger's 'mechanical' and 'psychological' effects characteristic of two-party systems (Duverger, 1987: 252), the PLN's ideological flexibility, the progressive transition of the majority of voters and of the two main parties towards the centre of the ideological spectrum, and, in the case of the 2002 elections, the emergence of the PAC. Consequently, after the 1948 Civil War and to date, leftist movements did never pose a serious threat to the PLN and the CA – later the PUSC – political hegemony.

As a way of summarising the historical development of Costa Rica's electoral institutions and the performance of the main parties or coalitions of its party families, Table 11.1. shows the results of the country's elections from 1953 to 2002.

Conclusions

The 1948 Civil War has been the most influential social and political event in modern Costa Rican history. No conflict has so strongly polarised political life and taken as many lives. However, it was precisely after the civil war that the country began an uninterrupted process of democratic rule and institutional maturity. It would be impossible to understand Costa Rica's current political configuration without studying the causes and outcomes of the civil war.

Costa Rica's true democratic history and popular, competitive, fraud-free elections can only be safely claimed to have begun after the end of the armed conflict. Second, the battle made it clear that the oligarchy had lost its political monopoly, having to share power with the working sectors and, particularly, with the rising middle class. In the third place, central political reforms like the weakening of the presidency and the strengthening of the congress, and the banning of the army were only accomplished after the civil war. Moreover, key electoral reforms from this period (which included the expansion of the electorate, the establishment of concurrent elections, and the reconstitution of the TSE and the National Registry) provided a stable political environment suitable for strong political parties to develop.

In the fourth place, the main figures of the civil war – Figueres-Ferrer and Calderón-Guardia – created political parties or party coalitions in order to canalise their popular support. Even if centred on their leaders, these political groups also had clear ideological groundings (social-democratic and social-christian). Later, these two parties – first the PLN and then the PUSC – became strong institutions and developed the capacity to integrate under their banners diverse social, economic, and political groups.

Finally, on a darker note, as the Communist Party was temporarily banned from electoral competition, it lost its historical momentum and its organisational strength. Nonetheless, the Left's exclusion certainly eased the way for ideological moderation and bipartism, two features largely responsible for Costa Rica's political stability during times of regional turmoil.

Costa Rica is arguably Latin America's most stable democracy. This nation's political system has been built on the institutions and the collective experience inherited from the civil war. The absence of a military, well-institutionalised parties, respected electoral institutions, and a strong parliament which assures a balanced distribution of power, have been central in promoting Costa Rica's political stability. As shown, the formation and development of these institutions, and of a political class evidently conscious of their importance, are legacies of the Civil War of 1948.

Table 11.1 Costa Rican election results, 1953–2002

Year	Party/coalition	Presidential election (percentage of votes and elected President)	Legislative election (percentage of seats)	Absenteeism	Percentage population registered to vote
1953	PLN	64.7 (José Figueres-Ferrer)	66.7	32.8	33.8
	PD	35.3	24.4		
	PRNI	–	6.7		
	PUN	–	2.2		
1958	PLN	42.8	44.4	35.3	33.7
	PUN	46.4 (Mario Echandi)	22.2		
	PI	10.1	6.7		
	Prep	–	24.4		
	Other	–	2.2		
1962	PLN	50.3 (Francisco Orlich)	50.9	19.1	38.7
	Prep	35.3	31.6		
	PUN	13.5	15.8		
	PAD	0.9	1.7		
1966	PLN	49.5	50.9	18.6	36.6
	CUN	50.5 (José J. Trejos)	45.6		
	Other	–	3.5		
1970	PLN	54.8 (José Figueres-Ferrer)	56.1	16.7	39.5
	CUN	41.2	38.6		
	PAS	1.3	3.5		
	Other	2.7	1.7		
1974	PLN	43.4 (Daniel Oduber)	47.4	20.1	45.9
	CUN	30.4	28.1		
	PAS	2.4	3.5		
	Other	23.8	21.0		
1978	PLN	43.8	43.9	18.7	50.4
	CU	50.5 (Rodrigo Carazo)	47.4		
	CPU	2.7	5.3		
	Other	3.0	3.4		

Year	Party	Presidential vote	Legislative vote		
1982	PLN	58.8 (Luis A. Monge)	57.9	21.4	53.9
	CU	33.6	31.6		
	CPU	3.3	7.0		
	Other	4.3	3.4		
1986	PLN	52.3 (Oscar Arias)	50.9	18.2	55.6
	PUSC	45.8	43.9		
	CPU	0.6	1.7		
	CAP	0.8	1.7		
	Other	0.5	1.7		
1990	PLN	47.2	43.9	18.2	57.2
	PUSC	51.5 (Rafael A. Calderón-Fournier)	50.9		
	CPU	0.7	1.7		
	Other	0.6	3.4		
1994	PLN	49.6 (José M. Figueres-Olsen)	49.1	18.9	58.2
	PUSC	47.7	43.9		
	PFD	1.9	3.5		
	Other	0.8	3.5		
1998	PLN	44.6	40.3	30.0	55.6
	PUSC	47.0 (Miguel A. Rodríguez)	47.4		
	PFD	3.0	5.1		
	Other	5.4	7.0		
2002	PLN	31.1	29.8	31.2	56.5
	PUSC	38.6 (Abel Pacheco)[a]	33.3		
	PFD	0.3	0.0		
	Other	30.0	36.8		

Sources: Author's own estimations based on TSE 2002.

Notes

Due to rounding, totals for each election may not add to 100 per cent.

a A runoff election was needed. Abel Pacheco (PUSC) got 58 per cent of the vote, defeating Rolando Araya (PLN) who obtained 42 per cent.

Note

1 I thank Alan Angell, Laurence Whitehead, and Forrest Colburn for their comments on drafts of this study.

References

Acuña, M. (1974) *El 48*, Costa Rica: Imprenta Lehmann.
Aguilar-Bulgarelli, O.R. (1993) *Costa Rica y sus hechos políticos de 1948: problemática de una década*, Costa Rica: Editorial Costa Rica.
Bell, J.P. (1979) *Crisis in Costa Rica: The 1948 Revolution*, Austin, TX: University of Texas Press.
Booth, J.A. (1998) *Costa Rica: Quest for Democracy*, Boulder, Co and Oxford: Westview Press.
Booth, J.A. (1999) 'Costa Rica: The Roots of Democratic Stability', in L. Diamond, J. Hartlyn, J.J. Linz, and S.M. Lipset (eds) *Democracy in the Developing World, Latin America*, Boulder, CO: Lynne Rienner.
Booth, J.A. and Seligson, M.A. (1993) 'Paths to Democracy and Political Culture of Costa Rica, Mexico and Nicaragua', in L. Diamond (ed.) *Political Culture and Democracy in Developing Countries*, Boulder, CO and London: Lynne Rienner.
Cañas, A. (1982) *Los ocho años*. Costa Rica: Editorial UNED.
Cañas, A. (17 May 1992) *Interview*. One of PLN's founders, former deputy (1962–1966 and 1994–1998), San José: His residence.
Cerdas-Cruz, R. (1992) 'Costa Rica', in L. Bethell and I. Roxborough (eds) *Latin America Between the Second World War and the Cold War, 1944–1948*, Cambridge: Cambridge University Press.
Cerdas-Cruz, R. (1997) 'Contribución al estudio comparativo de las relaciones cívico-militares en Centroamérica', in K. Casas-Zamora (ed.) *Relaciones cívico-militares comparadas*, Costa Rica: Fundación Arias para la Paz y el Desarrollo Humano.
Chalker, C. (1995) 'Elections and Democracy in Costa Rica', in M.A. Seligson and J.A. Booth (eds) *Elections and Democracy in Central America, Revisited*, Chapel Hill, NC: University of North Carolina Press.
Colburn, F.D. (September/October 2002) 'The Perils of Magical Realism: A Talk with Costa Rica's Ex-President', *New Leader*: 11–13.
Constitución Política de la República de Costa Rica (1999) 'Texto oficial vigente autorizado por Ministerio de Justicia', Costa Rica: La Nación.
Dahl, R.A. (2000) *On Democracy*, New Haven, CN and London: Yale University Press.
Duverger, M. (1987) *Los partidos políticos*, México: Fondo de Cultura Económica.
Fait, A. (20 May 1992) *Interview*, Former Vice-President (1986–1990) and member of the PLN, San José: His office.
Fernández, O. (1992) 'Elecciones en Costa Rica: ¿Repetición de una secuencia?', in R. Cerdas, J. Rial, and D. Zovatto (eds) *Elecciones y democracia en América Latina 1988–1991: una tarea inconclusa*, Costa Rica: IIDH-CAPEL, Friedrich-Naumann-Stiftung.
Fernández, O. (1996) 'Los partidos políticos: su interrelación y los rasgos centrales en la sociedad costarricense', *Anuario de Estudios Centroamericanos* 22(2): 147–166.

Figueres-Ferrer, J. (1987) *El espíritu del 48*. Costa Rica: Editorial Costa Rica.
Güell, R. (23 January 2002) *Interview*, President of the 1948 Civil War Veterans Association, former PLN member, San José: His residence.
Instituto Nacional de Estadística y Censos (INEC) (2002) 'Publicaciones', www.inec.go.cr/paginas/publicaciones.htm.
Jonas-Bodenheimer, S. (1984) *La ideología Social Demócrata en Costa Rica*. Costa Rica: EDUCA.
Kirchheimer, O. (1966) 'The Transformation of West European Party Systems', in J. LaPalombara and M. Weiner (eds) *Political Parties and Political Development*, Princeton, NJ: Princeton University Press.
Knight, A. (2001) 'Democratic and Revolutionary Traditions in Latin America', *Bulletin of Latin American Research* 20(2): 147–186.
Latinobarómetro (1996–2003) 'Informes de prensa', www.latinobarometro.org/.
Lehoucq, F.E. (1998) *Instituciones democráticas y conflictos políticos en Costa Rica*. Costa Rica: Editorial UNA.
Mainwaring, S. and Scully, T. (1995) 'Party Systems in Latin America', in S. Mainwaring and T. Scully (eds) *Building Democratic Institutions: Party Systems in Latin America*, Stanford, CA: Stanford University Press.
Mcdonald, R. (1971) *Party Systems and Elections in Latin America*. Chicago, IL: Markham Publishing Company.
Molina, I. and Lehoucq, F. (1999) *Urnas de lo inesperado: fraude electoral y lucha política en Costa Rica*. Costa Rica: Editorial UCR.
Peeler, J.A. (1985) *Latin American Democracies: Colombia, Costa Rica, Venezuela*, Chapel Hill, NC: University of North Carolina Press.
Peeler, J.A. (1996) 'Democratización inicial en América Latina: Costa Rica en el contexto de Chile y Uruguay', *Anuario de Estudios Centroamericanos* 22(2): 65–90.
Peeler, J.A. (1998) *Building Democracy in Latin America*, Boulder, CO and London: Lynne Rienner.
Pérez-Brignoli, H. (1999) *Historia del Partido Unidad Social Cristiana*. Costa Rica: INCEP, Fundación Konrad-Adenauer.
Proyecto Estado de la Nación (PEN) (2001) *Auditoría ciudadana sobre la calidad de la democracia*. Costa Rica: Proyecto Estado de la Nación.
Rodríguez, F., Castro-Méndez, S., Estrada-Mena, V., Rosales-Valladares, R., Solano-Bentes, J., and Zeledón-Torres, F. (April 2002) 'Radiografía de una indecisión: estudio político electoral en la semana previa a las elecciones de febrero del 2002', Costa Rica: PROCESOS, Programa de Posgrado Centroamericano en Ciencias Políticas (UCR).
Rojas-Bolaños, M. (1979) *La lucha social y la guerra civil en Costa Rica*, Costa Rica: Editorial Porvenir.
Rovira-Mas, J. (January–June 1998) 'Elecciones generales: Costa Rica, 1 de febrero de 1998', *Boletín Electoral Latinoamericano* XIX: 9–70.
Salazar, J.M. (1981) *Política y reforma en Costa Rica, 1914–1858*, Costa Rica: Editorial Porvenir.
Sánchez, F.F. (2001) 'Sistema electoral y partidos políticos: incentivos hacia el bipartidismo en Costa Rica', *Anuario de Estudios Centroamericanos* 27(1): 133–168.
Sánchez, F.F. (2003) 'Dealignment in Costa Rica: A Case Study of Electoral Change. D. Phil. Thesis', in *Department of Politics and International Relations*, Oxford: University of Oxford.
Schifter, J. (1981) *La fase oculta de la guerra civil en Costa Rica*, Costa Rica: EDUCA.

Schifter, J. (1982) *Costa Rica, 1948: análisis de documentos confidenciales del Departamento de Estado*, Costa Rica: EDUCA.

Seligson, M.A. (1987) 'Costa Rica and Jamaica', in M. Weiner and E. Ozbudun (eds) *Latin American Politics and Development*, Durham, NC: Duke University Press.

Seligson, M.A. (2001a) 'Costa Rican Exceptionalism: Why the "Ticos" are Different', in R.A. Camp (ed.) *Citizens Views of Democracy in Latin America*, Pittsburgh, PA: Pittsburgh University Press.

Seligson, M.A. (2001b) '¿Problemas en el paraíso? La erosión en el apoyo al sistema político y la centroamericanización de Costa Rica 1978–1999', in J. Rovira-Mas (ed.) *La democracia de Costa Rica ante el siglo XXI*, Costa Rica: Editorial UCR.

Shugart, M.S. and Carey, J.M. (1992) *Presidents and Assemblies: Constitutional Design and Electoral Dynamics*, Cambridge: Cambridge University Press.

Stone, S. (1975) *La dinastía de los conquistadores*, Costa Rica: EDUCA.

Thibaut, B. (1993) 'Costa Rica', in D. Nohlen (ed.) *Enciclopedia electoral latinoamericana y del caribe*, Costa Rica: IIDH.

Tribunal Supremo de Elecciones (TSE) (2002) 'Información electoral y declaratorias oficiales', http:www.tse.go.cr.

Urcuyo-Fournier, C. (1990) 'Costa Rica: consolidación democrática, desafíos del presente y del futuro', in R. Alfonsín (ed.) *Agenda para la consolidación de la democracia en América Latina*, Costa Rica: IIDH-CAPEL, Friedrich-Naumann-Stiftung.

Vega-Carballo, J.L. (1989) 'Partidos, desarrollo político y conflicto social en Honduras y Costa Rica: análisis comparativo', *Síntesis* 8: 363–383.

Vega-Carballo, J.L. (1992) 'Political Parties, Party Systems and Democracy in Costa Rica', in L.W. Goodman, W.M. LeoGrande and J. Forman (eds) *Political Parties and Democracy in Central America*, Boulder, CO and Oxford: Westview Press.

Wilson, B.M. (1998) *Costa Rica: Politics, Economics, and Democracy*. Boulder; London: Lynne Rienner.

Yashar, D.J. (1995) 'Civil War and Social Welfare: The Origins of Costa Rica's Competitive Party System', in S. Mainwaring and T. Scully (eds) *Building Democratic Institutions: Party Systems in Latin America*, Stanford, CA: Stanford University Press.

Zumbado, O. (22 January 2002) *Interview*, 1948 Civil War veteran, PUSC militant, Heredia: His office.

12 Democracies, disengagement, and deals

Exploring the effect of different types of mediators in civil conflict

Isak Svensson[1]

Introduction

In April 1993, the civil war was raging in Bosnia. Soldiers were killed on the battlefield, civilians fled, and the country was devastated. In that context, the European Union strived to bring the conflict to an end through mediation. The mediators, the former British member of Parliament and Foreign Secretary Lord David Owen, together with a representative from the United Nations, former US Secretary of State Cyrus Vance, facilitated communication between the parties, held meetings with the leadership and designed a peace plan, called the Vance-Owen Plan. The belligerents initially signed the plan, but the Bosnian Serb Assembly soon after failed to ratify it. The mediators were deemed inefficient and unsuccessful (Greenberg and McGuinness, 2001). The failure was partly due to the fact that the third party mediators possessed very little leverage over the belligerents. Although a strategy for the mediators to increase the leverage over the belligerents would have been to threaten to disengage from the conflict and leaving the parties to their own destiny, such a strategy could not be used since their commitment to the mediation effort itself hindered them to withdraw. Indeed, Burg (2005) argues that the right response of the mediators to the failure of the conflicting parties in Bosnia to accept the Vance–Owen plan should have been withdrawal from the third party efforts. However, 'the sponsoring states had committed troops, treasure, and prestige to the mediation effort, leading them to block any alternative other than to continue that effort' (Burg, 2005: 206). Paradoxically, the mediators' commitment to the mediation process made them in some sense less efficient as mediators.

The example from Bosnia illustrates that the threat of withdrawal may be one potential strategy for third parties involved in finding peaceful solutions to armed conflicts. It is also an illustration that some types of third parties have problems to employ this strategy, making them less efficient as mediators. All types of mediators cannot make termination threats with the same degree of credibility. In this chapter, I suggest that one plausible explanation for why threat of withdrawal cannot be efficiently employed by some types of mediators is to be found in the high value mediators attach to the peace process and their own role in that regard. In this particular case, the European countries valued the existence of a peace process, and their own role of being the mediator in such a process, to such an extent that they were unable to credibly threaten to terminate their mediation efforts. This chapter explores the dynamics of mediation termination threat.

Mediation theory identifies the threat of mediation withdrawal as one of the most important strategies mediators may use in order to get the parties in conflict to a negotiated settlement. Leverage refers to the power a mediator may possess over the belligerents. It can stem from different mediation strategies, one of which is the threat to end the mediation process (Touval and Zartman, 2001). A mediator's leverage over the belligerents has been suggested by previous mediation research as the main explanation for the ability to move the parties towards a settlement (Assefa, 1987; Bercovitch, 1991; Crocker et al., 2004; Kleibor, 2002; Zartman, 1995b). Touval even argues that leverage on part of the mediators is a prerequisite for successful mediation: 'To be successful, mediators require leverage' (Touval, 1992: 233). Hence, mediation efficiency is partly conditioned upon the third party's ability to threaten belligerents with costly breakdown of negotiations if they do not reach agreement.

However, previous research has not explored the conditions under which the threat of mediation termination can be made in a credible manner. Put differently, previous mediation research has not adequately addressed the question of why belligerents would believe in the mediator's threat to disengage from a peace process. Whereas mediators may mount pressure on the parties by threatening to disengage if the parties do not settle their conflict, such a threat will only be efficient under two general conditions. First, the alternative to mediated agreement must be costly conflict. Warring parties may be assumed to relate the costs of peaceful settlement to the costs of conflict. If the continuation of the unresolved conflict is bearable, then the prospect of mediators disengaging will not seem threatening. Second, a mediator must be able to convince the parties that they will follow through on a threat of disengagement. I argue that mediators with internal audiences – democracies – will be less tolerant to be associated with failed mediation, as they may suffer punishment from their own internal audiences due to failed mediation attempts. Given the value mediators with internal audiences attach to the process and outcome of mediation, such mediators will be less credible in their threats of withdrawal. The counter-intuitive implication is that we should expect non-democracies to outperform democracies as peace brokers in costly conflicts.

The purpose of the chapter is to examine which types of mediators are associated with negotiated settlement in internal armed conflicts. This chapter explores the implications of a credibility problem that the mediators may encounter due to their concern for their reputation as mediators in relation to their own audience. This study contributes to an ongoing debate concerning what conditions mediation will be credible (Fearon, 1998; Gilady and Russett, 2002; Kydd, 2003; Smith and Stam, 2003). In addition, this study contributes to the literature dealing with conflict and democracy, which has suggested that the existence of internal audience can be beneficial from a conflict resolution perspective (Fearon, 1994; Guisinger and Smith, 2002; Schultz, 1999). Quite to the contrary, this study suggests that democracies, unfortunately, due to the existence of internal audience carry a systematic disadvantage as mediators compared to non-democracies.

The chapter is divided in four sections. First, the theoretical argument is presented in relation to previous research on mediation. In the second section, the research design is laid out. I present the operationalisation of the dependent as well as the independent variables. I also describe the data on mediation in all intrastate armed conflicts during the period 1989–2003 that is used for this chapter. The results are presented in the third section of the chapter. I address two questions. The question of where mediation occurs is addressed by searching for systematic patterns of selection into various conflict situations by different sorts of mediators. Mediators do not choose where to mediate at random. Therefore, I start with the question of where mediation occurs in order to diagnose to what extent problems of strategic selection can influence the effect of mediation. Overall, no conclusive evidence can be found in this respect. Both democratic and non-democratic mediators intervene in conflicts where parties approach power parity, in stronger rather than weaker states and in conflicts of long duration. The only indication of selection between types of countries that we can observe in the data is that non-democracies, in contrast to a democratic mediator, are significantly more likely to intervene if there is more than one rebel group fighting the government. The second question deals with what effect different types of mediators have on the likelihood of a negotiated settlement, controlling for the effect of mainstream explanatory variables in civil war termination literature. Mediation is considered successful if warring parties reach a peace agreement and violence ceases for at least one year. When including non-active conflicts in the analysis, both democracies and non-democracies have a significant effect on the likelihood of a negotiated settlement. However, in active conflicts, only non-democratic mediators have a positive effect on the likelihood of negotiated settlements. Hence, non-democratic mediators seem to be better than democratic mediators at bringing governments and rebel groups to a peaceful settlement in costly conflicts. In the fourth and final section of the chapter, I discuss the results and their theoretical implications.

Theoretical framework

Previous mediation research emphasises leverage as the most important explanation for successful mediation. By having the power of sticks, carrots or information about the other side, a mediator may bring the parties to a negotiated settlement. Leverage is both the 'ticket to mediation' (Touval and Zartman, 2001: 436) and the main explanation for its success. Mediators 'can only help the parties or produce an agreement if they have leverage' (Touval and Zartman, 1985: 13). There are three ways in which mediators may increase the chance of settlement (Bercovitch and Langley, 1993; Touval and Zartman, 2001; Zartman, 1995a). First, mediators may facilitate sharing of information between the warring parties. Mediators can provide information about the other side's willingness to settle for peace rather than continue to fight. Hence, mediators can decrease the informational asymmetries between the warring parties by supplying information about the other side's resolve (Gilady and Russett, 2002; Kydd, 2003). The second way a mediator may increase chance for negotiated settlement is to make peace pay. Mediators can increase the relative value of a negotiated settlement, for example, by facilitating the exploration of potential solutions to a conflict, or by using side-payments in order to pull the parties towards peace. Third, mediators can increase chance for negotiated settlement by making continuous war costly. By decreasing the probability of winning, the cost for fighting the conflict to its final end, or the value at stake, a mediator can increase the relative value of negotiated settlements. To sum up, there are three basic measures a mediator may implement in order to increase the chance for peace, that is, sharing information, use of carrots and use of sticks.

Mediation theory asserts that the threat of mediation withdrawal is one of the most important sources of leverage and, therefore, one important way that mediators can push the parties to peace. Zartman states that 'conflict resolution depends on a sense of urgency', and argues that this can be created by the third parties artificially, and enforced by 'a threat to withdraw from the conciliation process'. (Zartman, 1985: 233). As a source of leverage, termination threat 'lies in the mediator's ability to withdraw and leave the parties to their own devices and their continuing conflict' (Touval and Zartman, 2001: 437). Hence, mediators who are able to threaten to leave the parties to themselves if they do not agree to settle their conflict will be more efficient peace brokers.

From a bargaining perspective, the leverage explanation is insufficient because it has not adequately addressed the question of why the belligerents would believe in the mediators. Given that all parties – the primary as well as third parties – have incentives to deceive the others, the puzzle is how mediators can be credible, in their promises, pressures, or in the information they reveal. The credibility of the mediator may be increased, according to some scholars, if they have a mediation reputation to consider. For instance, Gilady and Russett assert that some mediators have an interest in keeping their 'mediation reputation' in front of an audience, and that 'any breach of this reputation might be costly for the mediator, which has an incentive to only supply reliable information – an incentive that enhances the mediator's credibility' (Gilady and Russett, 2002: 398). Hence, the existence of internal audiences, according to these arguments, serves to increase the probability of mediation success. In this chapter, I dispute the beneficial role of internal audiences for third party efficiency. If we take the threat of mediation withdrawal as the theoretical point of departure, concern about their own mediation reputation in front of an internal audience may decrease, rather than increase, the chances of peaceful settlement of armed conflicts.[2]

I suggest that mediation termination threats will be efficient under two general conditions. First, the alternative for the belligerents to a mediated negotiated settlement should be costly conflict. In line with previous research, I assume that warring parties relate the costs of peaceful settlement to the costs of no-agreement, that is, to continued conflict (Mason and Fett, 1996). Internal armed conflicts do not necessarily need to be costly for the primary parties. Armed conflicts can be non-costly in the sense of providing an acceptable status quo for both sides. The second condition for termination threats to be efficient is that the mediators must be able to carry it through. I argue that mediators vary in their ability to make a threat of mediation disengagement in a believable manner. The argument presented here builds on the assumption that internal audiences in democracies in general reward mediation, mediation attempts and successful mediation, but will punish mediators who are associated with failed mediation. In democracies, the political opposition may exploit failed mediation attempts by the government as a way of picturing the government as ineffective. Mediators with internal audiences will therefore be less tolerant to be associated with failed mediation, as they may suffer punishment from their own internal audiences. The termination threat in mediation is a brinkmanship strategy. The mediator must be able to credibly threaten to withdraw – with failed mediation as a result – if the warring parties are to be pushed to sign an agreement. An effective mediator must therefore stand ready to sacrifice the positive externalities that follow with a mediation process. Those mediators that are too attached to the mediation role, and that can be punished if a mediation effort fails, will have incentives to keep on trying to get the parties to reach a settlement. Anticipating this, the belligerents have little reason to believe in the threats to withdraw from the mediation attempts. Consequently, those actors without internal audiences will be more capable to credibly threaten to terminate the mediation efforts.

This argument has implications for which types of mediators we should expect to be successful. Previous research has shown that democracies, due to their relatively higher audience costs, may be more efficient when signalling their intentions and capabilities (Fearon, 1994; Guisinger and Smith, 2002; Schultz, 1999; Smith, 1998). This applies to conflicts where the primary parties are democracies, whereas in this chapter, I examine the effect of democratic mediators. In international conflicts, internal audiences will punish a leadership that backs down from a commitment. When it comes to mediation, the internal audience is generally in favour of mediation attempts by the political leadership. Democracies are influenced by the 'norms of dispute resolution integral to the democratic process' (Dixon,

1993: 42), which makes them favourably attuned to the mediation role. Put differently, to be a peace broker generates political credit. Just as democracies must take into consideration their own internal audience when they act in international crisis, they must take into consideration their image as peace brokers when they mediate in other countries' internal conflicts. Thus, democratic countries, due to a high payoff for mediation, cannot make credible commitment to mediation withdrawal, and they therefore have a systematic disadvantage as mediators. In contrast, non-democratic countries are generally unconcerned about their own audience. Consequently, non-democratic countries are able to make their mediation disengagement threats credible and should be expected to outperform democracies as efficient peace mediators, if the alternative is continuous conflict.[3] This explanatory logic entails the novel empirical proposition that *mediators, that are non-democratic countries, rather than democratic countries, should be more likely to successfully bring the parties to a negotiated settlement in costly conflicts.*

Research design

The empirical analysis covers all intrastate armed conflicts, during the period 1989–2003. An armed conflict is defined as a contested incompatibility that concerns government or territory where the use of armed force between two parties, of which at least one is the government of a state, results in at least 25 battle-related deaths in one calendar year.[4] The unit of analysis is conflict-dyad-year.[5] During this time-period, there were 204 conflict-dyads in 67 countries. The total number of observations is 1,431.

Previous quantitative research on war termination has mainly used the conflict, or the conflict-year, as the level of analysis (for example, Bercovitch and Schneider, 2000; DeRouen and Sobek, 2004; Regan and Stam, 2000; Walter, 2002).[6] In Table 12.1, the distribution of conflict-dyad-years is described. We can see the frequency of conflict-dyad-years for conflicts with only one rebel group compared to conflicts with several rebel groups. Given that more than half of the conflict-years, during the time-period 1989–2003, occurred in conflicts with more than one rebel group, it is reasonable to argue that conflict-level is not an appropriate level of analysis. Mediators may engage themselves in some conflict-dyads, while not others within the same conflict. Some rebel groups may choose to settle the

Table 12.1 Distribution of conflict with one or several rebel groups

More than one dyad in the incompatibility?	Frequency	Percentage	Cumulative
No	659	46	46
Yes	772	54	100
Total	1,431	100	

conflict, while others may continue to fight. Using these variables on the higher level of aggregation may therefore be potentially misleading. Hence, the dyadic level provides us with a more accurate level of analysis, when examining the effect of mediations.

The way conflict is defined evolves around the notion of incompatibility. Incompatibility refers to the stated incompatible positions of the warring parties. As long as the incompatibility is unresolved, the conflict is included in the data. This way of measuring armed conflicts implies the inclusion of several non-active armed conflicts, which other projects may consider terminated. As the theoretical expectation is that termination threats would only be efficient where the alternative to mediated settlement is continuous costly conflict, I estimate the model on a subset on the data, including only active conflict years. Costly conflicts are operationalised as conflicts with battle-related deaths above the threshold of 25 per year.

Dependent variable

There is a vast amount of literature on what constitutes mediation 'success'. Frei (1976) defines it in terms of the belligerents' acceptance of mediation, Regan and Stam (2000) as conflict duration, and in Bercovitch (1991) success is defined as settlement (partial or full) or ceasefire. Touval and Zartman define success as the conclusion of an agreement promising the reduction of conflict (Touval and Zartman, 1985), whereas Greig (2001) also includes long-term changes in rivalry relationships. In sum, there seem to be no consensus within previous literature on what constitutes mediation success.

Mediation success is defined in quite ambitious terms in this project. The dependent variable in this study is negotiated settlement (SETTLEMENT), which is defined as a situation where the primary parties have signed a peace agreement, and the conflict-dyad did not reach the threshold of 25 battle-related deaths the following calendar-year. An agreement between the primary parties is considered to be a peace agreement if it addresses the problem of the incompatibility, by regulating or resolving all or part of it.[7] I want to examine whether mediation is able to produce a transformation in conflicts, that is, a turning point, in which an armed conflict is transformed into more peaceful relationships. This should be a turning point both in terms of the conflict issue and in terms of the conflict behaviour. This is the rationale for using battle-related deaths in the year following an agreement as an indicator whether the peace agreement could be coded as negotiated settlement, or not.[8]

Independent variables

Mediation is defined as efforts to help the primary parties to regulate the incompatibility. Mediation efforts may imply, for example, providing good offices, leading or facilitating talks, or in other ways participating in negotiations between the primary parties. Common to previous research's definitions of mediation is that it is voluntary, made in order to regulate or settle their conflict and is performed by an actor who stands outside the conflict. I use the category 'third party' from Uppsala Conflict Data Programme (UCDP), but make three amendments in order to make the coding compatible with previous definitions of mediators, namely to exclude peacekeeping operations, mediators from within the conflict, and mediation attempts that are clearly rejected.[9]

The theoretical argument proposed in this chapter expects a variation in mediation success for non-democratic mediators compared to democracies. In order to measure whether a country is democratic (DEMOMED), the combined score of Polity IV is used. In line with previous studies on democratic intervention (Gleditsch et al., 2004), the threshold for being coded as a democracy is that a country has a score of 6 or more on the combined polity score. A mediation attempt is coded as democratic if at least one democratic country is involved in the mediation. DEMOMED is coded as 1, when there is mediation by democratic countries, and 0 otherwise. Consequently, a non-democratic mediator (NONDEMOMED) is a country that is defined as mediator and that has a score of 5 or less on the combined polity score. DEMOMED and NONDEMOMED are not mutually exclusive. I estimate them both simultaneously in order to control for the potential overlapping effect of different mediators mediating simultaneously. Democratic countries are coded as mediating in 77 cases, whereas non-democratic mediators are coded as mediating in 102 cases.[10] There are also situations where both democratic and non-democratic countries mediate simultaneously. There are 61 cases where such joint mediation occurred.

Control variables

Mediation can be conducted by third parties that are not countries, and therefore cannot be divided into the dichotomy democracy or non-democracy. There are cases where mediation is performed by non-country mediators, for example, non-governmental organisations or regional or global inter-governmental organisations. I therefore include a variable (ORGMED) that is coded as 1 when there is mediation by non-country mediation.[11]

There are several variables suggested in previous literature that may have an effect on both the dependent and independent variables, and that therefore seem reasonable to include as control variables. In this study, I control for great power mediation (Crocker et al., 2004; Kleibor, 2002; Touval, 1992), the duration and intensity of the conflict (Mason and Fett, 1996), number of rebel groups (Crocker et al., 1999), military balance (Zartman, 1995b), level of democracy (DeRouen and Sobek, 2004), territorial dimension (Toft, 2004) and the strength of the government's army (Balch-Lindsay et al., 2006; DeRouen and Sobek, 2004). Great power mediation (POWERMED) is measured by examining whether a mediator was a country, which is a permanent member of the UN Security Council.[12] Intensity is measured with a dummy-variable (WAR) that is coded as 1 if conflict reached the threshold of 1,000 battle-related deaths during the year, and 0 otherwise.[13] Duration of the conflict (DURATION) is measured by counting the number of years since the conflict-dyad started.[14] In order to control for a curvilinear relationship, in line with the reasoning in Mason et al. (1999), a squared term (DURATION^2) of the duration variable is included. Moreover, the number of warring rebel groups (DYADS) is coded by counting the number of rebel groups fighting the government in the same conflict incompatibility. The relative strength between the parties' troop numbers is measured (MILBAL).[15] Whether the country of the conflict was democratic (POLITY), is measured with data from Polity IV.[16] Data for the variable (GDP) is taken from Gleditsch's dataset (Gleditsch, 2002).[17] The incompatibility in conflict is captured (TERR) by coding 1 if the incompatibility is territorial, and 0 if the incompatibility is governmental.[18] The size of government army (GOVTARMY), is measured by taking the total amount of military personnel in thousands.[19] Controls for temporal dependence is estimated with the use of 'cubic splines' (Beck et al., 1998).

Results

The results will be discussed in two parts. First, the question of whether the systematic selection between different types of mediators is addressed. Second, the effect of mediation on the probability of negotiated settlement is estimated, while controlling for the explanatory factors suggested in previous literature. Probit analysis is used as statistical technique estimating these relationships. As a criterion for statistical significance, a p-value of 0.05 is used. Given that the observations are not independent from each other (there are many observations in the same conflict-dyad), the standard errors have been clustered on the country level.[20]

Where do mediators go?

We first address the question of whether mediators select themselves to different conflict contexts. Do mediators separate themselves according to the contexts of conflicts, in which they choose to mediate? In Models 1, 2 and 3 in Table 12.2, we can see the effect of a set of explanatory, contextual variables on the occurrence of mediation by democracies, non-democracies and organisations.

Both democratic and non-democratic mediators tend to intervene into more balanced situations compared to conflict situations where the power relationship between governments and rebels were highly asymmetric. Hence, the different types of mediators reveal a similar systematic pattern of

Table 12.2 Where do mediators mediate?

	DEMOMED	NONDEMOMED	ORGMED
MILBAL	0.452*	0.860**	0.844**
	(0.205)	(0.191)	(0.199)
WAR	0.203	0.051	0.518**
	(0.168)	(0.167)	(0.184)
GOVTARMY	−0.000**	−0.000*	−0.000**
	(0.000)	(0.000)	(0.000)
DURATION	0.053*	0.055*	0.007
	(0.021)	(0.027)	(0.033)
DURATION^2	−0.001*	−0.001	−0.001
	(0.000)	(0.001)	(0.001)
DYADS	0.040	0.127**	−0.025
	(0.057)	(0.038)	(0.050)
GDP	−0.010	−0.057	−0.317**
	(0.126)	(0.100)	(0.121)
TERR	0.238	−0.031	0.209
	(0.215)	(0.221)	(0.238)
POLITY	−0.011	−0.030	0.026
	(0.021)	(0.018)	(0.018)
Constant	−1.614	−1.084	1.218
	(0.986)	(0.735)	(0.954)
Observations	692	692	694

Notes
Robust standard errors in parentheses. Standard errors are adjusted for clustering on dyads. * significant at 5 per cent; ** significant at 1 per cent.

intervention in this regard. Moreover, non-democratic mediators as well as democratic mediators tend to occur in conflict countries with relatively less military capacity. The fewer the troops in a state in conflict, the higher the probability of getting mediation by non-democracies as well as democracies. Yet another empirical pattern that we can observe is that both democracies and non-democracies intervene in longer, rather than shorter, conflicts. Previous research has found that conflicts are more likely to be peacefully settled the longer they continue (for example, Mason and Fett, 1996). In this sense, both democracies and non-democracies select the least demanding cases and choose to intervene when they anticipate that they have a good chance to help the parties reach a settlement. The negative and significant effect of the squared terms of duration (DURATION^2) indicates that the effect of duration on the likelihood of democratic mediation is not linear. Conflict duration increases the probability of mediation by democracies, but this effect decreases over time.

There is one variable that can be interpreted as indicating a selection effect between different types of mediators. Non-democracies tend to mediate in conflicts with more than one conflict-dyad. More rebel groups

Democracies, disengagement, and deals 237

should largely increase the complexity and degree of difficulty in reaching agreement (Crocker *et al.*, 1999). Hence, if there is indeed a selection effect, then non-democracies intervene in the most demanding conflict situations.

Turning to mediation by organisations, we can observe that four variables indicate a systematic pattern of occurrence of mediation. As with countries, organisations mediate in conflict situations where the parties are relatively balanced, in the sense of military capability. Likewise, as with countries, the effect of the size of the government's army is also negative and significant, indicating that the fewer troops on the government's side, the more likely that mediation by organisations will occur. There are two explanatory variables that indicate that organisations mediate in other settings than those where countries mediate. Organisations tend to mediate in the most intense conflict situations. WAR has a negative and significant effect on ORGMED. Moreover, mediation by organisations tends to occur in less wealthy states. GDP is significant and negative, indicating that the less state resources in the country involved in conflict, the more likely that an organisation will mediate.[21] These two variables taken together illustrate an interesting pattern: mediation by organisations tends to occur in the cases where the state is weak, rather than strong, and in intense conflict situations. These are the situations where the probability of reaching a negotiated settlement is probably the least likely. The overall picture is that there is more evidence of a selection between countries and organisations, than a differential selection between types of countries.

Measuring mediation success

In Table 12.3, we can see the results of the estimations on the probability of negotiated settlement. The expectation derived from the argument in this chapter is that mediators that are non-democratic countries, rather than democratic countries, should be more likely to successfully bring the parties to a negotiated settlement in costly conflicts. In Model 1, mediation by non-democracies (NONDEMOMED) is positively related to the probability that antagonists will sign an agreement and stop fighting each other; this effect is statistically significant.[22] Democratic mediators, on the other hand, seem to be less effective. The effect of democratic mediation (DEMOMED) on the likelihood of parties reaching a peace agreement and ceasing their battles is not significant. To exemplify, Russia succeeded to mediate a negotiated settlement in Tajikistan in 1997 and Libya was successful as a mediator in Chad at the beginning of the new millennium. On the other hand, Norway has hitherto failed to get the parties in Sri Lanka to reach a negotiated settlement, and the Netherlands was unsuccessful in their attempts to peacefully resolve the territorial conflict in Nagaland in India.

The overall relationship between mediation and negotiated settlement remain robust when control-variables are included. In Model 2, non-democratic mediation has a positive effect, whereas democratic mediators

Table 12.3 Measuring the effect of mediation

Settlement	(1)	(2)	(3)	(4)
NONDEMOMED	0.852**	0.772*	0.925**	0.779**
	(0.271)	(0.367)	(0.214)	(0.293)
DEMOMED	0.205	−0.207	0.402*	0.109
	(0.234)	(0.463)	(0.187)	(0.305)
ORGMED	−0.012	0.157	0.058	0.274
	(0.330)	(0.313)	(0.216)	(0.263)
POWERMED	–	0.701	–	0.433
		(0.632)		(0.384)
MILBAL	–	0.446	–	0.203
		(0.273)		(0.211)
WAR	–	−1.188**	–	−1.260**
		(0.449)		(0.393)
GOVTARMY	–	0.000	–	−0.000
		(0.000)		(0.000)
DURATION	–	−0.048	–	−0.011
		(0.036)		(0.021)
DURATION^2	–	0.000	–	0.000
		(0.001)		(0.000)
DYADS	–	−0.027	–	0.010
		(0.075)		(0.032)
GDP	–	0.167	–	−0.034
		(0.151)		(0.123)
TERR	–	−0.292	–	−0.192
		(0.258)		(0.183)
POLITY	–	−0.033	–	0.012
		(0.027)		(0.018)
Time since last settlement	–	0.370	0.508*	0.269
		(0.258)	(0.254)	(0.282)
(Cubic splines not shown)				
Constant	−2.185**	−3.501**	−2.512**	−2.002*
	(0.139)	(1.177)	(0.249)	(0.870)
Observations	803	692	1,426	951

Notes
Robust standard errors in parentheses. Standard errors are adjusted for clustering on country. * significant at 5 per cent; ** significant at 1 per cent.

have no significant effect. As we can see in Model 2, mediation by organisations (ORGMED) fails to have a significant effect. In line with the aforementioned reasoning, this lack of effect can be due to organisations mediating in the most demanding situations. Furthermore, mediation by great powers (POWERMED) are not associated with any significant effect. It could be argued that the capacity of the mediators should be taken into consideration, and not only their political system. Great powers are strong actors on the mediation scene and have military, political, and economic resources at their disposals, which can be brought to bear on the parties in order to increase their incentives for a peace settlement. But in contrast to what we may expect from such reasoning, POWERMED fails to have a significant effect on the likelihood of a negotiated settlement. Moreover, the military balance between the parties does not have an effect on the likelihood of a negotiated settlement. We have seen that more militarily balanced situations tend to attract mediation, and that this applies to all types of mediators. Although military balance may increase the chance for mediation, it does not seem to have any effect on the likelihood of settlement. Furthermore, we can see that conflict intensity (WAR) is negatively related to the likelihood of negotiated settlement. Higher intensity tends to decrease the chance for negotiated settlement. We can interpret this in many ways. The intensity of the conflict may be an indicator of how much the parties are committed to the cause they are fighting for. Alternatively, the intensity of the warfare may, by itself, create mistrust and a sense of insecurity between the belligerents that decreases chances for negotiated settlement. Moreover, several of the control-variables fail to have an effect on the likelihood of settlement. The duration of conflict, the size of the government's army, the number of warring groups, the wealth of the country in conflict and the type of incompatibility do not seem to matter when it comes to the likelihood of reaching a negotiated settlement. There is also no evidence suggesting a temporal dependence in the data.[23] This non-significance of several explanatory variables that previous research has found to be important, indicates that when utilising dyadic levels of analysis, results from the more aggregated conflict level may not be able to be replicated.

The theoretical expectation in this chapter is that mediation termination threats would only be efficient in the context of the costly conflicts. As described in the research design, the data used in order to capture the notion of costly conflicts is conflicts with battle-related deaths above the threshold of 25 per year. Those mediation processes that take place after the parties have ceased their fighting (such as, for example, Western Sahara or Chittagong Hill Tract in Bangladesh) therefore fall outside such an analysis. If non-active conflict-years are included, the picture is different. In Model 3, mediation is estimated on both active and non-active conflicts increasing the number of observations. Here we can see that both democracies and non-democracies have an effect on the likelihood of negotiated settlement. Hence, democracies can sometimes be efficient peace brokers. However, the effect of democracies is highly dependent upon the specification of the model. We can see that when control-variables are included (Model 4) then the effect of democratic mediators (DEMOMED) is no longer statistically significant.[24]

Discussion

Under what conditions does mediation increase the likelihood of negotiated settlement in internal armed conflicts? This study has shown that non-democratic mediators outperform democratic mediators in terms of their effect on the probability of negotiated settlement in costly conflicts. The hypothesis suggested in this chapter is empirically supported.

Termination threat should only be efficient under the condition that the alternative to mediated agreement is a costly conflict. That is not always the case in armed conflicts. Some conflicts are not active in the sense of involving battle-related deaths, but still active in the sense of being unresolved. When the non-active years are included in the empirical analysis, democracies and autocracies alike have an effect on the chance of negotiated settlement. The implication is that the results in this chapter should be interpreted with caution. Democracies may be efficient peace brokers, but it is dependent on the dynamics of the conflicts. Democracies may deliver the deals, but in active conflicts, however, they tend to be less effective. I suggest that this depends on their need to consider the reaction of their own internal audience when performing their mediation efforts. These audiences want to see their representatives being useful, bringing peace or, at least, trying to do so. This makes them less effective to issue termination threats in costly conflicts.

Can the difference in performance between democratic and non-democratic mediators be a result of a selection effect? Theoretically, we could imagine that the reason why democracies do not have a significant effect while non-democracies do is that democracies take on the most difficult cases of conflict. Drawing inferences from the data, however, that is not the empirical pattern that we can observe. A strong case for selection bias would have shown different signs between the different types of actors, and effects that were significant.[25] This is not the case. What we can observe, however, it that non-democracies systematically select themselves into situations where there is more than one dyad. Democratic mediators revealed no such systematic pattern in relation to the number of challengers to the government. Overall, this indicates that, as far as we can go to diagnose a selection effect between types of mediators we can conclude that if there is a selection process, then non-democratic mediators tend to mediate in the most demanding situations. Hence, the strategic selection hypothesis has difficulty in explaining the difference in performance of democracies compared to non-democracies.

Elaborating on the question of selection, we saw that organisations tend to mediate in the most demanding situations, in terms of high conflict intensity and low level of income. Bercovitch *et al.* (1991) find that leaders of governments are more efficient mediators compared to any other actor. The explanation suggested by Bercovitch *et al.* is that of a strategic selection process: international organisations have to engage themselves in especially intractable cases, precisely because countries are reluctant to mediate in those cases. This study provides some support to that idea, in the sense that there is a significant trend indicating a selection process for mediation by organisation *vis-à-vis* other types of mediators.

This study has theoretical implications for the discussion about conflict resolution within the rationalist framework. For example, Gilady and Russett (2002) assert that some mediators have an interest in keeping their 'mediation reputation' in front of an audience, and that this serves as an incentive that enhances the mediator's credibility. The argument explored in this chapter implies that mediation reputation may have another effect than that predicted by Gilady and Russett. The theoretical starting point is the termination threat. By decreasing the credibility of withdrawal threats, the mediators' concern about their mediation reputation in front of their internal audience decreases, rather than increases, the probability of their success.

The relationship between democracy and peaceful resolution of conflicts is complex. While democracies may be better equipped than other types of countries to manage their own conflicts (Hegre *et al.*, 2001) or conflicts among themselves (Dixon, 1993, 1994; Raymond, 1994), this chapter indicates that they are less efficient when mediating in other countries' conflicts. We know from previous studies that democracies have a general preference for third party resolution of disputes. Disputes between democracies are more likely to be peacefully settled than other types of disputants (Dixon, 1994), dyads of democracies are more likely to refer their interstate disputes to binding third-party settlement (Raymond, 1994) and they are also more likely than others to accede to the involvement of conflict managing agents (Dixon, 1993). Moreover, previous research has shown that democracies, due to their relatively higher audiences costs, may be more efficient when signalling their intentions and capabilities (Fearon, 1994; Guisinger and Smith, 2002; Schultz, 1999; Smith, 1998). My contribution to this debate is to show that democracies seem to be less efficient than non-democracies when acting as mediators in internal armed conflicts. Audience costs plays an opposite function when the political leadership is involved in mediation exercises, compared to crisis bargaining. These findings can be related to each other in order to generate a coherent picture of the role of democracy and peaceful settlement of violent conflicts: the mechanism that makes democracies better equipped to peacefully manage their own conflicts – that is, the attachment of audience cost to their signals – is also the mechanism that makes democracies less efficient as mediators.

The threat of mediation withdrawal is not the only source of mediation leverage and, hence, not the only tool a mediator can use in order to get the parties to a negotiated settlement. Leverage may also stem from the mediators' ability to, for example, pay side-payments or threaten to take sides. Yet, evidence in this study suggests that other sources of leverage may be less important than previously suggested. As resource-rich and powerful actors, great-powers are supposedly the best equipped for using several of the other mediation strategies, and should therefore be expected to be successful peace brokers (Crocker, 1992; Crocker *et al.*, 2004; Touval, 1992). Interestingly, however, this study shows that great power mediation does not have an effect on the likelihood of parties reaching a negotiated settlement.

Conclusions

Mediation as a way of managing conflict has recently received increased attention by both the research community and by policymakers (for example, Crocker et al., 2004). This chapter is an example of how the bargaining approach with its emphasis on credibility may help us deepen the analysis of previous theories, and derive untested hypotheses that shed new light on a well-studied phenomenon (Gilady and Russett, 2002; Reiter, 2003; Werner et al., 2003). This study examines under what conditions mediation increases the chance that belligerents in internal conflicts will reach negotiated settlements. Based on previous mediation theory, the threat of mediation withdrawal is identified as one important factor for successful mediation. I suggest that all types of actors cannot make this termination-threat in a believable manner. Democracies have internal audiences that they seek to satisfy. In front of these audiences, mediation gives benefits in terms of a beneficial political reputation, but audiences can also punish failed mediation. In contrast, non-democracies do not have to pay audiences costs if they fail with their mediation efforts. They can therefore credibly threaten to withdraw from their mediation attempts. Hence, building on this logic, non-democracies should be expected to outperform democracies when it comes to the capability of bringing the warring parties to a negotiated settlement in costly conflicts. This is supported by an empirical analysis of all intrastate armed conflicts, 1989–2003. Democracies can have an effect on the likelihood of negotiated settlements, when including non-active years in the analysis. However, in contrast to democratic mediators, non-democracies have an effect on negotiated settlement when the parties are still fighting each other.

Lastly, a caveat should be put forward on how to interpret these results in terms of policy relevance. There may be several paths to successful mediation, of which threat of mediation withdrawal is just one. Mediators may facilitate transparency in the conflict, assist with economic resources, offer security guarantees for the parties or threaten the parties with different sorts of coercive measures. This chapter does not identify all the conditions under which mediation leads to negotiated settlement, but rather to test the empirical implication derived from my theoretical argument. Different strategies may work in different situations. This chapter shows that in costly conflicts democracies tend to be less efficient than non-democracies. Unfortunately, those that are most eager to take on the role of the mediator can be the ones that – under some circumstances – are the ones that are the least likely to be successful mediators.

Notes

1 I acknowledge that this chapter has benefited from the valuable comments from Patrick Regan, Allan Stam, Mattiew Hoddie, Kaare Strøm, Mats Hammarström, Desireé Nilsson, Erika Forsberg, and Lisa Hultman on earlier drafts. All errors are my own.
2 This echoes the situation when third parties are heavily biased towards one side and therefore are not able to credibly threaten with abandonment (Schmidt, 2005)
3 Note from the outset that I do not argue that the threat of withdrawal is the only source of influence a mediator may exercise. Mediation is a complex social process, in which several social, political and cultural factors influence the chance of getting the parties to peace. There may be several other strategies that a mediator may use that may also induce the parties to settle their conflict (Touval and Zartman, 2001). However, bearing this caveat in mind, I still expect the argument to have observable empirical implications.
4 This definition is from the Uppsala Conflict Data Programme. The data used in this chapter can be found at www.ucdp.uu.se (version as of April 2005).
5 A conflict dyad consists of a government and a rebel group. In other words, there can be several conflict-dyads within one conflict.
6 To use mediation attempt as level of analysis (Bercovitch 1991) may lead to selection bias. For a critique on those lines, see Regan and Stam (2000).
7 Peace *process* agreements, in which parties agree how to design the peace process, are not considered to be peace agreements.
8 Ideally, battle behaviour during the year the peace agreement was signed should be examined. However, this has not been possible given that monthly data on battle-related deaths does not yet exist. Why parties return to armed conflict after a peace settlement has been reached is partly another question, which falls outside the ambitions of this project.
9 Whereas third parties are coded only on the conflict level in the UCDP, I have disaggregated these data to the dyadic level.
10 Note that cases here refer to conflict-dyad-years.
11 When formal leaders of countries, or groups of countries, are mediating (even if they represent an organisation) they are coded as separate countries. When a secretariat of an organisation or emissaries for organisations' Secretary Generals mediates, given that they are not head of a country, that is coded as ORGMED. Mediations by presidents, prime ministers, foreign ministers, or ambassadors, are coded as mediations by the country they represent.
12 This variable and the main independent variables are not mutually exclusive, as some mediators may be both democratic (or non-democratic) and great powers.
13 It would have been preferable to have raw-numbers on battle-related deaths, but these figures do not exist (or are not reliable), when it comes to dyadic data, including minor armed conflicts.
14 The start of the dyad is the first year when the conflict behaviour resulted in a minimum of 25 battle-related deaths. As a robustness check, I also coded a variable (DURATIONCONFLICT) that counts the number of years since the conflict – that is, the incompatibility, not necessarily the dyad – reached 25 battle-related deaths. In another specification (DURATIONCONFLICT^2) this variable was also squared. Including these specifications of duration in the model does not substantially alter the results.
15 Measuring military balance in internal armed conflicts must take into account the fact that governments commonly face several challenges, both internal and external. Subsequently, a ratio of 4:1 is used in this study, dividing the number of the government's troop with the number of rebels' troop. This variable

indicates that if a government has four times more troops than the rebels, or less, then the conflict dyadic relationship is defined as being balanced. More than four times greater manpower indicates a great asymmetry between the government and the rebels. As this is an arbitrary threshold, I tried different cut-off points, but such changes did not substantially affect the results. Data has been collected from Military Balance, the SIPRI Yearbook, and UCDP. Missing data has been interpolated.

16 The combined polity score from Polity IV is used, which has a scale ranging from −10 to +10, where higher scores indicate a higher level of democracy. The values of transition has been converted to conventional POLITY scores.
17 Data for the two last years has been interpolated. The variable has been logged in order to account for decreasing marginal effects.
18 In UCDP, Sudan (Southern Sudan) is coded as Government/Territory. I have coded this as a governmental conflict.
19 Data on military personnel is taken from the World Bank Development Indicators Database and missing data is supplemented from Military Balance's yearly reports.
20 In order to check for the robustness of the results, however, I have tested clustering on the country level, but this does not substantially change the results.
21 The relationship is not linear, as the marginal effect of GDP is highest for the least wealthy states.
22 A conflict that has a non-democratic mediator is 9 per cent more likely to reach a negotiated settlement, compared to a conflict that has no mediator at all. Predicted probabilities are available from the author upon request.
23 The cubic splines were not significant when tested jointly.
24 The reason why the number of observations drops dramatically in this regression is that there is missing data in the MILBAL.
25 A proper test of selection effect would be to use a two-step selection model (such as censored probit). Unfortunately, statistical models for simultaneous equations are at the current stage of technical development not able to distinguish between different types of mediators in both the first and second equation simultaneously. Ultimately, we would want a model that differentiates between different types of mediators in regard to both mediation and settlement simultaneously, but that is beyond the scope of this study, and must await further technical developments.

References

Assefa, H. (1987) *Mediation of Civil Wars: Approaches and Strategies – The Sudan Conflict*, Boulder, CO and London: Westview Press.

Balch-Lindsay, D. (Late), Enterline, A.J., and Joyce, K.A. (2006) *Third Party Intervention and the Civil War Process*, typescript: Department of Political Science, University of North Texas.

Beck, N., Katz, J.N., and Tucker, R. (1998) 'Taking Time Seriously in Binary Time-Series-Cross-Section Analysis', *American Journal of Political Science* 42(4): 1260–1288.

Bercovitch, J. (1991) 'International Mediation and Dispute Settlement: Evaluating the Conditions for Successful Mediation', *Negotiation Journal* 7(1): 17–30.

Bercovitch, J. and Langley, J. (1993) 'The Nature of the Dispute and the Effectiveness of International Mediation', *Journal of Conflict Resolution* 37(4): 670–691.

Bercovitch, J. and Schneider, G. (2000) 'Who Mediates? The Political Economy of International Conflict Management', *Journal of Peace Research* 37(2): 145–165.

Bercovitch, J., Anagnoson, J.T., and Wille, D.L. (1991) 'Some Conceptual Issues

and Empirical Trends in the Study of Successful Mediation in International Relations', *Journal of Peace Research* 28(1): 7–17.
Burg, S.L. (2005) 'Intractability and Third-Party Mediation in the Balkans', in C.A. Crocker, F.O. Hampson, and P. Aall (eds) *Grasping the Nettle: Analyzing Cases of Intractable Conflicts*, Washington, DC: United States Institute of Peace Press.
Crocker, C.A. (1992) 'Conflict Resolution in the Third World: The Role of Superpowers', in S.J. Brown and K.M. Schraub (eds) *Resolving Third World Conflict: Challenges for a New Era*, Washington, DC: United States Institute of Peace Press.
Crocker, C.A., Hampson, F.O., and Aall, P. (1999) 'Multiparty Mediation and the Conflict Cycle', in C.A. Crocker, F.O. Hampson and P. Aall (eds) *Herding Cats: Multiparty Mediation in a Complex World*, Washington, DC: United States Institute of Peace Press.
Crocker, C.A., Hampson, F.O., and Aall, P. (2004) *Taming Intractable Conflict: Mediation in the Hardest Cases*, Washington, DC: United States Institute of Peace Press.
DeRouen Jr, K.R. and Sobek, D. (2004) 'The Dynamics of Civil War Duration and Outcome', *Journal of Peace Research* 41(3): 303–320.
Dixon, W.J. (1993) 'Democracy and the Management of International Conflict', *Journal of Conflict Resolution* 37(1): 42–68.
Dixon, W.J. (1994) 'Democracy and the Peaceful Settlement of International Conflict', *American Political Science Review* 88(1): 14–32.
Fearon, J.D. (1994) 'Domestic Political Audiences and the Escalation of International Disputes', *American Political Science Review* 88(3): 577–592.
Fearon, J.D. (1998) 'Commitment Problems and the Spread of Ethnic Conflict', in D.A. Lake and D. Rotchild (eds), *The International Spread of Ethnic Conflict*, Princeton, NJ: Princeton University Press, pp. 107–126.
Frei, D. (1976) 'Conditions Affecting the Effectiveness of International Mediation', *The Papers of the Peace Science Society (International)* 26: 67–84.
Gilady, L. and Russett, B.M. (2002) 'Peacemaking and Conflict Resolution', in W. Carlsnaes, T. Risse, and B.A. Simmons (eds) *Handbook of International Relations*, London: SAGE Publications, pp. 392–408.
Gleditsch, K.S. (2002) 'Expanded Trade and GDP Data', *Journal of Conflict Resolution* 46(5): 712–724.
Gleditsch, N.P., Siljeholm-Christianse, L., and Hegre, H. (2004) 'Democratic Jihad? Military Intervention and Democracy', Paper Prepared for the Workshop on 'Resources, Governance Structures, and Civil War', ECPR Joint Sessions of Workshops, Uppsala, Sweden, 13–18 April.
Greenberg, M.C. and McGuinness, M.E. (2001) 'From Lisbon to Dayton: International Mediation and the Bosnia Crisis', in M.C. Greenberg, J.H. Barton, and M.E. McGuinness (eds) *Words Over War: Mediation and Arbitration to Prevent Deadly Conflict*, New York: Rowman & Littlefield Publishers, Inc.
Greig, M.J. (2001) 'Moments of Opportunity: Recognizing Conditions of Ripeness for International Mediation Between Enduring Rivals', *Journal of Conflict Resolution* 45(6): 691–718.
Guisinger, A. and Smith, A. (2002) 'Honest Threat: The Interaction of Reputation and Political Institutions in International Crises', *Journal of Conflict Resolution* 46(2): 175–200.
Hegre, H., Ellingsen, T., Gates, S., and Gleditsch, N.P. (2001) 'Towards a Democratic Civil Peace? Democracy, Political Change, and Civil war, 1816–1992', *American Political Science Review* 95(1): 33–48.

Kleibor, M. (2002) 'Great Power Mediation: Using Leverage to Make Peace', in J. Bercovitch (ed.), *Studies in International Mediation: Essays in Honor of Jeffrey Z. Rubin*, New York: Palgrave Macmillan.

Kydd, A. (2003) 'Which Side Are You On? Bias, Credibility, and Mediation', *American Journal of Political Science* 47(4): 597–611.

Mason, D.T. and Fett, P.J. (1996) 'How Civil Wars End: A Rational Choice Approach', *Journal of Conflict Resolution* 40(4): 546–568.

Mason, D.T., Weingarten, J.P., and Fett, P.J. (1999) 'Win, Lose, or Draw: Predicting the Outcome of Civil War', *Political Research Quarterly* 52(2): 239–268.

Raymond, G.A. (1994) 'Democracies, Disputes, and Third-Party Intermediaries', *Journal of Conflict Resolution* 38(1): 24–42.

Regan, P.M. and Stam, A.C. (2000) 'In the Nick of Time: Conflict Management, Mediation Timing, and the Duration of Interstate Disputes', *International Studies Quarterly* 44: 239–260.

Reiter, D. (2003) 'Exploring the Bargaining Model of War', *Perspectives on Politics* 1: 27–43.

Schmidt, H. (2005) 'When (and Why) do Brokers Have to be Honest? Impartiality and the Effectiveness of Third-Party Support for Negotiated Civil War Settlements, 1945–1999', Paper prepared for the delivery at the 63rd Annual National Conference of the Midwest Political Science Association, Chicago, IL, 7–10 April.

Schultz, K.A. (1999) 'Do Domestic Institutions Constrain or Inform? Contrasting Two Institutional Perspectives on Democracy and War', *International Organization* 53(2): 233–266.

Smith, A. (1998) 'International Crises and Domestic Politics', *American Political Science Review* 92(3): 623–638.

Smith, A. and Stam, A. (2003) 'Mediation and Peacekeeping in a Random Walk Model of Civil and Interstate War', *International Studies Review* 5(4): 115–135.

Toft, M.D. (2004) *The Geography of Ethnic Violence: Identity, Interests, and the Indivisibility of Territory*, Princeton, NJ and Oxford: Princeton University Press.

Touval, S. (1992) 'The Superpowers as Mediators', in J. Bercovitch and J.Z. Rubin (eds) *Mediation in International Relations*, New York: St. Martin's Press, pp. 232–248.

Touval, S. and Zartman, I.W. (1985) *International Mediation in Theory and Practice*, Conflict Management Studies, SAIS, Boulder, CO and London: Westview Press.

Touval, S. and Zartman, I.W. (2001) 'International Mediation in the Post-Cold War Era', in C.A. Crocker, F.O. Hampson, and P. Aall (eds) *Turbulent Peace: The Challenges of Managing International Conflict*, Washington, DC: United States Institute of Peace Press, pp. 427–443.

Walter, B.F. (2002) *Committing to Peace: The Successful Settlement of Civil Wars*. Princeton, NJ and Oxford: Princeton University Press.

Werner, S., Davis, D., and Bueno de Mesquita, B. (2003) 'Dissolving Boundaries: Introduction', *International Studies Quarterly* 5(4): 1–7.

Zartman, I.W., (1985) *Ripe for Resolution: Conflict and Intervention in Africa*, Oxford: Oxford University Press.

Zartman, I.W. (1995a) 'Dynamics and Constraints in Negotiations in Internal Conflicts', in I.W. Zartman (ed.) *Elusive Peace: Negotiating an End to Civil Wars*, Washington, DC: The Brookings Institution, pp. 3–29.

Zartman, W.I. (ed.) (1995b) *Elusive Peace: Negotiating and End to Civil Wars*, Washington, DC: The Brookings Institution.

13 Rebels on the outside

Signatories signaling commitment to durable peace

Desirée Nilsson[1]

Introduction

In the aftermath of a peace agreement, the signatories sometimes stick to peace, but in other instances, renewed cycles of violence follow in the wake of a deal. Why are some peace agreements successful in ending civil wars, while others fail? The role of spoilers has been highlighted in previous research (e.g. Stedman 1997, 2003). According to Downs and Stedman (2002: 56), 'The presence of spoilers in peace agreements poses daunting challenges to implementation.' More generally, several studies suggest that rebel groups on the outside of a peace agreement pose a threat to peace settlements (Ayres 2006; Kydd and Walter 2002; Newman and Richmond 2006, forthcoming; Stedman 1997; Zahar 2003, 2006).[2] However, this issue has largely been left unexplored in the quantitative research on durable peace. Therefore, little is known about the general patterns by which rebel groups on the outside of a deal may influence whether the signatories stick to peace or engage in violence.[3]

This study aims to fill this lacuna by examining the conditions under which the signatories, faced with a rebel group on the outside, stick to their peace agreement. More specifically, I will explore if the signatories, that is, the government and one or more rebel groups, are more likely to remain committed to their deal if they are faced with at least one excluded rebel group that is militarily strong vis-à-vis the government. Most research dealing with this question of rebel groups on the outside of a deal, has tended to concentrate on the groups that try to sabotage the peace agreement by using violent tactics (e.g. Ayres 2006; Darby 2001; Stedman 1997). This only gives part of the picture. It is also of interest to know if excluded groups that do not engage in violence can influence the signatories' decision to renege on their deal, or if the exclusion of such groups has no effect on the signatories' commitment to peace. Therefore, this study does not limit the analysis to the actors that challenge settlements by violent means, but explores the conditions under which rebel groups on the outside of a deal influence whether the signatories stick to peace or not. Hence, this study deals with potential outside spoilers to a peace agreement.[4]

Based on the logic of costly signaling, I propose that the military capabilities of the excluded rebel groups can play a role in this context, as the presence of a strong rebel group on the outside of a deal may help the signatories in signaling conciliatory intent to each other, and thereby make peace more likely to last. This draws on the work by Hoddie and Hartzell (2005) who analyze how signatories may commit to peace by engaging in costly signaling.[5] They suggest that the signatories can signal their commitment to peace by taking on costs in terms of sticking to the peace process even when challenged by parties on the outside of the peace agreement.[6] Hoddie and Hartzell illustrate these theoretical expectations through a case study of the peace process in the southern Philippines.

I take this costly signaling argument one step further and propose that we should expect to see this dynamic when at least one of the rebel groups on the outside is strong vis-à-vis the government. The reason is that signatories who go ahead with a peace process, despite the presence of a strong challenger, are taking on costs that they would be unwilling to suffer if they did not have sincere intentions to uphold the peace agreement. In other words, parties that sign on to an agreement, while anticipating that a strong rebel group may continue to engage in violence demonstrates that they are committed to peace. This signaling effect is likely to be less apparent if the group is weak. I utilize a Cox proportional hazards model to analyze this argument using new data on warring parties and peace agreements in internal armed conflicts during 1989–2004. While not conclusive, the results show support for this claim.

The chapter is outlined as follows. First, I will briefly discuss previous literature on durable peace which has dealt with the issue of the inclusion and exclusion of rebel groups, as well as the role of spoilers in peace processes. In the second section, the bargaining perspective is outlined and the commitment problem is discussed. Here I also introduce the main argument of this chapter, which focuses on the role that costly signals can play in the post-settlement phase, and in particular, how the signatories can signal conciliatory intent to each other. Third, the research design is described, followed by a section where I present and analyze the results. Finally, conclusions are drawn.

Research on durable peace

In the aftermath of a settlement in a civil war, what determines if the warring parties engage in violence or whether peace endures? The last decade has seen an increasing body of literature dealing with this particular question. Many studies, in particular quantitative studies, have concentrated on the provisions of the peace agreement and the role that third parties can play in the post-settlement phase to reduce the risk of renewed warfare (e.g. Fortna 2003; Hampson 1996; Hartzell and Hoddie 2003; Walter 2002).[7] Most quantitative research on conflict termination has focused on only two parties – the government and opposition – when explaining why some settlements are successful and others are not.[8] But by treating the opposition side as a unitary actor, important dynamics are lost. While many case studies recognize the need for a more refined view of the rebel side, aspects pertaining to the complexity of the rebel side are largely absent in the quantitative literature. One exception is Nilsson (2006), who shows that it is pivotal to consider all rebel groups on the opposition side when studying the duration of peace in the wake of a peace agreement.

Case studies demonstrate that various factors such as spoiler dynamics, and whether parties are standing on the inside or outside of an agreement, can influence the prospects for peace in the wake of a peace agreement. Some researchers have proposed that whether all or some warring rebel groups have signed an agreement or not may influence the duration of peace (e.g. Hampson 1996). Indeed, it is argued that an inclusive agreement, in which all actors with the potential to resume hostilities take part, is more likely to provide a sustainable solution (Ohlson and Söderberg 2002). Furthermore, Darby and Mac Ginty claim that: 'A lasting agreement is impossible unless it actively involves those with the power to bring it down by violence.' They suggest a principle of 'sufficient inclusion', meaning that the parties representing a significant part of the community, together with actors that have the capacity to destroy an agreement, should be included in the agreement (Darby and Mac Ginty 2000: 254). Thus, they argue that the exclusion of parties from settlements can affect the prospects for durable peace.

When considering the issue of inclusion and exclusion of parties, the dynamics involving warring parties that act as spoilers in the wake of a negotiated settlement becomes relevant. The role of spoilers has been proposed to influence the prospects for peace following a peace agreement (e.g. Stedman 1997, 2003; Zahar 2003). Stedman (1997: 5) defines spoilers as: 'leaders and parties who believe that peace emerging from negotiations threaten their power, worldview, and interests, and use violence to undermine attempts to achieve it'. Furthermore, Stedman (1997: 5–8) makes a distinction between inside spoilers, actors that are part of the peace agreement and choose to defect, and outside spoilers, which never have been part of the settlement. That some parties act as spoilers while others agree to peace illustrate the importance of going beyond a unitary conceptualization of the opposition. Indeed, the spoiler dynamics seem to suggest that the implementation of a peace agreement may be considerably more complex than what an analysis of the rebel side as a unitary actor allows for. The concept of spoilers has, however, received considerable criticism, for instance, it has been argued that spoilers have not been possible to identify 'ex ante' (Zahar 2003: 114). One way of dealing with this problem is to study all groups excluded from a peace agreement – thereby not limiting the analysis to those that end up using violence following the agreement. By doing so, we can identify which groups can be excluded without the signatories being triggered into violence. Hence, in this study all warring parties are seen as potential spoilers. To summarize, there are many case studies that suggest that the exclusion of rebel groups and spoiler dynamics may influence the prospects for peace, but so far, quantitative studies have not explored these issues.[9]

Signaling conciliatory intent

The bargaining perspective has increasingly been used to analyze the causes, dynamics and resolution of war (Reiter 2003). Whereas most research has focused on how bargaining models can be used to explain the outbreak of war, there is a growing literature on how this perspective can help us understand the termination of armed conflicts (e.g. Fortna 2004; Walter 2002; Werner 1999; Werner and Yuen 2005). The bargaining perspective is useful as it provides an answer to the puzzle of why rational actors may go to war even though it is a costly action. Indeed, since wars are costly the parties should prefer a settlement instead of first fighting, but war still occurs. Hence, a logically coherent explanation for why parties choose to pursue their ends by violent means must address this puzzle.[10]

The commitment problem has been suggested to play a pivotal role in explaining bargaining failures and why rational actors may end up in war even though it is a costly action.[11] While the parties would like to avoid the costs of war, they may be unable to uphold an agreement due to fears that the other party may renege on the deal (Fearon 1995). In such a situation, at least one of the parties is unable to credibly commit not to take advantage of its future position, and the other party, in fear of what can happen in the future, has incentives to strike in the present. Walter (2002) has argued that parties in a civil war face a commitment problem which they need to overcome in order to be able to reach a negotiated settlement that will last. The implementation phase of a peace agreement leaves the belligerents vulnerable to defection from the other side, and the parties may find it difficult to credibly commit to a peace deal without guarantees from a third party.

Hoddie and Hartzell (2005) suggest that third parties may not be a panacea for peace, as there are both instances where the parties go back to the battlefield when third parties are present, and cases where the signatories stick to peace even without any guarantees from a third party. There may be other ways in which the parties may overcome problems of uncertainty and commitment following a civil war. Indeed, while Walter proposes that third parties can help the parties overcome this commitment problem, such an argument does not address the question of what the parties themselves may do to credibly commit to peace.

Costly signals can play an important role in communicating information. Fearon (1992: 162) identifies costly signals as a means for the parties to reveal information to each other, stating that: 'Costly signals are instruments for revealing one's preferences.' Thus, through the use of costly signals parties can share information about their intentions. Furthermore, Fearon

(1995: 397) stresses that in order to be informative a signal should 'be costly in such a way that a state with lesser resolve or capability might not wish to send it'. Hence, costly signals can serve to provide the parties with information about each other.

There are a number of studies that have begun to explore how the parties may signal their conciliatory intent. For instance, Kydd (2000) develops a model exploring how parties may overcome mistrust by engaging in a process of conciliatory gestures. But the value of costly signals in the post-settlement phase has also been questioned. Walter (1999: 136) argues that costly signals are not likely to be effective in the post-settlement phase due to a party's fears that the others will take advantage of its vulnerability. She argues that such signals 'either expose the sender to such danger that even peace-loving groups would avoid using them or they are too easy to mimic by more Machiavellian groups to have the desired effect of relaying peaceful intentions'.

Hoddie and Hartzell (2005) analyze the role of costly signaling in peace processes and how the parties at the various stages of this process may take on costs that can signal conciliatory intent. They propose that the logic of costly signals can serve to provide the parties with information about each other. Hoddie and Hartzell outline a theoretical framework focusing on how parties can show that they are sincere in their efforts to make peace stick through the use of costly signaling. It is by taking on costs that the signatories can signal that they are committed to peace, since actors that are unwilling to abide by an agreement would be unlikely to take on such costs. When actors sign on to agreements they may suffer costs by having to compromise. For instance, whereas the government may concede some of its powers, the rebels may have to give up any aim of achieving control over the state, in return for a share in power. Furthermore, governments as well as rebel groups may come under increasing pressure from dissatisfied parties. Hoddie and Hartzell further propose that in the post-settlement phase these costs become readily apparent to the warring parties, as they begin to implement the agreement.

One intriguing conclusion from their study is that the presence of recalcitrant actors may, in fact, have a positive effect on the signatories' commitment to peace. The reason is that the parties in such an environment more easily can signal their conciliatory intent to each other, than in a situation where such actors are absent. Hoddie and Hartzell provide the following rationale for this, viewing parties that:

> actively oppose the peace process as a potentially valuable resource because when such critics of efforts at peace emerge, they provide the occasion for those involved in designing a settlement to prove their dedication to the agreement by enduring and effectively managing these challenges.
>
> (Hoddie and Hartzell 2005: 37)

Hoddie and Hartzell illustrate these dynamics with the peace process in the southern Philippines. In 1996, the government reached a peace agreement with the MNLF, while the Abu Sayaff, as well as MILF, with its 12 000 men strong army was standing outside of that deal. The fact that the signatories remained committed to the agreement in spite of protests that followed in the wake of the agreement from actors outside of the deal, served to reassure the signatories of their conciliatory intent (Hoddie and Hartzell 2005: 34; BBC 2003).[12]

Hoddie and Hartzell (2005) have made an important contribution by showing how the presence of spoilers may facilitate the signaling of conciliatory intent between the signatories, but they do not take into account the capabilities of these potential spoilers. Facing a party on the outside may not in itself be sufficiently costly to serve as a strong signaling device. I propose that the military capabilities of the rebel groups that are standing on the outside of a deal may influence the strength of the signal between the signatories. The fact that the signatories are willing to take on the costs of facing strong pressure from a rebel group on the outside can help the parties signal their conciliatory intent to each other. The point is that excluded rebel groups that are strong rather than weak can serve to reinforce the signal of conciliatory intent made by the signatories to the settlement. A strong rebel group on the outside of a deal is difficult to ignore, and if the signatories take on costs by implementing the terms of their agreement, this demonstrates their willingness to stick to the deal. If the parties sign an agreement while anticipating that a strong group on the outside may continue to engage in violence, this may serve as a signal that they are committed to peace.

Moreover, while a strong rebel group is likely to pose a real threat due to its military capabilities, it may also exert pressure on the signatories in other ways. The argument does not presuppose that the parties on the outside use violence, but suggests that the mere presence of a strong excluded party may influence events. To exemplify, the protests that followed the peace agreement in the Philippines was followed by massive demonstrations where many Muslims gathered to voice their demand for a separate state (Hoddie and Hartzell 2005: 33). In contrast, a small faction outside of a deal, may not be able to create the same pressure on the signatories, nor be perceived as the same threat to the peace process. Admittedly, while smaller groups may compensate their military strength by other means, on average, it is still reasonable to expect that strong parties should be more likely to influence the parties inside the deal. Faced with a strong rebel group on the outside the signatories should be able to signal their conciliatory intent more successfully as the costs are likely to be higher in such a situation. Based on this reasoning, the following hypothesis can be proposed.

Hypothesis: The signatories to a settlement are more likely to stick to the peace agreement if there is at least one *strong* rebel group standing on the outside of the deal.

Research design

Internal armed conflict

Most research on conflict termination is carried out on negotiated settlements signed in civil wars that reach at least 1000 battle-related deaths per year (e.g. Hartzell and Hoddie 2003; Walter 2002). The Uppsala Conflict Data Program (UCDP) has the advantage of not only focusing on the civil wars above this level, but also contains data on all internal armed conflicts reaching at least 25 deaths per year.[13] Therefore, I include all those conflicts that have reached this level and where at least one peace agreement has been signed in the post-Cold War period. The UCDP defines an internal armed conflict as a contested incompatibility over government and/or territory, between a government and at least one opposition organization.

Peace agreement

The existing lists of peace agreements use several different criteria for inclusion. The negotiated settlements that receive most attention are often the ones that to some extent have been successful: the conflict behavior has ended for some time, or some efforts have been made toward implementing the agreement (e.g. Hartzell 1999; Licklider 1995; Wallensteen 2002). However, by examining only the agreements that have lasted for a certain period of time, previous research might have introduced an unnecessary bias. Wallensteen points out that there is a need to include other agreements in a more systematic analysis of conflict resolution processes, and he argues that these failed agreements also can provide valuable information (Wallensteen 2002: 80–82). Furthermore, some lists of peace agreements require that all, or the major warring parties, have signed the settlements (Walter 1999: 127, 2002: 52).

The Uppsala Conflict Database, covering the period 1989–2004, includes data on all peace agreements including those that fail in the short term and the long term. Moreover, this database does not make any restrictions based on which warring parties, other than the government, have signed the agreement. Note, however, that all peace agreements are signed by at least two warring parties, consisting of the government and one or several rebel groups. This data is thus suitable for this study since it does not exclude agreements where only some of the rebel groups are signatories, an aspect that is pivotal to my argument. For the purposes of this chapter, a peace agreement should address the incompatibility by settling all or part of it, and 'address more than just the termination of the use of armed force' (Sollenberg 2002: 14). More specifically, a peace agreement should meet one of the following criteria: '(a) comprehensive agreement signed by all parties regulating or resolving the incompatibility; (b) partial peace agreement (agreement signed by all parties regulating or resolving part of the incompatibility); (c) dyadic agreement (comprehensive agreement signed by the parties, but not in all dyads, regulating or resolving the incompatibility)' (Sollenberg 2002: 14).[14] There were 82 peace agreements signed during the period under study here, and of these, 34 peace agreements excluded one or more rebel groups. To exemplify, in the conflicts in Burundi, Chad, Colombia, Sudan and the southern Philippines, one or more rebel groups were standing on the outside of the settlements reached.

Data and unit of analysis

All data used in this chapter comes from the Uppsala Conflict Data Program if not otherwise mentioned. For each of the internal armed conflicts included in the UCDP dataset, there may be two or more warring parties fighting, of which one always is the government. These have all been involved in an armed conflict that has reached the level of 25 battle-related deaths in at least one year. I focus on the warring parties, since these have been involved in the armed struggle and at some point had both the incentives and capabilities to use armed violence. In this chapter, a party that met this criterion of 'warring parties' *prior* to the peace agreement is of interest, and each of the rebel groups may, or may not, have signed a peace agreement in the conflict. A rebel group is seen as a signatory if the rebel group signed a peace agreement, or previously signed a peace agreement, and then refrained from using violence. Otherwise, the rebel group is seen as excluded from a settlement.

The unit of analysis is the signatory dyad-year. In order to examine if the signatories fight after the settlement, the dataset was constructed with the *dyad* in focus, consisting of the government and a rebel group. All rebel groups that have signed an agreement with the government enter the dataset. Each dyad that has signed a deal is studied from the first year after 1989 that a peace agreement has been reached in an armed conflict until the end of the observation period. An incompatibility consists of one or several dyads, where the government remains the same in each dyad. For every peace agreement signed in the conflict, there is at least one dyad-peace agreement signed by the government and a rebel group. In this dataset, each signatory dyad-year constitutes a row. This makes it possible to explore if the government and a particular rebel group that has signed a peace agreement over time become engage in violence or stick to peace. The dyads may resort to violence after the respective settlements, and then later sign another peace agreement. If a signatory dyad engages in post-settlement violence, this dyad re-enters the dataset if they sign another peace agreement and is then observed till they experience another event (i.e. post-settlement violence) or till the observation period ends.

Statistical technique

Duration analysis (also called hazard or event history analysis) is preferable when there is a need to take into account so-called censored observations (i.e.

the ones that at the end of the observation period still are at peace), and there is an interest in exploring the duration of time up to some event (Box-Steffensmeier *et al.* 2003). A duration model is therefore well suited for the purposes of this study. The model estimates the effects of the independent variables on the risk of experiencing armed conflict after a settlement, given that peace has lasted up to that particular point in time.

Many of the control variables vary over time, which makes it appropriate to use a model with time-varying covariates in order to study changes over time. Since the dyad is observed every year after the signing of a peace agreement until the end of the observation period, there are multiple observations for each of the 26 dyads. In this study, the dyads are at risk of experiencing an event from the signing of a peace agreement in the incompatibility until the observation period ends on December 31, 2004.[15] I employ a Cox proportional hazards model which, in comparison to other hazard models, has the advantage of not assuming a specific parametric form for its distribution (Box-Steffensmeier and Jones 1997: 1422).

Dependent variable

The event of interest is post-settlement armed conflict involving a government and a rebel group that results in at least 25 battle-related deaths.[16] The post-settlement armed conflict is measured the year following the peace agreement in order to ensure that the violence has taken place *after* the agreement was signed.[17] The dependent variable *Peace Duration* measures the number of years without armed conflict for each dyad. Since all dyads involve the government and one rebel group this variable captures armed conflict between these two signatories.

Independent variables

A rebel group's relative military strength to the government is central to the argument presented in this chapter. Jeffrey Dixon (2001; 2002) argues that troop strength can serve as an indicator of military strength. The data for this variable has been collected based on Military Balance, SIPRI Yearbook, and the Uppsala Conflict Database.[18] Where possible, the same source has been used to code the number of troops of the government and the rebel group.

It can be difficult to assess the numbers of rebel troops with a high degree of precision, but it can at least be determined whether the group is militarily strong or weak in relation to the government. I use a ratio of 5:1 to assess strength based on how the data is dispersed.[19] I consider a rebel group to be weak if the government has a relative military strength that exceeds 5:1, otherwise the rebel group is considered to be strong. The independent variable *Outside Strong* captures whether a rebel group on the outside of a deal is strong. Hence, the variable is coded 1, if there is at least one excluded rebel group that is strong relative to the government, and is otherwise coded 0.

Control variables

I include a number of control variables. To begin with, the control variable *Strong* captures the relative military strength between the signatories to the deal, in other words, whether the signatory rebel group can be seen as strong or weak in relation to the government. The relative military capability of the signatories is one aspect that could explain if they stick to peace or not. This is coded in a similar fashion as the independent variable *Outside Strong*. Hence, the variable *Strong* is coded 1 if a rebel group that has signed onto a settlement is strong, and coded 0 if the rebel group is weak. Furthermore, some previous findings suggest that the number of warring parties increases the risk of renewed conflict (e.g. Downs and Stedman 2002; Doyle and Sambanis 2000). It is therefore appropriate to control for *Number Parties* which is measured as the number of warring parties in the conflict in a given year. Moreover, the intensity of the conflict has been argued to influence the likelihood of armed conflict after a peace agreement. The underlying theoretical arguments mainly concern the costs of war and war weariness (e.g. Doyle and Sambanis 2000: 787; Fortna 2004; Hartzell *et al.* 2001: 202). The variable *Intensity* is coded 1 if a particular dyad has reached the level of war prior to the agreement, meaning more than 1000 battle-related deaths in a year, and is otherwise coded 0.

According to Page Fortna (2003), peacekeeping has a significant effect on the risk that peace breaks down following an agreement. Moreover, Zahar (2003: 117) argues that the UN peacekeepers may be more 'neutral' than what sometimes is the case for regional peacekeepers. Thus, I include a control variable *UN Peacekeeping*, which is coded 1 if a peacekeeping operation under the United Nations was in place in a given year, 0 otherwise. I also constructed a variable that measures the presence of peacekeeping forces other than the UN. The *Non-UN Peacekeeping* variable is coded in the same fashion as the *UN Peacekeeping* variable. For these variables I rely on a dataset compiled by Birger Heldt.[20]

In line with findings from previous research I found it appropriate to control for the type of deal reached. To this end, a comprehensive dataset covering the terms of peace agreements reached in the post-Cold War period was used.[21] It is expected that peace agreements which entail power sharing, in comparison to those that lack such provisions, should be more likely to see peace endure. Hence, the dummy variable *Power Sharing* was coded 1 if the agreement contained at least one pact concerning the sharing of power, that is, either military, territorial or political power, otherwise it was coded 0. This variable is coded in line with the criteria for power-sharing pacts used in Walter's (2002) war termination dataset.

In addition, lower levels of economic well-being have been found to be associated with an increased risk of renewed conflict (Walter 2004). The variable *GDP* is intended to capture this aspect. I use the real GDP per capita in constant US dollars with the base year 1996. In order to account for decreasing marginal effects, the variable is logged. This data is available from the Expanded Trade and GDP Data, which are based on the Penn World Tables (Gleditsch 2002).[22] Finally, I also control for the number of peace agreements signed in the conflict. It is conceivable that if the dyad in question, or other dyads in the conflict, have signed an agreement, this could make the signatory dyad less likely to engage in post-settlement violence. It is also possible that a higher number of agreements indicates that the conflict is more difficult to resolve and therefore at greater risk for a return to violence. Hence, the variable *Number Agreements* is included to capture the number of peace agreements previously reached in the conflict. In addition, some alternative specifications are carried out where I control for variables such as the type of political system, the duration of the conflict, and the type of incompatibility, that is, whether the conflict is fought over government or territory.[23]

Results

The results concerning the hypothesis can be found in Table 13.1. The hazard ratios are reported: a ratio below one indicates a decrease in the risk that peace fails, a value above one indicates an increase in the risk that peace breaks down. To exemplify, a hazard ratio of 0.5 means that the risk of peace failing is decreased by 50 percent, whereas a hazard ratio of 1.5 indicates

Table 13.1 Exclusion of rebel groups and the hazard of peace failing

	Model 1	Model 2
Outside strong	0.241** (−2.45)	−
Exclusive agreement	−	0.774 (−0.73)
Strong	5.351*** (2.68)	2.118* (1.85)
Number parties	1.851** (1.97)	1.362** (2.16)
Intensity	6.059** (2.18)	1.150 (0.44)
UN peacekeeping	0.364 (−1.16)	0.954 (−0.11)
Non-UN peacekeeping	0.699 (−0.53)	1.455 (0.99)
Power sharing	0.215 (−1.24)	0.568 (−1.28)
GDP	0.907 (−0.50)	0.834 (−1.31)
Number agreements	0.824 (−1.50)	0.983 (−0.21)
Observations	127	323
Number of failures	12	29
Log likelihood	−29.273	−110.481

Notes
A Cox proportional hazards model is employed. Hazard ratios rather than coefficients are reported, with robust z statistics (given in parentheses) clustered on dyad. A ratio above 1 indicates an increase in the risk that peace fails, while a value below 1 decreases the risk that peace fails. *Statistically significant at the 0.10 level. **Statistically significant at the 0.05 level. ***Statistically significant at the 0.01 level. Two-tailed tests are used.

that the risk of peace failing is increased by 50 percent. The dataset contains 157 dyad-years, but due to missing data on some of the variables the estimations are made on the remaining 127 dyad-years for which there is data.[24] It should be noted that the focus is on agreements where at least one rebel group is excluded. This makes it possible to assess whether the strength of excluded groups affects the behavior of the signatories.

The argument that strong excluded rebel groups reduce the risk of conflict is supported by the empirical results. The results in Model 1 in Table 13.1 show that the variable *Outside Strong*, controlling for all other variables, has a hazard ratio below one and is statistically significant. In other words, the risk of peace failing is decreased if one or more of the excluded parties is strong rather than weak. More specifically, if there is at least one strong rebel group on the outside of the agreement, the risk of post-settlement armed conflict involving the signatories, is decreased by 76 percent.[25] Thus, the hypothesis is supported by the findings. Indeed, this result is in line with the theoretical expectation that the signatories to an agreement may be able to signal their conciliatory intent more successfully if there is at least one rebel group that is standing on the outside of a deal. This is an interesting finding as it is easy to imagine an opposite pattern whereby the stronger rebel groups on the outside of an agreement should be able to pose a more significant threat to peace among the signatories than weaker groups. However, the results here suggest just the opposite and the logic of costly signals provide an explanation for a finding that otherwise might seem counterintuitive.

Furthermore, it is also interesting to see that this result holds when controlling for variables such as the number of parties to the conflict, as well as the relative military capabilities of the signatories themselves. Of the control variables only *Strong*, *Number Parties* and *Intensity* display statistically significant effects. Thus, dyads where the signatory rebel group is strong rather than weak are significantly more likely to go back to the battlefield. Furthermore, if there are a higher number of parties involved in the conflict there is also an increased risk that peace concerning the signatories will fail. Moreover, dyads that have reached the level of full-scale war are significantly more likely to go back to the battlefield.

I have also estimated some alternative models (not reported here). For instance, as a robustness check I included a variable that captures how many of the warring parties in the conflict signed on to the deal. Certainly, it could be the case that peace agreements that leave out a strong excluded rebel group tend to include fewer parties, which could explain why the signatories may find it easier to commit to peace. But the results are robust to such specifications.[26] I also estimate some alternative models where I control for the type of political system, the duration of the conflict, as well as the type of incompatibility. In these models the effect of the variable *Outside Strong* remains statistically significant. At the same time, it should be noted that the results are somewhat sensitive to alternative model specifications, and in some of these the Cox proportional hazards assumption is violated. In addition, when employing a Weibull model instead of a Cox model, the variable *Outside Strong* is no longer statistically significant. The fact the results are sensitive to these alternative specifications may be due to the small sample, and the results should be seen as tentative. Nevertheless, this study can serve as a valuable first step in terms of exploring how the presence of excluded parties may affect the conflict behavior of those parties that have signed on to an agreement.

It can also be of value to take a step back and examine if the mere exclusion of rebel groups, regardless of how strong they are, influences the signatories' commitment to peace agreements. Indeed, Hoddie and Hartzell (2005) proposed that we should expect that the signatories are more successful in signaling their conciliatory intent if the signatories are faced with groups that oppose the agreement. So far, the statistical analysis of the present study has been performed on a sample covering the peace agreements where one or more rebel groups were excluded from the settlement. But if we instead estimate a model with all signatory dyad-years regardless of whether a party was excluded or not, it becomes possible to explore if the mere exclusion of parties influences the signatories' peace duration. To examine this issue, an alternative model is estimated which consists of a sample of 323 observations, instead of the 127 observations that were used to evaluate the main hypothesis.[27] Thus, in contrast to the previous dataset used to estimate the hypothesis, this one includes all signatory dyads regardless of whether a rebel group has been excluded from the deal or not. In this model a dichotomous variable *Exclusive Agreement* is incorporated, which captures whether or not a particular settlement excludes one or more rebel groups. These results reveal that the exclusion of rebel groups from settlements does not show any significant effect on the likelihood of the signatories remaining at peace.[28] Hence, while Hoddie and Hartzell (2005) argued that the signatories can more successfully commit to peace when faced with opposition to a peace agreement, the results reported here demonstrate that the effect of one or more rebel groups being excluded is conditional on the capabilities of the excluded rebel groups. This is in line with the theoretical argument of this chapter, which proposes that if the signatories are facing strong pressure from a rebel group on the outside, this can make it easier for them to signal their conciliatory intent. To summarize, the hypothesis stating that signatories that are faced with a rebel group on the outside are more likely to stick to the peace agreement is supported by the findings.

Conclusions

This study set out to explore the conditions under which the signatories that are faced with a rebel group on the outside stick to their peace agreement. It was argued that the military capabilities of the excluded rebel groups can play a role in this context, as the signatories more successfully can signal their conciliatory incentives in the presence of a strong rebel group on the outside of a deal. By taking on costs in terms of upholding the settlement, even when faced with an excluded rebel group that is strong vis-à-vis the government, the signatories can reveal that they are committed to peace. Although not conclusive, the results showed support for these theoretical expectations. Indeed, if a strong rebel group was excluded from a deal, the signatories were significantly less likely to engage in post-settlement violence. Moreover, it was shown that the mere exclusion of a party did not have a significant effect on the signatories' commitment to peace. This supports the argument presented here that the strength of a signal is conditional on the military capabilities of the parties. In other words, if the signatories are faced with an excluded rebel group that is strong, this can serve to reinforce the signaling effect, thereby demonstrating that the signatories are committed to their peace agreement.

These intriguing findings suggest avenues for further research. To begin with, as the sample is small, making the model somewhat sensitive to alternative specifications, it would be valuable to collect more information in order to explore these dynamics further. At present, dyadic data is only available for the post-Cold War period; it would be of interest to examine if these patterns hold if the time period were to be extended. Furthermore, it could be fruitful to explore the mechanisms by which strong rebel groups can affect the duration of peace for the signatories. This could entail a closer look at the interaction between non-signatories and signatories, and study if the signatories remain committed to peace if they come under violent attacks from the excluded groups. In addition, it can be valuable to identify to what extent the non-signatories simply continue to fight, or if they actively are trying to disrupt the peace agreement. An inquiry into these patterns could shed light on the processes by which signatories stick to their agreement or return to violence, when one or more rebel groups is standing on the outside of the deal. To conclude, efforts toward making peace with only some rebel groups may be worthwhile even if the signatories are faced with a strong rebel group on the outside of the deal. Hence, the findings demonstrate that peace is possible, even if some rebel groups are left out of a peace agreement.

Notes

1. The author wishes to thank Isak Svensson, Birger Heldt, Magnus Öberg, Kristine Eck, Lisa Hultman and Hanne Fjelde for valuable suggestions and comments.
2. Some of these studies consider spoilers on the inside as well as on the outside of a peace agreement. To be clear, this study does not attempt to identify which of the signatories may renege on the deal.
3. Ayres (2006) examines this issue, but focuses more specifically on violent attacks to the peace, and considers the whole peace process rather than after peace agreements. To my knowledge no statistical results have been presented.

Rebels on the outside 261

4 Rebel groups on the inside are sometimes referred to as included parties, and the groups on the outside as excluded parties.
5 They base their theoretical framework on the work by Fearon, who has developed the logic of costly signaling as a means for revealing information (e.g. Fearon 1995, 1997).
6 Hoddie and Hartzell discuss the role of challengers to an agreement, which I understand as primarily pertaining to parties that are excluded from a settlement.
7 See Licklider (2001) for a review of the conflict termination literature.
8 There are examples of work that consider several parties, but these explore other aspects of civil wars (e.g. Cunningham 2005; Walter 2003).
9 For an exception, see Nilsson (2006). While the study considers the issue of excluded rebel groups from peace agreements, it does not specifically explore how the military capabilities of parties on the outside of a deal may affect the conflict behavior of the signatories.
10 As noted by Reiter (2003: 37) the most direct challenge to the bargaining approach lies in the notion that the fighting as such is valued. While this is a legitimate concern, I would argue that it is reasonable to assume that actors generally fight to acquire some other value rather than viewing war as something desirable in itself.
11 Other rationalist explanations for armed conflicts are private information and incentives to misrepresent that information, or when stakes are indivisible (Fearon 1995). It has also been argued that most commitment problems are in fact based on information problems (Gartzke 1999).
12 It should be noted that armed conflict also came to involve the MNLF faction that emerged, whereas MNFL can be seen to have remained committed to peace. MNFL stands for the Moro National Liberation Front and MILF is the acronym of the Moro Islamic Liberation Front.
13 For definitions of concepts, see the Uppsala Conflict Data Program (2006).
14 In line with previous research I will not include 'peace process agreements' since these are merely 'outlining a process for regulating or resolving the incompatibility' (Sollenberg 2002: 14).
15 Some dyads drop out of the data earlier either because the incompatibility is resolved in other ways than through a peace agreement or due to the fact that the party ceases to exist. For instance, if a rebel group completely dissolves or takes over the government the dyad drops out of the data set.
16 I focus on the parties that were active prior to the signing of the agreement and therefore new parties that later emerge are not taken into account.
17 Since the dependent variable is measured from the year following the peace agreement, data for 2004 are also used for this variable.
18 This is the result of a joint coding effort by the author, Isak Svensson and Lisa Hultman. Isak Svensson was responsible for India; Lisa Hultman for Somalia, Djibouti and Sudan; and the author for the remaining conflict locations.
19 In the range of 0–5:1 there is a large cluster of observations, and changing the ratio from 5:1 to either 6:1, or to 7:1 does not alter the sub-sample by much.
20 Data on peacekeeping operations has been supplied by Birger Heldt of the Folke Bernadotte Academy. I would like to extend my thanks to Birger Heldt for generously sharing this data. For a definition of peacekeeping and a list of all operations, see Heldt and Wallensteen (2006).
21 This dataset forms part of a research project carried out by the author and Isak Svensson, where Ralph Sundberg collected data on the terms of all peace agreements in the Uppsala Conflict Database (UCDB). For the codebook and definitions, see Nilsson *et al.* (2006).
22 See Gleditsch (2002) for coding rules. The dataset was only available for the period up till 2000 (version 4.1), and the values for the following years have

therefore been imputed. This variable is fairly stable over the years and mostly varies between rather than within cases.

23 It has been suggested that a democratic system can reduce the risk of recurring civil war (Walter 2004). In order to control for this effect the variable *Political System* was created which is coded based on the Polity IV data set which uses a scale ranging from −10 to +10, where a higher score indicates a more democratic system. I use the Polity2 variable where values of transitions have been converted to conventional polity scores (Marshall and Jaggers 2002). Since this effect may be curvilinear, I also introduce the variable *Political System^2*, which is the square of the *Political System* variable, in order to account for such a relationship. I also control for the duration of the conflict. The data in this study is at the dyadic level and *Duration* is measured as the number of years since the dyad first reached the threshold of 25 battle-related deaths. Given that many conflicts have started several decades ago, the data collection for this variable extends back prior to 1989. Moreover, the variable *Incompatibility* is included in the alternative specifications and is coded 1 if the conflict is fought over government rather than territory.

24 There is some missing data on the relative military strength of the parties. Since data on strength is missing for some of the rebel groups, and some observations therefore, drop out of the analysis, could potentially bias the results.

25 This result is obtained by clustering on dyads, but the result is roughly the same when clustering on conflict or country. The statistical literature encourages that the proportional hazards assumption is to be tested (e.g. Box-Steffensmeier and Jones 2004: 132). The results show no violations in either the covariate specific tests or the global test for the main models, but do so for some of the alternative specifications.

26 Furthermore, the main result is also robust to other alternative specifications. The result is almost identical when instead clustering on conflict or country. By clustering on dyad, conflict and country, it is possible to learn if the observations are independent across these different groups.

27 The original sample consists of 498 observations but because of missing data the estimations are made on the reduced sample of 323 observations.

28 It should though be noted that this variable, similar to the variable *Outside Strong*, indicates a decreased risk that peace will break down.

References

Ayres, R.W. (2006) 'No Peace At Any Price: The Effectiveness of Spoilers in Intrastate Conflicts', paper presented at The Annual Meeting of the International Studies Association, San Diego, CA, March 22–25.

BBC (2003) Guide to the Philippines Conflict, available at news.bbc.co.uk/2/hi/asia-pacific/1695576.stm (accessed March 17, 2003).

Box-Steffensmeier, J.M. and Jones, B.S. (1997) Time is of the Essence: Event History Models in Political Science, *American Journal of Political Science* 41(4): 1414–1461.

Box-Steffensmeier, J.M. and Jones, B.S. (2004) *Event History Modeling: A Guide for Social Scientists*, Cambridge: Cambridge University Press.

Box-Steffensmeier, J.M., Reiter, D. and Zorn, C. (2003) Nonproportional Hazards and Event History Analysis in International Relations, *Journal of Conflict Resolution* 47(1): 33–53.

Cunningham, D. (2005) 'Veto Players and Civil War Duration', paper presented at The 101st Annual Meeting of the American Political Science Association, Washington, DC, September 1–4.

Darby, J. (2001) *The Effects of Violence on Peace Processes*, Washington, DC: United States Institute of Peace.

Darby, J. and Mac Ginty R. (2000) 'Conclusion: The Management of Peace', in J. Darby and R. Mac Ginty (eds) *The Management of Peace Processes*, London: Macmillan Press Ltd.

Dixon, J.S. (2001) 'Intervention, Capabilities, Costs, and the Outcome of Civil Wars', dissertation, Rice University, Houston, Texas.

Dixon, J.S. (2002) 'Governments, Issues and War Type: Addressing the Role of Nonstate Actors in War', paper presented at The Annual Meeting of the International Studies Association, New Orleans, LA, March 24–27.

Downs, G. and Stedman, S.J. (2002) 'Evaluation Issues in Peace Implementation', in S.J. Stedman, D. Rothchild and E.M. Cousens (eds) *Ending Civil Wars: The Implementation of Peace Agreements*, Boulder, CO and London: Lynne Rienner Publishers.

Doyle, M.W. and Sambanis, N. (2000) 'International Peacebuilding: A Theoretical and Quantitative Analysis', *American Political Science Review* 94(4): 779–801.

Fearon, J.D. (1992) 'Threats to Use Force: Costly Signals and Bargaining in International Crises', dissertation, University of California, Berkeley, CA.

Fearon, J.D. (1995) 'Rationalist Explanations for War', *International Organization* 49(3): 379–414.

Fearon, J.D. (1997) 'Signaling Foreign Policy Interests: Tying Hands Versus Sinking Costs', *Journal of Conflict Resolution* 41(1): 68–90.

Fortna, V.P. (2003) 'Inside and Out: Peacekeeping and the Duration of Peace after Civil and Interstate Wars', *International Studies Review* 5(4): 97–114.

Fortna, V.P. (2004) 'Does Peacekeeping Keep Peace? International Intervention and the Duration of Peace after Civil War', *International Studies Quarterly* 48(2): 269–292.

Gartzke, E. (1999) 'War Is in the Error Term', *International Organization* 53(3): 567–587.

Gleditsch, K.S. (2002) 'Expanded Trade and GDP Data', Version 4.1, available at weber.ucsd.edu/~kgledits/exptradegdp.html (accessed January 2005).

Hampson, F.O. (1996) *Nurturing Peace: Why Peace Settlements Succeed or Fail*, Washington, DC: United States Institute of Peace Press.

Hartzell, C.A. (1999) 'Explaining the Stability of Negotiated Settlements to Intrastate Wars', *Journal of Conflict Resolution* 43(1): 3–22.

Hartzell, C. and Hoddie, M. (2003) 'Institutionalizing Peace: Power Sharing and Post-Civil War Conflict Management', *American Journal of Political Science* 47(2): 318–332.

Hartzell, C., Hoddie, M. and Rothchild, D. (2001) 'Stabilizing the Peace After Civil War: An Investigation of Some Key Variables', *International Organization* 55(1): 183–208.

Heldt, B. and Wallensteen, P. (2006) *Peacekeeping Operations: Global Patterns of Intervention and Success, 1948–2004*, 2nd edn, Sandöverken: Folke Bernadotte Academy Publications.

Hoddie, M. and Hartzell, C. (2005) 'Signals of Reconciliation: Institution-Building and the Resolution of Civil Wars', *International Studies Review* 7: 21–40.

Kydd, A. (2000) 'Trust, Reassurance, and Cooperation', *International Organization* 54(2): 325–257.

Kydd, A. and Walter, B.F. (2002) 'Sabotaging the Peace: The Politics of Extremist Violence', *International Organization* 56(2): 263–296.

Licklider, R. (1995) 'The Consequences of Negotiated Settlements in Civil Wars, 1945–1993', *American Political Science Review* 89(3): 681–690.

Licklider, R. (2001) 'Obstacles to Peace Settlements', in C.A. Crocker, F.O. Hampson and P. Aall (eds) *Turbulent Peace: The Challenges of Managing International Conflict*, Washington, DC: United States Institute of Peace Press.

Marshall, M.G. and Jaggers, K. (2002) Polity IV Project, Political Regime Characteristics and Transitions, 1800–2002, available at: www.cidcm.umd.edu/inscr/polity/ (accessed February 1, 2005).

Newman, E. and Richmond, O. (2006) *Challenges to Peacebuilding: Managing Spoilers during Conflict Resolution*, Tokyo: United Nations University Press.

Nilsson, D. (2006) 'In the Shadow of Settlement: Multiple Rebel Groups and Precarious Peace', dissertation, Report No. 73, Department of Peace and Conflict Research, Uppsala University, Uppsala.

Nilsson, D., Svensson, I. and Sundberg, R. (2006) 'The Terms of Peace Agreements Data (TOPAD), Codebook', Department of Peace and Conflict Research, Uppsala University, Uppsala.

Ohlson, T. and Söderberg, M. (2002) 'From Intra-State War To Democratic Peace in Weak States', Uppsala Peace Research Papers, Department of Peace and Conflict Research, Uppsala University, Uppsala.

Reiter, D. (2003) 'Exploring the Bargaining Model of War', *Perspectives on Politics*, 1(1): 27–43.

Sollenberg, M. (2002) 'The Uppsala Conflict Data Project: A Background Note for the Internet Database', Department of Peace and Conflict Research, Uppsala University, Uppsala.

Stedman, S.J. (1997) 'Spoiler Problems in Peace Processes', *International Security* 22(2): 5–53.

Stedman, S.J. (2003) 'Peace Processes and the Challenges of Violence', in J. Darby and R. Mac Ginty (eds) *Contemporary Peace Making: Conflict, Violence, and Peace Processes*, Basingstoke: Macmillan Press Ltd.

Uppsala Conflict Data Program (UCDP) (2006) Available at: www.ucdp.uu.se (accessed June 2006).

Wallensteen, P. (2002) *Understanding Conflict Resolution: War, Peace and the Global System*, London: Sage Publications.

Walter, B.F. (1999) 'Designing Transitions from Civil War: Demobilization, Democratization and Commitments to Peace', *International Security* 24(1): 127–155.

Walter, B.F. (2002) *Committing to Peace: The Successful Settlement of Civil Wars*, Princeton, NJ and Oxford: Princeton University Press.

Walter, B.F. (2003) 'Explaining the Intractability of Territorial Conflict', *International Studies Review* 5(4): 137–153.

Walter, B.F. (2004) 'Does Conflict Beget Conflict? Explaining Recurring Civil War', *Journal of Peace Research* 41(3): 371–388.

Werner, S. (1999) 'The Precarious Nature of Peace: Resolving the Issues, Enforcing the Settlement, and Renegotiating the Terms', *American Journal of Political Science* 43(3): 912–934.

Werner, S. and Yuen, A. (2005) 'Making and Keeping Peace', *International Organization* 59(2): 261–292.

Zahar, M.-J. (2003) 'Reframing the Spoiler Debate in Peace Processes', in J. Darby and R. Mac Ginty (eds) *Contemporary Peacemaking: Conflict, Violence and Peace Processes*, London: Palgrave Macmillan.

Zahar, M.-J. (2006) 'Political Violence in Peace Processes: Voice, Exit, and Loyalty in the Post-Accord Period', in J. Darby and R. Mac Ginty (eds) *Violence and Reconstruction*, Notre Dame: University of Notre Dame Press.

Part IV
Conclusions

14 Conclusions

Magnus Öberg and Kaare Strøm

Introduction

The preceding chapters have explored the role of resources and governance structures in the onset, incidence, and termination of civil conflict. In various ways they detail the ways in which resources and governance regimes play important roles in the onset and the termination of civil conflicts. The contributions in our volume also highlight the importance of various forms of outside interventions. Several chapters further suggest that the importance of resource endowments and resource distributions is indeed often contingent on governance structures. Thus, the lesson to be drawn is not simply that both resource and governance matter to civil conflict, but also that we often cannot understand the impact of one without paying careful attention to how it interacts with the other. Our contributors have identified and examined a number of mechanisms that affect the interplay between governance structures and resources. Below, we describe these findings in terms of the conceptual apparatus developed in Chapter 1, and suggest some questions that deserve further examination in future research.

Resources and civil conflict

The distribution of resources in society

Perhaps the oldest and most widely held belief about the causes of civil conflict is that economic inequalities and disparities are one of its major causes. Rebels often refer to inequalities as motivating their cause, but decades of research on the relationship between economic inequalities and civil conflict have failed to demonstrate any stable link between measures of resource distribution at the national level and civil conflict (cf. Collier and Hoeffler, 2004; Cramer, 2003). Relatively poor data on resource distributions may be one reason why no stable patterns have been found. There are reasons, however, to suspect that the lack of association may stem from more fundamental problems than poor data quality. As Collier and Hoeffler have pointed out, if rebels engage in addressing inequalities they are providing a public good, which in turn implies that they face serious collective action problems (Collier and Hoeffler, 2004). Therefore, we should expect that rebellions based purely on such collective grievances will be difficult to organize and sustain. Rebels will be more likely to succeed if they can offer something more than public goods, or if they can find credible ways to target their appeals and their redistributive commitments. Ethnicity may provide groups with structures and organizations that sometimes can produce sufficient selective incentives and information to police free-riding problems. A few recent studies indicate that there is a link between group level inequalities and civil conflict (Regan and Norton, 2005; Østby, 2005). Thus, economic inequalities generate a significantly increased risk of civil conflict when these inequalities coincide with group lines.

Evidence from William Noël Ivey's contribution to this volume suggests another set of conditions under which rebellion or insurgency motivated by inequalities may be sustained. In societies, or parts of societies, where the government fails to enforce contracts and protect the poor from abuse there is a market for protection. A rebel organization can fill this market niche, providing protection and retribution in return for taxes. While this type of insurgency may not be capable of changing the fundamental distribution of resources or authority in society, it may have the capacity to address some of the negative effects of these distributions. Ivey also finds, however, that if resource disparities are too large, the poor may be unable to mount a sustained rebellion or insurgency. This implies that resource inequalities may have a curvilinear relationship to civil conflict, such that the risk of civil conflict is relatively lower at the extremes of high and low disparities, and relatively higher inbetween, where there is a moderate level of social inequality. It is also possible that severe inequalities are most likely to depress rebellion in very poor societies, so that the curvilinear relationship is more pronounced the poorer the society is. Thus, there may be relationships between country-level inequalities and civil conflict that have not showed up in previous research due to the curvilinear nature of the relationship. At the very least, there is every reason to look forward to further research on these relationships.

Yet, civil conflict is not a one-way street, or rather, a situation in which strategic rebels fight a non-strategic government. In the existing literature, the problem of civil conflict has mostly been viewed from the aggrieved population's point of view, i.e. from the potential rebels' perspective. From this vantage point the issue is about seeking redress for an unfair distribution of wealth and resources in a country. This can often be achieved without major bloodletting through normal political activities, protests, and even threats of rebellion. Yet, the ubiquity of inequality and the mixed findings regarding inequalities suggest that we may get a better understanding of how inequalities affect civil war if we look not just at how inequalities may motivate potential rebels, but also at how governments can try to avoid rebellion.

From the government's point of view, the issue is how to avoid rebellion at some cost less than fighting a war. To avoid a rebellion motivated by unequal distribution of wealth and resources, the government can try to redistribute enough that potential rebels do not find it worthwhile to take the considerable risks and costs that rebellion entails. But such redistribution is costly and the regime may also try to control dissent through various forms of repression, preventing the aggrieved from organizing a rebellion. A further problem with redistribution is that it may trigger violent opposition from segments of society that stand to lose. As Fernando F. Sánchez points out in Chapter 11, this has been seen as a contributing factor in the origins of the 1948 civil conflict in Costa Rica. Thus, the government needs to find a balance between concessions and repression, redistribution and control, such that no group or segment of society finds rebellion worthwhile. The government's willingness and ability to avoid rebellion through redistribution or repression is likely to be conditioned by a number of factors related to governance, such as the government's knowledge of the distribution and strength of citizen preferences, its ability to raise revenues, and its dependence on resource rents or the citizens' productive investments.

Avoiding rebellion through a redistribution of resources may also carry with it another risk. Grievances based on deep-seated cultural, social, and religious discrimination may persist, and a redistribution of resources that empowers the aggrieved but does not address these other grievances and discriminatory circumstances may actually increase the risk of civil conflict. Evidence from the Naxalite cases suggests that in societies with highly skewed resource endowments, in which the majority of the population directly depends upon natural resources for their subsistence, civil conflicts will tend to be localized and of short duration. Only when and where some form of redistribution of natural resources creates opportunities for insurgents to sustain an insurgency and reduce the power of the resource controllers should we expect to see sustained insurgencies.

Natural resource endowments

The availability of natural resource endowments may act as an incentive for war, as many natural resources provide tempting targets for self-enrichment as well as a means to overcome collective action problems. If potential rebels can extract these resources, they can use them to provide selective incentives, pay their troops, purchase arms, bribe arms traders or government officials, buy off potential competitors, and the like. Yet, rich natural resource endowments do not necessarily promote civil conflict. Their effects are contingent on governance structures. Resource endowments is an advantage for responsive governments as it helps them provide public goods and a social safety net to satisfy citizen demands, and at the same time, to develop effective means of national defense and public order, so as to deter conflict and banditry.

However, natural resource endowments may indirectly exacerbate civil conflict by perverting patterns of revenue collection or infrastructure development in such ways that social inequalities are created, or that the state loses its ability to tax its population effectively and equitably (cf. Humphreys, 2005; Ross, 2001). Thus, Fearon and Laitin (2003) argue that the rents from natural resources weaken the state and increase the value of controlling the state, thereby increasing the risk of conflict.

Weak states with ineffective and inefficient governance structures have been found to increase the risk of civil war (Ayoob, 1995; Azam, 2001; Holsti, 1996; Migdal, 1988). The ability to govern effectively is crucially dependent on the ability to raise revenues, and findings suggest that governments that are strong in this sense are much less likely to experience civil conflict (Benson and Kugler, 1998). But, despite these potential revenues, resource-abundant states are not necessarily effective or efficient. Nor are they necessarily more responsive of fair. On the contrary, the literature on natural resource dependence and governance suggests that resource dependent states tend to have slower economic growth, higher poverty rates, higher levels of corruption, and more authoritarian government (Ross, 2004a; see also Ross, 2004b for a recent overview).

Several aspects of political governance may thus be adversely affected by particular forms of mineral resource abundance (cf. Dunning, 2005; Snyder and Bhavnani, 2005). When resources are concentrated in particular regions and this location distorts government policy, the risk of civil conflict may increase because of (perceived or real) problems of fairness in governance (Ross, 2001, 2004a). Thus, in Nigeria it is paradoxically the populations of the oil-rich regions in the Niger delta that complain that while most of the benefits of the oil economy flow to the national government, the costs of environmental degradation are born by the local population. Resource abundance may also weaken another aspect of political governance, namely its efficiency (Fearon and Laitin, 2003). When graft and corruption flourish in resource-extractive industries, such problems often follow, as public offices are filled with cronies of dubious competence, or these same offices disproportionately attract the greedy, through some process of adverse selection of government personnel.

In his investigation of the origins of the civil conflicts in the Sudan Aleksi Ylönen argues that natural resource rents contribute to the highly contested nature of the state in the Sudan. He finds that natural resource rents played a significant role in the origins of the civil conflicts, albeit not by providing opportunities for would-be rebels. Instead, Ylönen argues that government economic opportunism and extraction policies led to the political and economic marginalization of southern Sudan. Repressive government policies, including cultural oppression and the dispossession of land and water resources, fuelled grievances that led to rebellion in the south. More recently, similar policies in the Darfur region have generated another civil conflict. Thus, Ylönen's findings lend support to earlier arguments suggesting that extraction policies is an important mechanism through which natural resource wealth may generate civil conflict (Humphreys, 2005; Swanson, 2002; Switzer, 2001). What Ylönen observes in Sudan seems to be part of a more general pattern. In a recent article Macartan Humphreys identifies and describes six distinct mechanisms that have been argued to link natural resource endowment to the onset of civil conflict: the greedy rebels mechanism, the greedy outsiders mechanism, the grievance mechanism, the feasibility mechanism, the weak states mechanism, and the sparse networks mechanism (Humphreys, 2005). Although Humphreys is unable to test the affects of all six mechanisms empirically and comparatively, his findings suggest that grievance plays an important role.

If natural resource endowments and dependence on natural resource rents are important in bringing about civil conflict, it seems reasonable to assume they would also affect conflict duration and termination. In Chapter 5 of this volume William Noël Ivey examines the linkages between resource distribution, the availability of lootable resources (in this case precious timber), and civil conflict in the Indian Naxalite insurgencies. The Naxalite cases suggest that in societies in which much of the population depends directly upon natural resources, civil conflicts will tend to be localized and of short duration. But if natural resources create opportunities for insurgents to sustain an insurgency by wresting away control over these resources, the outcome may differ and we may indeed see sustained insurgencies. Again, therefore, this case suggests that the relationship between resource endowments and conflict duration may not be straightforward or linear.

The problem of natural resource dependence has not yet had an impact on the conflict termination literature. In one of the first attempts to study the effects of natural resource dependence on conflict termination, Margareta Sollenberg in Chapter 10 analyzes the conditions under which civil conflict ends through competitive elections. She finds that dependence on natural resource rents reduces the likelihood that civil conflict will end through competitive elections. It is significantly more likely that a civil conflict will end through competitive elections when the parties are dependent on the citizens' productive investments. This is so, she argues, because civil conflict leads to excessive expropriation of citizens' productive investments. This in turn causes investments to shrink and the economy to stagnate. Thus, the situation resembles a tragedy of the commons, which gives the parties an incentive to end their conflict and regulate expropriation. If, on the other hand, the parties derive most of their income from natural resource endowments rather than the citizens' productive investments, these incentives no longer apply. Therefore, conflicts in such societies are less likely to be solved through democratic means.

Governance and civil conflict

Effectiveness

Ineffective governance structures can open up opportunities for entrepreneurs or predators to establish competing authority structures. The most straightforward impact of ineffective governance structures on the risk of civil conflict is in terms of the state's ability to police or combat rebel mobilization and activities. This is obviously important for deterring insurgency, maintaining order, and preventing the establishment of competing authority structures. In Chapter 6 Enric Martínez-Herrera shows that improvements in Spanish policing effectiveness significantly decreased ETA violence. A law-ruled repression policy, better targeted measures, and international cooperation all increased the effectiveness of the Spanish counter-insurgency efforts. The joint effect of these interventions was to reduce ETA's fighting abilities, and led to significantly reduced levels of violence in the Basque conflict.

Ineffective governance structures can affect the risk of civil conflict in less obvious ways as well. Governance structures that are ineffective in meeting citizen needs create a potential market for private sector actors to meet these unfulfilled needs. This is perhaps obvious with respect to needs such as, for example, health care, schooling, food, and transportation. But it may also apply to more basic functions of the state such as the exercise of authority. Such functions include policing, contract enforcement, adjudication of disputes, and even prescribing norms or laws.

Lack of effectiveness creates incentives and opens up a market niche for insurgents to provide redress for perceived wrongs. In so doing, the insurgents are effectively exercising authority in lieu of the government. Ivey's findings on the Naxalite insurgency suggest that while filling this niche was not the original motivation of the insurgents, it has become an important activity from which they derive both resources and legitimacy. They provide contract enforcement and protection, as well as remedies for social wrongs and abuse suffered. Like the state and organized crime they also engage in taxation (or extortion) to fund their activities. Thus, insurgents may step in and fulfill erstwhile government functions, in effect replacing or complementing ineffective governance structures. In return for their services they receive and extract resources from the local population and companies in their area of operations.

Ivey shows that in the Naxalite case the ability of insurgents to establish themselves in this market niche is contingent on the distribution of resources in society. Only when the resource stratification has been diminished have Naxalite insurgents been able to sustain themselves and act as informal authorities. On this account, the Naxalite case may be at the extreme end of a continuum. If the poor are so poor that all their resources are needed for their immediate survival, there are no buyers in the market for protection, whatever the price may be.

The importance of this mechanism for establishing an insurgency is that it shows how the market created by ineffective governance structures may allow even rebels without access to lootable resources to overcome the collective action problem of rebellions. In short, such rebels can succeed by becoming service providers to some part of the population that is (more or less) willing to pay for it. The public good produced by their activities, if any, is largely a positive externality. This way of organizing and funding an insurgency may also reduce some of the problems with adverse selection of personnel that Jeremy Weinstein has identified. Weinstein points out that natural resource endowments enable rebel leaders to attract followers by offering short-term rewards, but they risk being flooded with opportunistic recruits. In resource poor environments, on the other hand, such short-term benefits are not forthcoming and recruits will tend to be less opportunistic and more willing to invest time and energy in the hope of reaping larger gains in the future (Weinstein, 2005). In other words, under these particular circumstances an insurgency may be largely grievance based, rather than greed based, and still overcome collective action problems.

There is one more possible twist to the story if we take this reasoning beyond the establishment of an insurgency. To the extent that the government is ineffective in subduing or policing the insurgency, it creates a market for protection for resource holders. This would help explain why in many cases we see private militias being created in response to insurgents. These may, or may not, collude with the government, but the end result of government ineffectiveness is the generation of several competing authority structures. This has happened in many conflicts around the world since 1945, including the Naxalite insurgency and several cases in Latin America that have economic structures resembling those in the Naxalite case. Thus what we see in the Naxalite case may in fact be an example of a more general pattern that occurs in largely agricultural societies with large resource disparities and ineffective governance structures.

Finally, conflict termination involves the re-establishment of effective national governance structures. This may happen through victory and defeat (elimination of competing authorities), or through some kind of peace agreement. The function of peace agreements is to regulate the incompatibility, govern the transitions to peace, and re-establish effective authority over the country in question. It has often been argued that to accomplish these tasks all warring parties, or at least all the significant ones, have to be included in the peace agreement (cf. Darby and Mac Ginty, 2000; Hampson, 1996). For peace to endure among signatories, effective governance has to be re-established over the whole country. If any seriously competing authority structure is left out of the agreement, chances are that this group will spoil the agreement and throw the country back into civil conflict. However, Desirée Nilsson's findings in Chapter 13 show that peace agreements may endure even if they are not inclusive, and that peace agreements that exclude strong rebel groups last significantly longer than other peace agreements.

Thus, partial peace is possible and may even last longer than an inclusive peace. However, partial peace comes with a high risk of continued conflict with excluded parties. Thus, a partial peace agreement may not be able to deliver effective governance structures and the essential public good: peace in all parts of the country.

Efficiency

Efficient governance structures are important in maintaining government legitimacy, and by extension for maintaining civil peace. Perhaps the most widespread form of inefficiency is corruption, which not only tends to undermine the legitimacy of the government, but also harms economic growth and thus the future prospects of the population. Not surprisingly then, corruption tends to generate popular discontent. Thus, alleged or real government corruption and economic mismanagement provide fertile grounds for competing elites and political entrepreneurs to mobilize opposition to the government. There are many examples of this from around the world, often leading to protests, confrontations and sometimes civil conflict. Fernando F. Sánchez's study of the origins of the civil conflict in Costa Rica illustrates the process well. Not without reason, the incumbent president Calderón was accused of corruption, nepotism and unrestrained spending on public works supplied by his friends. The public discontent generated by these practices allowed competing elites to mobilize opposition to his rule, challenge him in elections and, when elections failed to settle the issue, ultimately to overthrow his regime by force.

Responsiveness

It is by now well established both that states with inconsistent regime characteristics and states undergoing transitions to democracy have an increased risk of civil conflict (cf. Hegre *et al.*, 2001). The explanation for this pattern can be put in terms of effectiveness and responsiveness. States that have neither consistently democratic nor consistently autocratic governance structures tend to be less effective than autocracies in deterring rebellion and less responsive to citizen demands than democracies. Thus, in states with these governance characteristics there are both incentives to rebel and less effective structures to prevent rebellion, leading to an increased risk of civil conflict.

The findings presented by Enric Martínez-Herrera in Chapter 6 illustrate this pattern. Martínez-Herrera also shows how over time, the establishment of democracy in Spain produces new governance structures that have been more responsive to Basque nationalist demands. The democratization period was accompanied by an increase in violence, but Martínez-Herrera finds no significant effects on the levels of violence from democracy in and of itself. However, democracy has had an indirect effect on violence by allowing for a decentralization of authority and the establishment of far-ranging Basque autonomy. This decentralization of power produced governance structures that were perceived as being more responsive to Basque interests, thereby undermining the legitimacy and political support for ETA's violent struggle against the Spanish state. Thus, the establishment of more responsive governance structures helped significantly reduce the level of violence in the Basque conflict.

Fairness

Politics involve considerable amounts of contestation. In situations where much is at stake for some or all groups, governance structures have to secure the consent of actual or potential losers, or risk that civil peace breaks down. Aleksi Ylönen's study of the origins of civil conflicts in the Sudan illustrates this problem. The government's struggle to control the country's resource endowments, notably oil, land, and water resources, have been biased in favor of the northern Arab–Muslim population and elites. Ylönen argues that over the past fifty years political and economic marginalization has generated grievances in the south as well as in Darfur. Policies implemented to secure the extraction of resources and control over oil deposits has led to the dispossession of land and water resources in the south. After the discovery of oil deposits we see a similar pattern in the Darfur region. Clearly, in both cases, the affected populations perceived the policies as seriously biased in their conferral of costs and benefits, prompting many of them to choose outside options. They organized mutinies and rebellions leading to civil conflict, or they fled their homes seeking refuge elsewhere.

Competitiveness

Having competitive governance structures may be important both in generating civil conflict and in ending it. Margareta Sollenberg argues in Chapter 10 that when the warring parties depend on the citizens' productive investments in inconclusive civil conflicts, they have incentives to end the conflict through competitive popular elections. However, warring parties will only agree to settle their dispute through popular arbitration if there is some uncertainty about the outcome. Thus, competitiveness is a critical component in ending civil conflicts. As Sollenberg's findings suggest, this may be a particularly vexing problem in ethnically polarized societies like Bosnia and Herzegovina, where post-conflict voting tends to follow ethnic lines, which makes electoral outcomes highly predictable.

The civil conflict in Costa Rica in 1948 described by Fernando F. Sánchez in Chapter 11 shows how a lack of competitiveness may also contribute to causing civil conflict. Significant irregularities in the 1948 elections were an important catalyst in the outbreak of civil conflict. The prior elections in 1944 and 1946 had also been riddled with irregularities, and the opposition had claimed fraud. While these elections did not lead to civil conflict, they did generate protest, strikes, and in 1947 it was agreed that the opposition appoint the three members of the Electoral Tribunal that would oversee the upcoming presidential election. In 1948 the elections was again riddled with irregularities, but this time the Electoral Tribunal declared the opposition candidate Ulate the winner. The incumbents claimed fraud, the government-controlled congress nullified the election, and Ulate was imprisoned. Together with the irregularities in previous elections, this greatly undermined trust in the electoral system. The outcome of the elections was no longer seen as uncertain. Consequently, the opposition leader Figueres came to the conclusion that the crisis could not be resolved through elections. A short but intense civil conflict followed.

If electoral fraud was a key catalyst in bringing about the civil conflict, the establishment of an electoral system that could be trusted was critical to bringing peace and long-term stability to Costa Rica. The post-conflict constitution adopted in 1949 established a Supreme Electoral Tribunal (TSE) with absolute political and economic independence and wide-ranging authority over the electoral process, including control of the police forces during elections. The establishment of the TSE and the expansion of the electorate made electoral outcomes uncertain once again, allowing the parties to settle their differences through competitive contests. These electoral reforms, Sánchez argues, are key factors underlying the long post-war stability of Costa Rica, which is unrivalled in Latin America. The outcome of the civil conflict in Costa Rica also nicely illustrates some of Sollenberg's findings discussed above.

Externalities and international governance structures

Even though civil conflict by definition takes place between inhabitants of one and the same state, its causes and consequences are by no means always contained to that state. In Chapter 4, Kristian S. Gleditsch and Idean Salehyan point out that there has been an unfortunate analytical separation between civil conflicts and international conflicts. The effects of civil conflicts are not contained to the country in question, and international factors affect the onset, duration and termination of civil conflicts. Gleditsch and Saleyhan show that civil conflicts are an important source of international disputes, and the authors describe a range of mechanisms by which civil conflict may generate militarized disputes between states. First, civil conflicts are often fought in the vicinity of international borders, and rebels often seek refuge across international borders. Hence, counterinsurgency operations may lead to border violations that generate disputes with neighboring countries. Second, it is not uncommon that insurgents receive international or transnational support from governments or even private citizens. This may also generate international disputes. Third, civil conflicts may cause or threaten to cause an irregular change of government, which in turn may trigger reactions from other states that see their interest being threatened. Fourth, human rights violations and maltreatment of minorities in civil conflicts may provoke outside interventions. Finally, civil conflicts create negative externalities by generating refugee flows, reducing economic growth in neighboring countries, and threatening to interrupt or disturb the supply of strategic resources. Thus, affected countries have incentives to intervene to terminate the conflict, thereby increasing the risk for an international dispute. Thus, there are a number of reasons why outside powers might intervene to re-establish political order in a country ravaged by civil conflict.

However, as Scott Gates and Håvard Strand show in their contribution to this volume, the historical record of interventions is not always encouraging. Military interventions to support governments in civil conflicts do not significantly affect the political stability of the country in question, and new regimes installed through military intervention tend to be short-lived. On the other hand, interventions to democratize a country in civil conflict have often been at least partly successful. Yet, democratization does not insure political stability. Gates and Strand find that the long-term effect of democratization is negligible and that partial democratization is destabilizing.

Even if intervention is often futile, states are often tempted to intervene in simmering civil conflicts. Theodora-Ismene Gizelis shows in Chapter 9 that even if the externalities generated by civil conflict create incentives to intervene, reducing the externalities is a public good. This may be a particularly vexing problem when, as is often the case, long-term international guarantees are required to settle a civil conflict (Walter, 1999, 2002). Gizelis argues that to solve this problem there must be a dominant or privileged international actor willing to bear the costs of enforcing a settlement. When such an actor is missing, or when there is more than one actor vying for dominance, settlement may not be possible. This may be part of the explanation for the pattern observed in Chapter 2, that the rate of conflict termination, especially through peace agreements, increased dramatically after the end of the Cold War.

However, intervention in civil conflict need not be as costly as military intervention, and international governance structures may attempt to promote peace in less costly ways. A more common form of intervention is mediation, that is, to provide assistance in negotiating a peace agreement that can re-establish peaceful governance. In Chapter 12, Isak Svensson shows that such interventions do contribute significantly to conflict resolution. He also finds that mediation by non-democracies is more efficient than mediation by democracies. The reason, Svensson argues, is that non-democracies have lower audience costs for failing in their mediation efforts and can therefore more credibly commit to withdraw their assistance. The leaders of such states can more easily withdraw from efforts they have made to solve the conflict. This gives them more leverage over the conflict parties, and hence a higher likelihood of producing an agreement.

Concluding remarks

The preceding chapters have thrown new light on many issues concerning the interplay between governance structures, resources, and civil conflict, but many questions remain. Dependence on rents from natural resource endowments rather than on citizens' productive investments generates a number of problems for governance structures that may increase the risk of civil conflict. First, dependence on resource rents tends to produce less responsive and fair governance structures (cf. Humphreys, 2005). This may create problems of the kind that Ylönen describes in his chapter on the civil conflict in Sudan. But since there is no stable general association between primary commodity dependence and civil conflict, we need a better understanding of what specific circumstances we should expect this particular mechanism to play out. Second, dependence on resource rents tends to produce less effective governance structures, with poorly developed state apparatus (Fearon and Laitin, 2003). This may open up a market for competing authorities, along the lines suggested by Ivey in Chapter 5. It may also increase the value of controlling the state, thus raising the stakes in any contest for authority. Previous research shows that raising the stakes increases the probability that a contest escalates to large scale civil conflict (Öberg, 2002). Ivey's study suggests circumstances under which we should expect local insurgencies to arise when governance is ineffective, but under what circumstances may such local insurgencies grow to a contestation over the central government? Third, dependence on natural resource rents may affect conflict endings. Sollenberg's contribution to this volume shows that it significantly reduces the likelihood of inconclusive civil conflicts ending through competitive elections. Previous research shows that natural resource conflicts end more quickly and more often in victory or defeat (Humphreys, 2005). But how does it affect post-conflict governance structures? Is an elite bargain that excludes popular influence the most likely outcome, as the literature on resource dependence and governance structures implies? If so, this may help us understand why civil conflict recurs with depressing regularity in some countries.

The chapters in this volume have thus in various ways helped uncover the mechanisms underlying the interplay between institutions, resources, and preferences in civil conflict, thereby adding to a growing literature on these important matters. Still, much remains to be done. The mechanisms that have been described in this volume need to be more precisely described and understood, and their effects must be subjected to rigorous empirical testing. The field needs rigorous theoretical models, as well as intensive empirical study, of the relationships with which this book has been concerned. We are confident that such efforts will play an important part in future research on civil conflict.

References

Ayoob, M. (1995) *The Third World Security Predicament*, Boulder, CO: Lynne Rienner.
Azam, J.P. (2001) 'The Redistributive State and Conflicts in Africa', *Journal of Peace Research* 38(4): 429–444.
Benson, M. and Kugler, J. (1998) 'Power Parity, Democracy, and the Severity of Internal Violence', *Journal of Conflict Resolution* 42(2): 196–209.
Collier, P. and Hoeffler, A. (2004) 'Greed and Grievance in Civil War', *Oxford Economic Papers* 56(4): 563–595.
Cramer, C. (2003) 'Does Inequality Cause Conflict?', *Journal of International Development* 16(4): 397–412.
Darby, J. and Mac Ginty, R. (2000) *The Management of Peace Processes*, Basingstoke: Macmillan Press Ltd.
Dunning, T. (2005) 'Resource Dependence, Economic Performance, and Political Stability', *Journal of Conflict Resolution* 49(4): 451–482.
Fearon, J.D. and Laitin, D.D. (2003) 'Ethnicity, Insurgency, and Civil War', *American Political Science Review* 97(1): 75–90.
Hampson, F.O. (1996) *Nurturing Peace: Why Peace Settlements Succeed or Fail*. Washington, DC: United States Institute for Peace Press.
Hegre, H., Ellingsen, T., Gates, S. and Gleditsch, N.P. (2001) 'Toward a Democratic Civil Peace? Democracy, Political Change, and Civil War, 1816–1992', *American Political Science Review* 95(1): 33–48.
Holsti, K.J. (1996) *The State, War and the State of War*, Cambridge Studies in International Relations, Cambridge: Cambridge University Press.
Humphreys, M. (2005) 'Natural Resources, Conflict, and Conflict Resolution: Uncovering the Mechanisms', *Journal of Conflict Resolution* 49(4): 508–537.
Migdal, J.S. (1988) *Strong Societies and Weak States: State-Society Relations and State Capabilities in the Third World*, Princeton, NJ: Princeton University Press.
Öberg, M. (2002) 'The Onset of Ethnic War as a Bargaining Process: Testing a Costly Signaling Model', Ph.D. dissertation, Department of Peace and Conflict Research, Uppsala University, Uppsala.
Østby, G. (2005) 'Horizontal Inequalities and Civil War', paper presented at the Annual National Political Science Conference, Hurdalsjoen, Norway, January 5–7.
Regan, P.M. and Norton, D. (2005) 'Greed, Grievance, and Mobilization in Civil Wars', *Journal of Conflict Resolution* 49(3): 319–336.
Ross, M.L. (2001) 'Does Oil Hinder Democracy?', *World Politics* 53(April): 325–361.
Ross, M.L. (2004a) 'How Does Natural Resource Wealth Influence Civil War? Evidence from 13 Cases', *International Organization* 58: 35–67.
Ross, M.L. (2004b) 'What Do We Know About Natural Resources and Civil War?' *Journal of Peace Research* 41(3): 337–356.
Snyder, R. and Bhavnani, R. (2005) 'Diamonds, Blood, and Taxes: A Framework for Explaining Political Order', *Journal of Conflict Resolution* 49(4): 563–597.
Swanson, P. (2002) 'Fuelling Conflict: The Oil Industry and Armed Conflict', Fafo, Program on International Co-operation and Conflict Resolution.
Switzer, P. (2001) 'Armed Conflict and Natural Resources: The Case of the Minerals Sector', International Institute for Environment and Development.

Walter, B.F. (1999) 'Designing Transition from Civil War', in B.F. Walter and J. Snyder (eds) *Civil Wars, Insecurity, and Intervention*, New York: Columbia University Press, pp. 38–69.

Walter, B.F. (2002) *Committing to Peace. The Successful Settlement of Civil Wars*. Princeton, NJ: Princeton University Press.

Weinstein, J. (2005) 'Resources and the Information Problem in Rebel recruitment', *Journal of Conflict Resolution* 49(4): 598–624.

Index

Abu Sayaff 272
accommodation 104, 121n17
action, manners of 103; of the
  intervening party 31–2; sectors of 103
Addis Ababa Peace Agreement (1972)
  133–7
Afghanistan 10, 26; Soviet invasion of
  29, 33, 47, 69, 71, 147, 152
Africa 26–9, 35, 53, 125, 129, 130,
  142, 172; Central 68; Great Lakes
  region; 52, 60 Western; 47, 70, 189
age of ongoing conflict *see* conflict
Aguilar-Bulgarelli, Oscar R. 207
aid 26, 29, 30, 48, 52, 67, 88, 192,
  194, 195, 212; developmental
  assistance 188, 192, 194
Albania 58, 68–70
alliances 10, 64, 82, 83, 206, 208, 209,
  210, 212, 213, 218; informal 10
Al-Qaeda 10, 58, 200n12
Americas 26–8, 35
ammunition 106, 111
amnesties 113, 121n15
Amnesty International 10
anarchy 30, 59, 60, 81, 82
ancient cultural hatreds 5, 126
Angola 33, 69, 125, *198*
anocracies 31, 39n2, 50
anti-government organization 152
Arab Gathering (1987) 140
arbitration 83, 85, 94, 96, 99n3, 277;
  agencies 12; internal 180, 183
arbitrator 178, 180, 186
Arévalo, Juan José 211
Arias, Oscar *203*
Aristide, Jean-Bertrand 70
army 6, 7, 72, 131, 134, 207, 211–14;
  size of 235, 237, 239; strength of
  234, 252

arrest 62, 81, 106, *111*, 112, 115;
  extraordinary 115; ordinary 115, 120,
  122n17
Asia 26, 27, 28; Central 53, 172, 89;
  Southeast 173
audience costs 228, 240–2, 279
authority 9–11, 59, 102–3, 149, 270,
  274, 275, 277, 278, 280;
  concentration of 149; political 6, 9,
  153
autocracy 12, 15, 39n2, 105, *111*, *120*,
  141n11, 148, 149, 155, 160n5;
  operability of 110; regression
  towards 118; strong 148; transition to
  31, 50
autocratic institutions 63, 149, *154*,
  276; polities 39n2, 50, 147; societies,
  systems 12, 13, 153
autocratization 148, 153, 155, 160n6

Balkans 33, 60, 172, 174
banditry 30, 45, 82, 271
bandits, stationary 82
Bangladesh *32*, 69; Chakma minority in
  172; Chittagong Hill Tract 239
bargain(ing) 14, 20, 71, 74, 165, 168,
  173, 176n9, 230, 241, 248, 250,
  261n10, 280; models of 250
Basque(s) 101; appeasement of 117;
  Batallón Vasco Español (BVE) *101*,
  113; conflict 13, 101, 105, 107, 274,
  177; Eusko Alkartasuna 111;
  executive 108; folklore 109; Grupos
  Antiterroristas de Liberación (GAL)
  113, 122n16; language 108, 109;
  nationalist insurgency 102, 105;
  Pact of Lizara (1999) 110, 117;
  parliament 108; quotas 109;
  regional police force 108;

Basque(s) *continued*
regional self-government institutions 108; transfer of political power towards 117; Triple A 113; Unión del Centro Democrático 113; vernacular 109; *see also* Euskadi ta Askatasuna (ETA)
Basque Autonomous Community 137, 141n9
Basque Autonomy Law (1979) 108
Basque country 101, 103, 105–7, 109, 112, 113, 118; assassination in 105, 107
Basque National Liberation Movement (MLNV) 106
Basque Nationalist Party (PNV) 110
battle deaths 23, 28, 29, 30; definition of 28
battle-to-war-dead ratio 30
Beck, Nathaniel 64, 202n29
Belgium 166
Bercovitch, Jacob 233, 240
Bhattacharyya, Buddhadeb 77
Bhojpur 85, 86, 88, 89, 90, 91, 92, 99
Bihar 77, 79, 85, 86, 88, 89, 90, 91, 92, 93, 94, 96, 97n2
black market goods 36, 47
blame attributions 49
Bogotá 62
Booth, John 205, 214
borders, international 38, 86, 71, 278; national boundaries 52, 60, 66; natural boundaries 66
Bosnia 148, 159, 165, 172–5, 176n10, 277; Bosnian Muslim government in 173; Bosnian Serb Assembly in 227; civil war in 227; constitutional autonomy 173; Croats in 174; Gorazde corridor 174; Muslims in 173, 174, 176n9; self-administration privileges in 174; Serbs in 173, 174, 176n8, 176n10, 176n11; territorial division 173, 174
Bosnia-Herzegovina 167, 170, 173
Bosnian conflict 176n7; importance for region 174
British East Africa 130
Buhaug, Halvard 37
Burg, Steven L. 227
Burma 29, 30, 97; Karen insurgency in 4, 26; Thailand and 67
Burundi 92, 97, 254

Cairo Conference 131
Calderón-Fournier, Rafael Ángel 216, 218
Calderón-Guardia, Rafael Angel 206, 221
Cambodia 29, 33, 47, 67, 97; Khmer Rouge in 67
Cañas, Alberto 207, 218
Capone, Al 78, 84–5, 93, 95
car bomb 107, 122n21, 216
Cararabo 61
Carazo, Rodrigo 222
Carrington Proposal 169
carrots (and sticks) 229–30
Carter, Jimmy 35
case studies 18, 47, 48, 148, 165, 172, 248, 249, 250
casualties 4, 68, 78, 81, 84, 86, 152; tolerance to 171
causal relations (links) 66, 80, 111; hidden 114; spurious 114
ceasefire 8, 24, 37, 38, 39, 40n16, 168, 233
Center for International Development and Conflict Management (CIDCM) 110
center–periphery relationship 128
Central America 33, 60, 211
Chad 138, 97, 237, 254
Chavez, Hugo 62
Chhattisgarh 79, 86
China 3, 36, 67
Chinese Civil War 28
civil conflict 5, 9, 18, 28–9, 34, 37, 51, 53, 54, 60, 61, 62, 77–84, 125–6, 143, 149, 166, 270, 280; causes 4–7, 12–13, 17, 47, 48, 50, 79, 126, 128, 271–3, 275–80; definition 3, 79; duration 8, 16, 51; economic cost 4; factors conducive to prolonging 38; global average 28; global patterns 23, 24, 38; international intervention in 15, 17, 31, 33, 279; interstate conflict and 3, 4, 62–6, 68, 72; length of 4, 26; likelihood of 5, 7, 13–14; number of 24–5, 26–7, 30, 38, 157; probability of 27, 50, 280; scope of 17, 24, 30, 78; termination of 12, 15, 39, 269; *see also* conflict; ethnic conflict
civil disobedience 49
civil society 149
civil war, closed-country model of 60;

economic factors in 5, 7, 46–9, 51, 53–4, 68, 79–84, 86, 90–6, 125–34, 136, 137–43, 157, 167; empirical studies of 58, 60, 62, 179, 280; international disputes and 17, 58–9, 63–6, 71–2, 278; military intervention in 15, 33, 67, 69, 147–50, 159, 279; predictors of onset 45–7; primordialist explanations for 51, 54; role of geography in 52–3, 66, 83, 129, 214
civilians 3, 28, 30, 53, 61, 69, 138, 140, 88, 212, 214, 227
coalition governments 110, 212, 218
coding 39, 60n8, 89, 96, 234, 235, 261n18, 261n22; bias 36
coercive means 16, 78, 83
coexistence 129, 166, 178; disposition to 105
cohesion, internal 51, 217
Colburn, Forrest 205
Cold War 6, 23–6, 28, 29, 30, 33–5, 37, 38, 39, 148, 154, 159, 168, 175, 211, 253, 260; end of 3, 15, 24, 25, 38, 45, 50–1, 69, 77, 153, 279
collective action, armed 113; problem 6, 7, 17, 81, 165, 167, 169, 270, 271, 275
collective good 165, 167, 168, 169, 171, 173
Collier, Paul 7–8, 18n4, 36, 45, 46, 47, 48, 52, 125, 126, 127, 201n22, 203n38, 269
Colombia 4, 26, 31, 32, 61–2, 80, 200n17, 254
colonial powers 14
colonies, former 10, 14
commitment problems 165, 166, 250, 261n11
Committee on World Food Security 31
Commonwealth of Independent States (CIS) 89
communal violence 3
communist movements 51, 219
compromise(s) 102, 103, 105, 171, 251; mutual compromises 102
concessions 112, 129, 135, 137, 271; unilateral 103
Condon Fors, Heather 7
conflict, accumulation of 25, 26; age of 23, 25, 26; armed 3, 6, 18, 24, 25, 28, 58, 63, 179, 84–7, 95, 99n1, 200n11, 206, 208, 210, 218, 219, 227, 228, 229, 232, 239, 241, 242, 248, 253–6, 258; colonial conflicts 28, 133; costly 228, 229, 231, 233, 239, 240, 242; cultural bases of 102; definition 23, 92n1, 152; duration 4, 7–9, 16, 17, 23, 25, 26, 33, 38, 48, 29, 51, 52, 78, 81, 96, 186, 190, 195, 199, 202n29, 233–6, 238, 239, 243n14, 257–8, 262n23, 271, 273, 278; escalation of 91, 104, 126, 137–42, 168; extrasystemic 28; high intensity 84; inconclusive 8, 14, 15, 49, 80–1, 83–4, 86–7, 89–90, 92–6, 178, 200n10, 277, 280; internal 24, 45, 60, 61, 62, 63, 68, 126; interstate 3, 10, 28, 38, 40n16, 58, 59, 60, 63, 64, 66, 67, 73n7; islands and 52, 153; linkages 58, 65, 66, 68, 71; low-intensity 84; magnitude of 4, 17, 23, 28–31; management 25, 185; motivations to engage in 52, 81; onset 6, 7, 12–14, 23, 37, 39, 46, 48, 49, 52, 53, 126, 127, 129, 261, 273; opportunity structure for 12, 78, 82, 91; over government 38, 84, 199n1, 262n23; spatially clustered 52; solved through democratic means 92, 200n17, 273; spillover of 52, 65, 171, 174; studies 59; symptom of 50, 103; termination 5, 8–10, 14–18, 23–5, 27–9, 37–8, 229, 231, 232, 248, 250, 253, 269, 273, 275, 278, 279; territorial 38, 84, 199n1, 237; zones 66
conflict diamonds 36
conflict-dyads 232, 233, 235, 236, 263n5
Congo 7, 171; see also Democratic Republic of Congo
Congo-Brazzaville 92
consent of political actors 11, 14, 180
consistency of institutional arrangements 13
consociational democracy 13, 103
consociativism 104
consolidation mechanisms 150
constitutional and legislative initiatives 101
constitutional engineering 13, 17, 103, 104
contiguous states, districts 64, 78, 86, 153
contraband 29, 38, 46, 48, 52

conventions 10
cooperation, international 13, 17, 112, 274
co-optation 104
Correlates of War 72n7, 73n11, 73n15, 152, 184
corruption 12, 18, 36, 47, 135, 206, 207, 272, 276; state 47
cost functions 170, 171
Costa Rica: adoption versus development of democracy 206; Alajuela 208; Alianza Popular (AP) 220; American Embassy in 211; anti-liberacionistas 217; assassination 210; bankers in 206; bipolar system 217; Brigadas de Choque (Hit Brigades) (also linieros) 212; calderonistas 209; capitalists in 209; Cartago 208; catch-all parties 217; causes of civil war 209; central cleavage 209; centre-left party 217, 219, 220; Church in 206; Civil Registry 215; Civil War of 1948 205–11, 216, 220, 221; class conflict in 207; class division 208; classes 208; Coalición Pueblo Unido (CPU) 220; Coalición Unidad (CU) 218, *222*; coffee plantations 208; coffee producers in 206; communist party 206, 208, 214, 221; Constituent Assembly (1949) 213, 214, 219; Constitution (1949) 214, 215; corruption 206, 207, 211; economic development 208; economic failures 207; economic mismanagement 207, 276; eight-year regime 206, 207, 210, 213; Ejército de Liberación Nacional (ELN) 207, 211, 212, 213, 214; election (1948) 206, 209, 213; electoral concurrence 214; electoral fraud 206, 207, 209, 210, 211, 278; electoral process 205, 209, 210, 211, 215, 240, 278; electoral reforms 214, 215, 216, 221; entrepreneurs in 206, 208; Figueres–Ulate Pact (1948) 213; figueristas 219; First Republic 205; fiscal mismanagement 206; foundational conflict of party system 216; general elections in 205; governing junta 213, 214; government alliance 206; Heredia 208; liberacionistas 217; liberal democracy in 205; middle class in 208, 221; military dictatorship 212, 213; Ministry of Labor 219; National Registry 209, 221; nepotism 207, 276; Nicaragua and 211, 212, 220; non-doctrinary neoliberals 217; oligarchy 206, 208, 221; opposition coalitions 217; Pacto del Caribe 211; Partido Acción Ciudadana (PAC) 220; Partido Acción Democrática Popular (PADP) 219; Partido Acción Socialista (PAS) 220; Partido Comunista de Costa Rica (PCCR) 219; Partido del Progreso (PP) 220; Partido Frente Amplio (PFA) 220; Partido Fuerza Democrática (PFD) 220; Partido Republicano (PRep) 207–10, 217, 218; Partido Revolucionario de los Trabajadores en Lucha (PRTL) 220; Partido Social Demócrata (PSD) 206, 209, 210, 213, 216; Partido Unión Nacional (PUN) 206, 207, 210, 213, 217, 218; Partido Vanguardia Popular (PVP) 206, 219, 220; political hegemony 220; political persecution 206; political repression 207, 208; progressive social reforms in 206–8; redistributive economic policies 217; revolution 209, 211; Second Republic 205; social welfare guarantees 217; Social-Democratic Republic 217; Supreme Court of Justice 215; Tribunal Supremo de Elecciones (Electoral Tribunal) 206, 207, 209, 210, 214, 215; two-party system in 214, 218, 219, 220; ulatistas 209, 210; Unidad Móvil (Mobil Unit) 212; Unificación Nacional (UN) 218; as uninterrupted democracy 205, 221
Cote d'Ivoire 68
counter-insurgency 13, 17, 66, 69, 139, 274, 298
counter-terrorism 101; collaboration of governments 114
coup d'etát 38, 50, 70, 72, *111*, 113, 117, 118, *120*, 135, 140, 142
courts 12, 61, 96, 104, 118, 135, 215
Cox proportional hazards model 248, 255, 259
credible commitment problems 165, 166
Croatia 173, 174, 176n8
cross-border strikes 66, 71

cultural groups, communities 49, 51, 165; heritage, preservation of 104; repression 143; traits 101, 133, 165
culture 54, 103, 106, 108, 131, 135, 214; and violence, conflict 102, 103
Czech republic 166
Czechoslovakia 104, 212

Dahl, Robert, A. 105, 185
Darfur 126, 128, 136–44, 272; Arab interests in 140, 142; political marginalization in 141, 142, 277
Darfurians, African 143; Arab 140, 143
Davis, Nathaniel 212
Dayton, Ohio, agreement at 173, 176n11
decentralization 101–5, 108, 109, *111*, 115, 118, 120, 123, 214, 277
decision-making power 9; transference of 104
demilitarization 147
democracy(ies) 12, 14, 15, 17, 18, 72, *111*, 113, 141, 148, 157, 172, 178, 180–1, *199*, 199n3, 205–7, 213, 216; and civil conflict 11, 13, 18, 24, 32, 49–50, 59, 61, 64, 110, 121, 228–9, 231–2, 234–7, 239–42, 276, 279; conditions necessary for emergence of 182; degree of 12, 157, level of 12, 50, 59n2, 179, 185, 190, 193–4, 202n31, 234, 244n16; measure of 31, 50, 73n11, *154*, 185, 186, 201n21; persistence of 105, 219, 221; strong 12–13; as tool for settling armed conflict 39, 105, 179, 192, 195–6, 200n17, 273
democratic government 147, 149; external imposition of 147–55, 199n4, 200n10, 221
democratic peace 61, 64
democratic polities 149, *158*, 214
Democratic Republic of Congo (DRC) 30, 66, 71
democratization 15, 17, 50, 101, 102, 103, 105, 110, 118, 147, 157, 178–9, 181–2, 279; aggressive 148, 159; Japan and 147–8, 159; literature 118, 182; operationalization of 115, 120; processes 178–9; through conquest 17, 147–55, 159; trend toward 31, 51, 107
demography, debate over 51–2
Deng, Francis 129, 132

deprivation, as force behind rebellions 7, 18n3, 77, 133
developing countries, societies 34, 53, 165, 205
development (economic) 4–5, 33, 49, 54, 86, 110, 128, 130, 132, 134, 137, 141, 143, 149, 151, 153, 157, 208
devolution 104
diamonds 7, 36, 37, 47, 80, 83
diaspora 48, 127, 133
dictator(ship) 110, 114, 149, 153, 182, 207, 211, 212, 213
direct taxation 36, 47
discrimination 49, 78, 81, 92, 131, 179
disease 28, 30
disparity, inter-group *see* horizontal inequality
dispute 5, 18, 23, 58, 59, 60–71, 73n13, 73n17, 94, 138, 147, 206, 220, 244, 278–9; definition of 72n1; mechanism to arbitrate, settle 17, 138, 169, 178, 185, 231, 241, 277
dispute resolution, norms of 231
diversionary theory of war 61
diversity (in society) 51, 54, 127
division(s) 51, 82, 95, 126, 206, 208, 210–12, 216
Dixon, Jeffrey 255
Downs, George 247
Doyle, Michael 8, 179, 192–4, 202n31
duration analysis (hazard or event history analysis) 254–5
Duverger, Maurice 240

Eastern Europe 105
Echandi, Mario *202*
economic agenda, as cause of internal conflict 125–7
Economic Community of West Africa (ECOWAS) 69–70; monitoring group (ECOMOG) 189
economic development *see development*
economic embargo arrangements 10
economic growth 4, 46, 53, 68, 82, 149, 157, 217, 272, 276, 279
economic interdependence 59, 64
education 47, 49, 53, 103, 104, 108, 130, 146, 147, 172
El Salvador 29, *197*, 199n2, 200n16
Elbadawi, Ibrahim 45, 49

election(s) 11, 51, 105, 119, 131, 133, 135, 155, 173, 181, 202n38, 205, 206–7, 208–10, 211, 213, 214, 215–20, 276–8; broad enfranchisement and 149; competitive 12, 14, 18, 178–9, 182–6, 188–90, 192–3, 195–6, *197*, 198, 199n2, 200n10, 200n16, 200n17, 201n19, 201n21, 202n31, 273, 280; electoral districts 110; electoral system 105, 110, 214–16, 221, 278; electorate 183, 214, 221, 278; fair 15; fraud 14, 206, 207, 209–10, 278; free and contested 15, 92, 149; participation in 151, 185, 205
elite(s) 128, 130, 131, 132, 136, 139, 141, 206, 218, 220
employment 46, 82, 91, 94
endogeneity problems 53, 73n17, 153
enforcement of settlement *see* settlement
enforcer of last resort 170
entrepreneur(s) 6, 89, 206, 208, 274, 276
Eritrea 68
Ethiopia 29, 68, 132, 136, *197*
ethnic affiliation, rebel groups and *see* rebel groups
ethnic conflict 17, 51, 103, 104, 105, 118, 121n5, 127, 138, 141, 165–77; definition 165; internationalized 61, 167–8; settlement of 17, 165–75; spread of 167; *see also* civil war; civil conflict; conflict
ethnic(ity), diversity and violence 137, 183, 140, 143; dominance 14, 15, 79, 129, 141; fractionalization 188, 189, 193–5, *198*; fragmentation 14, 183; heterogeneity 15, 188, 193, 194, 195–6, 222n38; homogeneity 15
ethno-nationalist violence, conflict 101–2, 105, 110
Europe 9, 10, 26–8, 35, 69, 86, 176n11, 228
European Union (EU) (also European Community) 35, 160n1, 169, 170, 173–4, 227
Euskadi ta Askatasuna (ETA, Basque Country and Freedom) 106, 117, 119, 274; active recruitment by 113; Algiers negotiations and *111*, 113, 117, 122n21; arrests of members 106, 112; communication with 113;

ETA-m (military) 111, 113; ETA-pm (political-military) 113, 118; negotiations with 112, 119; penal concessions to 112; penal matters 117; reintegration 112, 113, 115, 117, 121n13, 121n14; renunciation of violence 113, 117, 118; satellite structures 118; unilateral cease-fire, truce 111, 117
exclusion 125, 128, 131, 133, 139, 221, 249, 259, 260; of rebel groups 16, 18, 248, 270, *257*
executive 118, 119, 153, 160n5, 215; recruitment of 13, 149, 151, 200–1n18
executive authority, constraints on 149
exploitation 14, 16, 78, 94, 96, 128, 129, 133, 136, 140, 231
expropriation 93, 128, 180, 181, 199n6, 173
external actors 170, 174–5, 176n10, 181; incentives to facilitate settlement 165, 167–9
external enforcement 165, 168, 180–1, 183–4, 188
external involvement 166, 167, 172, 177
externality(ies) 68, 71, 72, 73n16, 80, 167, 168, 170, 181, 231, 278, 279
extraction 7, 17, 56, 47, 82, 89, 128, 129, 132, 134, 139, 143, 183, 271, 272, 273, 274, 297
extremism 102–3, 105–8, 110–12, 117–19, 122n22

Fait, Alberto 217
Falkland War 152
famine 30, 31, 45
Fearon, James D. 36, 45–7, 52, 188, 202n38, 250, 261n5, 272
feasibility mechanism 273
Federal Yugoslav Republic (FYR) 174
federalism 104
Fernández, Oscar 216
fighting, cost of 168
Figueres-Ferrer, José 206–7, 210, 211–14, 216, 218, 221, *222*, 278
Figuerres-Olsen, José María 216, *223*
food-for-oil program 10
forced migration 4, 20, 68
forest products 78, 83, 91
Fortna, Page 256
France 10
free ride 81, 270

Freedom House index of political freedoms 110–11, 115, 120, 141n10
Frei, Daniel 233
Fudenberg, Drew 169

games, incomplete information 169; zero-sum 95, 103
Gandhi, Jennifer 50,
Gandhi, Rajiv 172
Garang, John 136, 137
Garzón, Baltasar 118
gem(s) 36, 37, 83
Geneva Talks 174
genocide 3, 4, 28, 140, 202n32
geographical displacement 4, 30, 140
Germany 3; West Germany 148,
Ghana 79
Gilady, Lilach 230, 241
Gilmore, Elisabeth 36
Gleditsch, Nils Petter 148, 155
global power(s) 168, 169–71
governance structure(s) 5, 9–13, 14, 16–17, 101, 269, 271, 274–80; competitiveness of 11–12, 14–15, 277; domestic 94, 157; definition of 9; effectiveness of 9, 11–14, 102, 180, 215, 231, 272, 274–6, 280; efficiency of 11–12, 14, 18, 207, 213, 214, 216, 272, 276; fair 280; ineffective 274–5, 280; inefficient 272; international 10, 72, 279; openness, of 12–14, 36, 50; post-conflict 15, 280; properties of 274–9; responsiveness of 9, 11–14, 101–4, 107–8, 110–11, 121n2, 271, 272, 276–7, 280; stable 31
government, predatory 46; restructuring of 101–2, 104, 117
government repression 66, 69, 80, 86, 117–18, 207, 271, 274
Granda, Rodrigo 62
Great Britain 31, 89
great power(s) 11, 28, 234, 235, 238, 241, 243n12
Greece 32, 68
greed versus grievance 7–8, 78–80, 126–7, 275
greedy outsiders mechanism 273
greedy rebels mechanism 273
Greig, Michael J. 233
grievance(s) 7–8, 13, 46, 52, 80–1, 125–7, 136–7, 142–3; grievance mechanism 273

gross domestic product (GDP) 36, 46–8, 53, 64, 80, 153, *154*, 157, 160n4, 87, 90, 95, *199*, 235, *236*, 237, *238*, 244n21, 256–7, 270–3, 275, 277
group quotas 104
Guatemala *197*, 199n2, 200n16, 211
Gulf War (1991) 10

Haiti 30–1, *32*, 70, 147, 148, 152, 159, 175, 176n6, *217*
Harbom, Lotta 33, 40n8
Hartzell, Caroline 248, 250–2, 259, 261n6
Hay, Richard A. 114
health 30, 104, 108, 274
Hegre, Håvard 45, 121n5
Heldt, Birger 34, 40n9, 89, 261n19
Herman, Margaret G. 148
hierarchy 59–60, 88–90, 102–3, 129, 169–72, 174–5
Hindu(s) 79, 172
historical narrative 127–8
HIV/AIDS 45
Hoddie, Matthew 248, 250–2, 259, 261n6
Hoeffler, Anke 7, 18n4, 36, 45–8, 52, 125–8
Honduras 211
Human Development Index 86
human rights 112; abuses 85; violation(s) 69, 153, 279
Human Security Report 30
humanitarian crises 28, 30
Humphreys, Macartan 273
Hungary, 69
Hurd, Douglas 173
Hussein, Saddam 10, 147, 152
Hutu rebels 66

Ibrahim, Khalil 139
identity 12, 127, 128, 132, 205
illicit drugs 7, 80; and conflict duration 26
inbetween regime types 13
incentives 6, 13, 52, 83, 105, 126, 128, 142, 165, 181, 182, 230, 231, 250, 276, 277, 279
inclusiveness 103, 214
income, per capita 46, 126
inconsistent political institutions 13, 153, 155, 157, 159, 276
Index of Democratization (ID) 185

index on ethno linguistic
  fractionalization (ELF) 188, 201n24
India 32, 69 70, 79, 84, 88, 89, 94, 95,
  97–8, 170, 172; access to capital and
  credit in 93; Adivasi (tribals), 84, 88,
  90, 91; agriculture in 77, 84, 88–91,
  93–4; Andhra Pradesh 77, 86, 88,
  89–92, 100; 79, 86; Chota Nagpur
  Tenancy Act 89; Communist Party of
  India (Maoist) 84; Communist Party
  of India (Marxist) 84; dalits in 79, 85,
  86, 96; Dandakaryana 91, 92; forestry
  companies in 77; fragmented
  landholdings in 93; Green revolution
  in 88, 90, 93; Gujarat 92; Haryana
  89; Hyderabad Presidency 88;
  Kamma caste 90; Kerala 85; Koeris
  89; Kurmis 89; land reforms in 78,
  93, 96, 98; land seizures in 84;
  landowners (landlords) in 77–8,
  84–5, 89, 90, 91, 94, 96; lower-caste
  77, 89, 96; Madhya Pradesh (MP) 79,
  86, 91, 92; Maharastra 85, 86; Maoist
  Communist Centre (MCC) 84;
  martial law (1977) in 85, 90, 91;
  Nagaland 237; Naxalbari 84–6;
  Orissa 86, 88, 90–2; panchayats 94;
  People's War Group (PWG), 77, 86,
  91–2; private militias in 77, 275;
  Reddys 90; as regional power 169,
  172; rural banks in 94; Santal
  Parganas region 89; Punjab 85, 89;
  scheduled castes in 79, 92; Senas
  (landlord-funded militias) in 85,
  97n3; sharecropper(s) 88, 94; Siliguri
  85; South 172; Srikakulam 86, 90;
  stratification in 96, 274; Tamil Nadu
  85, 89, 172; Telengana 86, 88–92;
  United Front in 94; United
  Liberation Front of Assam 92;
  untouchables 77, 79; Uttar Pradesh
  85, 88, 89–90, 97n1; West Bengal
  77, 84–5 88–90, 93–5, 97n1; Yadavs
  85, 89, 90
Indian land tenure systems 88–9
indigenous communities 77
Indochina 53, 67
Indonesia 49, 51
inequality(ies) 5–6, 80, 91, 125–7,
  269–70; economic 48–9, 51, 269–70;
  group level 270; income 48–9;
  individual 126; gender 47; global 48;
  horizontal 48–9, 51; political 49

information 71, 85, 112, 115, 168,
  229–30, 250–1, 253, 261n5,
  261n11, 270
infrastructure 4, 30, 47, 66, 88, 106,
  112, 149, 272
instability 13, 17, 46, 48, 50, 53, 140,
  142, 148, 150, 167
institutional reform 18, 205
institutions 5, 10, 12–13, 14, 58, 60,
  63, 104, 108, 109, 149, 151, 153,
  159, 183, 205, 216, 221; legislative
  50
insurgency(ies) 4, 5, 8, 13, 17, 26,
  29–30, 36, 38, 46, 52, 58, 66, 67,
  69, 77–9, 81, 84, 86, 88, 90, 93, 95,
  96, 98, 101, 103, 105, 125–8, 133,
  136, 137, 139, 142, 270, 278, 280;
  opportunity for 82–3, 271, 273–5
interaction effects 189–90, 192, 194,
  201n26
Inter-American Court of Human Rights
  61
intermediate political types 148, 182
international community 45, 166, 174,
  176n9, 176n11
International Crisis Group 136
International Peace Research Institute,
  Oslo (PRIO) 23, 28, 63, 200n12
international disputes see disputes
international organization(s) 23, 34
intervention(s) 10, 14, 16, 23, 24, 33,
  36, 39, 73n7, 80, 94, 103, 112, 134,
  155, 172, 174, 213, 218, 229,
  234–7, 269, 279; biased 15, 32–3; by
  secondary supporting parties 33;
  economic 15, 16; effects of 15, 154,
  274; interstate, international
  intervention 31, 61, 67–8, 70–2,
  73n15 148, 166, 167–9, 193, 199n4,
  200n10; military 8, 15, 17, 33, 69,
  147–53, 157–9; neutral 15, 34;
  secondary warring party 33; third
  party 14–15, 34–5, 40n12, 165, 184,
  188, 196, 200n10, 220, 227, 230–1,
  234, 241, 243n2, 243n9, 248, 250;
  typology 31
intolerance 105
investment(s) 8, 180–3, 188, 195,
  199n5, 271, 173, 280
Iran 29, 67, 69, 70
Iranian revolution 70
Iran–Iraq war 29
Iraq 10, 29, 33, 67, 70, 136, 147, 152

irregular government change(s) 65, 70, 278
Islamic Brotherhood 139, 142
Islamic Jihad 68
Islamism 68, 135, 137, 139, 141
Israel 32, 62, 66
Israel–Palestine conflict 26, 84
Italy 148

Japan 147–8, 159
Jharkand 77, 79, 85, 89–90, 92, 93
Johnson Douglas H. 129, 131
Juba Conference (1947) 130
judicial decisions 11; procedures 118
junta 152, 213–14

Karen insurgency (Myanmar) 4, 26
Kashmir 70, 84
Keen, David 47, 128
Kegley, Charles W. 148
Kenya 67
Khmer Rouge *see* Cambodia
Khun Sa 67
Kimberley Process 39
kinship ties 69
Korean War 28, 30
Kosovo 20, 67, 69, 71, 159; Albanian population of 58, 69; Racak massacre 69
Kosovo Force (KFOR) 70
Kosovo Liberation Army 69
Kosovo War (1999) 147
Kurdish rebellion 49
Kydd, Andrew 251

Laitin, David D. 36, 45–7, 52, 73n14, 203n38, 272
land reform(s) 18, 78, 89, 93, 94, 96
language 104, 109, 130, 131, 133, 140
Latin America 205, 214, 216, 221, 275, 278
League of Nations 11
Lebanon 62, 66, 97
Legión Caribe (Caribbean Legion) 211–13
legislation 89, 103, 118, 135
legislative institutions *see* institutions
legitimacy 83, 113, 274, 276, 277
Lemke, Douglas 169, 175
leverage 18, 107, 172, 227–30, 241, 279
Leviathan 180, 181, 199n6
Liberia 30, 68, 69, 125, 178, 197

Libya 135, 138, 237
Lijphart, Arend 104, 121n3
Linz, Juan J. 105, 121n4
looting 6, 126, 138, 140, 141
Lujala, Päivi 37

McCleary, Richard 114
macro studies 45, 48, 51, 53–4
mafia(s) 78, 83
majoritarian systems 13, 14, 105
Mandela, Nelson 34–6
Maoist insurgent groups 51, 77
Marandi, Babulal 77
marginalization 125–6, 128–30, 132–3, 137, 141–3, 272, 277
massacre(s) 3, 30, 69
Matthews, Robert O. 130
mediation 23, 30, 34–5, 227, 230, 232, 235–6, 240, 242, 243n3, 243n6, 243n11, 244n25, 279; definition of 233; diplomatic 15; by organizations 234, 237–8; success 229, 231, 233–4, 237, 242; termination threats 228–9, 231, 239; theory 228, 230, 242; threat of withdrawal 230, 232, 241, 242
mediator(s) 18, 228–31, 234, 237, 241, 242, 244n22; influence of 18, 243n3
Meernik, James 148
Middle East 26, 27, 28, 35, 136
migration 130, 167, 172
Miguel, Edward 43
military, aid 28–30, 38, 48, 212; capabilities 64, 236, 237, 252, 256, 258, 259, 260, 261; defeat 17, 159; technology 28; victory 22, 31, 37, 38, 39, 280
Military Balance 234, 239, 243n15, 244n15, 244n19, 255
Military Interstate Dispute (MID) data 63–5, 67–71, 73n8, 73n13
military intervention *see* intervention
militia(s), private 77, 275
Milosevic, Slobodan 167
Mindanao rebellion 26
mineral(s) 7, 36, 77, 78, 90, 92, 97n2, 183, 272
minority(ies) 13, 50, 51, 65, 69, 104, 108, 110, 166, 168, 169, 172, 173, 174, 175, 279
mobilization 6, 14, 18n2, 81, 82, 92, 95, 96, 137, 141, 167, 274
Mogadishu 30

Monge, Luis A. 218, 223
Mora, Manuel 206, 209, 212, 219
Moro Islamic Liberation Front (MILF) 252, 261n12
Moro National Liberation Front (MNLF) 252, 261
mortality 23, 28, 29, 46, 107
Mozambique 29, 178, *197*, 219n2, 220n16
Mullah Omar 152
multiethnic societies 14, 105, 172
multilateral intervention 34, 38, 184, 188, 189, 200n10
Murdoch, James C. 68
Musharraf, Pervez 70

Naidu, Chandrababu 77
Namibia, 29
national boundaries *see* boundaries
national interest(s) 168, 172, 174, 279
National Liberation Army (ELN) 61, 211–14
nationalism 101, 119, 130, 172, 173
natural resources *see* resources
Naxalite 8, 17, 77–9, 84–6, 88–93, 95–6, 271, 273–5; definition of 84; history 84; incidents 78, 86, 95, 97n1, 97n3
Neeman, Zvika 179–80
negotiated settlement *see* settlement
negotiations, direct 112, 187
neighborhood effects 52, 157
Nepal 51, 172; civil war (1996) 51
nepotism 18, 207, 276
Netherlands 237
Nicaragua 29, 178, *197*, 199n2, 200n16, 211, 212, 220
Niger delta 272
Nigeria 7, 31, *32*, 68, 69, 70, 89, 172
Nile river valley 134
non-governmental organizations, actors 10, 11, 94, 230
non-state actors 33, 34, 60
norms 149, 231, 174
North, Douglass C. 149
North Atlantic Treaty Organization (NATO) 10, 58, 67, 70, 173
Northern Ireland 84
Norway 237

Oduber, Daniel 222
oil 7, 8, 10, 17, 36, 47, 133–4, 136–7, 143–4, 183, 272, 277

oligarchic domination 110
Olson, Mancur 182
Olson, Ola 7
Oneal, John 63–4, 73n9, 73n12
opportunism 128, 133, 137, 143–4, 272
opportunity cost of rebellion 5, 12–13, 46–7, 92, 106, 113, 115, 126
order, transition to 180, 182, 279
Ovares, Julio César 210
Owen, Lord David 227

Pacheco, Abel 223
Pact of Lizara (1999) *see* Basque
Palestine Liberation Organization (PLO) 62
Panama 32, 148, 159, 97, 211
peace, agreement 16, 37, *38*, 40n16, 67, 135, 137, 166, 179, 229, 233, 237, 243n7, 243n8, 247–50, 252–60, 260n2, 260n3, 261n9, 261n21, 275–6, 279; broker(s) 91, 228, 230, 232, 239, 240–1; civic 54; durable 247–9; permanent 129; process 228, 243n7, 248, 251–2, 260n3, 261n14
peacekeeping 10, 17, 23, 30, 34, 35, 59n3, 40n11, 40n13, 188–9, 94, 95, 98, 201n25, 234, 256, 257, 261n20
peacekeepers 34, 256
Pearson, Frederic 151
peasant(s) 29, 85, 89, 93, 97n2
Peceny, Mark 148
Penn World Tables 257
People's Union for Civil Liberties (PUCL) 97n3
People's Union for Democratic Rights (PUDR) 97n3
periphery 38, 104, 139, 142–4
petro-states 36
Philippines 26, 248, 252, 254, 262
Picado, Teodoro 206, 209, 212
Pickering, Jeffrey J. 151–2
pluralism 103, 104
Plurinational polities, states 104–5
Polarization 33, 39n6, 51, 53, 125, 126, 138, 140, 160n1, 277
police, policing 60, 67, 77, 82–5, 90–1, 93, 96, 97n2, 108, 112–13, 117–18, 121n7, 121n8, 131, 135, 184, 188, 209–10, 212, 215, 270, 274, 278
political economy 126, 130; classical 182
political institutions *see* institutions

political openness *see* governance structures
political opportunity structure 12, 78, 82, 91
political participation 13, 80–1, 83, 104, 131, 139, 168, 185–7, 201n19, 201n20, 212, *215*, 219, 220
political parties 71, 72, 84, 92, 98, 110–11, 135, 139, 152, 179, 185–6, 196, 198–9, 201n19, 205, 206, 208, 212, 213–14, 216–21
political rights 50, 104, 131, 166, 173, 199n3
political subculture *see* culture
political system(s) 11, 13–14, 23, 50, 101, 103–7, 110, 142, 180, 184, 201n20, 208, 214, 216, 217–21, 238, 257–8; autocratic 153; caesaristic 153; democratic 153, 178–9, 182, 192, 195–6, 200n17, 200n18, 201n18, 262n23; duration of 150, 153, 157; institutionally inconsistent 153; stability of 106, 148–9
political transformations 130, 148, 149, 210, 233
political variables 49, 54
polity 52, 206, 150–1, 153, 157
polity scale, dataset 39n2, 50, 64, 73n11, 152, 160n3, 200n10, 200n18, 234–5, *236*, *238*, 244n16
polyarchy data, project 160n3, 185, 200n17
population density 52, 93
Port Sudan 134
poverty 5, 29, 91, 130, 132–3, 272
power, aerial 28; political 40n16, 48, 58–9, 70, 89, 90–2, 94–6, 102, 104, 110, 117, 125, 128–30, 133–5, 137, 139, 141–4, 147, 151, 153, 173–4, 178–60, 184–6, 199, 206n2, 211, 213, 214, 218, 219, 221, 235, 256, *257*, 277; ratio(s) 58, 71; seizure of 70, 84
power relationship, asymmetric 235, 244n15
power-sharing 10, 49, 104, 180, 186–7, 199n6, 256, *257*
predation 7, 8, 30
primary commodities 7, 47, 80, 127, 187, 189, 192, 194, *198*, 280
privileged actor 16, 18, 168–9, 175
profit 47, 88, 126, 127, 142

property rights 11, 166, 173, 182
proportional representation 13, 50, 110
Przeworski, Adam 153, 182
public good(s) 7, 12, 16, 17, 36, 47, 165, 168–71, 175, 270–1, 275–6, 279

Qatar 70

rapprochement 111
rebel group(s), movements 6–9, 16–18, 34, 46, 52, 60–2, 67, 72, 83, 127, 132, 138–9, 141, 185, 229, 232, 234–6, 243n5, 245–60, 261n4, 261n9, 261n15, 262n24, 270, 274–6; *see also* incentives
rebellion, opportunity for 125–8, 133, 137, 143; as rational behavior 126, 250
redistribution 8, 79, 89, 93–6, 104, 141, 217, 270, 271
refugee(s) 30, 52, 60, 68, 69, 70, 71, 73n16, 167, 172, 175, 279
Regan, Patrick M. 15, 233, 243n6
regime 10, 12, 17, 29, 39n2, 58, 103, 105, 121n5, 133–8, 141–2, 149, 155, 185, 205–7, 210–13, 271; change 70, 72, 81, 143, 147–8, 151–5, 159, 276; resource dependent 36, 47; stability, instability 50, 53, 140, 144, 149–55, 157, 159, 279; strongman 149, *154*, 157; type and civil conflict 12–13, 15, 17, 31, 50, 110, 148, 269
religion 14, 34, 35, 51, 54, 103, 104, 125–7, 129, 135, 140, 141, 171–2, 183, 188, 202n38, 203n38, 271
rentier states 36
rent-seeking 8, 36
repression 12, 17, 47, 50, 66, 69, 70, 80, 86, 101–3, 107, 110–12, 115, 117–18, 121n2, 121n13, 126, 127, 141–3, 207, 208, 210, 220, 271, 272, 274
resource(s): abundance 8, 80, 82–4, 192, 272; access to 78, 95, 87; allocation 101, 102, 104, 107, 108, 109, 117; availability 8, 53, 82, 272, 273; distribution of 5, 6, 8, 78, 80, 82, 88, 90, 91, 92, 93, 94, 96, 104, 217, 269–71, 274; extraction 7, 17, 36, 47, 89, 132, 134, 143, 183, 272, 273, 277; lootability of 6, 7, 8, 26,

resources *continued*
  36, 47, 48, 127, 83, 87, 92–5,
  202n31, 273, 275; natural 5, 7, 8,
  16, 17, 24, 36, 39, 46–7, 49, 77–84,
  106, 91–6, 126, 133, 178, 182, 183,
  187, 192, 194–5, 202n31, 271–4,
  280; natural resource economies 49,
  52, 78, 90; obstructability of 7;
  scarcity 78, 80, 83, 84, 94, 138
revolutionaries 77, 211–12, 220
Revolutionary Armed Forces of
  Columbia (FARC) 61, 62
revolution(s) 38, 49, 61, 70, 72, 72n2,
  77, 79, 88, 95, 209, 211, 220
Reynal-Querol, Marta 13, 50
Rice, Condoleezza 168
Robin Hood 77, 78, 84, 93, 95
Rodríguez, Miguel A. 223
Romania 69, *197*
rule of law 59, 149
Russett, Bruce, M. 63–5, 73n9, 73n12,
  230, 241
Russia 3, *32*, 36, 176n11, 189, *197*,
  237
Rustow, Dankwart A. 105
Rwanda 4, 66, 80, *197–8*, 202n32

Saideman, Stephen M., 105, 121n5
Sambanis, Nicolas 8, 45, 49, 60, 179,
  192–4, 201n22, 202n31, 202n34
Sanabria, Monsignor Victor Manuel
  206, 207, 210
sanctions 10, 102, 106, 113, 174, 181
Sandler, Todd 68
Sanhueza, Ricardo 153
Sartori, Giovanni 79
Saudi Arabia 70
scarcity 78–80, 83–4, 94, 96, 98, 138
Schifter, Jacobo 208
secession 23, 36, 47, 52, 105, 107,
  167–8, 175n2, 176n7, 176n11
secondary supporting, warring, parties
  32–4, 37, 39n4, 39n7, 40n8, 187–9,
  193, *198*, 201n23, 201n25
security 30, 39n4, 45, 46, 49, 77, 82,
  94, 106, 112–15, 135, 138, 149,
  165, 167, 168, 183, 188, 239;
  guarantees 16, 58, 61, 67, 69, 72,
  178, 181, 184, 189, 196, 200n9, 242
Seligson, Mitchell, A. 216
semi-democracy 15, *154*, 155
September 11 attack (2001), 58, *111*,
  120, 159

settlement 15–18, 24, 38, 40n16, 59,
  69, 140, 165–75, 175n5, 176n10,
  176n11, 179, 181–4, 187, 190, 194,
  195, 196, 199n2, 200n9, 200n16,
  202n31, 228–33, 235–42, 242,
  243n8, 244n22, 247–60, 261n6,
  279; enforcement of 10, 16, 18, 59,
  165–75, 176n11, 180–4, 188, 279;
  negotiated 34, 38, 40n16, 149, 166,
  167, 175, 228–33, 235, 237,
  239–42, 264n22, 249–50, 253
Sharif, Nawaz 70
Sierra Leone 30, 70, 125, *197*
signal(ing) 32, 169–71, 175, 180, 231,
  241, 249, 250–2, 258–60, 261n5
Sivard, Ruth, L. 3
Slovak republic 166
Slovenia 173
Söderbom, Måns 52
Somalia 30, 148, 159, 175, 176n6, *197*,
  261n18
Somoza, Anastasio 212
South Africa 35, 80, 201n25
sovereign 9, 59, 66, 152, 180
sovereignty 62, 66, 68, 147
Soviet Union (USSR) 3, 25, 29, 40,
  104, 175n4, 201n24
Spain 13, *32*, 101, 106, 108, 110, *111*,
  112, 118, 119, 121n4, 121n8, 208,
  274, 276, 277; Bidart operation
  (1992) *111*, 112, 115, *120*, 121n14;
  Constitution (1978) 108
Spanish Civil War (1936–1939) 108
spoilers 247–50, 252, 260n2
Sri Lanka *32*, 165, 169–70, 172, 173,
  177, *197*, 237
stability 8, 13–18, 46, 48, 50, 53, 138,
  140, 142, 147, 149–50, 153, 155,
  157, 159, 167, 175, 176n6, 216,
  221, 278, 279
Stam, Allan 73n8, 233, 243n6
state apparatus 135, 136, 142, 166,
  209, 280
state capacity 5, 36, 92
State Failure Task Force 45
state(s): building 182; failed 12, 29,
  126, 147, 151; weak 30, 46, 47, 92,
  272, 273
Stedman, Stephen J. 247, 249
Stewart, Frances 48
Stockholm International Peace Research
  Institute (SIPRI) Yearbook 244n15,
  255

strategic selection hypothesis 229, 240
Studenmund, A.H. 119
Sudan 8, 17, 67, 125–44; Anglo-Egyptian Condominium 130; Disputes 68; Animist 125, 136; Arab communities 125–43; Baggara 137–8; black Africans in 129, 137; Chad and 138; civil war 125–8, 132, 137; Closed Door Ordinances 130; Democratic Unionist Party 135; Dinka ethnic group 134, 136, 139; Fur 138, 141; insurgency 17, 126–8, 133, 136, 137, 139, 143; Islam in 125, 132, 135–9, 141–3; Islamic Brotherhood 139, 142; Janjaweed militia 139–41, 143; Jonglei canal 134, 137; Justice and Equality Movement (JEM) 141; Khartoum regime 141–2; Masaleit 137, 141; Missairia (Baggara) 138; Murahaleen (government militia) 139; Muslim Brotherhood 135–6; National Congress Party (NCP) 139–42; National Islamic Front 136, 139; National Reconciliation 135; Nimeiri regime 133–7; Northern domination in 130–2, 136, 143; oil 8, 133–4, 136–7, 142–4; oppressive policies 128–9, 136–7, 142, 144, 272; People's Assembly 135; People's National Congress (PNC) 139; Rezaiqat (Baggara) 138; Southern Equatoria Corps (SEC) mutiny 133, 143; Sharia (Islamic law) 135–6; southern rebellion 128, 131, 133, 138, 143; SPLA-Fur offensive (1991–1992) 138; State Security Organization 135; Torit 132; Transition Zone 139; Umma 135; Unity Province 134; war in 125–7, 138, 141; Zaghawa 137, 141; Zurga 137–8, 141
Sudan Administrative Conference (SAC) 130
Sudan National Legislative Assembly (NLA) 131
Sudan People's Liberation Army (SPLA) 137–8, 141
Sudan People's Liberation Movement (SPLM) 137
Sudanization 131, 133
superpower rivalry 6, 25–6, 28, 45

Taisier, M. Ali 130
Tajikistan *197*, *198*, 237

Taliban 10, 58, 147
taxation 6, 29, 36, 47, 53, 80, 91, 96, 108, 133, 139, 181, 182, 188, 208, 270, 272, 274
termination threats *see* mediation
terrorism 39n6, 45, 101, 105–7, 112–14, 117–18, 121n6, 122n22
Thailand 36, 67
third party intervention *see* intervention
Thucydides 5
Tinoco, Federico, and José Joaquin 212
Tirole, Jean 169
Tito, Josip Broz 173
Togo 69, *198*
Touval, Saadia 228, 233
trade 22, 58, 64, *65*, 71, 130, 135, 149, 190, 195, *199*, 257, 271
trafficking 36, 45, 52, 62, 182, 199n8, 207; cocaine 36; heroin 36
tragedy of the commons 180, 273
transparency 36, 205, 215, 242
Treaty of Paris (1995) 173
Treaty of Westphalia (1648) 9–10
Trejos, José 222
Tres Bocas 62
Turabi, Hassan 136, 139–40, 142–3
Tures, John A. 148

Uganda 67–8, 132, *198*
Ulate, Otilio 206, 210, 211, 213, 218, 278
Ulster agreement 111
United Nations 10, 11, 35, 38, 174, 184, 227, 256; peacekeeping operations (PKOs) 23, 34, 40n13, 188–9, 194–5, 256; Security Council 235
United States (US) 10, 35, 39n6, 48, 168, 207, 211–12, 227; intervention by 35, 58, 73n7, 147–8, 152, 159, 171–5, 175n4, 175n6, 176n11, 212–13
Uppsala Conflict Data Project (UCDP) 23, 31, 36–8, 39n2, 39n5, 40n7, 40n11, 40n15, 184, 187–8, 190, *198*, 200n11, 200n12, 201n23, 234, 243n9, 244n15, 244n18, 253–4
USSR *see* Soviet Union

Valverde, Carlos Luis 210
Vance, Cyrus 174

Vance–Owen plan 227
Vanhanen, Tatu 185–6, 190, 201n19, 201n20
Venezuela 32, 36, 61–2, *198*
Vietnam 28, 33, 40n16, 73n8
Von Hippel, Karin 148
Vreeland, James 50

Wallensteen, Peter 33, 40n8, 40n9, 189, 200n13, 253, 261n20
Walter, Barbara F. 16, 175n3, 200n9, 250, 251
Waltz, Kenneth N. 59
Wantchekon, Leonard 8, 15, 178–82, 192, 195, 196, 199n4, 199n5, 199n6, 199n7, 200n10
war 3–4, 6, 10, 14 , 23–6, 28–9, 30–3, 35, 37–9, 45–54, 58–64, 66–9, 71, 73n9, 73n17, 77, 84, 86, 95, 105, 108, 125–7, 138, 147–54, 157, *158*, 159, 168, 175n4, 176n8, 178–81, 183–7, 189–90, 192–5, *197*, 199n1, 200n9, 200n10, 200n11, 200n17, 201n21, 202n31, 202n32, 205–13, 215–21, 227, 229, 230, 232, *236*, 237, *238*, 250, 253, 256, 260, 261n10, 262n23, 270, 272, 278; interstate 29, 61, 73n7 148–50, 152, 157, 166; proxy 29, 30; *see also* civil war
War against Terror 39n6, 118
war crimes 10, 28; tribunals 10
Warsaw Pact 69
wealth, political stability and 5, 7, 8, 31, 46, 49, 52, 64, 95, 104, 128, 132, 153, 157, 178, 217, 239, 244n21, 270–1, 273
Weinstein, Jeremy 275
West Africa 29, 47, 70, 189
Western Sahara 239
Wilson, Bruce M. 209
winners and losers 11–12
World Bank 45, 49, 69, 89, 190, 212, 244n19
World War I 3, 59, 212
World War II 3–4, 24, 28, 31, 45, 53, 59, 73n9, 149, 173

Yashar, Deborah J. 216
Yugoslav People's Army 173
Yugoslavia 25, 58, 69–70, 104, 147, 166, 173

Zahar, Marie-Joëlle 256
Zaire/DRC 66, 69, *198*
Zartman, I. William 175n2, 230, 233
Zumbado, Omar 209

eBooks – at www.eBookstore.tandf.co.uk

A library at your fingertips!

eBooks are electronic versions of printed books. You can store them on your PC/laptop or browse them online.

They have advantages for anyone needing rapid access to a wide variety of published, copyright information.

eBooks can help your research by enabling you to bookmark chapters, annotate text and use instant searches to find specific words or phrases. Several eBook files would fit on even a small laptop or PDA.

NEW: Save money by eSubscribing: cheap, online access to any eBook for as long as you need it.

Annual subscription packages

We now offer special low-cost bulk subscriptions to packages of eBooks in certain subject areas. These are available to libraries or to individuals.

For more information please contact webmaster.ebooks@tandf.co.uk

We're continually developing the eBook concept, so keep up to date by visiting the website.

www.eBookstore.tandf.co.uk

For Product Safety Concerns and Information please contact our EU
representative GPSR@taylorandfrancis.com
Taylor & Francis Verlag GmbH, Kaufingerstraße 24, 80331 München, Germany

www.ingramcontent.com/pod-product-compliance
Lightning Source LLC
Chambersburg PA
CBHW052149300426
44115CB00011B/1592